Deep Mediations

THINKING SPACE IN CINEMA AND DIGITAL CULTURES

Karen Redrobe and Jeff Scheible, Editors

University of Minnesota Press
Minneapolis
London

MINNESOTA

A condensed version of chapter 10 was originally published as "Sinkholes," *JCMS: Journal of Cinema and Media Studies* 58, no. 2 (Winter 2019): 169–74; copyright 2019 by the University of Texas Press; all rights reserved.

Published by the University of Minnesota Press
111 Third Avenue South, Suite 290
Minneapolis, MN 55401-2520
http://www.upress.umn.edu

ISBN 978-1-5179-0889-8 (hc)
ISBN 978-1-5179-0890-4 (pb)

A Cataloging-in Publication record for this book is available from the Library of Congress.

Printed in the United States of America on acid-free paper

UMP BmB 2021

DEEP MEDIATIONS

In Memoriam:
Edward Branigan
Douglas Crimp
Jonathan Kahana

CONTENTS

PREFACE

In January 2019, the *New York Times* published an article in which op-ed columnist Thomas Friedman eleven months prematurely declared his choice for 2019's word of the year. Friedman writes,

> Even though it's early, I'm ready to declare the word of the year for 2019. The word is "deep." Why? Because recent advances in the speed and scope of digitization, connectivity, big data and artificial intelligence are now taking us "deep" into places and into powers that we've never experienced before—and that governments have never had to regulate before. I'm talking about deep learning, deep insights, deep surveillance, deep facial recognition, deep voice recognition, deep automation and deep artificial minds. Some of these technologies offer unprecedented promise and some unprecedented peril—but they're all now part of our lives. Everything is going deep.[1]

If "everything is going deep," then when were things not deep? Some sort of periodization would be useful to chart the different meanings, paths, and valuations of depth that have historically accompanied the concept in order to understand its significance today.

An increasing cultural awareness of the Anthropocene, climate change, and mass extinction points to one identifiable marker that reintroduces a centrality of depth that was viewed as having receded with postmodernity. There seems to be scientific consensus that we have now entered a phase of the earth's geologic history that is indelibly shaped by the impact of human life. This appraisal is accompanied by a sense of urgency for taking questions of deep time more seriously in order to make sense of the planet's future in a *longue durée*. With this heightened environmental sensibility, we become acutely aware of all the history, material goods, and knowledge that humans have accumulated during their relatively brief stay on this planet. But at the same time that many scholars within the environmental humanities as well as the natural sciences are responding to an apparently new recognition of the scale of human devastation to the planet and beyond, scholars working within the realms of black studies, Indigenous studies, and decolonial theory are critiquing the paradigm of what Kathryn Yusoff calls the "White Anthropocene" or "White Geology" with its "racial" and "willful blindness" and its stratigraphic mode of thinking. Asking for more precision around the "anthros" implied by the idea of the Anthropocene, Yusoff writes,

> White Geology continues to propagate imaginaries that organize Blackness as a stratum or seismic barrier to the costs of extraction, across the coal face, the alluvial planes, and the sugar-cane fields, and on the slave block, into the black communities that buffer the petrochemical industries and hurricanes to the indigenous reservations that soak up the waste of industrialization and the sociosexual effects of extraction cultures. If the Anthropocene proclaims a sudden concern with the exposures of environmental harm to white liberal communities, it does so in the wake of histories in which these harms have been knowingly exported to black and brown communities under the rubric of civilization, progress, modernization, and capitalism.[2]

For Yusoff, the Anthropocene names a process of white people noticing an extinction that they have "chosen to overlook" in the making of modernity and freedom, suggesting that the contemporary attention to deep, ecological time is not incompatible with, and indeed may be paradoxically dependent on, other kinds of historical repression.[3] As she notes elsewhere, "Capitalism is a social machine that digs deep and wide into the substratum of the earth to find its *charge*."[4] She provocatively claims that "political questions are shot through with geologic forces, far below and in excess of topologies of power *into* the substratum of the earth, and tied to the force of those flows as much as they are to the forms of their expressions on the surface. . . . Reigniting a stratigraphic imagination in social theory can disrupt topological accounts that tend towards horizontal or surface-led interpretations of power relations; stratigraphic thinking temporalizes rather than simply spatializing (planetary) changes in material states and forces."[5] Depth may be reemerging as a hermeneutical optic to make sense of histories and information that postmodernists have suggested we had forgotten about, but this is, as we have just noted, a contested move. From geologic strata to data to politics, it appears vital that we dig deep to properly understand the range of stratifications structuring our world; but such stratigraphic thinking must also be held in tension with critiques of depth models and its blind (and deaf) spots, raising questions about what alternative approaches to technoecological disaster might look like.

At the same time, it seems altogether too tidy to say, for example, that depth was unpopular to think about in the 1990s and is now in the 2020s newly in fashion again. Does such an account reinscribe or reorganize master narratives around collections of thinking that are always in fact diverse, heterogeneous, and nonlinear? Indeed, it is challenging to think of a word more versatile and persistent across multiple paths of humanistic inquiry than "depth." To answer the most pressing questions about the ways the mind works, the economic organization of societies, representations of time and space, or the reaches of our critical capacities, scholars have for centuries developed and worked with deep-structure models to approach a range of objects and areas of study. Marx's figuration of base and superstructure is one notably influential depth paradigm, while Freud's insistence on multiple levels of consciousness is another whose lasting influence on our understanding of psychic processes would be impossible to overestimate. These models are examples of what Paul Ricoeur once described as a "hermeneutics of suspicion," whereby surface-level phenomena distract us from or, in a more generous spirit, might only be part of, what is *really* going on. Depth models, so the logic goes, allow the critical thinker to see the fuller, bigger picture. They provide one with a way to understand the "true" situation—not so unlike what André Bazin, describing the power of cinematic depth of field (film's ability to represent multiple planes of an image), famously called "the ambiguity of reality."

Following this logic, one can see why when truth itself is held suspect, as in many postmodernist theories, depth paradigms might seem to have less explanatory power. Now that phenomena like fake news and a reality TV president have become serious concerns and are viewed as threats to democracy, there has understandably been a backlash against some of the more hyperbolic claims of postmodernism—that we live in a "desert of the real" or that truth and fiction are impossible to distinguish. Rather, for a large number of scholars, it seems more important than ever to precisely locate where truth is and is not located. This context surely accounts for one reason that there is a discursive return to depth as we are propelled further forward into the twenty-first century. Several essays included here pursue different facets of this return as it relates to the status of truth in contemporary media and culture.

Yet to merely call this a "return" to depth in the early twenty-first century would be to overlook striking differences between accounts of depth that preceded the postmodern turn and those that follow its celebration of surfaces. For instance, while there is undeniably a *discursive* return to depths and deepness in relation to computing technologies, geology, and temporality today, the *valuation* of these depths is not marked by the same level of optimistic potential that deep-structure models seemed to offer for Marxist and Freudian ideology critique. Cultural critic Dick Hebdige has identified three ways to characterize postmodernist thinking and art. One of these is that they are "against utopia": a fundamental belief in the possibility of a better world that undergirded the modernist imagination no longer seems detectable in postmodernist contexts. He writes,

> There is a strongly marked vein of skepticism concerning any collective destination, global framework of prediction, any claims to envisage, for instance, the "ultimate mastery of nature," the "rational control of social forms," a "perfect state of being," "end of all (oppressive) powers." This anti-utopian theme is directed against all those programs and solutions (most especially against Marxism and fascism) which have recourse to a bogus scientificity, which place a high premium on centralized planning/social engineering, and which tend to rely heavily for their implementation on the maintenance of strict party discipline, a conviction of ideological certitude, etc.[6]

Rather than having returned to this belief in utopia, the contemporary registers of depth circulating in critical thought today instead seem more somber, reminiscent of a line from Racine repeatedly invoked by Alain Badiou at UCLA in November 2016 as he spoke in the immediate wake of Donald Trump's election: "It was during the horror of a deep night."[7]

A parallel point could perhaps be made on the level of the cinematic image. With the revitalization of 3D technologies in mainstream cinema spurred by the massive success of James Cameron's *Avatar* (2009) becoming the highest-grossing movie of all time, Hollywood reintroduced 3D technologies into films and movie theaters, hoping to draw dwindling audiences back in with the unique cinematic potentials of depth afforded by this technology that could be explored much more fully in film than in television. And yet, while 3D is still being marketed in mainstream cinema, it seems by 2020 to have lost steam and perhaps has come, once again, to be viewed with critical and popular disdain, even as immersive effects take on new life both through the rise of virtual reality (VR) in art venues, such as with the introduction of an annual VR competition at the 2017 Venice Biennale or with Tsai Ming-Liang's haunting adoption of VR in *The Deserted* (2017), and through the phenomenal, if partly accidental, box office success of a film like Bi Gan's *Long Day's Journey into Night* (2018), the final fifty-nine minutes of which are shot in a single, 3D long take.[8] As filmmaker Sebastian Buerkner, who works creatively with stereoscopy, put it anecdotally in 2015, there is a general "disinterest" in the technology: "When I mentioned the word 3D, everyone sort of rolled their eyes and stopped listening."[9] While the sources of this critical pushback are surely multifaceted (ranging from the limitations of Hollywood cinema's imagination to the high price of movie tickets), the added layers of visual depth afforded by 3D technology do not seem to hold lingering seductive powers.

On the one hand, then, the legacy of deep-structure models and technical experimentations with visual depth is far-reaching; on the other hand, it seems like it is time to take stock of some of the twists and turns concepts and practices of depth have taken on in the cultural, social moment after postmodernism, whatever we wish to call it. One of the goals of this volume is to provide space for examining the different ways in which scholars now, as we move into the 2020s, are engaging this legacy, particularly as it impinges on the realms of cinema and media studies. As evidenced by the endurance of nineteenth-century thinkers like Marx, Freud, and Nietzsche, deep-structure models have proved overwhelmingly formative to ideas of what good, proper scholarship looks like—and, in turn, to ideas of what more promiscuous and less rigorous scholarship looks like. Think of how often, for example, scholarly work is dismissed for not being "deep" enough. This collection seeks to make sense of what one might call a critical fixation on depth by considering the term's use across a range of conversations, and to ask what its status is in relation to today's mediascape and critical methodologies.

Meanwhile, discourses of postmodernity suggest that surfaces, often conceptualized in conjunction with depthlessness, reign supreme. And our lived realities would seem to bear this out. In cities around the pre-COVID-19 world, we increasingly found ourselves among crowds of people gazing downward at their cell phone screens; scrolling through news headlines, social media feeds, and dating profiles; texting friends in group chats; checking e-mails; and playing games, blending work with leisure in the information economy that Jonathan Crary describes as 24/7 capitalism.[10] Screen interfaces seem to form a barrage of images and imaginaries that distract us from the "deep." But one of our aims here is to think twice about the kinds of critical thinking that too-hasty rejections of depthlessness close off and to instead examine multiple types of depth and depthlessness that might be parsed out and seen for the ways in which they relate to one another and to our worldviews in less neatly delineated manners. We do not take for granted that depth is positive and that its (variable) opposite is negative, and hope the essays in this book offer opportunities to consider more nuanced mechanisms by which, rather than inherently containing any particular attributes, depth in fact is instead discursively imbued with them.

Recent turns to the surface embed productive critiques of depth paradigms, bound up as they are with their white, patriarchal progenitors. In her book *Pretty: Film and the Decorative Image,* for example, Rosalind Galt shows how the field of film studies has established cinema's value and specificity by prying "the image away from its connotations of picturesque, decorative surface" and aligning it instead "with meaning and depth."[11] Galt explicitly positions herself as building on Dudley Andrew's work on iconophobia in film studies, *The Image in Dispute* (1997), as well as Martin Jay's *Downcast Eyes: The Denigration of Vision in Twentieth-Century French Thought* (1993), arguing that "the rhetoric of cinema has consistently denigrated surface decoration" and demonstrated more "concern for (active) meaning over (passive) spectacle."[12] She quotes Andrew identifying Marxists and feminists as "among the chief iconoclasts of our era," but through her attention to the superficial category of "pretty," Galt discovers queer, feminist, and antiracist value in the decorative and often commercial surface where ornament, color, and texture reside.[13]

While alternatives to depth epistemologies abound, there has surprisingly yet to be any synthetic or sustained consideration of the phenomenon of depth itself in a single monograph or edited collection, despite widespread acknowledgment of its significance and, at times, its insidiousness. This volume proposes to fill this critical gap, and as such, it aspires to be useful for scholars and students in a wide range of fields across the humanities: not only cinema and media studies but also art and art history, philosophy, psychology, literature, music, history, science studies, cultural studies, and more. Indeed, to examine questions of depth in cinema and media studies is at once to suggest the exciting potentials of discovering unexpected but productive points of connection across disparate fields at a moment when the field feels increasingly decentralized and to remember how interdisciplinary the field has always been.

Given depth's persistence and variability, particularly as it shapes and is shaped by thinking about media and visual culture, we invited a range of film and media scholars to reflect on questions pertaining to the status of depth today. This means widely divergent things for different contributors: for some, it means revisiting histories of aesthetic practices and theoretical debates that reorient or contribute to our understanding of spectatorship and perception; for others, it means searching for paradigms that help us understand how questions of visuality, history, geography, subjectivity, politics, and belonging are renegotiated in "deep" sites: mines, oceans, sinkholes, and outer space. These are particular examples of the "thinking spaces" to which our subtitle refers, but the thinking spaces navigated across this book exceed the physical dimensions of the term "space."[14] The essays collected here seek also to create intellectual running room by exploring how epistemological paradigms and methods shape and at times restrict the ways we comprehend relationships between depth and media. To help forge paths across these different contexts and approaches, we have asked contributors, whenever possible, to foreground and define the kinds of depths they are talking about; to be especially mindful of how connections between depth as a visual concept, as a medial concept, and as a philosophical concept might play into the particular valuations of depth they are writing about; and to locate points of connection and disconnection between historical and contemporary mediations of depth.

We have organized the essays into four overarching parts: I. Depths of the Moving Image: Perception, Spectatorship, and Film Theory; II. Depth Hermeneutics and Surface Turns; III. Deep Space, Deep Time; and IV. Deep Networks. Neither exhaustive nor mutually exclusive, these categories illustrate the range of scales at which ideas and discourses of depth operate and also where they are most generative in relation to film and media. Readers may opt to approach each part as a self-contained dossier, and the brief section introductions offer some frameworks for considering connections and themes across the essays contained within them. However, when read in order and from beginning to end, the book's chapters reflect a more particular narrative about a changing discipline that has always been in search of its object and mindful of, if not anxious about, its shifting and uncertain boundaries. The book's first half, for example, is in general more methodologically invested in readings of individual films, while the second half reflects the influence of contemporary debates in and around cinema and media studies that push our thinking beyond the aesthetic contours of the film text.

As an ensemble, these essays suggest how within cinema and media studies, the concept of "depth" seems to have been hiding in plain sight as one of the few core ideas that has managed to retain a central place in a continuously changing field. This persistence of depth's significance and value across the evolving landscape of the field makes the discourse around the term simultaneously, and almost paradoxically, both a red thread of continuity—the ground of the field—and a figure or index of change.

Notes

1. Thomas Friedman, "Warning! Everything Is Going Deep: 'The Age of Surveillance Capitalism,'" *New York Times,* January 29, 2019, https://www.nytimes.com/2019/01/29/opinion/artificial-intelligence-surveillance.html.

2. Kathryn Yusoff, *A Billion Black Anthropocenes or None* (Minneapolis: University of Minnesota Press, 2018), xiii.

3. Yusoff, xiii.

4. Kathryn Yusoff, "Geosocial Strata," *Theory, Culture and Society* 34, no. 2–3 (2017): 122.

5. Yusoff, 122.

6. Dick Hebdige, "Staking out the Posts," in *Hiding in the Light: On Images and Things* (London: Routledge, 1988), 196.

7. Alain Badiou, *Trump* (Cambridge, UK: Polity Press, 2019), 1–2

8. For the 2019 VR lineup at the Venice Biennale, see https://www.labiennale.org/en/cinema/2019/venice-virtual-reality. For a more detailed discussion of Bi Gan's use of 3D, see Iggy Cortez's book manuscript, "Night on Earth: The Nocturnal Sensorium in World Cinema." See also Catherine Shoard, "Chinese Arthouse Film Breaks Box Office Records after Viewers Mistake It for Romcom," *The Guardian,* January 2, 2019, https://www.theguardian.com/film/2019/jan/02/chinese-arthouse-film-breaks-box-office-records-marketing-bi-gan-long-days-journey-into-night.

9. Sebastian Buerkner, "Adjusting the Promise of Stereoscopy," *Ars Electronica,* September 5, 2015, https://vimeo.com/138849142.

10. Jonathan Crary, *24/7: Late Capitalism and the Ends of Sleep* (London: Verso, 2014).

11. Rosalind Galt, *Pretty: Film and the Decorative Image* (New York: Columbia University Press, 2011), 53.

12. Galt, 2–3. See also Dudley Andrew, ed., *The Image in Dispute: Art and Cinema in the Age of Photography* (Austin: University of Texas Press, 1997), vii–8. Andrew in turn positioned himself as responding to W. J. T. Mitchell, *Iconology: Image, Text, Ideology* (Chicago: University of Chicago Press, 1986).

13. Andrew, *The Image in Dispute,* viii, quoted in Galt, *Pretty,* 3.

14. For media scholarship that overlaps with this book's concerns but that is more explicitly about the concept of "space," see Nick Couldry and Anna McCarthy's important collection, *MediaSpace: Place, Scale, and Culture in a Media Age* (London: Routledge, 2004) as well as *Media Fields Journal* (mediafieldsjournal .org).

PART I

Depths of the Moving Image

Perception, Spectatorship, and Film Theory

Had we been film scholars writing in the late 1980s, it might have seemed adequate, or at least obvious, to think about the use of "depth" primarily as depth of field. By that point, the critical discussion of this concept was already extensive and nuanced, holding a central place in classical, realist, and apparatus theories. There is a tendency to summarize each of those strands of film theory as having a homogeneous position on depth of field, but since the mid-1970s, which might be considered a "peak moment" in the history of the theorization of depth in cinema, discussions of the term have continued to evolve even as the field has expanded its historical and geographic reach, its objects of study, and theoretical frames of reference. We might think of the concept of depth of field "as an instructive lens through which to review multiple moments of film theory and the different sets of priorities and ways of talking about cinema found in each."[1]

Because of the importance of depth of field to the development of film theory, as well as to cinema and media studies, we want to trace some of the key developments in this conversation. We do this not to entrench certain narratives of depth of field in our minds but rather to remember the rich but historically specific pluralism of depth in this realm of scholarship, in spite of the sometimes-caricatured versions of these debates, before asking how we might put these earlier theorizations of depth in dialogue with other, more contemporary uses of the term. One need only think of the early scenes in *Citizen Kane* (Orson Welles, 1941), where we find some of the most prized shots for film theory's discussion of staging and shooting in depth coinciding with a narrative about the conversion of mining capital into mass media infrastructure, of the centrality of the Western genre to film theory's attempt to grapple with cinematic space, or even simply of the implicit extractivism of "the silver screen," to understand how imbricated and implicated cinema and media systems (including our systems of thought) are in the rhetoric and politics of depth.

We can find a drive to delineate elements of depth, perspective, and dimensionality from film theory's very beginning, as, for example, when Rudolf Arnheim declared, "The effect of film is neither absolutely two-dimensional nor absolutely three-dimensional, but something in between. Film pictures are at once plane and solid."[2] Yet few voices are as closely associated with depth of field as that of André Bazin, followed first by reactions to his and other "realist" theories in the apparatus theory of the 1970s, and then by reactions to apparatus theory in the 1990s. In his essay "The Myth of Total Cinema" (1946), Bazin invokes the film historian P. Potonièe's emphasis on stereoscopy more than photography as the discovery that "opened the eyes of the researchers," sending inventors in search of the "picture of life" and a "faithful copy of nature."[3] Then, in the composite of three essays written in the 1950s, published under the title "The Evolution of the Language of Cinema," he attends to the "plastics" of the cinematic image using a vocabulary that draws repeatedly on concepts of depth and surface. Over the course of the essay, it becomes clear that these are terms Bazin uses to think about how relationality functions in film. To view the plastics of Murnau's images as expressionistic would, Bazin claims, "be a superficial view." He continues, "The composition of his image is in no sense pictorial. It adds nothing to the reality, it does not deform it, it forces it to reveal its structural depth, to bring out the preexisting relations which become constitutive of the drama."[4] Bazin highlights Orson Welles and William Wyler as key filmmakers who challenge established styles of editing through the development of shooting in depth after 1939, although he recognizes that Jean Renoir's use of deep focus set an important precedent (30, 34). Through Renoir, Bazin stresses that the cinematic tradition of depth is not only spatial in nature but also temporal; this later becomes an issue of key importance both for Gilles Deleuze in *Cinema 2* and for Philip Rosen's examination of cinema's historicity in *Change Mummified*.[5] Bazin quotes a 1939 statement by Renoir: "The more I learn about my trade the more I incline to direction in depth relative to the screen," before commenting, "In [Renoir's] films, the search after composition in depth is, in effect, a partial replacement of montage by frequent panning shots and entrances. It is based on a continuity of dramatic space *and, of course, of its duration*."[6]

Bazin claims that the use of composition in depth is quite different in the 1940s from its use in the 1910s, where, he argues, shooting in depth primarily offered in exterior shots "the best vantage point to view the action" (34). By contrast, he sees Wyler's and Welles's handlings of depth of field constituting "not just a stock in trade of the cameraman like the use of a series of filters or of such-and-such a style of lighting" but rather as "a capital gain in the field of direction—a dialectical step forward in the history of film language" (35). Shooting in depth, Bazin argues, brings critical attention to several types of relationships within the film experience. Through Wyler's shooting in depth, "Objects and characters are related in such a fashion that it is impossible for the spectator to miss the significance of the scene" (34–35); this development in film language also, he claims, "affects the relationships of the minds of the spectators to the image" (35). While this "depth of focus brings the spectator into a relation with the image closer to that which he enjoys with reality," making the structure of such images "more realistic," for Bazin, this form of increased realism through depth also in some ways loosens the spectator's grasp on reality. Although we often tend to associate shooting in depth with increased focus and visual clarity in the image, the main quality this form of realism introduces at the cognitive level, at least for Bazin, is "ambiguity" (35–36).

Given the centrality of depth to Bazin, it is perhaps not surprising that, in 1971, Jean-Louis Comolli made depth of field the primary vehicle through which to execute his attack on Bazin's idea of an autonomously evolving aesthetic language of cinema, arguing that this position, which he described as "idealist," repressed the way that economic, political, and ideological factors interact to shape the technological and aesthetic development of cinema. In "Technique and Ideology: Camera, Perspective, Depth of Field [Parts 3 and 4]," Comolli also troubles Jean Mitry's technically determined and genealogical history of film. While he agrees with Mitry that "it's most often in exterior filming that the field achieves depth in this period [before 1915]," the two diverge on the question of how to approach the technical question.[7] Mitry points out that before 1915, only medium focal length lenses were available; Comolli follows up on this observation by asking what led to this situation in which only medium focal lenses were used during cinema's early years in the first place. Comolli concludes that these lenses were "authorized" over other focal lengths because of the "depth of field which they allowed," a depth of field that, he claims, upheld that society's "codes of analogy and realism," noting parenthetically that "other codes corresponding to other social demands would have produced other types of lenses" (433). Similarly, while Mitry attributes the "abandonment" of depth between

1925 and 1940 "in favor of intensive fragmentation" largely to the decreased sensitivity of the first panchromatic film emulsions, Comolli resists a style of argument that "explains technical transformation through other technical transformations" and is instead interested in why, during the development of the new emulsion, "apparently no pressure was exerted to preserve deep focus."[8] Perhaps most important for this volume and for a wider disciplinary history, Comolli's attempt to think historically in this essay about the uneven and complex use of depth of field in cinema results in his call for an end to "linear" histories of cinema—or at least an awareness of the ways in which these linear histories are underpinned by "another history," one itself made up of layers and depth, "a recursively stratified history of *significances*."[9] Various essays in this volume participate in this legacy of earlier depth conversations that aspire to open up nonlinear, recursive, and alternate pathways through film and media history.

Over the course of the 1970s, the question of depth of field continued to dominate anglophone film theory, with 1976 marking another key moment of engagement with the publication of Edward Branigan's essay "The Space of *Equinox Flower*" and Kristin Thompson and David Bordwell's "Space and Narrative in the Films of Ozu," both of which appeared in *Screen* (Summer 1976). These essays were followed swiftly in the next issue by another key contribution to the theorization of cinematic depth: Stephen Heath's "Narrative Space" in *Screen* (Autumn 1976).[10] Like his predecessors, Heath also discusses Bazin, Welles, and Wyler in the course of his reflections on narrative space and the screen, a part of the apparatus he describes as "one of the most stable elements in cinema's history" and "a pure expanse that can be invested with depth."[11] For him, the screen marks the spot where the differences that depth of field seem to make visible (differences that are arguably signaled by all Bazin's talk of relationships) are welded to each other through the "*narrativization* of film": "The terms, as they have been described here, are the terms of a constant welding together: screen and frame, ground and background, surface and depth, the whole setting of movements and transitions, the implication of space and spectator in the taking place of film as narrative" (397).

Though apparatus theory's understanding of a film viewer without agency—fixed in place by classical cinema's narrative and aesthetic codes—has now been displaced by more than half a century of less rigid thinking about spectatorship, it is worth noting that at this moment of discussing the welding of surface and depth, before Heath turns his attention to Japanese cinema (as Thompson, Bordwell, and Branigan all do) in search of other cinematic arrangements of space and depth of field, he briefly invokes the 1975 blockbuster *Jaws* (Steven Spielberg). Heath introduces this somewhat surprising example to illustrate the role of the "character-look" or point-of-view shot in the kinds of spatial weldings that concern him, describing how the camera aligns the spectator with Brody (Roy Scheider) as the new police chief of Amity Island flicks through picture books of sharks. It is, in many ways, an unremarkable moment in Heath's essay. Yet we flag it before discussing Japanese cinema's role in the anglophone conversation about depth of field because the presence of *Jaws* in this essay about narrative space retrospectively marks the possibility of "another history" (or other histories, and with it, other theories) to come: one attuned less to horizontal than vertical space, and perhaps not so centered in Anglo-American and Western European points of view. Although many of the publicity images for the film highlight the deep space that is of such theoretical concern at this moment through images of the smooth and expansive surface of the water that takes the viewer's eye out to the horizon, the film itself repeatedly emphasizes, visually and narratively, a vertical depth in both directions (up and down). Vertical depth dominates the film's aerial shots that peer dizzyingly down the line of the *Orca*'s mast at the ocean below, the unknown depth of which is marked by the rising and sinking barrels that have been shot into the body of the shark, as well as by the alignment of the shark itself, which often appears vertically, nose up. The film also draws spectatorial attention to the film's vertical axis through underwater shots reflecting the shark's point of view as it looks at the tasty swimmers and boats above the surface; and finally, through Quint's (Robert Shaw) onboard recollections of serving aboard the USS *Indianapolis* during World War II, delivering the atomic bomb that would be used in Hiroshima, and of the side of that ship being attacked by two torpedoes from a Japanese submarine. The tale is told by Quint (and Spielberg) as an American ocean tragedy, a story of horizontal underwater torpedoes and man against shark—only about three hundred of the twelve hundred men on board the USS *Indianapolis* survived. But this tale of oceanic depth also invokes, while simultaneously disregarding, another verticality: that of the atomic aerial warfare inflicted by the United States on Japan, where the combined death tolls of the acute effects of the bombs dropped on Hiroshima and Nagasaki range from 129,000 to 226,000. Heath would soon go on to publish his full review of *Jaws* in autumn 1976, where he addressed the film's resonance with Watergate and Vietnam and noted the atomic aesthetic of the final scenes of the shark's annihilation. But in the context of "Narrative Space," we merely glimpse the future possibility of a vertical turn, the kinds of histories and theories it has the potential to open up, as well as its imbrication in discussions of depth of field before Heath joins Bordwell, Thompson, and Branigan in a formal analysis of Japanese art cinema.[12]

Whatever the limitations of apparatus theory's engagement—some might call it obsession—with quattrocento perspective, it undoubtedly generated a new level of curiosity about the role of space in cinema. As Branigan recognized in "The Space of *Equinox Flower*," Yasujirō Ozu's spatial systems were quite different from the ones generally used in Hollywood (e.g., a 360-degree rather than a 180-degree model), often leading to experimentation: "Ozu even explores the possibility of confronting a three-dimensional perception of space with a two-dimensional mosaic of graphic qualities."[13] In the twenty-first century, as Alexander Zahlten argues in *The End of Japanese Cinema: Industrial Genres, National Times, and Media Ecologies* (2017), the Anglo-American formalist engagement of Japanese cinema that was, in part, a reaction to apparatus theory's universalization of the operations of cinematic space has now largely been replaced by other multimedia and "precisely delineated discursive histories" that move away from the national cinema model and rely on the "emergence of a generation of scholars fluent in Japanese and with access to historical documents."[14] Problematic as some of these formalist approaches might be, however, we recognize that the formalist approach, exemplified by a book like David Bordwell's *Figures Traced in Light: On Cinematic Staging* (2005), has generated a richer vocabulary for thinking about staging in depth and the formal variables available to and discovered by filmmakers: highlighting uses of planes as an alternative to diagonal staging; recognizing that foregrounds might be used in very different ways by filmmakers all still staging in depth; examining the role of lighting in creating depth effects; and so on.[15]

Thomas Lamarre's book *The Anime Machine: A Media Theory of Animation* (2009) makes a number of important interventions into several conversations within the field in the course of his landmark study of anime, and they are too numerous to summarize here. But for the purposes of our consideration of film and media theory's prior engagement with the concept of depth, it is useful to highlight some of these key points. Crucially, Lamarre rejects the technological determinism that is embedded both within positions that link geometric perspective to scientific modernization and within "superflat" theories that bind "Japanese structures of nonhierarchical distribution" to postmodernism in an essentializing way that leaves little room for thinking about, for example, Japanese modernism.[16] By focusing on animation, an area of study often defined by its focus on movement, Lamarre is able to notice first how often movement tends to be ignored in discussions of image composition (114) and, then, how movement can allow depth to be brought "to the surface" (132). Furthermore, by introducing examples of images that use orthogonal perspective and exploded projections, Lamarre helps to create space for thinking in less deterministic ways about depth: "What should concern us is the possibility that any structure of depth can be systematized or modernized, much as any language can be modernized. In other words, from a semiotic point of view, neither a mode of perspective nor a language affords any guaranteed dispensation toward or opposition to modernization. This is not to say semiotic structures do not have any potential for critical engagement, but they will not do the thinking for us" (122).

Animation offers different possibilities from live-action filming for representing 3D space in two dimensions. And as Nicholas Sammond points out in his recent study of blackface minstrelsy and American animation, the cinematically generated interaction between different dimensions, including how interactions are shaped by sound, is not merely an aesthetic issue, although it is also that. He notes, "Changes in the representation of narrative space were accompanied by alterations in production practices, and with them in understandings of the social and cultural geographies that those fictional spaces were meant to represent. Technological and aesthetic innovations that were developed in the jockeying for market share in animation during this period correlate to shifts in the spaces being represented on screen, but they also point to changes in how producers, exhibitors, and audiences understood the theatrical spaces in which cartoons appeared."[17] For Sammond, "complex play with depth, scale, and motion had less to do with creating stable regimes of cinematic realism and more to do with extending animation's performance of mastery beyond cartoon bodies to the very spaces they inhabited."[18] In this way, Sammond is aligned with a corrective trend in contemporary accounts of film theory that unfix positions assuming that any given techniques are tied to specific ideologies or aesthetics; it is precarious to claim, for example, that depth of field inherently gives way to a mode of realism. Ideas of what constitutes realism, instead, are equally shaped by a history of technical deployments, discourses, and artistic movements.

This collection begins with a series of essays that reflect on and at times rethink earlier moments in film history and film theory to offer new takes on some of these long-standing conversations about depth in cinema, particularly as they pertain to questions of perception and its intersection with flatness, animation, pictorial space, movement, time, perspective, value, truth, and spectatorship.

Notes

1. Edward Branigan and Warren Buckland, eds., *The Routledge Encyclopedia of Film Theory* (London: Routledge, 2013), 122.

2. Rudolf Arnheim, *Film as Art* in *Critical Visions in Film Theory: Classic and Contemporary Readings,* ed. Timothy Corrigan, Patricia White, and Meta Mazaj (Boston and New York: Bedford/St. Martin's, 2011), 282.

3. André Bazin, *What Is Cinema?,* ed. and trans. Hugh Gray (Berkeley: University of California Press, 1967), 20.

4. Bazin, 27.

5. Philip Rosen also stresses the importance of not mistaking Bazin's interest in depth of field for a naive concern with "perceptual-spatial accuracy or lack of accuracy," noting that "the function of perspective in Bazin's theory invites us to displace consideration of the special appeal of cinematic 'realism' from spatial similarity or dissimilarity between image and world to issues of temporality"; Rosen, *Change Mummified: Cinema, Historicity, Theory* (Minneapolis: University of Minnesota Press, 2001), 16. In *Cinema 2: The Time Image,* trans. Hugh Tomlinson and Robert Galeta (Minneapolis: University of Minnesota Press, 1989; first published in French in 1985), Gilles Deleuze distinguishes between two types of depth in the image. In the first, associated with sixteenth-century painting, depth takes place "in parallel and successive planes [*plans*], each autonomous, defined by characters or elements side by side" (107). But he identifies a second mode of depth arising in the seventeenth century, described as "a novel change, and crucial," "when an element of a plane refers directly to an element of a different plane, when characters address each other directly from one plane to another, in an organization of the picture along the diagonal, or through a gap which thus privileges the background and brings it into immediate touch with the foreground. . . . At this moment, depth becomes depth of field" (107). Deleuze maps this earlier history of art onto the history of film, with D. W. Griffith standing in for the sixteenth century, and Orson Welles, preceded by Renoir, embodying the seventeenth century. Deleuze seems clearly to be following Bazin here. Unlike the apparatus theorists, Deleuze notes that Bazin's realism is always "complex" (108). He notes that while Bazin gives depth "a function of reality," he "showed that this gain in reality could be achieved only through an 'excess of

theatricality'" (108). Deleuze then distinguishes this from his own position on depth in cinema by linking this spatial quality first to time, and then later, by extension, to memory: "We suggest that depth of field has many functions, and that they all come together in a direct time-image. The special quality of depth of field would be to reverse time's subordination to movement and show time for itself. . . . What must be noted is that depth of field sometimes shows us evocation in the act of occurring and sometimes virtual sheets of past that we explore in order to find the recollection sought" (109). Deleuze's discussion of a temporally charged depth of field emerges from his preceding meditation on the construction of time in the films of Alain Resnais, and the *fashioning* of time in animated films (104–5), preempting the way that animation constitutes one of the major forces challenging how film theory has dealt with depth of field. See, for example, Thomas Lamarre, *The Anime Machine: A Media Theory of Animation* (Minneapolis: University of Minnesota Press, 2009). Nevertheless, Deleuze's temporal notion of depth overlaps with and is continuous with Bazin's theorization of depth of field.

6. Bazin, *What Is Cinema?,* 34 (emphasis added).

7. Jean-Louis Comolli, "Technique and Ideology: Camera, Perspective, Depth of Field [Parts 3 and 4]," in *Narrative, Apparatus, Ideology: A Film Theory Reader,* ed. Philip Rosen (New York: Columbia University Press, 1986), 433.

8. Comolli, 435–37. Bazin mentions panchromatic stock in "The Evolution of the Language of Cinema" as contributing to the demise of shooting in depth; but he is never technologically determinist about it, and of shooting in depth outdoors, he notes, "Anyone could do it who really wanted to. So that it is less a question basically of a technical problem . . . than of a search for style"; Bazin, *What Is Cinema?,* 30.

9. Comolli, "Technique and Ideology," 424.

10. Stephen Heath, "Narrative Space," reprinted in Rosen, *Narrative, Apparatus, Ideology,* 379–420.

11. Heath, 393.

12. Stephen Heath, "*Jaws,* Ideology and Film Theory," *Framework: The Journal of Cinema and Media,* no. 4 (Autumn 1976): 25. The verticality of *Jaws* is also implicitly recognized in P. J. Capelotti's *Adventures in Archaeology: The Wreck of the* Orca II *and Other Explorations* (Gainesville: University Press of Florida, 2018).

13. Edward Branigan, "The Space of *Equinox Flower,*" *Screen: The Journal of the Society for Education in Film and Television* 17, no. 2 (Summer 1976): 105.

14. Alexander Zahlten, *The End of Japanese Cinema: Industrial Genres, National Times, and Media Ecologies* (Durham, N.C.: Duke University Press, 2017), 14.

15. A similar enrichment of depth vocabulary happens with the so-called historical turn in the realm of early film studies, exemplified by the 1990 volume

edited by Thomas Elsaesser with Adam Barker, *Early Cinema: Space, Frame, Narrative* (London: British Film Institute, 1990), and particularly Ben Brewster's "Deep Staging in French Films 1900–1914," 45–55.

16. Lamarre, *The Anime Machine,* 114–15.

17. Nicholas Sammond, *Birth of an Industry: Blackface Minstrelsy and the Rise of American Animation* (Durham, N.C.: Duke University Press, 2015), 173.

18. Sammond, 144.

CHAPTER ONE

From the Flat Plane, an Architecture of Light

Filming Space in Interwar Animation

Katherine Rochester

Hans Richter published the first issue of the avant-garde journal *G. Material for Elementary Construction* (*Material zur elementaren Gestaltung*) in Berlin in July 1923. In it, a collection of manifestos aimed at defining clear categories and trajectories for the arts abutted each other in a bold, graphic layout. Prominently placed on the bottom right quadrant of the first page was a treatise by Theo van Doesburg titled "Toward Elementary Construction" ("Zur Elementaren Gestaltung") (Figure 1.1). Advocating the clear separation of the arts as an antidote to baroque confusion and individualistic expression, van Doesburg outlined general principles for painting, sculpture, and architecture that could spur artists away from "decorative taste" toward "monumental artistic production."[1] Each art was identified by its "primary (elementary) means" and illustrated with a variation on the square. Four flat, black squares for painting suggest "form-time-color"; four cubes with high-contrast shading symbolize the "space-time-line-surface-volume" attributes of sculpture; four outlined cubes for architecture denote "space-time-line-surface."

Van Doesburg did not mention film, but a filmstrip from one of Richter's experiments bridged the gap (Figure 1.2). Hugging the entire length of the upper border of the second and third pages, it ran parallel to van Doesburg's article in the manner of a decorative border. Indeed, with the individual film frames displayed in succession and flattened across the surface of the broadsheet, Richter's filmstrip provided an ornamental variation on the motif of the square, which chimed with the larger squares and cubes that illustrated the flatness of painting, the modeling of sculpture, and the spatial logic of architecture in van Doesburg's article. As van Doesburg had with his diagrams, Richter annotated his filmstrip to

Zur Elementaren Gestaltung.

I.

Es wird notwendig zwei einander entgegengesetzte Ausdrucksweisen scharf zu trennen: die dekorative (schmückende) und die monumentale (gestaltende).

Diese zwei Ausdrucksweisen bestimmen zwei gänzlich verschiedene Kunstauffassungen: die der Vergangenheit und die der Gegenwart. Richtet das dekorative Prinzip sich nach Zentralisation, so kennzeichnet Dezentralisation das Prinzip des Monumentalen.

Die bisherige Kunstentwicklung durchläuft alle Stadien vom Individualismus bis zur äußersten Verallgemeinerung.

Individualismus			Verallgemeinerung
	Dekoration	**Monumentalität**	
	Vergangenheit	**Gegenwart**	
	Zentralisation	**Dezentralisation**	

In dieser Spannung liegt das Problem der neuen Kunstgestaltung, des neuen Stils.

In der dekorativen Auffassung war die schöpferische Tätigkeit abhängig von persönlichem Geschmack, Willkür oder intuitiver Wertung der Elemente des Kunstwerks. Diese launenhafte Arbeit entsprach aber nicht der Forderung unserer Zeit: **PRÄZISION.**

Diejenigen nun, die diese Forderung (z. B.) intellektuell begriffen haben, glauben den Widerspruch zu überwinden, indem sie ihre ebenso launenhafte wie spekulative Arbeit mit dem Worte „Problem" bezeichnen. Sie stellen fest, daß es sich in der bildenden Kunst nicht mehr um „künstlerische Komposition", sondern um „problematische Konstruktion" handeln müsse. Ich nehme an, daß der Unterschied zwischen Komposition (Zusammenstellen) und Konstruktion (Zusammenfassen) eine nicht zu unterschätzende Zeiterscheinung ist, aber weder das eine, noch das andere kann zu einer fruchtbaren, monumentalen

THEO VAN DOESBURG
GENERALBASS DER MALEREI

FIGURE 1.1. Illustration of painting principles. Theo van Doesburg, "Toward Elementary Construction" ("Zur Elementaren Gestaltung"), G. *Material zur elementaren Gestaltung* 1 (July 1923).

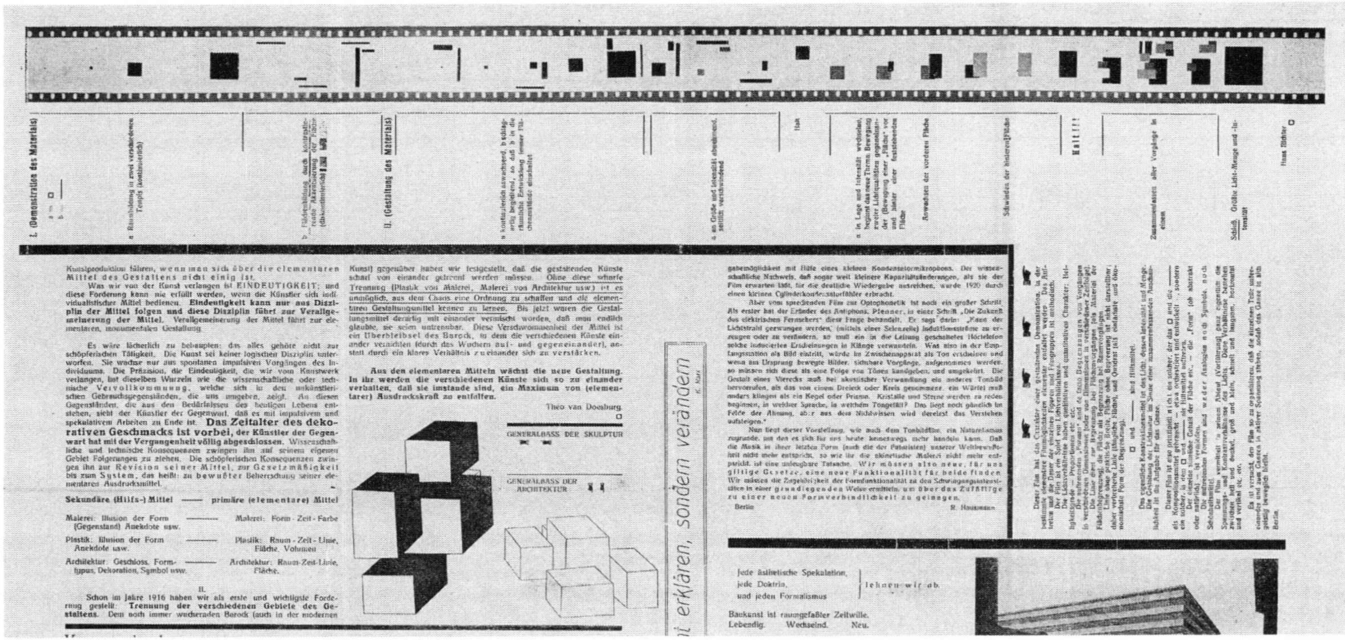

FIGURE 1.2. Hans Richter's annotated filmstrip above Theo van Doesburg, "Toward Elementary Construction" ("Zur Elementaren Gestaltung"), *G. Material zur elementaren Gestaltung* 1 (July 1923).

clarify its material and essential principles. Using time and rhythm to produce a new spatial logic, he intended his animated squares and lines to "create the construction of a surface by contrasting accentuation of the plane."[2] In previous essays, Richter had described his film work with the painter Viking Eggeling as a breakthrough for painting.[3] Film allowed for the clarification of painting principles in time-based media: "The clear organization of the formal vocabulary makes it possible to use it to create not just a picture—a static work—but to apply this vocabulary to time, a dimension hitherto inaccessible to the fine arts."[4] Writing in *De Stijl* a few months before he released the first issue of *G,* Richter buckled down on his conviction that time, not space, was an essential principle of film construction: "Film's rightful sphere is that of 'moving' space, 'moving' surface, 'moving' line. . . . This space is not architectonic or plastic, but rather temporal."[5]

In 1923, then, Richter was clearly committed to the widespread view that the essential properties of the animated film were time, rhythm, and flatness—or, rather, a dynamic intersection of planes that continuously reoriented the diegetic space of the film in relation to the rectangle of the screen, the horizontal surface of the animation table, and the vertical plane of the wall on which the image was projected. The Absolute Film Matinee of 1925 variously bore his thesis out with screenings of Viking Eggeling's *Diagonal Symphony* (1921/1924); Richter's own *Film Is Rhythm* (1921–1925); and Walter Ruttmann's *Opus 2, Opus 3,* and *Opus 4,* but by then the terms had begun to shift. Correcting the 1923 omission of film from "Toward Elementary Construction," van Doesburg soon supplied a definition that in every way contradicted Richter's thesis on the flat qualities of film in *G.* Acknowledging by name the artists who had advanced film to the stage of "film poetry" exhibited in the Absolute Film Matinee, van Doesburg declared that such attempts had ultimately fallen flat in their pursuit of the "purely constructivist film" (*rein gestaltender Film*). They faltered on account of their constrained spatial orientation, since they "operate strictly within the frame of the screen, not in *space.*"[6] Eggeling, Richter, Man Ray, Dudley Murphy, and others had created a "film ornament" (*Filmornamentik*) that emphasized flatness and pictorial rhythm, attributes more appropriate to the painted canvas than to the projected film.[7] Van Doesburg isolated flatness as a formal interloper, a medial stowaway whose continued presence thwarted true film construction: "Now this plane must be *exploded* in order to discover beyond it *new depth,* the space-time film continuum. Therein and nowhere else lies the creative realm of the constructive film!"[8] Earnest experiments in this direction by László Moholy-Nagy, Richter, and Kazimir Malevich soon followed, but despite van Doesburg's widely circulated statements and their swift ratification, the avant-garde's swerve into deep space has been overlooked.

What was at stake in the sudden constructivist insistence on depth over flatness? How were spatial properties theorized and mapped onto corresponding intellectual values in avant-garde film? Focusing on artists associated with various experimental animation practices, this essay will examine the efforts of the avant-garde to negotiate their own optics in pursuit of a new vision. Very often, this meant distinguishing between hapticality and opticality, terms that were constantly renegotiated as artists turned away from the "movie-canvas" or pictorial plane toward theorizing film as a projection of light into space. Viennese art historian Aloïs Riegl first theorized the haptic and the optic as poles of visual perception.[9] These poles described tactile (haptic) or visual (optic) encounters dictated by material, technique, and proximity. Hapticality connoted nearness and flatness, as observed in Egyptian hieroglyphics, which were sharply delineated ornaments on a self-contained plane; opticality, in contrast, suggested vision in deep space. Its most exemplary epoch was the Renaissance, where illusionistic space was painted with perspectival accuracy. Riegl's terminology was variously deployed during the interwar period, most famously by Walter Benjamin, who sought to analyze historical shifts in human perception by studying corresponding changes in artistic production.[10] As products of mechanical reproduction and mass consumption, cartoons initially played a starring role in Benjamin's formulation of the optical unconscious. The first draft of "The Work of Art in the Age of Its Technological Reproducibility" features Mickey Mouse as "the figure of a collective dream," whose absurd antics unfolding in a world of pure fantasy offered audiences instant catharsis.[11] Through collective laughter, Benjamin argued that "Disney films trigger a therapeutic demolition of the unconscious."[12] Coterminous with the advent of the optical unconscious was a new and characteristically modern desire to "bring things closer."[13] Benjamin's analogy of the filmmaker who "penetrates deeply into the tissue of reality" to a surgeon whose hand "moves among the organs," only to later stitch the pieces into an eventual whole, describes with graphic clarity the relationship that animators had to the cartoon body.[14] In film, Benjamin discerned a recalibration relative to the haptic and the optic, a distinctly modern reorientation in space crystallized specifically in animation.

Indeed, the centrality of animation to Benjamin's canonical essay on visual perception suggests that an exploration of space in Weimar film might begin with the animation table. Its flexible spatial orientation lent itself to a variety of artistic practices, which variously claimed to embrace or resist its logic as a material support. Indeed, media theorist Thomas Lamarre has contended that the multiplane camera has no de facto spatial properties but can—like so many machines—be put to various uses: "The animation stand, as a multiplanar machine, invites different ways of . . . thinking about and inhabiting the technologized world."[15] Writing about Japanese animation, Lamarre observes that the animation stand can either perpetuate or stymie the depth-seeking mission to which commercial animators broadly applied the multiplane camera. Style may seem to issue from support, but it often proceeds in wildly different directions. For example, film studies has characterized the multiplane camera as a three-dimensional object thanks to its multiple layers of glass and the perspectival realism that Disney achieved with it; but the multiplane camera was just as easily theorized as a flatbed concurrent with the flat surface of the animation table and therefore with decorative patterns that emphasize the flat planes of the film screen. Which direction artists pursued was motivated by a host of aesthetic, philosophical, and ideological convictions whose intertwining logics and constantly moving targets preoccupied the experimental film community in Weimar Germany. Far from being a bulwark against the hegemony of spatial realism on film, this essay will consider the avant-garde as an early and vocal agent in what has been considered the uniquely commercial drive to "evolve" film from primitive flatness to realistic depth in narrative cinema.

Evolving Film: From Primitive Flatness into Deep Space

In film studies, the deep focus shot has long been associated with more advanced and sophisticated cinema, whereas the flat or "theatrical" stationary shot has been associated with the "primitive" days of early film.[16] Histories of mainstream animation narrate an apparatus-driven evolution from flatness to depth that hews to a similar narrative.[17] Beginning with the lightning sketches popularized by John Stuart Blackton and the line drawings of Émil Cohl, animation progressed from lively cartoons that cavorted on the page to mimetically real characters situated in the perspectivally accurate world generated by Walt Disney's multiplane camera. While the treatment of deep space in Disney's *Snow White and the Seven Dwarfs* (1937) has been celebrated as a benchmark in animation studies, flatness—as both an aesthetic and an ideological choice—has been widely recognized as characteristic of avant-garde film.[18] Film scholar Esther Leslie argues that animation appealed to the ideologically motivated artists of the European avant-garde as a method for challenging the social order.[19] These artists believed that modernity demanded new forms to spur new modes of perception, and the peculiar logic of the animated world provided a model for envisioning an alternate reality.[20] "All sorts of anti-academic and experimenting artists found that cartoons touched on many things that they too wished to explore: abstraction, forceful outlines, geometric forms and flatness, questioning of space and time and logic."[21] Indeed, so crucial is the embrace of flatness and the rejection of perspectivally accurate space to Leslie's theorization of the avant-garde that she regards Disney's eventual simulation of depth with the multiplane camera as a politically reactionary move.[22] However, Leslie's argument as it relates to the avant-garde ascribes rather too much resistant power to the so-called flatness of their animations. Indeed, as mentioned earlier, van Doesburg advocated a plunge into deep space in 1927, a good ten years before *Snow White* premiered. I would therefore like to draw attention to the fact that while the avant-garde advocated abstraction over figurative realism, they were also susceptible to a host of prejudices that associated flatness with primitivity and decoration, qualities they explicitly strove to eliminate from their films on their way to creating the "new vision."

In their disdain for flatness, the avant-garde was actually very much in line with the status quo. Film historian Noël Burch proposes the concept of "primitive externality," an umbrella term under which he gathers certain formal attributes of early film such as the flat tableau, "horizontal and frontal camera placement," and restive long shots (as opposed to quick editing), all of which evolve or obsolesce by the time cinema reaches the classical era.[23] Burch is certainly not alone in adopting an evolutionary model for thinking about cinema. In an essay that organizes early film by formal traits, film historian Barry Salt maintains that "rapid developments in the formal aspects of film in these early years see some analogies with biological evolution, in the way that novel features which suddenly appear like mutations are sometimes rapidly taken up in other films, forming a line of descent, while on other occasions original devices die out because they have some unsuitability of a technical, commercial or artistic nature."[24] Salt proposes that these "unsuitabilities" of primitive film might be considered "evolutionary dead-ends" (31). Tracing this line of reasoning to its logical origin, film and literature historian Assenka Oksiloff has identified what must surely be the limit case of "primitive" cinema in a convincing examination of early ethnographic film practices. Drawing attention to the conventions of anthropological films, Oksiloff suggests that "the interplay of the panoramic and the close-up in picturing the primitive body is a key factor in understanding the notion of primitive cinema and its relationship to ethnography."[25] Showing how the flatness of "primitive" cinema was often compounded by the supposed primitiveness of the subjects it shot, Oksiloff delivers an important check on accepted definitions of how early cinema might be described in relation to its technical capabilities and formal properties. Hers is a useful reminder that the primitive connotation of flatness in film studies may not simply be ascribed to the shortcomings of its early apparatus.

Far from being "primitive," many animators in the 1920s who deliberately chose flatness over depth delivered films of extraordinary sophistication. These films, made by women and non-Westerners, and often taking fairy tales or "oriental" themes as their subject, were technically innovative but aesthetically and thematically problematic for the avant-garde, who sought to stringently differentiate their own experiments from these precedents. Lotte Reiniger, who began making animated films in 1919, choreographed her silhouettes like "arabesques of ornaments" to maximize their expression on a flat plane.[26] In her first published essay, she reiterated the importance of the animation table's flat surface: "The puppets lie flat on the surface. They lack the original center of gravity of marionettes, which gives them such a rich irreality. They lack the coming and going, the play of facial expressions that cartoons can have. Instead, they *rule* the plane and their flexible maneuverability knows no bounds."[27]

Reiniger draws an unequivocal distinction among marionettes, line-drawn cartoons, and silhouettes. Marionettes are vertically oriented, exist in real space, and obey the rules of gravity. Cartoons, such as Disney's, exist in a simulated but mimetically realistic version of three-dimensional space drawn on cels. Reiniger's silhouettes, in contrast, were cut from paper and laid on a flat surface, with no attempt made to move them through a mimetic world of deep space. The gravity that bears them down on the table is reversed through the animation process, insofar as their flatness (their absolute adherence to the surface of the animation table) becomes the engine for their movement on axes that traverse the screen and are later flipped into vertiginous verticality when projected in a movie theater. Like Richter's annotated filmstrip in *G*, the work surface of Reiniger's animation table is transformed into a flat plane on film. This transformation charts a critical shift from a set of specifically engineered creative conditions to a register of theoretical possibilities generated by the planar universe on screen.

FIGURE 1.3. Page from Lotte Reiniger's chinoiserie notebook, featuring a sketch for a wedding procession. Graphite pencil on paper (1923–26). Stadtmuseum Tübingen, Lotte Reiniger Nachlass, R 665. Copyright 2019 Artists Rights Society (ARS), New York / VG Bild-Kunst, Bonn.

Preparatory sketches for a scene from Reiniger's full-length feature, *The Adventures of Prince Achmed* (1926), reveal the indivisibility of flat ornament from her approach to animation. For example, a carefully annotated sheet from one of her "chinoiserie" sketchbooks reveals the coordination required between movement, music, and camera in order to animate an intricately designed wedding procession (Figure 1.3). Twenty-two small figures are drawn in parallel rows. They march in opposite directions, the bottom row toward the right side of the page and the top row away from it. Under each figure Reiniger jotted down a number that corresponded to the beat on which she would adjust particular joints of individual bodies in time to the score (which was composed by Wolfgang Zeller in close coordination with Reiniger's animation).[28]

Once animated, this scene in *The Adventures of Prince Achmed* is rhythmically entrancing, with royal attendants marching in a boisterous file along a series of bridges and stairways that crisscross the screen (Figure 1.4). Palettes and lanterns tip and sway as they ostensibly advance across a supposed cityscape. But Reiniger interrupts the field of vision before we can identify a foreground and a background, opting, instead,

FIGURE 1.4. *The Adventures of Prince Achmed* (*Die Abenteuer des Prinzen Achmed*) (Lotte Reiniger, 1926). Stadtmuseum Tübingen, Lotte Reiniger Nachlass, R 1998-19. Image courtesy of Christel Strobel.

for a series of repetitions that confuse and delight the eye in a manner typical of wall coverings designed in the Chinese style.[29] Pagodas are cropped and jostled, bridges echo each other in similar humps and arches, and figures neither recede nor advance but remain constant regardless of their position in the landscape. The scene—as is typical of so many in Reiniger's films—pushes figures to the edge of abstraction by testing the limits of the eye to distinguish individual silhouettes amid multiplying patterns of ornamentation. While neither ornament nor animation stand was inherently flat, each offered an intriguing proposition about flatness as either aesthetic principle or material condition. What Reiniger used from ornamental design generally, and from oriental motifs and chinoiserie more specifically, were those elements that lent themselves to emphasizing movement on a two-dimensional plane.

Other experimental filmmakers worked the animation stand for similar effects. In Japan, Noburo Ofuji developed a method for animating origami and washi paper cutouts, the frontally lit surfaces of which extended ornate patterns of ornamentation across the screen. *Burglars of Baghdad Castle* (1926) and *The Story of the Monkey King* (1927)

FIGURE 1.5. Example of a cinematic pan effect (reading from left to right, top to bottom) achieved through scrolling. *Burglars of Baghdad Castle* (Noburo Ofuji, 1926).

display a remarkable use of scrolling to simulate the effect of cinematic pans (Figure 1.5). *Chiyogami*, Ofuji's visually resplendent technique, was engineered to maximize flatness by pulling the paper scene across the surface of the animation table. Inspired by Reiniger, Ofuji turned to oriental themes, interpreting the *Arabian Nights* from a Japanese perspective filtered through German Orientalism.

The avant-garde was wary of such ornamental effects. Indeed, carefully engineered rhetoric published in journals such as *G* often worked to give film space a gendered dimension, linking flat ornamentation to frivolous decoration and exotic decadence. Viewed in this light, van Doesburg's call to forsake the decorative art of the past in favor of new forms of construction was hardly a novel formulation. When the vogue for chinoiserie ebbed in the late eighteenth century and the modernist rejection of ornament surged, the imbrication of the oriental and the ornamental was so thorough as to be practically synonymous.[30] From art critic Karl Scheffler's popular book *Woman and Art* (*Die Frau und die Kunst. Eine Studie*, 1900) to architect Adolf Loos's short screed "Ornament and Crime" (1908), modernism was defined in sexist, racist, and homophobic language that called for an abandonment of ornament.[31] Linking the expungement of ornament to the development of modern, European man, Loos admitted that he could "tolerate" the ornaments produced by "the Chinese carvers," "the Kaffir who weaves ornaments into his fabric," and "the Persian who weaves his carpet" only because their cultures had failed to advance.[32] Unlike the degenerate Orient, however, Europe had aesthetics: "We have art, which has taken the place of ornament" (24). According to Loos, art could be produced only in the West, where creativity had been sanctified by racial and cultural superiority. Anyone who failed to expunge decoration undermined the very fabric of a healthy society. More than simply passé, modern ornament was "a pathological phenomenon" (24). Loos's solipsistic conclusion was that "freedom from ornament is a sign of spiritual strength" (22).

Flatness or hapticality and its relationship to European constructions of the exotic have recently been reconsidered by a number of scholars seeking to challenge the biases inherited from an evolutionary model of film and art history. Tracing the period theorization of early screen space back to Riegl's writings on late Roman art and Dutch portraiture, film historian Antonia Lant situates early film theory as a discourse that accounted for both the formal treatment of compositional elements and the psychological engagement of the viewer.[33] Noting the popularity of Egyptian themes in early film, Lant draws our attention back to Riegl's work on haptic Egyptian art. Its flatness and pictographic force modeled haptic possibilities for the "unclear identities of figure and ground" that characterized early cinematic space, even as its psychological attributes appropriately suggested the dawn of a new era of perception (46). Lant elaborates: "Egypt could not help but stand for ideas of emergence and evolution in style itself because of its place within [Riegl's] chronologies as the initial or primitive form, from which there could only be a progression" (51). According to Lant, early cinema was therefore winkingly primitive, playful, and full of potential. When the paper jungle set in Georges Méliès's *The Palace of the Arabian Nights* (1905) folds layer over layer to envelop a wandering group of travelers, Lant perceives the reflexive acknowledgment of cinema's illusory space insofar as "the surfaces of the forest seem to reconstitute the plane of the screen, the film briefly declaring itself the decorated canvas it always is" (45).

Film historian Rosalind Galt likewise draws extensively on Riegl to lay the groundwork for her study on the decorative in live-action film. She considers color, camera movement, and queer aesthetics, rightly linking the prejudice against flatness in cinema to a host of phobias that have historically been associated with the decorative: "The rhetoric of cinema has consistently denigrated surface decoration, finding the attractive skin of the screen to be false, shallow, feminine, or apolitical."[34] Galt notes that the connection between the decorative and the oriental is often commensurate to a rejection of the racialized Other, and she stakes out the territory of the pretty as denigrated terrain urgently in need of recuperation: "The politics of the pretty is therefore always engaged in a critique of gender, sexuality, and race as these terms have been imagined and codified through visual culture."[35] Yet while Riegl has repeatedly been invoked by film theorists eager to challenge the evolutionary argument of cinematic progress from theatrical flatness/narrative shallowness to deep focus/dramatic sophistication, Riegl's beneficiary and younger colleague Wilhelm Worringer was more frequently cited by avant-garde artists and theorists in the 1920s—and for causes specifically at odds with feminist and postcolonial critiques.

Unlike Riegl's suggestion that the haptic and optic may be present in different measures at different times in the artwork of different peoples, Worringer insisted that the haptic and optic anchored opposing poles of an evolutionary trajectory. Although largely a recapitulation of Riegl's theory of ornament, Worringer's *Abstraction and Empathy: A Contribution to the Psychology of Style* (*Abstraktion und Einfühlung: ein Beitrag zur Stilpsychologie*, 1908) was a touchstone for the filmmakers associated with the absolute film and supportive critics. Worringer's innovation was to sharpen Riegl's distinction between the haptic and the optic by associating the haptic with an empathic mode of perception and the optic with abstract thinking. He insisted that empathy and abstraction were opposing psychic processes with concrete values attached. Although the urge to abstraction had begun as an instinct in primitive man to still the psychic chaos wreaked by a pantheistic worldview, it had evolved as the human spirit passed "along the whole course of rationalistic cognition," to its apotheosis in the crystalline forms of the Gothic period.[36] Worringer adopted a mystical tone that resonated with modern artists seeking new paradigms for form. Reading him, the artists associated with the absolute film were gratified to find substantiated their own conviction that "a spiritual-intellectual penetration of abstract form" (19) was "the ultimate product of cognition" (18). The fitness of a theory of abstraction rooted in stasis for the study of animation seems not to have bothered the avant-garde. Nor did the worrisome entrenchment of concepts such as organic primitiveness and cerebral advancement, which art historian Ernst Gombrich has suggested proved ideologically pliable for the racially motivated politics of the Nazis.[37] These trajectories were rarely straightforward. And yet they were indicative of a period of backlash against haptic ornament, which theorists increasingly defined against spiritual purity and opticality. While this dynamic between hapticality and opticality played out across various media, its specific history in relation to avant-garde film is instructive for grasping the evolving stakes of the modernist vision more broadly.

Projections in Space, Film in Theory at the Bauhaus: László Moholy-Nagy, Hans Richter, and Kazimir Malevich

Although notorious for having neither a film nor an architecture department, the Bauhaus was a vocal advocate for film's constructive, spatial responsibilities and became a proving ground for filmmakers and theorists committed to discovering the possibilities of the new medium.[38] Viking Eggeling, Hans Richter, and Walter Ruttmann recruited Bauhaus students Erna Niemeyer, Werner Graeff, and Lore Leudesdorff to help animate their films, while students Ludwig Hirschfeld-Mack and Kurt Schwerdtfeger devised a series of protocinematic colored light plays, which they premiered at the Bauhaus and subsequently toured around Germany.[39] Bauhaus master Oskar Schlemmer's famous soirées often featured film screenings, and Richter eventually offered a series of lectures on film at the Bauhaus accompanied by select screenings. Although not affiliated with the Bauhaus, Theo van Doesburg was an early and frequent interlocutor. Moving to Weimar in 1922, van Doesburg cast himself as an agitator against what he perceived as the school's expressionist shortcomings. He heckled the faculty, recruited curious Bauhaus students to his own rival courses, and organized the 1922 Constructivist Summit, which flooded Weimar with his intellectual compatriots. Among those in attendance was László Moholy-Nagy, whom Walter Gropius hired shortly thereafter to lead the Bauhaus Preliminary Course. His ascendancy as one of the school's most influential masters during its shift from expressionist leanings to constructivist principles was characterized by extensive research into optical perception. Art historian Robin Schuldenfrei has argued that while his colleague Joseph Albers focused on the haptic qualities of various materials in the Preliminary Course, Moholy-Nagy assigned students exercises designed to hone spatial awareness.[40] Departing decisively from Albers's *Materie* and *Material* studies, which revolved around surface texture, Moholy-Nagy encouraged students to consider transparency, reflection, extension, and balance. Like van Doesburg, he couched the modernist project in terms that liberated the mind (by way of the eye) from decorative hapticality. Rather than painterly composition, Moholy-Nagy advocated for dematerialized construction, which he understood to be a direct result of cerebral calculation. "In comparison to composition," which he associated with outmoded approaches to painting, Moholy-Nagy stated that "construction demands intellectual engagement."[41] Light was the element that could elucidate and iterate these optical-spatial relationships. Indeed, it carried a quasi-moral valence. Moholy-Nagy was hopeful that, thanks to constructive design, "the hygiene of the optical, the health of the visible is slowly filtering through."[42] Light was immaterial, and its application across a broad range of media, from advertising signs to photography to film, meant that art might finally forget about medium specificity and escape its bondage to the material plane altogether. As early as 1922, he challenged the flat, "formal play" of Eggeling's, Richter's, and Ruttmann's films. Instead, he called for a dynamic extension in space free from material supports: "The way forward here is the designing of movement in space without reliance on direct formal development."[43] This central tenet of optical dematerialization was later animated in both the English and German titles that Moholy-Nagy chose for his 1929 book: *Von Material zu Architektur,* which translates as "From Material to Architecture," was officially released in English under the title *The New Vision*. Lost in translation—or, rather, sublimated—haptic materials were superseded by architectural structures, which pushed opticality into three-dimensionality and thus created a "new vision."

Marcel Breuer's humorous graphic from 1926 "a bauhaus film, five years long" ("ein bauhaus-film, fünf jahre lang"), provided a telling illustration of this constructivist vision (Figure 1.6). Proposing, like Moholy-Nagy, that the future of film lay in the abandonment of all material supports, Breuer recounted the history of the Bauhaus as a film that evolved from primitive flatness toward spatial construction. The story began with Gunta Stölzl's "African Chair" (1921), frontally shot to maximize its decorative surfaces; progressed through Breuer's chair (1925), shot at an angle to emphasize its planar construction; and arrived at a future of pure spatiality ("19??"), where a reclining body hovered languidly in space without the support of any chair at all. On the eve of the school's move from Weimar to Dessau, Breuer's thesis seemed to be that the progression from primitive hapticality to advanced opticality was linear, logical, and spatial. But what kind of space did constructivist film seek to build? After all, Breuer had punctuated the final chapter of his Bauhaus film with not one but two question marks, leaving its ultimate trajectory a mystery.

Having narrated themselves into a progressive history where film evolved from painterly flatness to advanced opticality, the avant-garde project to precipitate a new kind of vision demanded a more ambitious spatial agenda than one-point perspective could provide. In 1929, van Doesburg set the course. He challenged filmmakers to abandon one-point perspective, which belonged to outdated modes of painting and decorative ornamentation but was nevertheless observable in film: "Film builds itself

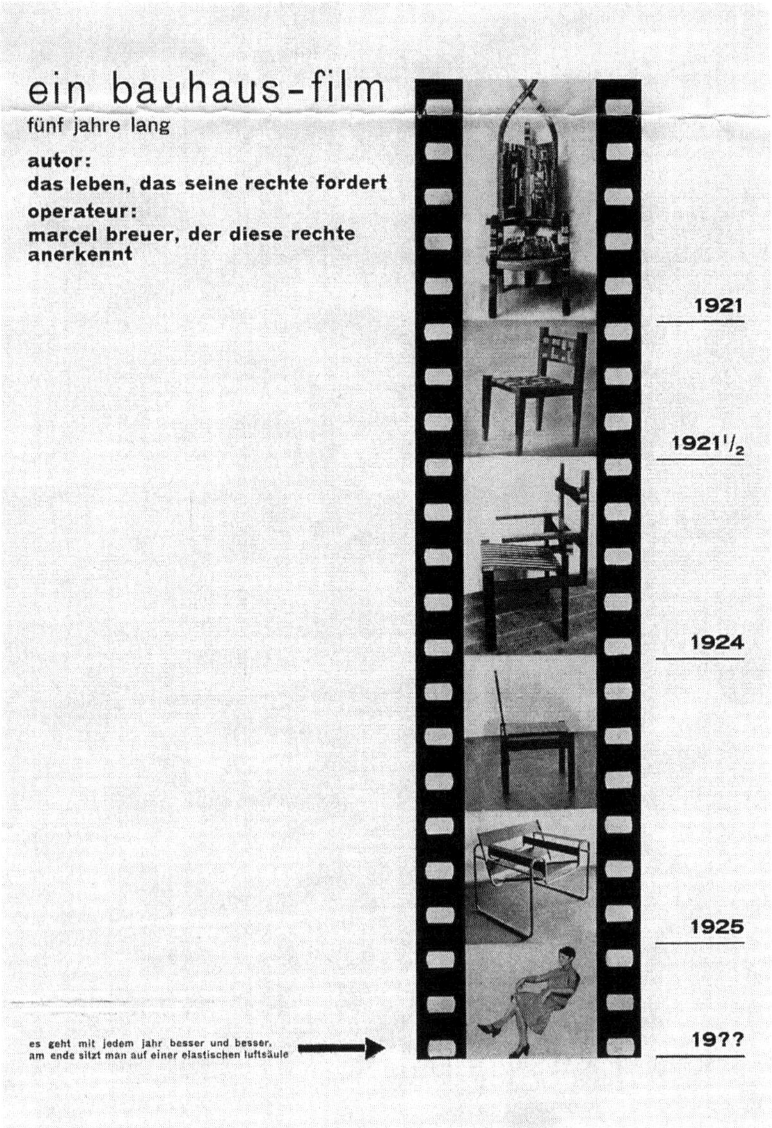

FIGURE 1.6. Marcel Breuer, "a bauhaus film, five years long" ("ein bauhaus-film, fünf jahre lang"), *Bauhaus. Zeitschrift für Gestlatung,* no. 1 (1926). Offset lithograph print. Bauhaus-Archive Berlin. Image courtesy of Thomas Breuer.

around a central axis, much like a Renaissance painting. The time-moment is expressed through the repetition of a theme just as in classical music (or ornamental carpet patterns), with no other success than the creation of a moving ornament. The eye moves only from left to right, from above to below; it moves within a two-dimensional plane."[44]

Van Doesburg declared that film's new depths would proceed from a fuller understanding of the medium's essential principles: light, movement, and shadow. Indeed, he concluded, film must be an architecture of light. No doubt inspired by Moholy-Nagy's experiments at the Bauhaus, van Doesburg stated: "The new attempts will be subject to an almost architectonic construction of polydimensional film space."[45] *Light Prop for an Electric Stage (Light-Space Modulator)* (1922–30), a kinetic metal and glass sculpture that Moholy-Nagy filmed in action to produce *Lightplay: Black, White, Gray* (1930), was a proof of concept. Its constantly shifting perspective repelled vision off reflective metallic planes only to reel the eye into deep space through layers of transparent glass. And, yet, it was a real object, rotated in real space, and filmed in real time. The question remained: Could animation, with its alternate space-time logic, offer a still more ambitious contribution to the production of polydimensional film space?

Galvanized by van Doesburg's critique of his early film experiments, Hans Richter was eager to prove himself a truly constructivist filmmaker. The opportunity came in 1927 when Kazimir Malevich conscripted Richter to animate a series of drawings titled "Art and the Problems of Architecture: The Emergence of a New Plastic System of Architecture."[46] Malevich and Richter developed an ambitious and extensively annotated film script. "Various Suprematist Elements" such as black, red, and white squares would spin into circles, whose rotation and diagonal transversal of the screen would yield color changes that corresponded to their movements. These circles would collapse into lines, which would again form into squares, the angles of which would expand into three-dimensional space to form cubes: "The forms built in this way make architectonic fragments; out of these architectonic fragments come architectonic systems; these systems produce the problems posed by the new architecture."[47] "Problems" certainly characterized the constructivist predicament. Art historian Magdalena Nieslony gives a detailed account of the Richter-Malevich collaboration, which was supposed to definitively illustrate Malevich's progression from a painter of flat planes to an architect of multidimensional space (Figure 1.7). Although the film script arrived at a formulation of the spatial challenges posed by the new architecture, she suggests that producing a solution on film proved more difficult. Richter attempted animating

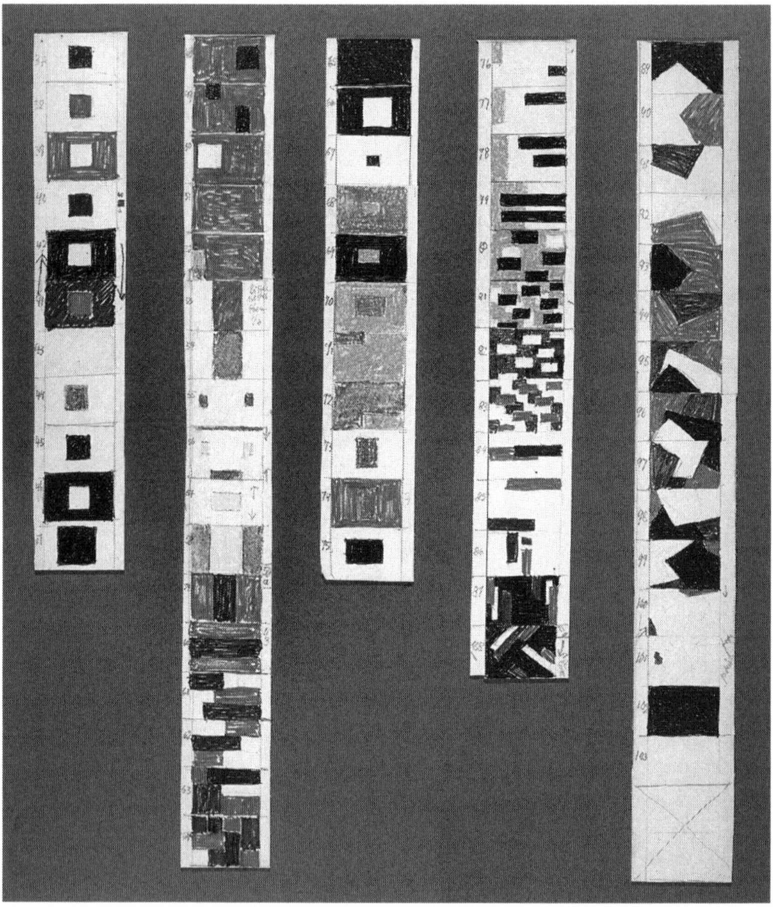

FIGURE 1.7. Hans Richter, storyboard for the Malevich animation, part 2, ca. 1970. Pencil and ink on cardboard. Getty Research Institute, Los Angeles (970021). Copyright estate of Hans Richter.

the scenario in fits and starts, ultimately abandoning the project on account of disappointing results. Whether square, circle, cross, or cube, Richter found that their animation on film was decidedly un-architectonic. According to Nieslony, this spatial conundrum had less to do with the failings of film than with the fact that constructivist principles were actually best suited to painting: "The space of most of Malevich's two-dimensional works cannot be reconstructed in a three-dimensional model, as the compositions contain deliberate spatial inconsistencies and ambiguity."[48]

In other words, constructivist, polydimensional space was, ironically, only possible to evoke on the flat plane of the canvas.

In their pursuit of dematerialized opticality, the avant-garde had constricted themselves to a narrowly defined vision for how new spatial dimensions might emerge on film. Predicated on the rejection of primitive flatness, Richter's pursuit of pure opticality had nevertheless led him back to the drawing board. Moholy-Nagy came perhaps closest to defining the promise of polydimensionality. As if aware that neither his sculpture *Light Prop for an Electric Stage* nor his film *Lightplay: Black, White, Gray* entirely achieved the spatial effects he imagined, Moholy-Nagy assumed a more speculative position. Describing his experiment in *Lightplay,* he claimed that "light—as a spatial projection—is an outstanding aid in attaining virtual volume."[49] With this statement, he intuited what few in the avant-garde seemed willing to admit: that polydimensional film space was perhaps possible only insofar as it was also virtual.

Notes

1. "Das Zeitalter des dekorativen Geschmacks ist vorbei" and "zu einer fruchtbaren, monumentalen Kunstproduktion führen." Theo van Doesburg, "Zur Elementaren Gestaltung," *G. Material zur elementaren Gestaltung* 1 (July 1923): n.p. Unless otherwise noted, all translations are my own.

2. "Flächenbildung durch kontrastierende Akzentuierung der Fläche." Hans Richter, "(Demonstration des Materials)/(Gestaltung des Materials)," *G. Material zur elementaren Gestaltung* 1 (July 1923): n.p.

3. Hans Richter and Viking Eggeling met through Dada circles in Zurich in 1918 and worked together to animate a series of scroll drawings when they decamped to Germany in 1919. See Louise O'Konor, *Viking Eggeling 1880–1925. Artist and Filmmaker. Life and Work,* trans. Catherine G. Sundström and Anne Bibby, Acta Universitatis Stockholmiensis/Stockholm Studies in Art History 23 (Stockholm: Almqvist & Wiksell, 1971). Theo van Doesburg saw their film during his visit to the Richter and Eggeling studio in Klein-Kolzig, Germany, and took it with him to Paris, where he held a small screening, "Soirée du coeur à barbe," at the Théâtre Michel. See Stephen C. Foster, ed., *Hans Richter: Activism, Modernism, and the Avant-Garde* (Cambridge, Mass.: MIT Press, 2000), 80. Richter was notorious for backdating his films and even later forging work that he claimed he made with Eggeling. See Holger Wilmesmeier, *Deutsche Avantgarde und Film. Die Filmmatinee "Der absolute Film" (3. und 10. Mai 1925),* Reihe Kunstgeschichte Bd. 25 (Münster: LIT Verlag, 1994), 17–30.

4. "Die übersichtliche Organisation der Formsprachmittel ermöglicht es, diese Mittel nicht auf den Aufbau eines Bildes: eines statischen Werkes zu

verwenden, sondern dieselben auch in einer der bildenden Kunst bisher nicht zur Verfügung stehenden Dimension, der Zeit, anzuwenden." Hans Richter, "Film" (1922), reprinted in Christian Kiening, *Der absolute Film: Dokumente der Medienavantgarde (1912–1936)* (Zurich: Chronos Verlag, 2012), 90.

5. "Die eigentümliche Sphäre des Films ist die des 'bewegten' Raumes, der 'bewegten' Fläche, der 'bewegten' Linie . . . Dieser Raum ist nicht architektonisch oder plastisch, sondern zeitlich." Richter, 92.

6. "Sie wirken nur innerhalb des Rahmens der 'Leinwand,' wirken aber nicht im *Raum*." Theo van Doesburg, "Film als reine Gestaltung," *Die Form. Zeitschrift für gestaltende Arbeit* 4, no. 10 (1929), reprinted in Kiening, *Der absolute Film,* 241.

7. Van Doesburg, 247.

8. "Aber gerade diese Fläche muß *gesprengt* werden, um hinter ihr die *neue Tiefe,* das raumzeitliche Filmkontinuum zu entdecken. Dort und nirgends anders liegt die schöpferische Sphäre des gestaltenden Films!" Van Doesburg, 247.

9. Aloïs Riegl, *Problems of Style: Foundations for a History of Ornament* (Princeton, N.J.: Princeton University Press, 1992).

10. A number of scholars have observed that Walter Benjamin's formulation of the optical unconscious in "The Work of Art in the Age of Its Technological Reproducibility" (1936) was inspired by Riegl's theories of art. See Walter Benjamin, *Illuminations: Essays and Reflections,* ed. Hannah Arendt, trans. Harry Zohn (New York: Schocken Books, 1968), 225; Miriam Hansen, "Of Mice and Ducks: Benjamin and Adorno on Disney," *South Atlantic Quarterly* 92, no. 1 (Winter 1993): 27–61; Antonia Lant, "Haptical Cinema," *October* 74 (Autumn 1995): 45–73; Michael W. Jennings, "Walter Benjamin, Siegfried Kracauer, and Weimar Criticism," in *Weimar Thought: A Contested Legacy,* ed. Peter Eli Gordon and John P. McCormick (Princeton, N.J.: Princeton University Press, 2013), 204; Giles Peaker, "Works That Have Lasted . . . Walter Benjamin Reading Aloïs Riegl," in *Framing Formalism: Riegl's Work,* ed. Saul Ostrow, Critical Voices in Art, Theory and Culture (Amsterdam: G+B Arts International, 2001), 291–310.

11. See Hansen, "Of Mice and Ducks," 27–61. Hansen shows how through successive edits with Adorno's feedback Benjamin removed all references to Mickey Mouse by the second draft. All three versions of the essay have now been published. The first version, reprinted in *Grey Room* and translated by Michael W. Jennings, was written in 1935: Walter Benjamin, "The Work of Art in the Age of Its Technological Reproducibility (First Version)," trans. Michael W. Jennings, *Grey Room* 39 (Spring 2010): 11–37. The second version was revised in 1936. The third and most widely read version, revised between 1938 and 1939, was edited by Hannah Arendt and published in Benjamin, *Illuminations: Essays and Reflections,* 217–51.

12. Benjamin, "The Work of Art in the Age of Its Technological Reproducibility (First Version)," 31.

13. Benjamin, *Illuminations*, 223.

14. Occurring first with scissors (many of the animations examined here were made with cut paper) and then at the level of the filmic edit, such cuts and sutures extended from intimate haptical interventions at the level of the shot to technologically reproducible montages spliced together to form a film. Benjamin argued that films created in this way were the polar opposite of paintings, which always "keep a natural distance from reality" (223). For Benjamin, film plumbed psychological depths by collapsing the distance traditionally maintained between art and the spectator, providing viewers with an immediate—indeed, imperceptibly mediated—"permeation of reality" (234).

15. Thomas Lamarre, *The Anime Machine: A Media Theory of Animation* (Minneapolis: University of Minnesota Press, 2009), 25.

16. For a useful overview of film theoretical positions on space in "primitive" versus classical cinema, see the section "The Organisation of Space and Time: Theatricality and Deep Staging," in Thomas Elsaesser's "Introduction" to Thomas Elsaesser and Adam Barker, eds., *Early Cinema: Space, Frame, Narrative* (London: British Film Institute, 1990), 12–15. Elsaesser establishes that "shot length and editing speed have been the hallmarks of cinematic sophistication and modernity," while "the oldest (and usually pejorative) distinction made between primitive and classical cinema [is]: the charge that early films were 'theatrical'" (11, 13). Sections I and II of the book anthologize essays from a range of film scholars who both assert and dismantle the association between primitive theatricality and classical deep focus. See, in particular, Barry Salt, "Film Form 1990–1906," 31–44; Ben Brewster, "Deep Staging in French Films 1900–1914," 45–55; and Noël Burch, "A Primitive Mode of Representation?," 220–27.

17. For a discussion of depth and realism in film in the context of animation, see Lev Manovich, "'Reality' Effects in Computer Animation," in *A Reader in Animation Studies*, ed. Jayne Pilling (Sydney: J. Libbey, 1997), 5–15. Manovich states that the eventual drive toward "cinematic realism was maintained through the effects of depth" in early animation, subjecting animation to the same laws of perspective later enshrined by André Bazin in his writings on realism in the cinema (7). In animation studies, the progression toward mimetic realism achieved through the simulation of depth is often tied to the multiplane camera. Narrative complexity and increasing character dimensionality are accompanied by progressive shifts in the animation apparatus. Jeff Lotman provides a standard narration: "One of the many contributions Disney brought to animation was the advent of the multi-plane camera. . . . This equipment helped to give the illusion of more depth to the filming of a cartoon." Jeff Lotman, *Animation Art: The Early Years 1911–1953* (Atglen, Pa.: Schiffer Publishing, 1995), 35. This approach to simulating depth became widespread. Jayne Pilling states that "following Disney's audacious gamble on the animated feature film *[Snow White and the Seven Dwarfs]*, animation became

defined by the Disney model." Jayne Pilling, ed., *A Reader in Animation Studies,* xi. Thomas Lamarre observes that apparatus theory has dominated histories of animation, contributing to the hegemony of the American Disney model even in the face of diverse and international animation practices: "The West often receives priority when one insists on Disney as the standard of animation, as the inventor of the apparatus. Apparatus theory is frequently in collusion with an emphasis on Western origins." Lamarre, *The Anime Machine,* 25.

18. Numerous animation studies have tied a shift in Disney's aesthetics to his adoption of a division of labor post-1930 modeled on the Hollywood studio system. This reorganization brought animation closer in line with the aesthetics of classical cinema. In a recent reprisal of this view, Maureen Furniss identifies a shift in Disney's aesthetic beginning with *Snow White and the Seven Dwarfs,* one that "showcased the development of Disney artists." The new style was defined by fast cuts, character development, sophisticated story lines, and deep focus (achieved by the multiplane camera): "In *Snow White and the Seven Dwarfs,* the multiplane system is used to create dimensionality and drama in various scenes to impressive effect." Maureen Furniss, *A New History of Animation* (London: Thames & Hudson, 2016), 106, 105.

19. Esther Leslie, *Hollywood Flatlands: Animation, Critical Theory and the Avant-Garde* (London: Verso, 2004).

20. Lotte Reiniger gives an early formulation of this view in her essay "Lebende Schatten. Kunst und Technik des Silhouettenfilms (1926)," reprinted in *Filmblatt* 10, no. 27 (Frühjahr/Sommer 2005): 18–19. Subsequently, Sergei Eisenstein developed his notes on the plasmatic, which expounded on the formal pliability of Disney's cartoon bodies. See Sergei Eisenstein, *Eisenstein on Disney,* ed. Jay Leyda, trans. Alan Upchurch (London: Methuen, 1988). For more recent investigations of the laws of realism in the cartoon universe, see Stanley Cavell, *The World Viewed: Reflections on the Ontology of Film,* enl. ed. (Cambridge, Mass.: Harvard University Press, 1979); Scott Bukatman, *The Poetics of Slumberland: Animated Spirits and the Animating Spirit* (Berkeley: University of California Press, 2012); Scott Bukatman, "Some Observations Pertaining to Cartoon Physics; or, The Cartoon Cat in the Machine," in *Animating Film Theory,* ed. Karen Beckman (Durham, N.C.: Duke University Press, 2014), 301–16.

21. Leslie, *Hollywood Flatlands,* 19.

22. Leslie suggests that Disney's pursuit of mimetic realism belied his embrace of Fordist assembly-line principles in the commercial animation studio. By mimicking live-action film, Disney curbed animation's revolutionary potential and imposed the limitations of mimetic realism on a universe governed by other laws. For Leslie, *Snow White* is the chilling example of how deep space moralizes the fairy tale to maintain the status quo. This is a fruitful observation. Indeed, it provides considerable insight into why Disney maintained fascist favor much

longer than other subversive artworks and films of the period. See Leslie, *Hollywood Flatlands,* 123–57.

23. Burch, "A Primitive Mode of Representation?," 220.

24. Salt, "Film Form 1900–1906," 31.

25. Assenka Oksiloff, *Picturing the Primitive: Visual Culture, Ethnography, and Early German Cinema* (New York: Palgrave Macmillan, 2001), 19.

26. Lotte Reiniger, "Film as Ballet (1936)," reprinted in *The Red Velvet Seat: Women's Writings on the Cinema: The First Fifty Years,* ed. Antonia Lant (London: Verso, 2006), 168.

27. "Die Puppen liegen flach auf der Fläche. Ihnen fehlt der originelle Schwerpunkt der Marionette, der dieser eine so reizvolle Unwirklichkeit gibt. Ihnen fehlt das Verschwinden und Auftauchen, das Mienenspiel, das Zeichentricks haben können. Dafür aber *beherrschen* sie die Fläche, und ihrer weichen Beweglichkeit sind keine Schranken gesetzt." Lotte Reiniger, "Wie ich meine Silhouettenfilme mache," in *Das Kulturfilmbuch,* ed. E. Beyfuss and A. Kossowsky (Berlin: Chryselius & Schulz Verlag, 1924), 206.

28. For an expanded discussion of chinoiserie and Orientalism in Lotte Reiniger's films see Katherine Rochester, "Silhouette Films, Weimar Cinema, and Ornaments from the Orient," in *Lotte Reiniger, the Silhouette Artist,* ed. Rada Bieberstein (Marburg: Schüren Verlag, forthcoming 2021). On music in Reiniger's films, see Frauke Fitzner, *Lotte Reiniger: Zur Rolle der Musik im frühen Film,* Lotte-Reiniger-Schriften 2 (Tübingen: Stadtmuseum Tübingen, 2011).

29. For an exposition on the spatial characteristics of Chinese-inspired wall coverings, see Stacey Sloboda, "Surface Contact: Decoration in the Chinese Taste," in *Qing Encounters: Artistic Exchanges between China and the West,* ed. Petra ten-Doesschate Chu, Ning Ding, and Lidy Jane Chu (Los Angeles: Getty Research Institute, 2015), 248–63.

30. Anne Anlin Cheng offers an insightful reading of how the fusion of the ornamental and the oriental has persisted in the racialized and insufficiently dismantled fantasy of the "yellow woman": "We thus cannot talk about yellow female flesh without also engaging a history of material-aesthetic productions. The yellow woman's history is entwined with the production and fates of silk, ceramics, celluloid, machinery, and other forms of animated objectness." Anne Anlin Cheng, *Ornamentalism* (New York: Oxford University Press, 2019), xi–xii.

31. Karl Scheffler, *Die Frau und die Kunst: Eine Studie* (Berlin: J. Bard, 1900), 1976; Adolf Loos, *Ornament and Crime: Selected Essays,* ed. Adolf Opel (Riverside, Calif.: Ariadne Press, 1998). Loos delivered "Ornament und Verbrechen" as a lecture in Vienna in 1908. It was subsequently published in various languages, starting in 1910.

32. Loos, *Ornament and Crime,* 24.

33. Antonia Lant, "Haptical Cinema," *October* 74 (Autumn 1995): 45–73.

34. Rosalind Galt, *Pretty: Film and the Decorative Image* (New York: Columbia University Press, 2011), 2.

35. Galt, 20.

36. Wilhelm Worringer, *Abstraction and Empathy: A Contribution to the Psychology of Style* (Chicago: Ivan R. Dee, 1997), 18.

37. Gombrich argued that the impetus toward racial prejudice was already clear in the logic of Riegl's *Kunstwollen* in *The Sense of Order: A Study in the Psychology of Decorative Art* (London: Phaidon Press, 1984), 184, and in *Art and Illusion* (New York: Pantheon Books, 1960), 16.

38. An architecture workshop was established in 1927, eight years after the school's founding. Film was never taught, although a forthcoming book by Laura Frahm will be the first to deal seriously with the question of film and its preponderance at the Bauhaus.

39. For a discussion of how Viking Eggeling, Hans Richter, and Walter Ruttmann relied on female assistants to animate their films, see Katherine Rochester, "Visual Music and Kinetic Ornaments: Lotte Reiniger and the Animation Avant-Garde in Weimar Berlin," *Feminist Media Histories* 7, no. 1 (forthcoming January 2021). Kurt Schwerdtfeger and Josef Hartwig developed the *Reflektorisches Farbenlichtspiel* (1922) while Ludwig Hirschfeld-Mack devised his *Farben-Licht-Spiele* (1923), which premiered during the Bauhaus Woche of 1923, was included in the Absolute Film Matinee of 1925 and toured with Wassily Kandinsky as a visual aid on his lecture circuit. Hans Richter organized three film screenings at the Bauhaus in June 1930.

40. Robin Schuldenfrei, "Equilibrium, Space, and Materiality at the Bauhaus," "Bauhaus 100: Object Lessons from a Historic Collection," Harvard Art Museum, March 29, 2019.

41. "Darum erfordert die Konstruktion—im Verhältnis zur Komposition—ein plus des Wissensmäßigen." László Moholy-Nagy, *Von Material zu Architektur* (1929), ed. Hans M. Wingler (Berlin: Florian Kupferberg Verlag, 1968), 71.

42. László Moholy-Nagy, *Painting, Photography, Film,* trans. Janet Seligman (London: Lund Humphries, 1969), 38.

43. "Der weitere Weg ist hier die Gestaltung der Bewegung im Raume ohne Anlehnung an eine direkte Formentwicklung." László Moholy-Nagy, "Produktion-Reproduktion" (1922), reprinted in Kiening, *Der absolute Film,* 102.

44. "Die Filmgestaltung baut sich auf um eine zentrale Achse ungefähr wie ein Renaissancegemälde. Das Zeitmoment wird durch Wiederholung eines Themas genau wie in der klassischen Musik (oder wie bei den orientalischen Teppichmustern) zum Ausdruck gebracht, mit keinem anderen Erfolg als der Schaffung eines bewegten Ornaments. Das Auge geht nur von links nach rechts und von oben nach unten, es bewegt sich innerhalb einer zweidimensionalen Fläche." van Doesburg, "Film als reine Gestaltung," 247.

45. "Die neuen Versuche unterliegen den Gesetzen eines fast architektonischen Aufbaues des poly-dimensionalen Filmraums." Van Doesburg, 241.

46. A photocopy of Malevich's scenario and archival materials from Richter's attempted animation are housed at the Getty Research Institute, Arnold Eagle Papers and Film Related to Hans Richter's Malevich Animation, 970021, series VI.

47. Hans Richter's German translation of Kazimir Malevich's Russian scenario for "Art and the Problems of Architecture: The Emergence of a New Plastic System of Architecture" (1927), n.d., Getty Research Institute, 970021, box 5, folder 13.

48. Magdalena Nieslony, "Felicitous Failure: Hans Richter's Malevich," *Getty Research Journal,* no. 9 (2017): 152.

49. László Moholy-Nagy, *The New Vision,* trans. Daphne M. Hoffmann, The New Bauhaus Books 1 (New York: W. W. Norton, 1938), 142.

CHAPTER TWO

Locomotive Views

Lateral Movement and the Flatness of the Moving Image

Jordan Schonig

A hallmark of cinematic immersion, sensation, and shock, the "phantom ride" genre of early cinema produced an illusion of moving through a picturesque landscape by mounting a camera on the front of a moving train. Marked by a sense of virtual inhabitation thanks to its z-axis movement through deep space, the phantom ride caused the spectator to become caught up in the animation of the unfolding world in its incompleteness and openness. In Tom Gunning's words, the spectator of the phantom ride "[chases] the horizon into the *depth* of an ever-unfolding image."[1]

Scholarship on early cinema tends to present the phantom ride's immersive depth effects as an evolution from the flat views of space presented in actual train travel.[2] Restricted to the lateral view of space unrolling ribbon-like across the window, the train traveler was restricted to a view of space that was radically separated from her own physical emplacement in the train car. In what Wolfgang Schivelbusch calls "panoramic perception," the train traveler was treated not to a fantasy of immersion but to a perceptual confrontation with the landscape as a distant "painted surface."[3] It is this flatness and distance that the phantom ride transcended. According to Gunning, "The displacement from the lateral view provided by the train . . . to a head-on plunge into the centre of the image fundamentally transforms the distance Schivelbusch described as inherent in panoramic perception."[4] As a result, for Gunning, the phantom ride was both "more . . . dynamic" (55) and "more thrilling" (56) than the train traveler's view, for it "[realized] the centuries-old fantasy of penetration that had remained literally impossible in landscape painting" (58) and became "the richest and most dialectical experience offered by early cinema in its exploration of movement and point of view" (56).[5]

Such a clear valuation of the phantom ride as a fantasy of spatial exploration should seem familiar in light of the longtime privileging of deep space in film theory, from André Bazin's enthusiasm for deep-focus cinematography as an approximation of human perceptual freedom, to David Bordwell's analysis of the stylistic history of deep-space staging, to Vivian Sobchack and Jennifer Barker's emphasis on the imagined inhabitability and palpable volume of cinematic space.[6] But if the phenomenological structure of the phantom ride reinforces dominant models of cinematic perception grounded on fantasies of exploration and immersion, what might the train traveler's view offer as a competing model of cinematic perception, one in which the spectator confronts the *flatness* of the screen rather than sees through it? Indeed, while the train window has been often compared to the cinema screen as an apparatus for perceiving the world, my aim is not to extend analogies between cinema and train travel grounded on their shared "annihilation . . . of space and time" or their shocking sensations of speed and instability.[7] Rather, I will argue that by transforming the space outside the train into a blurred, two-dimensional abstraction, the passenger's window becomes a *moving image* whose phenomenological properties can help us rethink fundamental assumptions about cinematic space, camera movement, and the flatness of the screen.[8]

In order to explore this claim, I will juxtapose Schivelbusch's emphasis on the train traveler's perceptual separation from framed space with phenomenologies of perception offered by Maurice Merleau-Ponty and perceptual psychologist James J. Gibson, both of whom emphasize the role of the subject's imagined continuity—that is, anticipated possible action and inhabitability—with the perceivable space around them. I then analyze how the train traveler's experience anticipates the moving camera in particular, paying specific attention to the properties of lateral camera movement—namely, its flattening of space and visual rhythm—as radically distinct from movements into depth. Finally, by reading Schivelbusch alongside lateral movement sequences from the films of Leos Carax, Bruce Baillie, and Gus Van Sant, I not only identify an unacknowledged phenomenological similarity between the cinema and train travel but also help reconsider some entrenched intuitions about the ontology of moving images. Ultimately, I will show how integrating the screen's flatness into an account of cinematic experience and the moving camera is part of what it means to engage in a phenomenology of cinema as an *aesthetic* experience instead of merely as an analogy to natural perception.

Panoramic Perception as Proto-Moving Image

In his book *The Railway Journey*, Schivelbusch describes the novel experience of train travel in the nineteenth century as a function of its radical increase in speed, especially as compared with travel by horse and carriage. In what he terms "panoramic perception," the experience of train travel effaces the passenger's sense of bodily continuity with the world she inhabits by rendering the viewable foreground a blurred, two-dimensional abstraction. In Victor Hugo's firsthand account, "flowers by the side of the road" become "streaks . . . of red or white," and "grain-fields" become "great shocks of yellow hair."[9] The sheer speed of train travel, paired with a lateral point of view, dissolves the passenger's sense of being physically continuous with the foreground of her visual field. The viewed space appears as a discrete, flattened image unfurling within the window frame. Indeed, while the objects of the landscape far off in the distance retain their shape, they are radically separated from the body of the passenger by the "almost unreal barrier" of the blurred foreground.[10] Schivelbusch names this mode of perception "panoramic" because, much like the nineteenth-century visual entertainment of the same name, space unfolds as if it were a never-ending *flat* image.[11]

Schivelbusch's description lays the foundation for a phenomenology of the train traveler's view as radically distinct from the natural perception of space in everyday life. In fact, despite the thrills and shocks of the phantom ride, the train traveler's panoramic perception is a far more unfamiliar mode of perceiving space, undermining the terms of mobile perception described in Merleau-Ponty's phenomenology, Gibson's ecological theory of perception, and other action-oriented theories of perception.[12] This tension largely has to do with the distinct phenomenological expectations we attach to the visual perception of forward movement and lateral movement. For example, when I move forward through space—be it by foot, bicycle, or car—my sensation of moving is predominantly produced by optical stimulation alone, for, as Gibson writes, "The impression of forward movement of the observer can be produced optically without any contribution from the vestibular or the muscle sense."[13] It is partly for this reason that, regardless of whether I am actively moving my body forward or being passively moved forward as a car passenger, I associate the onrush of space in my optical field with the feeling of intentional self-propulsion. Moving *forward*—that is, moving in the direction we currently face—is intimately related to a feeling of moving *toward*, that is, movement felt as directed, purposeful, and intended.

Moreover, the optical flow of distant, unfolding space activated by forward movement emblematizes what Merleau-Ponty and other phenomenologists call a "horizon," the anticipated existence of that which I do not intend or directly perceive. Like the perceived line dividing land and sky, a horizon marks the end point of our perception but beckons us to go toward and beyond it. When moving forward—or when perceiving camera movements that penetrate into depth like the phantom ride—we experience a horizon of anticipation as space flows forth from a single point in the distance, creating an immersive image of the world's continuous unfolding.

By contrast, when my visual field is reduced to a lateral view, I severely limit my view upon the world as a horizon of anticipated movement. While I can anticipate the direction of the space that passes before me, the space itself is not so much anticipated as *unfurled*, as if spontaneously generated from the edge of the window. As a result, the lateral view of space outside a passenger window displays a circumscribed disruption of possible action, a rift in the traveler's sense of viewed space as a potentially inhabitable part of her *world*.[14] A space of potential action and mutual imbrication is thereby relegated to a space of sensation, becoming particularly available for aesthetic appreciation in the form of a surface display.

I want to suggest, then, that it is this very gap in the perceptual field, this suspension of embodied contiguity, that transforms the train passenger's view into a moving image. The train passenger's view is a moving image not simply because it mediates a mobile viewpoint with a rectangular screenlike boundary (i.e., the window) but because the framed visual field exhibits aesthetic autonomy as an *image*. In other words, the space appears to move on its own, separated from the space contiguous with the traveler's body. This sense of the train window's aesthetic autonomy is part of the very vocabulary of the firsthand accounts of train travel that Schivelbusch draws on. In Victor Hugo's account, trees do not pass by, as if passively displaced by the movement of the locomotive, but actively "perform a mingling dance on the horizon."[15] In becoming a flattened, unrolling abstraction—in the words of Dolf Sternberger, a "painted surface"—the space outside becomes an image rather than a view; the window becomes a framed image rather than an opening onto the world.[16] As Schivelbusch puts it, "Panoramic perception, in contrast to traditional perception, no longer belongs to the same space as the perceived objects: the traveler sees the objects, landscapes, etc. *through* the apparatus which moves him through the world."[17]

For these reasons, the rushing space in a passenger's window approaches the condition of what Noël Carroll has called a *detached display.* In Carroll's essay "Defining the Moving Image," in which he proposes five necessary conditions for something to be a "moving image," one of those conditions is that a moving image must be a "detached display," a visual array with which "we are unable to orient ourselves toward . . . in the space that is continuous with our own bodies."[18] For Carroll, this condition helps distinguish moving images from the visual arrays presented in optical devices such as mirrors, binoculars, telescopes, and, most crucially, windows. Unlike the visual arrays encountered through those devices, which depict spaces continuous with our bodies, the space presented in a moving image is radically severed or *detached* from the perceiver's embodied perception.[19] In fact, similar articulations of detachedness have been put forward by philosophers as a fundamental condition of *all* images. Drawing from the neurophysiology of vision, Mohan Matthen argues that pictures—particularly figurative ones—engage only the parts of the brain used for processing visual representations while suspending those parts of the brain used for motor action.[20] In Matthen's words, our space "stops just where the space of depicted objects begins."[21] Pictorial space lacks the feeling of presence—of inhabitability, actionability, and manipulability—that is felt in ordinary space.[22] Thus, whatever its material support—paint on canvas, gradations of value on photosensitive paper, or light flickering on a screen—an image is marked by its imagined spatiotemporal detachment from the inhabitable world that surrounds it.

What makes the train passenger's experience of viewed space so pertinent for this definition of an image is the way it distills this quality of detachedness by just barely achieving it. Its detachedness is not materially guaranteed (via a canvas or screen) but asymptotically approached as a result of the train's speed, the bodily and perceptual orientation of the train passenger, and the architectural configuration of the train's windowed views upon the passing landscape. Compare this with a range of other moving-image "detached displays" that were invented before or contemporaneously with the train traveler's panoramic perception, from the moving panorama and the zoetrope (and a range of other philosophical toys that created an illusion of movement), to the camera obscura (which projected a moving image of the outside world onto an interior space), to the Claude glass (a darkly tinted, convex handheld mirror that reflected "an image carefully framed and optically *lifted out* of an undifferentiated visual field").[23] What distinguishes train travel's "moving image" from its protocinematic contemporaries, precursors, and the cinema screen itself, and, more important, what makes it of interest to a phenomenological account of cinematic experience, is that it provides a limit case for the perceptual emergence of detachedness within a view of three-dimensional space. The train window is emphatically not a visual representation produced on a material surface but, conversely, the *apparition of a surface within three-dimensional space.*[24] The view's detachedness, then—the very criterion of its being an image—is achieved by the immaterial appearance of its flatness.

In this way, the train traveler's panoramic perception becomes an elucidating phenomenological model for incorporating an attention to flatness into our perception of cinematic space, which, throughout film theory, has often been discussed in terms of immersion.[25] Perhaps for this reason, most arguments for the protocinematic nature of train travel avoid comparisons concerning the representation of space. When likened to a locomotive, cinema is often presented as a medium of travel that functionally *transports* the spectator, immersing her in new worlds on screen. But what would it mean to see cinematic space the way the train passenger saw the rushing landscape, not as an inhabitable world but as a vibrating surface? In other words, when does the screen incorporate its ontological status as a flat spatial barrier into its representation of space?

Lateral Camera Movement as Panoramic Perception

If panoramic perception has a phenomenological equivalent in cinema, we will most certainly not find it in the phantom ride but rather in *lateral camera movement,* tracking shots that move sideways with respect to the direction the camera faces. By emulating the general perceptual orientation of the train passenger, lateral camera movements have the capacity to reproduce the flat, image-like quality Schivelbusch describes in his account of panoramic perception.

It may seem fairly obvious to draw a comparison between the train traveler's view of the rushing landscape and lateral camera movement. But what matters is not that lateral camera movements *resemble* the train traveler's view so much as they reproduce the phenomenological logic of panoramic perception in cinematic form, thereby creating the sense of a moving image within a moving image. In other words, lateral camera movements can make the detached display of the cinema screen also *feel* detached, image-like, and two-dimensional, tapping into an affordance unique to the flatness of the screen. It is for this reason that the particular perceptual qualities of lateral camera movement are rarely accounted for in most theories of the perception of the moving camera, which tend to emphasize the immersive, embodied illusion of moving through the world on screen that is effortlessly achieved by most z-axis camera movement.[26]

The spatially alienating effects of lateral camera movement can perhaps most clearly be seen in shots that deliberately attempt to reproduce the visual qualities of train travel. Walter Ruttmann's *Berlin: Symphony of a Great City* (1927), for example, begins with a rapid montage of lateral views from a speeding train that yield various linear patterns and flashing rhythms. The vibration of telegraph wires, the blur of bushes rushing by, and the rhythm of passing train tracks together give a sensation of overwhelming speed. What introduces these images is a nonphotographic abstract animation of pulsing horizontal rectangles and rotating semicircles, anticipating and acknowledging the visual patterns that follow. Decades later, Stan Brakhage's *The Wonder Ring* (1955) explores similar effects produced by New York's elevated "El" train, exploiting the abstractions produced by the train passenger's lateral view in order to yield a sense of poetic reverie lurking in the everyday.

While such films use lateral camera movements to deliberately evoke the radical perceptual effects of the train passenger's view, similar perceptual effects that suppress immersion and kinesthesia are produced in subtler ways by more conventional lateral tracking shots. Near the end of *The 400 Blows* (François Truffaut, 1959), for example, the minute-long lateral tracking shot that follows Antoine as he runs away to the ocean produces a sense of dynamic energy as it amplifies the movement of the background, but it equally forecloses a sense of progress and direction by blocking our view of what lies ahead. In *The Shining* (Stanley Kubrick, 1980), distant lateral traveling shots follow their subjects in order to emphasize the mazelike geometry of the Overlook Hotel, thereby producing a kind of movement that feels more architecturally than anthropomorphically determined. And in *Seven Chances* (1925), Buster Keaton uses the circumscribed view of space endemic to the lateral tracking shot for a self-reflexive gag. During the film's iconic chase scene, a lateral tracking shot of Keaton fleeing a horde of brides ends in an unforeseen collision with that very horde; the gag capitalizes on the fact that the lateral view unfurls space rather than anticipates it.

What unites these examples is their potential to suppress the aspects of embodied identification, kinesthesia, or perceptual anticipation endemic to z-axis movement. Indeed, observing these characteristics of lateral camera movement is a central insight of Brian Henderson's essay "Toward a Non-bourgeois Camera Style," in which he argues that particular lateral tracking shots employed in the post-1968 films of Jean-Luc Godard refuted the bourgeois ideology endemic to the camera's reproduction of Renaissance perspective. By unflinchingly scanning a flat plane of action and thus refusing a sense of anthropomorphic subjectivity and spatial depth, Godard's camera represents "a refusal to participate in bourgeois space."[27] Despite its political thrust, Henderson's argument stems from a basic phenomenological intuition about how lateral camera movements can withhold kinetic depth effects. Henderson notes that with Godard's tracking shots, "the viewer is not drawn *into* the image, neither does he make choices within it; he stands outside the image and judges it *as a whole*."[28]

Making similar observations about anime, Thomas Lamarre has argued that the lateral camera movements on display in such animated films as *Steamboy* (Katsuhiro Otomo, 2004), *Spriggan* (Hirotsugu Kawasaki, 1998) and *Castle in the Sky* (Hayao Miyazaki, 1986) make visible the play of multiple flat layers that constitute the apparatus of cel animation. Such effects contribute to what Lamarre calls *animetism,* a way of seeing and moving through space that is "not about movement *into depth* but movement *on and between surfaces*."[29] Just as Henderson reads Godard's camera movements as an antibourgeois style, Lamarre reads ideological implications into this way of representing space. Animetism, he writes, "implies a different way of *perceiving* things," one that considers the visible landscape as a space for distanced appreciation rather than as a space to be explored, penetrated, and plundered.[30]

Both Henderson and Lamarre posit their examples of lateral movement as exceptions to a dominant cinematic mode of representing space. For Henderson, Godard's antibourgeois lateral movements emblematize his political modernism. Similarly, for Lamarre, animetism is an aesthetic tendency that at once is uniquely expressive of the medium-specific affordances of cel animation (as distinct from live-action cinema) and is opposed ideologically and aesthetically to what he calls *cinematism,* a dominant mode of spatial representation that "[sustains] Cartesian perspectivalism in conjunction with camera movement."[31] Both arguments thus reinforce the ways in which visual strategies emphasizing flatness and depth have been loosely mapped onto modernist and realist aesthetic aims.

But as I will demonstrate, the surface effects of lateral camera movements in the history of the moving image cannot be contained by such dichotomies, nor can they be so easily mapped onto modernist or avant-garde impulses across all instances. My aim is less to show how lateral camera movements can be mobilized to oppose the ideological underpinnings of Renaissance perspective than it is to show how our perception of them can help develop a phenomenological understanding of the moving image more generally.

To see how this works, consider a sequence from Leos Carax's *Mauvais Sang* (1986) in which the camera laterally tracks alongside the jubilant running of Denis Lavant to the tune of David Bowie's "Modern Love." The sequence immediately follows a conversation between Alex (Lavant) and Anna (Juliette Binoche), in which Anna falls into a depression over her fiancé. Eager to proffer an emotional outlet for Anna, whom he secretly loves, Alex turns on the radio to a mournful ballad. As soon as the song ends, Bowie's thumping synth-pop tune begins, introducing a tonal dissonance to the melancholic scene. Alex exits the apartment, but Bowie's tune follows him even as he leaves its diegetic source. When we cut to a lateral view of Alex walking screen right, the camera begins to accelerate, and Alex's hunched-over posture steadily opens up, ultimately exploding into a propulsive dance down the street.

Most descriptions of the sequence focus on the sheer physicality and manic energy of Denis Lavant, whose acrobatic talents are on full display.[32] But to explain the effect of the sequence purely in terms of Lavant's performance would overlook the particular feeling of kinetic energy uniquely produced by the speed, trajectory, and angle of the moving camera. To describe this feeling in phenomenological terms, we should first note that we do not quite *feel* the kinesthetic pull of moving through space along with Alex. Had the camera followed Lavant from behind or tracked backward in front of him, the sense of kinesthetic participation would be different. In such a case, we might link up our fictional alignment with Alex to the kinesthetic pleasure of moving through space as he does.[33] But while the sequence's lateral movement lacks this kinesthesia, we still experience a pointedly *kinetic* excitement. This sequence is not simply a depiction of but a cinematic enactment of exuberant movement, an equally diegetic and formal antidote to what Anna says earlier in the scene: "Nothing *moves* anymore."

Such a kinesis, rather than kinesthesia, can be largely attributed not simply to Lavant's propulsive dancing but to the vibratory pulses of vertical lines that quickly pass along the screen in the opposite direction (Figure 2.1). In this, the selection (or fabrication) of the backdrop is key. Lavant runs in front of a series of corrugated surfaces with painted stripes,

FIGURE 2.1. Lateral camera movement and pulsing visual rhythm in *Mauvais Sang* (Leos Carax, 1986).

alternations of white and gray, which produce intense rhythmic movements that resonate with the pulsing soundtrack. With the camera moving at such a speed, the alternating vertical lines do not simply appear to be laterally displaced by the movement of the camera; in other words, their succession does not simply mark our movement through space (as would the interpolation of single static objects between the camera and Lavant). Rather, the blurred vertical lines presented in rapid succession become a nearly abstract moving image of pure visual alternation, similar to the beginning of Ruttmann's *Berlin.* Entranced by the rhythm of the moving composition, the monotonous repetition of light and dark, Lavant's body seems to simultaneously traverse space *and* run in place. In a sense, the background does not just move in a single direction but *flashes* like a strobe light. Thus, we experience Lavant's increase in speed through the increase in visual rhythm; the perceived energy and vitality of his body are amplified by, but also inseparable from, the audiovisual rhythm that propels and is propelled by his movement. The effect is exacerbated when we briefly cut to a closer framing: with even less spatial reference to identify the camera's directional movement, Lavant's speed is sensed through the pulsing rhythm of the background.

A similar sequence from Carax's *Holy Motors* (2012), with the same actor no less, helps clarify what is going on here (Figure 2.2). Performing

FIGURE 2.2. Spatial unfurling in *Holy Motors* (Leos Carax, 2012).

a series of acrobatic stunts in a motion-capture studio, Lavant runs on a treadmill as a digital screen behind him projects rectangular polygons of alternating shades of black and white that rapidly glide to the left, simulating Lavant's traversal of space. While Lavant here is literally running in place, and the camera's only movement is a subtle track forward, the optical effect is almost identical to the "Modern Love" sequence. Both sequences, regardless of their profilmic differences, produce an undeniable feeling of speed through the abstract, rhythmic pulsation of light and dark shapes. In doing so, they invite comparison to the rhythmic repetition of railside objects familiar to the experience of nineteenth-century train travel. As Schivelbusch puts it, in panoramic perception, "the objects [perceived through the window] were attractive in their state of dispersal."[34] Notably, physicians were concerned with the eye fatigue from "watching too many telegraph poles *flash* by a moving train."[35] In adopting this overwhelming rhythmic flashing, the two sequences encourage us to stand outside Lavant's spatial situation and experience the screen as a flat, imaged whole.

Beyond producing visual rhythm and speed, the flat vertical lines flashing in the background also strikingly parallel the vertical edges of the film frame, thereby foregrounding the geometric rigidity of the frame. In a sense, the soft edges of the screen become hardened. The rectangularity of the screen is no longer an arbitrary convention of our view upon the filmic world but is now, briefly, aesthetically integrated into the pictorial contents composed within; the frame and its rectangularity are thus made aesthetically necessary. To borrow a phrase from Michael Fried, the sequence might be said to "acknowledge" the rectangularity of the frame and the flatness of the screen, taking on the challenge of addressing these material properties as intrinsically formal facts of its aesthetic presentation rather than contingent conditions of its medium.[36]

One temporal consequence of this spatial feature is a sense of *presentness* that permeates the sequence. Such presentness should not be confused with the "present tense" that Christian Metz has attributed to the movement of the moving image.[37] It has more in common with the presentness Fried and Stanley Cavell have identified with modernist visual art or with the "impression . . . of a continuous present" with which Bruce Elder has characterized the later works of Stan Brakhage.[38] Despite the sequences' linear temporality, their compositions' flatness and rhythmic regularity give off the impression of a pictorial fullness, a sense of an image being all there at once, to be beheld in a kind of perpetual present devoid of progress or anticipation. In engaging the planarity and rectangularity of the screen, the flashing visual abstraction suppresses the inherent linearity of recorded time. Lavant is indeed *represented* as spatiotemporally situated, as running toward something off in the distance, but the immediate formal effect of the composition places him within a pulsing rectangle that we experience as totally there, all at once. That the lateral movement of the camera is the agent of this formal achievement evidences the range of aesthetic possibilities continuous with Schivelbusch's panoramic perception. Unhinged from its mimetic adherence to embodied vision and expressive of the medium's detached display, the moving camera harnesses the expressive possibilities of the screen's geometric limits.

We can see such effects employed to various uses across European art cinema, classical Hollywood cinema, and avant-garde film. In one of the most formally daring sequences of Mikhail Kalatozov's *The Cranes Are Flying* (1957), a lateral tracking shot shows the protagonist Veronika frantically running alongside a speeding train to attempt suicide (Figure 2.3). Though the sequence culminates in violently jerky handheld camera movements and fast motion, the dominant aesthetic feature of the sequence is the pulsing rhythm of motion-blurred fence slats rushing by, causing the entire screen to flash with an intensity that evokes Veronika's inner turmoil. Or, to take a far less virtuosic example, in a scene from Otto Preminger's *Carmen Jones* (1954) in which Carmen and Joe are shown traveling by Jeep in rear projection, a cut to a lateral view introduces a subtle sensation of speed that complements Carmen's growing vivacity. As Victor Perkins explains, "The fresh angle conveys . . . a much stronger feeling of

FIGURE 2.3. The rhythm of blurred fence slats in *The Cranes Are Flying* (Mikhail Kalatozov, 1957).

movement since it brings into play what the previous shot had suppressed, the rapid flow of the background scenery. Its fluid, varied pattern reinforces the free-ranging rhythms of Carmen's song."[39]

In the experimental film *All My Life* (1966), Bruce Baillie explores the poetic effects of lateral movement and visual rhythm without channeling the image's affective energy through a human figure (Figure 2.4). Accompanied by Ella Fitzgerald and Teddy Williams's lilting jazz tune "All My Life," the film simply consists of a lateral tracking shot that slowly moves along a dilapidated fence, blue sky, and brown grass, occasionally passing by brilliantly red rosebushes. Seemingly attuned to the pace of the music, the alternating fence pickets steadily emerge from the left side of the frame, producing a soothing visual rhythm. As with the Carax examples, the verticality of the pickets acknowledges the vertical edge of the frame; but without a human figure on screen, the left edge of the frame becomes the locus of action that draws our attention. Focusing on the continuous unfurling of the fence pickets, we are not so much keyed in to the unfolding of a cinematic world as we are the purely formal rhythmic regularity vibrating on the screen's surface. In effect, we are lulled into a

FIGURE 2.4. The lulling rhythm of unfurling fence slats in *All My Life* (Bruce Baillie, 1966).

kind of temporal loop that produces a feeling of continuity and flow devoid of progress and exploration.[40] We are, as the song's lyrics indicate, simply "waiting" for rather than anticipating the unforeseen radiance of red rosebushes and the culminating ascent into blue sky.

A still different example is the lateral tracking shot of Matt Damon and Casey Affleck walking together in Gus Van Sant's *Gerry* (2002), a film that tells the tragic story of two hiking companions who get lost in the desert (Figure 2.5). By tightly framing his two subjects in shallow focus, using a telephoto lens, and keeping the camera's speed perfectly uniform with the pace of the actors, Van Sant draws our attention away from the characters' locomotion and toward the vertical patterns of rhythmic motion produced by the actors' heads bobbing up and down.[41] Despite both the camera's and the actors' continuous movement to the left, we focus our attention not on their progressive movement through space but on their movements with respect to the upper and lower barriers of the frame. This *traveling* shot, then, does not so much depict locomotion as it does the various levels of audiovisual synchronicity and asynchronicity between the two protagonists. Instead of functioning as

FIGURE 2.5. Lateral camera movement and visual rhythm in *Gerry* (Gus Van Sant, 2002).

an infinitely displaceable horizon of perception, the mobile frame rigidly encloses—and aesthetically presents—the human figures in order to spatially choreograph their movements within a two-dimensional array. In reducing space to a flat plane of figure and ground, the shot opens up new expressive possibilities at a quiet but pivotal moment in the narrative: the suspension of mobile progression evokes the hikers' complete sense of disorientation, and their asynchronous movements suggest a fomenting discord between them.

In each of these examples, ordinary lateral camera movements encourage us to see relations of movement on the surface of the screen and the audiovisual rhythms such movements produce. Just as the train passenger sees that the world is moving by but is simultaneously presented with an autonomous moving image separated from that world, the spectator of lateral movement sees that the camera is moving through space but is simultaneously presented with abstract visual rhythms colliding with the frame. In both cases, suppressing the immersion of kinesthetic participation opens up the spectator to a mode of viewing uniquely attuned to the two-dimensional composition of screen space. Such a denial occasions the emergence of a moving image *seen as* a moving image.

How might we develop positive terms for this kind of perceptual experience afforded by cinema's detached display? Elsewhere, I have drawn on Richard Wollheim's account of the "twofoldness" of picture perception—according to which the *aesthetic* perception of a picture involves a simultaneous attention to its surface qualities as well as its depictive content—to conceptualize the perception of camera movement.[42] In this view, the moving camera is understood not only as a surrogate for the spectator's movement through the film's world but also as a kind of paintbrush for generating two-dimensional screen phenomena. The spectator's perceptual attention of camera movement is thus of a *twofold* nature, simultaneously aware of these two seemingly contradictory aspects of the moving image.

Such a conceptual apparatus is helpful to understand the unique perceptual qualities of lateral camera movements. In the "Modern Love" sequence, for example, the speed, angle, and trajectory of the moving camera produces the conditions for us to see a depictive twofoldness in the screen's representation of movement. If it is the conventional power of the moving camera to encourage our identification with its virtual movement through scenographic space—that is, to identify the subject of depiction as the unseen camera itself—here we experience a productive tension between the depictive content of camera and screen. Just as the rushing landscape appears to the train passenger as moving on its own, the vertical lines in the background of the "Modern Love" sequence seem to flash as autonomous rhythmic patterns of light and dark. And yet, as spectators, we never lose an awareness that those abstract patterns depict the camera's traversal through space. In Wollheim's terms, the configurational and recognitional elements of the moving image are simultaneously present to us. We do not oscillate between these two modes of experience, seeing one and then the other. Rather, both aspects are constitutive of a single experience.

Such a logic is already embedded in the novel experience of train travel as a proto–moving image, for the train window automatically and indiscriminately renders the rushing landscape a "painted surface" without dissolving the literal perception of the moving landscape as indicative of the train's movement. The filmmaker can similarly use the moving camera as an aesthetic resource to convert space into the painted surfaces of moving images. The camera need not only carry us through the world it inhabits and activate spectatorial fantasies of penetrating the depths of represented space; it can also create a moving image separated from that world. Put simply, the moving camera can "paint" the screen with the visual material it captures from its own movement. In this way, lateral camera movements not only reproduce the perceptual conditions of panoramic perception but also exploit those conditions for unique aesthetic effects.

As an inherently malleable apparatus for modulating perceptual experience, the cinema screen offers a wide spectrum of spatial phenomena, from thickly illusory spaces of depth that efface the screen's material flatness to abstract patterns of light and color that acknowledge and exploit that flatness. On the one hand, the desire to efface an attention to the flatness of the screen works to extend the long-held identification of the camera with the eye, an intuitive conviction about the nature of cinematic experience as an immersive simulation of being-in-the-world. On the other hand, lateral movement invites us to reacquaint ourselves with that flatness, confronting us with the strangeness of moving images as zones of experience radically disassociated from our bodies. In placing these two models side by side, we not only avoid the pitfalls of overly deterministic theories but help elucidate the problems at the heart of theorizing a phenomenology of cinematic space in the wake of entrenched aesthetic discourses that privilege illusions of depth.

Ultimately, what Schivelbusch's account of train travel offers the film theoretical discourse of cinematic space is a model for attributing aesthetic and perceptual possibilities not to the material substrate of a technology or medium but to a *form of movement*. With the train passenger's panoramic perception, the "moving image" is not a material medium that yields a certain perception of movement. Rather, the converse is the case: a certain way of moving through the world—one afforded by the speed of the locomotive and its lateral view—yields a moving image. Film theory stands to gain from this model of thinking, for while the "moving image" is generally conceived as the material ground on which cinematic forms are built, it is equally an aesthetic effect that can be suppressed or brought to life by those very forms.

Notes

1. Tom Gunning, "Landscape and the Fantasy of Moving Pictures: Early Cinema's Phantom Rides," in *Cinema and Landscape,* ed. Graeme Harper and Jonathan R. Rayner (Bristol: Intellect Books, 2010), 55 (emphasis added).

2. The distinction between the lateral view of train travel and the frontal view of phantom rides was in fact a well-advertised feature of phantom rides. For example, an Edison catalog for *Phantom Ride on the Canadian Pacific* (1903) states, "The view taken from the front of the train running at high speed is one even tourists riding over the line are not privileged to enjoy"; quoted in Gunning, "Landscape," 55. Moreover, the popular entertainment of Hale's Tours films, in which phantom rides were rear-projected onto the "windows" of simulated train carriages, almost exclusively used frontal views of moving space rather than lateral views. See Christian Hayes, "Phantom Carriages: Reconstructing Hale's Tours

and the Virtual Travel Experience," *Early Popular Visual Culture* 7, no. 2 (2009): 185–98.

3. Wolfgang Schivelbusch, *The Railway Journey: The Industrialization of Time and Space in the Nineteenth Century* (Berkeley: University of California Press, 2014), 61.

4. Gunning, "Landscape," 57.

5. Gunning, 55, 56, 58, 56.

6. See André Bazin, "Evolution of the Language of Cinema," in *What Is Cinema?*, vol. 1, trans. Hugh Gray (Berkeley: University of California Press, 2004); David Bordwell, "Exceptionally Exact Perceptions: On Staging in Depth," in *On the History of Film Style* (Cambridge, Mass.: Harvard University Press, 1998), 158–272; Vivian Sobchack, "The Scene of the Screen: Envisioning Photographic, Cinematic, and Electronic 'Presence,'" in *Carnal Thoughts: Embodiment and Moving Image Culture* (Berkeley: University of California Press, 2004), 135–64; and Jennifer Barker, *The Tactile Eye: Touch and the Cinematic Experience* (Berkeley: University of California Press, 2009), 69–106. The apparatus theory of Jean-Louis Comolli and Jean-Louis Baudry critiques such a privileging of deep space and its analogy with "natural vision," but it also reinforces the primacy of deep space in cinematic representation by presuming the camera's automatic reproduction of Renaissance perspective. See Jean-Louis Baudry, "Ideological Effects of the Basic Cinematographic Apparatus," trans. Alan Williams and Jean-Louis Comolli, "Technique and Ideology: Camera, Perspective, Depth of Field [Parts 3 and 4]," trans. Diana Matias, in *Narrative, Apparatus, Ideology: A Film Theory Reader*, ed. Philip Rosen (New York: Columbia University Press, 1986), 286–98, 421–43.

7. Schivelbusch, *Railway Journeys,* 33. It is important to note that Schivelbusch himself was preoccupied with positing the train traveler's radical discontinuity with the outside world as a loss of a Benjaminian aura of spatiotemporal presence or as an intensification and multiplication of visual impressions typical of urban modernity. See also Lynne Kirby, *Parallel Tracks: The Railroad and Silent Cinema* (Durham, N.C.: Duke University Press, 1997); and Dimitris Eleftheriotis, *Cinematic Journeys: Film and Movement* (Edinburgh: Edinburgh University Press, 2010), 22–25.

8. While comparisons between the cinema screen and the train window are common, they are often simply grounded on an observation that both exhibit a framed view of moving space. For example, Lynne Kirby has referred to the passenger's window as a "framed, moving image," in *Parallel Tracks,* 2; Mary Ann Doane writes that "the railway passenger, like the cinema spectator, is subjected to a succession of images mediated by a frame," in "'When the Direction of the Force Acting on the Body Is Changed': The Moving Image," *Wide Angle* 7, no. 1–2 (1985): 42.

9. Quoted in Schivelbusch, *Railway Journey,* 55.

10. Schivelbusch, 189.

11. I am referring specifically to the *moving* panorama (as opposed to the *circular* panorama), which scrolled laterally before the spectator. For a media archaeological study of the moving panorama, see Erkki Huhtamo, *Illusions in Motion: Media Archaeology of the Moving Panorama and Related Spectacles* (Cambridge, Mass.: MIT Press, 2013).

12. See, for example, Alva Noë, *Action in Perception* (Cambridge, Mass.: MIT Press, 2004).

13. James J. Gibson, "The Visual Perception of Objective Motion and Subjective Movement," *Psychological Review* 61, no. 5 (1954): 306.

14. In violating the continuity between and mutual imbrication of embodied self and world, the view interrupts what Merleau-Ponty terms the "I can" of consciousness or what Gibson termed "affordances," that is, the potential for acting upon and within the world. Maurice Merleau-Ponty, *Phenomenology of Perception,* trans. Colin Smith (New York: Routledge, 1962), 159; James J. Gibson, *The Ecological Approach to Visual Perception: Classic Edition* (New York: Psychology Press, 2014), 127–46.

15. Quoted in Schivelbusch, *The Railway Journey,* 55.

16. Schivelbusch, 61 (emphasis in original).

17. Schivelbusch, 37.

18. Noël Carroll, "Defining the Moving Image," in *Theorizing the Moving Image* (New York: Cambridge University Press, 1996), 63.

19. Describing a similar phenomenological condition of the moving image in the terms offered by Gibson's ecological psychology, Richmond calls this basic condition cinema's modulation and suspension of "perceptual covariation." By this, Richmond means that the contents of the screen do not vary with respect to my bodily movements in the movie theater. Scott Richmond, *Cinema's Bodily Illusions: Flying, Floating, and Hallucinating* (Minneapolis: University of Minnesota Press, 2016), 89.

20. Mohan Matthen, "Two Visual Systems and the Feeling of Presence," in *Perception, Action, and Consciousness: Sensorimotor Dynamics and Two Visual Systems,* ed. Nivedita Gangopadhyay, Michael Madary, and Finn Spicer (New York: Oxford University Press, 2010), 121.

21. Mohan Matthen, *Seeing, Doing, and Knowing: A Philosophical Theory of Sense Perception* (New York: Oxford University Press, 2005), 316. For a useful discussion of Matthen's work in conjunction with Carroll's notion of the "detached display," see Ian Bryce Jones, "Enough of a World: A Phenomenology of Videogame *Weltlichkeit*" (PhD thesis, University of Chicago, 2015), 167–68.

22. Writing from an entirely different philosophical tradition and with different aims in mind, Jean-Luc Nancy similarly proposes that the ontological specificity of the "image" be understood in terms of what he calls "the distinct": "[The image] must be detached, placed outside and before one's eyes," in *The Ground of the Image* (New York: Fordham University Press, 2005), 2.

23. Gunning, "Landscape," 35 (emphasis added). As a kind of mirror whose particular size, shape, and use encouraged the production of an autonomous image, the Claude glass is also a liminal case for the detached display.

24. In this sense, it might be apt to consider the image within the train window a "virtual" image, where the term "virtual" denotes "possessing a power of acting without the agency of matter; being functionally or effectively but not formally of its kind"; quoted in Anne Friedberg, *The Virtual Window* (Cambridge, Mass.: MIT Press, 2006), 8.

25. By immersion, I mean the illusion or feeling of occupying a space other than the one in which I am physically situated. This should not be conflated with *absorption,* which has more to do with the spectator's engagement with narrative development and character identification than spatial engulfment. This distinction particularly matters for understanding Gunning's reading of the phantom ride as exemplary of the "cinema of attractions," a mode of spectatorship whose series of shocks and exhibitionist displays place it squarely against an aesthetics of absorption. Thus, insofar as the phantom ride's sensationalist shocks may align it with a subversive avant-garde aesthetics, its representation of deep space reinforces immersion as the dominant cinematic mode of perception. See Tom Gunning, "Cinema of Attractions: Early Film, Its Spectator and the Avant-Garde," in *Early Cinema: Space, Frame, Narrative,* ed. Thomas Elsaesser (London: British Film Institute, 1990).

26. David Bordwell, for example, writes that "we can hardly resist reading the camera movement effect as a persuasive surrogate for our subjective movement through an objective world"; David Bordwell, "Camera Movement and Cinematic Space," *Ciné-Tracts* 1, no. 2 (1977): 23. And considering the implications of Bordwell's observation for theories of art, Arthur Danto finds that because "the experience [of camera movement] is of *ourselves* moving," the moving camera "seems to overcome . . . the distance between spectator and scene"; Arthur Danto, "Moving Pictures," in *Philosophy of Film and Motion Pictures: An Anthology,* ed. Noël Carroll and Jinhee Choi (Malden, Mass.: John Wiley, 2009), 110. For more on this tendency in theories of camera movement, especially its central role in the phenomenological film theory of Vivian Sobchack, Jennifer Barker, and Scott Richmond, see Jordan Schonig, "Seeing Aspects of the Moving Camera: On the Twofoldness of the Mobile Frame," *SYNOPTIQUE: An Online Journal of Film and Moving Image Studies* 5, no. 2 (2017): 57–78.

27. Brian Henderson, "Toward a Non-bourgeois Camera Style: Part-Whole Relations in Godard's Late Films," in *A Critique of Film Theory* (New York: Dutton, 1980), 80.

28. Henderson, 65.

29. Thomas Lamarre, *The Anime Machine: A Media Theory of Animation* (Minneapolis: University of Minnesota Press, 2009), 7 (emphasis in original).

30. Lamarre, 6.

31. Lamarre, 27.

32. See, for example, Fergus Daly and Garin Dowd, *Leos Carax* (Manchester: Manchester University Press, 1988), 95; and Jonathan Rosenbaum, "The Problem with Poetry: Leos Carax," *Film Comment* 30, no. 3 (May 1994): 12.

33. For an account of how theories of cinematic identification might have purchase on such camera movements, see Scott Richmond, "The Exorbitant Lightness of Bodies, or How to Look at Superheroes: Ilinx, Identification, and Spider-Man," *Discourse* 34, no. 1 (2012): 113–44.

34. Schivelbusch, *The Railway Journey,* 189.

35. Quoted in Kirby, *Parallel Tracks,* 48 (emphasis added). In fact, the perception of these flashes was a medical danger they associated with cinema spectatorship, as both visual activities put a "strain on the eye to follow the object it is looking at" (48).

36. Michael Fried, "Shape as Form," in *Art and Objecthood: Essays and Reviews* (Chicago: University of Chicago Press, 1998), 88.

37. Christian Metz, "On the Impression of Reality in the Cinema," in *Film Language: A Semiotics of the Cinema,* trans. Michael Taylor (Chicago: University of Chicago Press, 1974), 5–6.

38. See Michael Fried, "Art and Objecthood," in *Art and Objecthood,* 148–72; Stanley Cavell, *The World Viewed: Reflections on the Ontology of Film* (Cambridge, Mass.: Harvard University Press, 1979), 108–17; and R. Bruce Elder, *Image and Identity: Reflections on Canadian Film and Culture* (Waterloo, Ont.: Wilfrid Laurier University Press, 2010), 253.

39. Victor Perkins, *Film as Film: Understanding and Judging Movies* (London: Penguin, 1972), 80.

40. Rudolph Arnheim reminds us that "there are mobile works that are not sequential. A dance composition is likely to unfold logically from its beginning to its end, but a waltz in the ballroom is not. Similarly, certain kinds of music, intended to establish a particular mood, are stationary, without a beginning, end, or development. The movements of a sculpture mobile have no progression. They reveal the varieties of spatial relation within a set of jointed elements. . . . When sequence is confused with mobility, misinterpretations result"; Rudolph Arnheim, *Art and Visual Perception: A Psychology of the Creative Eye* (Berkeley: University of California Press, 2004), 376.

41. This shot is a clear homage to a similar shot in Bela Tarr's *Werckmeister Harmonies* (2000), but I have chosen to examine Van Sant's version because it places more emphasis on the oscillation between synchronicity and asynchronicity.

42. See Schonig, "Seeing Aspects of the Moving Camera."

CHAPTER THREE

Deep in the Cave

Jean Ma

Holy Motors (Leos Carax, 2012) begins with a credit sequence referencing the chronophotographic motion studies conducted by Étienne-Jules Marey and Georges Demenÿ in the late nineteenth century. In brief scenes that alternate with the credit titles, we glimpse darkened cell-like spaces with gridded floors in which nude bodies perform basic physical actions. In one of these scenes, lasting no more than two seconds, the body of a boy is propelled laterally and upward by the velocity of his gesture of throwing. Following this is an equally brief fragment of footage, repeated three times in a loop, in which an adult man steps forward and vigorously tosses an object to the ground (Figure 3.1). The deteriorated condition of these black-and-white images and the jerkiness of their motion situate them in an era of visual media far removed from our own. The final image shown in the opening credit sequence, however, shifts the time frame to a more proximate period. It consists of a color image of a mass of people who appear to be asleep while seated upright in uniform rows in a dim, cavernous space. At first it is unclear whether this is a filmic image or a photographic freeze-frame, given the perfect stasis of these dormant figures. But as the shot continues for the next thirty-five seconds, it becomes legible as a moving image of an unmoving, unconscious cinema audience. The reflected light from the screen before the audience washes over them, briefly exposing the red cushions of their seats. The sounds that echo in this dim space—traffic, footsteps, a man's voice shouting "No!," a gunshot—emanate from the film that, although not visible in the shot, is playing before them.

Holy Motors at once gestures to the beginnings of moving image technology in serial photography and to the subsequent development of the movies as an institution of collective reception; it reflects on cinema

FIGURE 3.1. *Holy Motors* (Leos Carax, 2012)

as means of making images and of assembling an audience. Yet the energetic actions of the performing bodies form an odd and striking contrast to the completely motionless bodies inside the picture palace. The flickering and jittery quality of the older footage further animates these images, suggesting an uncontainable energy that struggles to burst forth

FIGURE 3.2. *Holy Motors* (Leos Carax, 2012)

from within and shatter the photographic stillness of the individual frame. In the image of the film audience, however, it is as if the intervening refinements of filmic technology have returned us to a condition of nearly photographic stasis and an atrophy perhaps even more profound. *Holy Motors* begins with a distant beginning, the body on screen convulsed in movement and twitching with irrepressible animation, in order to arrive at, in a kind of reverse shot to the other side of the fourth wall, an audience inert and quiescent, wrapped up in a stifling darkness. Crossing over from the image on screen to the space of the theater, we encounter unresponsive bodies that seem to be the negative counterpart of the active body on screen (Figure 3.2).

In this introductory sequence, *Holy Motors* activates a long-standing association between the movie theater and the cave as architectures of obscurity, seclusion, and enclosure. To enter into the theater is as if to leave behind the lucid sunlit world and descend into a cavernous realm, obscure and indistinct in its contours with the exception of the screen's rectangle of light. Cut off from external reality and acclimating to these surroundings, the viewer is conditioned to a different disposition of the body and senses. She is launched along a trajectory of lowering consciousness, such that to fall asleep (as one is wont to do in darkened spaces) is to touch bottom. The comparison between movie theaters and caves, and between filmgoing and sleeping, was made repeatedly at a specific moment when cinema spectatorship became an object of intense theoretical scrutiny. Across the writings of various thinkers who connect the environmental conditions of film exhibition with particular perceptual and cognitive effects—including Robert Smithson, Jean-Louis Baudry, and Christian Metz, who are discussed in this essay, as well as several others who are not—the question of spectatorship takes shape around a model of depth.[1] In this model, depth designates the degree of the viewer's involvement, pointing to the loss of distance from the projected image that comes with intense absorption. Depth also designates the dangers that attend such a degree of involvement, evoking the threat of disorientation and getting lost; the descent into the cinematic cave carries the sense of a fall from a fully aware, alert state of consciousness into a state akin to dreams, stupor, or narcosis. In some respects, this depth model of spectatorship is fully consistent with the verdict on the film spectator that is typically attributed to "apparatus theory"—as a locus of deception and mystification, attesting to the inexorability of industrial cinema's ideological effects. A closer look at how the idea of depth is mobilized, however, reveals surprising differences within a network of discourses that are frequently collapsed together under this unitary rubric. Moreover, it also reveals insights offered by these discourses, which stem from a period when the cinema experience was dominated by the fixed form of theatrical film exhibition, to debates about spectatorship in a contemporary moment of proliferating formats of display and modes of reception.

The artist Robert Smithson anticipates the turn to depth in theories of the film spectator in his essay "A Cinematic Atopia" (1971). In this essay, Smithson imagines the film viewer as a kind of cave dweller, whose eyes "probe the screen," whose mind forgets everything else, and whose body is mired in the "murky" reflections cast by the luminous screen.[2] The ultimate film theater would be one constructed from an actual cave, he writes, while "the ultimate film goer would be a captive of sloth. Sitting constantly in a movie house, among the flickering shadows, his perception would take on a kind of sluggishness. He would be the hermit dwelling among the elsewheres, foregoing the salvation of reality. Films would follow films, until the action of each one would drown in a vast reservoir of pure perception."[3] Smithson's imagination of the filmgoer sunken in a state of torpor—"impassive, mute, still"—is visually echoed in *Holy Motors*' depiction of the audience in suspended animation, for whom the shelter of darkness seems to be an invitation to oblivion (105). Within the cinematic cave, it is not only the body that becomes captive to sloth but also the senses that succumb to the drag of inertia and gravity. Thus perception assumes "a kind of sluggishness," suffers a loss of acuity, and even erases the contours of the films that it grasps (107). If the films all blur together as they swarm in the cave's "vast reservoir" of perception, so too do the filmgoers of *Holy Motors* become indistinct within the common condition of a drowned vision. To be fully immersed in this fashion is to experience something like a loss of consciousness and responsiveness, as the film's depiction of the movie audience suggests; likewise, Smithson notes that the filmgoer might very well fall asleep, but that would not even matter.

For other thinkers, too, the analogy between the theater and the cave aptly captures the sense in which the experience of cinema involves not only a situation of display but also a process of submergence within a distinctive space, with all of its attendant implications of losing one's bearings, passing into an altered state, and disappearing into an elsewhere. In "The Apparatus: Metapsychological Approaches to the Impression of Reality," published just a few years later, Jean-Louis Baudry theorizes the apparatus of cinema in terms of locality—that is, as a particular reproducible condition that depends on a particular place. Here Baudry also sees the film theater as a kind of cave that confines the audience, suppresses their motor impulses, and produces a peculiar mode of perception. While Smithson's cave is a geologic object, Baudry's cave exists in the realm of philosophical parable, a feature of an imaginary topography that allegorizes the spectator's state of deception and distance from the truth. Thus he draws a by-now-notorious comparison between the film viewer and the prisoner in Plato's cave, both caught in a "state of confusion" that "makes them take images and shadows for the real." The immobility to which Plato's cave dwellers become accustomed—so much that they resist leaving the cave when freed from their chains—is the same immobility that the filmgoer seeks out in the cinematic cave, "that the visitor to the dim space rediscovers, leaning back in his chair."[4] Baudry, via Plato, relates the physical conditioning of the filmgoer to a hijacked vision that leads to deception rather than knowledge and brings about a paralysis of the intellect as well as the body.

Furthermore, the vision of those who linger in caves can be likened to the perceptions experienced during sleep rather than during a regular state of wakefulness. As in the examples of *Holy Motors* and "A Cinematic Atopia," here Baudry characterizes the filmgoer as a somnolent figure. Immobility in darkness "was not invented by Plato," he observes, but can also refer to "the forced immobility of the sleeper who we know repeats the postnatal state and even intrauterine existence."[5] Baudry refers to another kind of cave that is recalled by the activity of sleep, drawing from Freudian psychoanalysis. When human beings undress and prepare to sleep, in Freud's account, "they approach remarkably close to the situation in which they began life. Somatically, sleep is a reactivation of intrauterine existence, fulfilling as it does the conditions of repose, warmth and exclusion of stimulus; indeed, in sleep many people resume the foetal posture."[6] The psychoanalytic reading of sleep frames it as a return to the womb, in which the subject rediscovers warmth, darkness, repose, and the absence of external stimuli. While Smithson identifies the cave as a site of dissipation—where perceptual energies wind down to an entropic end point—in Freud's primordial description the cave is an origin, a site of resubmergence within a fetal state of nondifferentiation, and a locus of regression. To withdraw into the cave of sleep is to backpedal from the alert state of the fully developed ego, paving the way for a "relaxation of a certain deliberate (and no doubt also critical) activity which we allow to influence the course of our ideas while we are awake."[7] In this respect, Freud notes, sleep has much in common with other psychoneurotic states that involve "temporal regression," such as psychosis (which resembles dreaming in its hallucinatory wish fulfillment) and narcissism (suggested by the sleeper's lack of interest in the world).[8] These regressive dynamics play an important role in dreaming, a process that Freud characterizes in terms of the loss of the ability to differentiate between perceptions generated from within and those provoked by external stimulation—hence the dreamer's belief in the reality of the dream for as long as she is asleep.

In dialogue with both Plato and Freud, Baudry associates the movie theater with a series of spaces that all share the attributes of inhibiting motor response and cutting off direct contact with external reality: cave, chamber, bedroom, and womb. Deprived of such response and contact, the filmgoer occupies a position like that of the sleeper for whom, according to Freud, "the possibility of reality-testing is abandoned," perception being closed to the outside.[9] Cavernous spaces therefore give rise to effects that are quite distinct from "the activity of representation in a state of wakefulness."[10] The filmgoer falls prey to an "impression of reality"—both like the cave prisoner who confuses reflected shadows with reality itself and like the sleeper who is fully wrapped up in the dream (302). By simulating the economic conditions of dreaming, Baudry writes, the cinematic apparatus "brings about a state of artificial regression." By means of the darkness of the space, the compelled passivity of the viewer, and the projection of an image, the apparatus "artificially leads back to an anterior phase of his development—a phase which is barely hidden, as dreams and certain pathological forms of our mental life have shown" (313). Baudry closely follows Freud's theory of sleep and dreams in delineating how cinematic exhibition modifies the psychical system so as to detour the processes of consciousness in a waking state—reducing the reach of the senses, decapacitating cognition, and ultimately bringing about a state of deception like that experienced by the dreamer.

Taking up the construct of the cinematic cave, "The Apparatus" develops this construct as the basis for a depth model of spectatorship, describing an envelopment of the viewer that simultaneously obliterates her awareness of her surroundings. Baudry's theorization of spectatorship builds upon the deep structure of the psyche set forth in Freudian psychoanalysis, thereby linking spatial, architectural ideas of depth to temporal, developmental ideas of regression. If this essay stands out for its extreme position on the dangers of getting lost inside caves (as many of its critics have pointed out), it is nonetheless not alone in drawing such connections. "The Apparatus" was published alongside the work of Christian Metz, another emblematic thinker of film theory's turn to the resources of psychoanalysis. In "The Fiction Film and Its Spectator: A Metapsychological Study," Metz also imagines the theater as a cave that sucks the viewer into its torpor. In elaborating on the effects that follow from this plunge into a drowsy inertia, he likewise relies on Freud's definition of sleep as the "economic condition" that makes dreaming possible.[11] Even while starting from a similar set of premises, however, Metz arrives at a different view of spectatorship, one that emphasizes the volatility rather than the determinism of cinematic absorption.

According to Metz, consciousness becomes hazy from the moment that the filmgoer enters and takes a seat. The effect can perhaps be grasped most readily in retrospect, as the filmgoer emerges from the spell of the darkness: "In ordinary screening conditions, as everyone has had the opportunity to observe, the subject who has fallen prey to the filmic state . . . feels he is in a kind of daze, and spectators at the exit, brutally rejected by the black belly of the cinema into the bright, unkind light of the foyer, sometimes have the bewildered expression (happy or unhappy) of people waking up. To leave the cinema is a little like getting out of bed: not always easy" (116–17). This conditioning of the viewer paves the way for "perceptual transference," or what Metz calls "that dreamlike and sleepy confusion of film and reality" situated at the crux of the cinema's power (103). The soporific inducements of the darkness bring about the beginnings of psychic regression, in which one begins to mistake impressions for reality. For Metz, as for Baudry, the altered state of the filmgoer recalls that of the dreamer. Yet Metz stops short of advancing a direct analogy between the two activities. For him, spectatorial depth maps onto not just a linear trajectory of regression but also a free fall into a murky zone of lowered and intermediary states of consciousness—a zone designated by the sleepiness that so readily descends within the cinematic cave. And while sleep in a functional sense (defined as a set of modifications to normal perceptual processing) supports the analogy between filmgoing and dreaming, sleep in a more literal sense presents a stumbling block.

Both Baudry and Metz project the operations of a sleeping psyche upon the activities of a hypothetical viewer who is awake, her eyes open to the film, and for Metz, this contradiction warrants further scrutiny. Indeed, the very first sentence of his essay declares the incontrovertible difference between the dreamer and the spectator: "The dreamer does not know that he is dreaming; the film spectator knows that he is at the cinema: this is the first and principal difference between situations of film and dream. We sometimes speak of the illusion of reality in one or the other, but true illusion belongs to the dream and to it alone" (101). With this cautionary note in mind, Metz continues to develop the comparison between the metapsychology of the dream state and that of the filmic state. But even as he goes on to enumerate the similarities between them, he also constantly returns to the gaps that thwart the analogy he is constructing. For example, Metz observes that another major difference between these states concerns hallucinatory wish fulfillment. While the dream is made to the perfect measure of the wishes of the dreamer, the film can achieve only a poor fit, for "it rests on true perceptions which the subject cannot fashion to his liking." Unlike the dream, which is bound to the pleasure principle, the film cannot escape the reality principle (112–13). And, he writes, "filmic perception *is* a real perception (is really a perception)" that is experienced with other spectators; "it is not reducible to an internal psychical process," in the way of a "true illusion" or a "true hallucination" (109). Metz accordingly hedges his claims, describing the filmic state as a "semi-regression," versus the total regression of sleep (118).

Reservations such as these accumulate in the course of his discussion, congeal into a running counterargument to the explicit thesis of the essay, and consolidate around a central assertion: that the gap between the dream state and the filmic state boils down to the problem of sleep. As Metz writes, "The dominant situation is that in which film and dream are not confounded: this is because the film spectator is a man awake, whereas the dreamer is a man asleep" (109). If the economic transformations of sleep provide a theoretical armature for the dream metaphor, they also constitute the loose thread that unravels the metaphor altogether, for as Metz well recognizes, the moment that the regressive movement reaches its conclusion, when the filmgoer closes her eyes to the film and surrenders to sleep, the entire conceptual edifice collapses upon itself. In a remarkable passage, he describes this paradox as a kind of monster haunting the nightmares of the waking theorist:

> When we trace the obscure kinship relations (interwoven as they are by differences) of the film and the dream, we come upon that unique and methodologically attractive object, that theoretical monster . . . a dream, in short, like life. That is to say (we always come back to this), the dream of a man awake, a man who knows that he is dreaming, and who consequently knows that he is not dreaming, who knows that he is at the cinema, *who knows that he is not sleeping;* since if a man who is sleeping is a man who does not know that he is sleeping, a man who knows that he is not sleeping is a man who is not sleeping. (123)

The theorization of cinema as an impression of reality skates unsteadily on the razor edge of sleep. And, as Metz well demonstrates, he who invokes the imminence of sleep while simultaneously warding off its arrival might find himself tied into knots.

Metz takes the sleepy spectator as an equally central object of theoretical interest, the counterpart of the spectator who dreams with open eyes. This putative figure—a drowsy viewer wobbling unsteadily on the cusp of consciousness, adrift in the transitional zone in between sleeping and waking—becomes the genesis for an alternative line of investigation in the essay. "The Fiction Film and Its Spectator" cleaves at the point of sleep, splitting into two distinct critical tracks: on the one hand, a psychoanalytic account of film as dream and, on the other hand, a phenomenological account of sleeping in the theater. In order to arrive at the juncture of the filmic state and the dream state, it is not simply enough for Metz to map the viewing situation and the abstract spectator into a schema of simulated regression. Rather, his approach also requires an attention to the concrete variables of bodies perhaps already fatigued, minds more or less already emotionally spent, as these enter a space of darkness and encounter "a mill of images and sounds overfeeding our zones of shadow and irresponsibility . . . a machine for grinding up affectivity and inhibiting action" (107). By way of this line of reasoning, Metz arrives at another view of the relationship between sleeping and waking—less as a binary opposition between surrendering to depth and extricating oneself from it, and more as a sliding scale.

Tracing cinema's somnolent effects, Metz follows the movements of a hypothetical embodied viewer who exists in time up and down this sliding scale, drawing nearer to or retreating from the point of perceptual transference on a moment-to-moment basis. He describes scenarios in which, "for brief instances of fleeting intensity," the gap between the state of the dreamer (unaware that she is dreaming) and that of the filmgoer (aware that she is at the cinema) can diminish, and "the subject's consciousness of the filmic situation as such starts to become a bit murky and to waver, although this slippage, the mere beginning of a slippage, is never carried to its conclusion" (101). By way of example, Metz conjures an urbane adult filmgoer well habituated to conduct herself with silence and stillness in the theater, in contrast to children or country audiences inclined to respond with outbursts of voice and gesture. Such a filmgoer, especially if already "in a state of fatigue or emotional turmoil" and moved profoundly by the film, is likely to experience the slippage he describes (103). This viewer might experience an instance of perceptual transference, what Metz refers to as a dizziness or "psychical giddiness" aroused in a fleeting, anomalous moment when dreaming and seeing coincide, and the viewer dreams what she actually sees. Whether the moment of perceptual transference transpires depends on the audience member's preexisting state ("when one has not had enough sleep, dozing off is usually more a danger during the projection of a film" [107]) as well as social profile ("there is material here for a socio-analytic typology of the different ways of attending a film screening" [103]). Even while explicating spectatorship as a psychic regime of perception, Metz keeps other dimensions in play and fleshes out his hypothetical viewer with a body, history, and context. The dispositive of cinema is not a closed and static system, but open to the rhythms of the bodies it contains and made variable by their multiplicity.

On one side of sleep, there is this drowsy and sluggish filmgoer, her wakefulness ebbing as she succumbs to the cinema's invitation to relax, taking steps in the direction of sleeping and dreaming until she arrives at that brief flash of psychical giddiness. On the other side, Metz posits a counterpart to this figure, a dreamer who is only partially submerged in sleep. Much as wakefulness diminishes for the filmgoer, so sleep can loosen its grip on the dreamer. There are moments when "deep sleep steals away," when the dreamer acquires a lucid alertness to her situation and realizes, "I am in the middle of a dream." During such moments, the dream's illusion of reality splits open. As in the filmic situation, the perceptual transference of the dream is modulated by shifting degrees of wakefulness. In both cases, the normal regime of functioning can be momentarily interrupted by gaps—like the psychical giddiness of the filmgoer, or the lucidity of the dreamer. And it is here, in these gaps, that Metz identifies "a kinship at once more profound and dialectical" between the filmic state and the dream state: "The filmic and dream states tend to converge when the spectator begins to doze off . . . or when the dreamer begins to wake up" (108).

The drifting consciousness of sleep, then, leads to a surprising theoretical destination. It leads Metz to a consideration of depth that is more akin to that of Smithson than Baudry—one that is ambiguous and open-ended rather than suspicious and speleophobic. By way of this route, Metz goes beyond the notion of a transcendent spectatorial position that is typically attributed to both psychoanalytic film theory and apparatus theory, arriving instead at a view of reception that calls into question the inevitability of a uniform, totalized subject effect. Dreaming in the cinema is the product of an at-best tenuous equilibrium between disparate and contradictory states. The filmgoer hovers at a volatile juncture, shaped by processes of abstraction and disembodiment, but equally by intransigent materialities and opacities. For Metz, the special power of film is to momentarily reconcile regimes of consciousness that are typically distinct and mutually exclusive, to link them so as to allow for "overlapping, alternating balance, partial coincidence, staggering, and ongoing circulation" (138). In this account, vision never fully transcends corporeality, and absorption is interwoven with distraction. Rather than generating a specific regime of vision and knowledge in a deterministic fashion, the situation of projection gives rise to a state of attention in constantly varying depth, moving between levels of consciousness. The depth model of spectatorship Metz advances here is phenomenologically textured, modulated by ebbs and flows rather than funneled by the singular momentum of regression. As such, it is a model worth revisiting in a contemporary moment marked by a diffusion of spectatorship across multiple sites, platforms, and exhibitionary configurations. The question of depth discloses continuities between the fluctuating forms of attentiveness dominant in an earlier era of technologies and those emerging in the present, and thus offers a corrective to recent discussions that schematically oppose the immobility, fixity, and absorption of the theater against the more interactive, mobile, and distracted spectatorial practices arising in the postcinematic era.

In a pilot study looking into the seasonal variability of human sleep patterns, Thomas Wehr replicated the conditions of sleep as experienced by early cave dwellers with limited means of lighting. Over a period of fifteen weeks, he restricted the photo-exposure of his test subjects by confining them to an artificial cave, simulating the short days and long nights of the winter months. Under these circumstances, the sleep of the test subjects settled into a distinct bimodal pattern, consisting of roughly four-hour bouts of sleep alternating with extended periods of a state he calls "quiet rest."[12] Quiet rest, as Wehr found, is distinct from daytime wakefulness in its endocrinological profile, comparable to the altered state of meditation—indeed, perhaps accessible only through meditation and other practices of cultivating quiescence in an era when habits of sleep are thoroughly structured by the ready availability of artificial light and the strictures of the nine-to-five workday.[13] He interprets this as evidence of unfamiliar sleep patterns that reside latent in human physiology, deactivated and suppressed by a technological world that abolishes the natural variability of circadian rhythms. Wehr writes, "This situation has obtained for so many generations that modern humans no longer realize that they are capable of experiencing a range of alternative modes that may have once occurred on a seasonal basis in prehistoric times but now lie dormant in their physiology."[14] Buried under layers of social regulation and biotechnological management, these alternative modes of nocturnal life nonetheless persist. Once rediscovered, they dislodge preconceived notions of what constitutes "natural" sleep and disclose new, unfamiliar amalgamations of sleeping and waking.

The movie theater as conceived by Metz functions similarly to Wehr's cave, as a haven from the permanent vigilance demanded by perpetual daytime and therefore an inroad into these other modes of consciousness. Both share a sense that sleepy perception can be, besides a detraction from the waking state, something else or even something more. It can designate an open field of differential effects and varying wavelengths of attention—a field in which viewers' perceptions and bodily experiences can extend beyond their most familiar and habitual zones, unfurling toward edges and thresholds that are less commonly frequented. And cinema can provide an opportunity to further explore this unfamiliar territory, by carving out a space in which to prolong transitional states of awareness, and to linger at the edges of sleep in the presence of others. Perhaps there are other things to be discovered in its darkness, swimming with the other hermits in this "vast reservoir" of perception.

Notes

1. For an expanded discussion of this topic, see Jean Ma, *At the Edges of Sleep,* forthcoming.

2. Robert Smithson, "A Cinematic Atopia," in *The Writings of Robert Smithson: Essays with Illustrations,* ed. Nancy Holt (New York: New York University Press, 1979), 105.

3. Smithson, 107.

4. Jean-Louis Baudry, "The Apparatus: Metapsychological Approaches to the Impression of Reality in the Cinema," in *Narrative, Apparatus, Ideology,* ed. Philip Rosen (New York: Columbia University Press, 1986), 303.

5. Baudry, 303.

6. Sigmund Freud, *A Metapsychological Supplement to the Theory of Dreams,* vol. 14 of *The Standard Edition of the Complete Psychological Works of Sigmund Freud,* ed. James Strachey (London: Hogarth Press, 1953), 222.

7. Sigmund Freud, *The Interpretation of Dreams,* trans. James Strachey (New York: Basic Books, 2010), 127.

8. In *The Interpretation of Dreams,* Freud observes that dreaming can be likened to psychosis, as a state in which wishing ends in hallucinatory fulfillment (369). He further develops this link to psychoneurotic states throughout *A Metapsychological Supplement to the Theory of Dreams.*

9. Freud, *A Metapsychological Supplement,* 234.

10. Baudry, "The Apparatus," 308.

11. Christian Metz, "The Fiction Film and Its Spectator: A Metapsychological Study," in *The Imaginary Signifier: Psychoanalysis and the Cinema* (Bloomington: Indiana University Press, 1982), 99–148 (translation modified). As the titles of their essays indicate, both Baudry and Metz are indebted to Freud's considerations of the dreaming psyche.

12. Thomas A. Wehr, "A 'Clock for All Seasons' in the Human Brain," in *Hypothalamic Integration of Circadian Rhythms,* ed. R. M. Buijs, A. Kalsbeek, H. J. Romijn, C. M. A. Pennartz, and M. Mirmiran (New York: Elsevier, 1996), 321–42.

13. See Wehr; Natalie Angier, "Modern Life Suppresses an Ancient Bodily Rhythm," *New York Times,* March 14, 1995, https://www.nytimes.com/1995/03/14/science/modern-life-suppresses-an-ancient-body-rhythm.html.

14. Wehr, "A 'Clock for All Seasons,'" 337.

CHAPTER FOUR

On a Lonely Planet, Feeling-in-Depth

Wong Kar-wai's *2046* and Chris Marker's *Sans Soleil*

Jinhee Choi

> I'm leaving you a rather melancholic picture, but in the depths of my heart, I am happy.
>
> —*SANS SOLEIL*

One of the prevailing approaches to the question of depth and reality in film studies is still André Bazin's realism. Certain stylistic devices, including Orson Welles's use of deep focus in *Citizen Kane* (1941) or Jean Renoir's apparently spontaneous, fluid camera work and staging in *The Rules of the Game* (1939), foreground a quality of phenomenological reality: a space extending beyond the screen frame, inviting the spectator to construe this reality as continuous.[1] In this essay, I turn away from the spatially oriented notion of depth, to instead explore the depth of aesthetic object and feeling, following Mikel Dufrenne. Along with Maurice Merleau-Ponty, Dufrenne, a French philosopher of art, has influenced the development of a phenomenological approach within contemporary film theory, represented most notably by Vivian Sobchack.[2] Yet compared with Merleau-Ponty, Dufrenne's philosophy has not been widely adopted within film studies. Initially characterizing depth by differentiating it from intellectual difficulty, perceptual obscurity, and density, Dufrenne defines depth as the expressivity that an aesthetic object emits toward which the spectator's or listener's feeling is directed. In such feeling, the aesthetic object deepens the subject.[3]

While elaborating his view on aesthetic expressivity and experience, Dufrenne discusses several art forms, but in particular music and painting, mentioning film only in passing. He never explicitly elaborates on how the concept of the aesthetic object or depth could be construed in relation to film other than in a footnote; of film, he writes, "movement is its very matter and its means . . . film is the novel in movement, and it is in movement because it exists in the form of images."[4] Sobchack, inspired by Merleau-Ponty and Dufrenne, dwells on the co-substantiation or interobjectivity between subject and object, yet prioritizes the on-screen characters' devotion that has moved her rather than the film's formal strategies.[5] I will first introduce Dufrenne's notion of depth as a philosophical concept, then further explore its applicability in the analysis of the depth "of" film, drawing on Wong Kar-wai's *2046* (2004) and Chris Marker's *Sans Soleil* (1983). Because the two filmmakers are normally considered directors of neither long take nor deep focus—the film styles that are most frequently associated with depth—their films offer interesting case studies to consider here as alternatives to the dominant, spatial approach to depth. These films will be approached in terms of the depth of aesthetic object, and how they invite or block the spectator to "be-in-depth" or feel the depth of aesthetic object.[6]

Depth, Expressivity, and Inexhaustibility

Dufrenne's *The Phenomenology of Aesthetic Experience* has hardly been at the center of philosophical debates on aesthetic experience in English-language scholarship, despite his affinity with, and inspiration from, Merleau-Ponty and Immanuel Kant. The paucity of scholarship on Dufrenne, according to David G. Allen, could be rooted both in the delay of the English translation of his work and in the difficulty of his writing in terms of its scope and style.[7] Although Dufrenne's work appeared in the 1950s, contemporaneous with that of Susanne Langer, Benedetto Croce, and Rudolf Arnheim, who were more prominent in the analytic tradition of aesthetics and art history, his writing has been available in English only since the 1970s. Further, the enormous compass of Dufrenne's book, drawing from Edmund Husserl, Martin Heidegger, Kant, Jean-Paul Sartre, and Merleau-Ponty, challenges the reader unless one is well versed in an array of phenomenological approaches. Readers in English-language film studies might have encountered Dufrenne's name in passing. Dudley Andrew mentions Dufrenne in his addressing of the film world as experiential—a mode of experience—while Sobchack appeals to Dufrenne's idea of co-substantiation in her film ethics.[8] But such a brief mention of Dufrenne's phenomenology has hardly motivated many to delve into his thick book of more than five hundred pages. Daniel Yacavone is one of the few scholars who draw on Dufrenne's philosophy in order to develop an ontology of film's world, emphasizing the spectator's immersive experience of it, yet he focuses less on depth than on rhythm in cinema.[9]

One of the reasons to introduce and revisit Dufrenne's philosophy in the discussion of depth here lies in his contribution to the phenomenological reconfiguration of the relationship between subject and object. His idea of aesthetic feeling helps us to surpass the limits of intentionality—the postulation by the Husserlian phenomenological approach that construes consciousness as external to its object. Consciousness is often defined negatively, as a lack or absence from the world to which it is directed but of which it could not be part.[10] Dufrenne instead proposes, "Intentionality is no longer an aim or mere intention *toward* but a participation *with* . . . to lay myself open is not merely to be conscious of something, but to associate myself with it. Feeling is an act of communion to which I bring the entirety of my being" (406).

The intervention of Dufrenne should be found in his attribution to the aesthetic object of a special relationship with "the" world through its embodiment of "a" world. A work of art not only expresses but also is a physical object that exists within the world. For Dufrenne, given the fact that the subject stands co-substantially with a world of the aesthetic object, consciousness does not need to be considered as external to that which it is directed toward. His theory thus avoids the pitfall of modern philosophies of consciousness and its relationship to the world, which has haunted many philosophers and even film theorists.[11] Dufrenne's idea of "feeling as being-in-depth" in a world of the aesthetic object resonates with a Heideggerian "being-in-the-world" or Husserl's "natural attitude."[12] Yet to what extent this kind of immersion and immanence is facilitated by the *aesthetic object* and *experience* should be further fleshed out in Dufrenne's terms.

Dufrenne often characterizes the relationship between aesthetic feeling and the object through an analogy with interpersonal relations: generosity, intimacy, and love. Affective engagement with an aesthetic object presupposes a reciprocal relationship between subject and object: sensitivity on the side of the subject and affective qualities on the side of the aesthetic object. He writes, "It is no longer a question of pretending that Hamlet is real so that we may become interested in his adventures. Instead, we make ourselves present to Hamlet's world so that it may touch us and flow into us. Feeling has depth, therefore, by this type of generosity, this confidence which it inspires with regard to the object and which does not proceed without fervor."[13] We are invited to get to know a world—the fictional world—which characters inhabit not through making any conscious effort ("pretending") to be sympathetic with them but through the object's "generosity" to inspire the subject and the latter's intimacy with it ("touch" and "flow"). It depends on the capacity in me to be affected and to be involved. My sensitivity—"being capable of being affected"—enables me to exist co-substantially with a work; "the more I lay myself open to the work, the more sensitive will I be to its effects" (405).

This idea of intimacy or "reciprocity between intentionality and being-oneself" brings one's attention not only to consciousness's participatory nature but also to its immanence (405). An aesthetic object is not a springboard to retrieve one's past memory, but it "instruct[s] me by giving the work a greater hold over me, and myself a greater depth" (405). Depth as immanence consists in this very relationality of subject and object, which is neither completely external to the subject nor entirely sinking within one's interiority: "Aesthetic feeling is deep because the object reaches into everything that constitutes me. My past is immanent in the present of my contemplation and exists there as what I am—it is not the result of a history which would turn me into the final term of a causal sequence, but the seat of a duration in which I am conjoined with myself" (404). An aesthetic object possesses interiority or quasi subjectivity insofar as it expresses for the spectator and audience to engage with it. Dufrenne adds, "The depth must be sought in the object's power to express, through which it is the analogue (as a result of being the proxy) of a subjectivity" (411). Consciousness attributed to both the subject and an aesthetic object here is not, Dufrenne claims, "the power of negation" but "a power of affirmation" (404). The relationship between consciousness and the aesthetic object, according to Dufrenne, is comparable to love: "Is not love that expectation of a conversion by the attention we pay to the other, to what he is and expresses?" (406).

Because the expressivity of an aesthetic object is closely tied to aesthetic feeling rather than understanding, Dufrenne often uses nonrepresentational art, such as music, in his characterization of the aesthetic object and experience. Although understanding does not keep one from forming an inexhaustible relationship with an aesthetic object, the appeal of the musical form for Dufrenne lies in its being free from the burden of identifying an object represented and understanding its hidden meaning: "We face all art in fundamentally the same way as we face music, where *representation gives way to expression*. It is the particular—and formidable—privilege of music to awaken feeling without provoking reflection and to summon us to a depth which is not that of obscurity. There is no obscurity for feeling, which knows the expressed object, but only for understanding, which knows the represented object" (411; emphasis added). This is one of the principal reasons that Dufrenne constantly dissociates "depth" from other concepts that require an exercise of understanding. The depth of the aesthetic object should not be equated with antiquity (407), the hidden, strangeness (408), or difficulty (410), Dufrenne states. Depth would not disappear even after one understands an aesthetic object's longevity or its implicit meanings; aesthetic experience, for Dufrenne, neither requires a causal explanation of, nor seeks a solution to, that which a work of art presents to the subject (410). The aesthetic experience of *Citizen Kane,* for instance, would not disappear even after one identifies Kane's last word, "rosebud," which sets out the narrative enigma, or after one figures out how the depth of field is rendered in the famous shot of young Kane playing in the snow outside the window, while his mother signs papers with Thatcher in the foreground.

The depth of aesthetic feeling for Dufrenne is existential as well as experiential, both of which are unquantifiable and inexhaustible. It is based on the subject's intimacy with, and sensitivity to, the expressivity of an object. Dufrenne connects depth to both the intensity and the authenticity of the self. The subject's relation to an aesthetic object does not posit the transcendence of, or indifference to, the object. On the contrary, it is manifest through the "intensity" of a being (i.e., the subject's capability to be affected) and the "authenticity" of the self (i.e., the subject's entire history and immanence) (405, 411). Immanence here does not mean the self's reminiscence of a particular moment in time: "Depth can have a relationship with the present moment only to the extent that this moment is filled with my self, arising from a time which I am and not from one *in* which I am. That is, depth refers essentially to the self, to the plenitude and authenticity of my being, and depth is in time only to the extent that time *is* myself" (401; emphasis in original). This correlation between the authenticity of a being and temporality articulated earlier is further illustrated by Dufrenne's explanation of immersion in music; one is not reminded of a memory of the past but brings one's entire being to appreciate it: "This past which I am gives a density to my being" (404). This kind of "*nonmaterial density* of a deep and profound self" (405; emphasis added) is a precondition for the subject to participate in a relationship with the aesthetic object. The density of the self should then be differentiated from the material density of matter in a quantifiable sense, which is measured by extension. While describing the depth of the aesthetic object, Dufrenne contrasts it with the density of the sea. The latter's inexhaustible appearance or physical depth has more to do with its material density. And the subject's access to it is through understanding, not feeling; "this is why the sea is continually celebrated as the instructor of understanding, for understanding alone (i.e., thinking in terms of relations) is related to this radical exteriority" (412). Only when the sea expresses moods to us, through its affective qualities such as calmness and fury, does it then embody Dufrenne's depth: the "emergence of a for-itself" (404).

Aesthetic experience for Dufrenne is predicated on both density and depth. He claims, "It is essential that the aesthetic object always possess—on the level of the in-itself—the density of being by which it is nature" (412). One could recall the passage quoted earlier in which Dufrenne associates expressivity and depth with love, which I repeat: "Is not love that expectation of a conversion by the attention we pay to the other, to what he *is* and *expresses?*" (406; emphasis added). Like love that is based on both one's nonmaterial density ("is") and depth ("expresses"), aesthetic experience relies on both.

Here it would be useful to briefly compare and contrast Dufrenne's material sense of density with Bazinian "spatial density": to be exact, in Bazin's words, "the spatial density of something real."[14] Despite the apparent conflation of Bazinian realism with certain stylistic tropes, for him realism has to do with the evocation of the unity and homogeneity of space, an outcome of the interplay between the real and the imaginary (50). In the famous footnote where Bazin discusses *Where No Vultures Fly* (Harry Watt, 1951), the spectator's sudden surprise at, and acute sensing of, the impending danger of a boy near a lioness is thanks to the two-shot that follows the crosscutting between the two—an event that unfolds before the camera in "its physical and spatial reality" (49).

In contrast to the Bazinian spatial density of the profilmic reality, aesthetic depth is still unquantifiable. Dufrenne emphasizes: "Even the image of physical depth tends to mislead, however, to the extent that it suggests measurability and thus extension. The aesthetic object has depth because it is beyond measurement. The depth of the aesthetic object is measured by the depth of the existence to which it invites us. Its depth is correlative with ours."[15] If Dufrenne's notion of depth is an invitation, an interiority of an object as well as the co-substantiation between object and subject, its manifestation does not require any specific stylistic unfolding. Although for Bazin the aesthetic significance of realistic style is thanks to its phenomenological holding of the spectator—providing an "authenticity" to the scene in question—some Bazinian descendants have been tempted to be swayed under "technical dogma," reducing the cinematic phenomenological reality to stylistic correlates.[16] Some contemporary slow cinema practitioners appear to compete for the record of average shot length—the object of an understanding rather than a feeling or subjective experience.[17] As Thomas Elsaesser aptly notes, however, spatial density for Bazin could be exemplified by the long take and depth of field, but it is not identical with them.[18] If that is the case, there exists more affinity between Bazin and Dufrenne in terms of the relationship between depth and its various stylistic manifestations, yet Dufrenne's aesthetic theory of depth and feeling offers an alternative model for properly apprehending depth in philosophical, existential terms, instead of only in spatial, phenomenological terms: depth "of" film, rather than "in" film.

There certainly exist philosophical challenges to the aesthetic attitude and experience that Dufrenne endorses. Regardless of whether the emphasis is on the subjectivity of the object (Dufrenne) or the objectivity of the subject (Sobchack), as the latter notes, "we cannot avoid imbuing nonintentional objects with a quasi subjectivity . . . not as 'in-self' but rather 'for-itself.'"[19] That is, aesthetic experience is construed as fundamentally anthropomorphic.[20] In contrast to Dufrenne's belief that the interiority of an aesthetic object is a logical necessity for it to express, contemporary aestheticians avoid such a projection (or category mistake).[21]

The relationship between aesthetic category or quality and a world manifest in a work of art also needs careful unpacking. There exists a kinship between aesthetic qualities in an aesthetic object and the categories that the subject employs to feel them. Aesthetic qualities in a work are felt, through the subject's affective categories, which are given a priori, like Kantian space and time.[22] As Allen observes, "The categories are for reading the affective quality, not the quality itself."[23] Dufrenne, however, seemingly reduces the affective quality of a work, as if it is singular.[24] He writes, "We are able to feel the tragic in Racine, the pathetic in Beethoven, or the serene in Bach" (464). He continues, "In the tragic qualities of *Phèdre* we immediately recognize the tragic as such and understand that the word or idea 'the tragic' does not begin to exhaust" (471). If one understands this unity of a singular feeling, or better an atmosphere, as a means to illustrate the macro-level unity of a world expressed in a work of art, then yes; but if this means that Dufrenne equates a world expressed with a singular affective quality and category, this raises a serious question about its applicability; as I will show shortly through the analysis of *Sans Soleil,* it does not seem to do justice to articulating the aesthetic feeling of a work, either minimalistic or complex.[25] Even a single scene could emit various or even contradictory affective qualities simultaneously, not to mention an entire film. In what follows, by taking *2046* and *Sans Soleil* as two primary examples, I discuss the extent to which they both illustrate, as well as challenge, Dufrenne's notion of the depth of feeling and its relationship to immanence and density.

Depth of Film, Immanence, and Density

A reason for juxtaposing *2046* and *Sans Soleil* alongside Dufrenne's philosophy may not be immediately clear to the reader. Wong's films are known for their strong melancholic quality, romantic longing manifest through the unrequited love and sensuous style.[26] In contrast, Marker's modernist filmmaking often distances the spectator rather than intensely drawing him or her into the world depicted. I will explore the two films in light of the relationship between depth and its two correlates—immanence and density. I will discuss the mise en abyme structure in *2046* as an analogue of the depth of feeling in a world of aesthetic object through the character's "nonmaterial" density of being and time (immanence), while analyzing the organizational patterns of *Sans Soleil* via an oscillation between depth and material density—how the latter could undermine the depth initially felt to underscore the materiality of image and sound.

In *2046,* Chow Mo-wan, played by Tony Leung, is a disillusioned newspaper reporter whose past unrequited love with Su Li-zhen leaves him cold to the advances by women around him. As the film unfolds, Chow finds himself drawn to the daughter of the owner of the Oriental Hotel in which he is staying, Wang Jing-wen (Faye Wong), who is in love with a Japanese man (Kimura Takuya) visiting Hong Kong for work. Chow begins to write two stories, both of which are set in the future, named "2046" and "2047," respectively; in the former, everyone wants to go to the future, the year 2046, while in the latter, Tak (Kimura) tries to leave 2046 behind. The characters Chow has met in the past and interacted with in the present appear as fictional characters in the stories he writes, and the story of "2047" takes place on a futuristic train, where androids meet customers' various needs.

The motif of time, Stephen Teo notes, brings together Wong's films, in particular *Days of Being Wild* (1990), *In the Mood for Love* (2000), and *2046.*[27] The three films not only are set in the 1960s, a period about which Wong fondly reminisces in these films, but also are interconnected through characters that permeate their porous textual boundaries, such as Lulu/Mimi (Carina Lau), Chow Mo-wan (Tony Leung), Su Li-zhen

(Maggie Cheung). The film begins from the futuristic scenes set in the year 2046–47. Tak's voice-over informs us that he is the only one who has left the year 2046, in which everyone hopes to recapture lost memories. His voice-over continues that in 2046 nothing changes. This scene is repeated halfway into the film, and we learn that it is part of a novel being written by Chow. Now Chow repeats the same lines as Tak. As Chow is increasingly infatuated with Wang, he claims that he imagines himself to be the Japanese man in the novel "2047," who is attached to the android (also played by Faye Wong), and repeatedly inquires about her willingness to leave with him. This "transference of identities across bodies and narrative levels" between Tak and Chow, as Jean Ma puts it, entertains Dufrenne's union of subject and object.[28] As both the writer and the reader of "2047," Chow brings his "entire being" to the story, as Dufrenne would put it. Not merely the motif of time but also Chow's sensitivity to time—his past, present, and even future—constitute Chow's density of being as well as his depth: "Depth is in time only to the extent that time *is* myself."[29]

I want to further explore Dufrenne's feeling-in-depth through paying special attention to a particular sequence in *2046*. The idea of immanence, which Dufrenne finds essential to the aesthetic experience, nicely captures Chow's relationship to his story "2047." After the Christmas meal in 1968 with Wang, Chow takes her to his office so she can make a long-distance call to her boyfriend in Japan. The two days, Christmas Eve and Christmas Day, are transformed into a train car called 1224–1225 in "2047," which is an area, Chow's voice-over has earlier explained, that makes one require a little bit of warmth. As Chow's voice-over laments that he did not get any warmth around Christmas that particular year, there is a cut to Tak, who walks away from the middle ground of the shot toward the background (Figure 4.1), linking Chow in the present to his self as projected in "2047," Tak, who in the end gives up on receiving an answer from the android. A montage of the android in its static poses, not responding even after ten hours, a hundred hours, and a thousand hours since Tak has left, leads to Chow's realization that the delayed response of the android has to do with the fact that it loved somebody else. The camera flows back to Chow in the present, now on the hotel rooftop, against which he is seen alone—in contrast to an earlier scene of Chow and Wang together. The scene, accompanied by Vincenzo Bellini's "Casta Diva," concludes with a close-up of Wang against a white background (Figure 4.2), probably on her way to Japan, rendering her as an abstract image, outside of the clear spatiotemporal nexus. The scene

FIGURE 4.1. Tak (Kimura Takuya), in the story "2047," walks away, as he gives up on receiving an answer from the android (*2046,* Wong Kar-Wai, 2004).

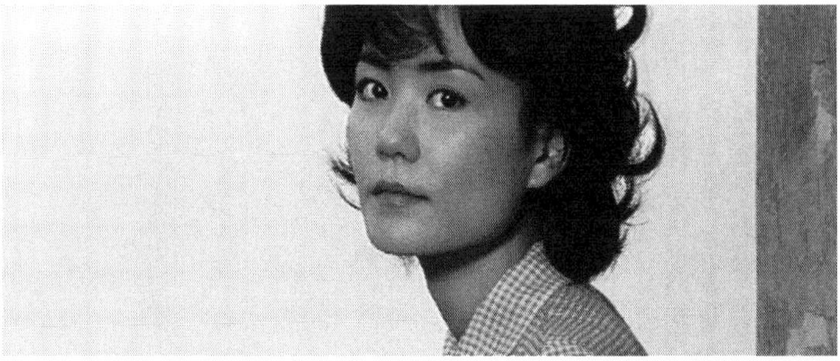

FIGURE 4.2. As Wang (Faye Wong) glances at the camera, a shot of her becomes an abstract image (*2046,* Wong Kar-Wai, 2004).

fluidly weaves through various characters—Chow, Tak, the android, and Wang, on disparate spatiotemporal planes—rendering Chow's experience of "2047" all the more immanent. Here time (Christmas Eve and Christmas Day) turns to space (1224–1225), while memory becomes still, as if it punctuates the end of Chow's aesthetic experience of the story he has written as well as love. After this scene, we learn from Wang's father that she read the story Chow had written and found the ending too sad; her father conveys Wang's wish to Chow, asking whether he could change it. Yet, we see Chow holding his fountain pen, unable to rewrite the ending, as if it becomes the aesthetic object with an internal necessity; as Dufrenne puts it, "It cannot be otherwise than it is."[30]

There is more to say about Wong's film style, which has ignited varying evaluations that view it either as a site of an "aesthetic of sensuous experience" or as the work of a postmodern, self-indulgent "aesthete."[31] I will sidestep here the debate on the material density of Wong's film style—luscious color, languid cinematography, nostalgic mise-en-scène, repetitive, swelling music, and expressive bodily movement and performance—that prepares the spectator's feeling of his achingly beautiful films, and the extent to which such stylistic devices and patterns may enhance or obstruct one's aesthetic perception and absorption.[32] In *2046*, the repeated staging through aperture framing or off-center composition with a disproportionately empty space left next to the interlocutor in the shot reverse shot certainly carries both narrative and aesthetic significance and function.[33] But the degree to which such a style enhances or blocks the spectator's aesthetic feeling of the film is certainly less than that in *Sans Soleil.* In the remainder of this essay, I focus on the constant push and pull of (material) density and (expressive) depth in Marker's *Sans Soleil,* as Marker loosens up causality to yield image and sound as more fragmented, disjointed, and enigmatic than that in Wong's film, foregrounding the film's density.

In her analysis of Marker's film, Carol Mavor emphatically states, "Watching *Sans Soleil* is to be in *Sans Soleil.* I find 'me' in a sunless place, in the black of the movie theatre, in communion with the youth (and the animals) that *Sans Soleil* celebrates."[34] This kind of feeling-in-depth is what Dufrenne must have in mind when he argues for the totality of subject and object in the feeling of aesthetic experience. Nonetheless, Marker constantly juxtaposes fragmented images out of specific time and space, turning their manifest affective qualities into a "non-image."[35] As Mavor observes, in Marker's film, opposite affective qualities are copresent: blue versus black or happiness versus death.[36] The bucolic Icelandic town in which the three children have been shot, for example, is later smeared and covered with black as the volcano erupts.[37]

One can notice not only visual but, I would add, also sonic transformation; the name of a missing cat of an elderly couple, "Tora," when repeated three times—"tora, tora, tora"—becomes the code name of Pearl Harbor for kamikaze fighters, not all of whom, as the letter informs the listener, participated voluntarily in their suicidal mission. Both events may invite the spectator to feel a kind of elegiac mourning, yet certainly not exactly the same kind. What underlies this kind of transformation of both the visual and the auditory is duration or repetition of time: time that passes, persists, and returns—as Mavor states, "undoing linear time, as if replaying time itself on the circularity of film on a reel"—"time . . . 'already swallowed by the spiral.'"[38]

Yet Marker's aesthetic here is more than putting together two opposite aesthetic qualities. The black film leader in the opening sequence is interspersed several times as in a structural film, between the image of the children in Iceland and other shots such as that of an airplane, before the voice-over that accompanies the black screen: "If they don't see the happiness in the picture, at least they will see the black." The recurrence of the black leader, in fact, points to the fact that it embodies more than a thematic opposite of the happiness, but could be seen further as a non-image, or the material density of the image.

In *Sans Soleil,* the push and pull between depth and density often lead the spectator to find oneself withholding or suspending an initial feeling.[39] The voice-over often introduces the spectator to a new site. Close-ups of the feet of a dancing girl in a Japanese neighborhood celebration invite the spectator to feel the energy and excitement. The camera turns its gaze from the girls' feet on wooden clogs onto their faces, then to the fast body gestures of either a single dancer or a group in unison (Figure 4.3). The ambient, synthesized noise is heard, as if sound is pixelated; the volume of footsteps gets louder, occasionally evoking the sound of military marching. As the rhythm of percussion to which the girls dance quickens, it is interspersed or overlaid with other sounds such as the song of an anime, *Doraemon* (Japan, 1969–96), which then turns lyrical when there is a cut to a shot of an elderly dancer. The fragmented hand gestures of dancers are now accompanied with an even more pronounced, higher-pitched synthesized sound that hovers. The sequence suspends the spectator's initial feeling of joy in the atmosphere and shifts, in Dufrenne's term, from its interiority to exteriority, turning the ritualistic gestures into mechanical movement: an unexpected superseding of an "in-itself" over the "emergence of a 'for-itself.'"[40] Some of these images of the sequence later return toward the end of the film, in a denser form as non-images, in which the spectator can barely notice the original referents (Figure 4.4).

An opposite passage from density to depth is also found. In a market scene in Bissau, after women in the market have been shown in many close-up shots, glancing at or looking or walking away from the camera, there are a couple of shots of rocks being passed around among a few men and women standing in a row. Unlike the shots in the market, these are shown in silhouette against the dusk. The speed of the women's bodily movements is slowed down, while the sound of a scale running from a high to a low note (or vice versa) gets quicker. The camera cuts to show a woman in the middle of the row in a one-shot, and the initial clumsy movement of her fumbling with a rock becomes playful, turning the women's labor into play. In what is possibly a reference to Dziga Vertov in *Man with the Movie Camera* (1929), in the factory sequence, the

FIGURE 4.3. Dancers in a neighborhood celebration (*Sans Soleil,* Chris Marker, 1983). The camera focuses on their body gestures.

speed of a female worker's hands folding a cigarette box is accelerated: the movement takes on a different feeling as well as meaning.

In the film medium, Dufrenne would say that depth and density cohabitate like any other aesthetic object. Marker's film particularly makes the spectator more acutely aware of its duality and their interplay. In "the Zone," which is a reference to Andrei Tarkovsky's *Stalker* (1979), images and sound become denaturalized when an alleged Japanese friend of Krasna—Yamaneko Hayao—feeds them to a synthesizer. Catherine Lupton notes, "Hayao's Zone is initially introduced as a mechanism that can

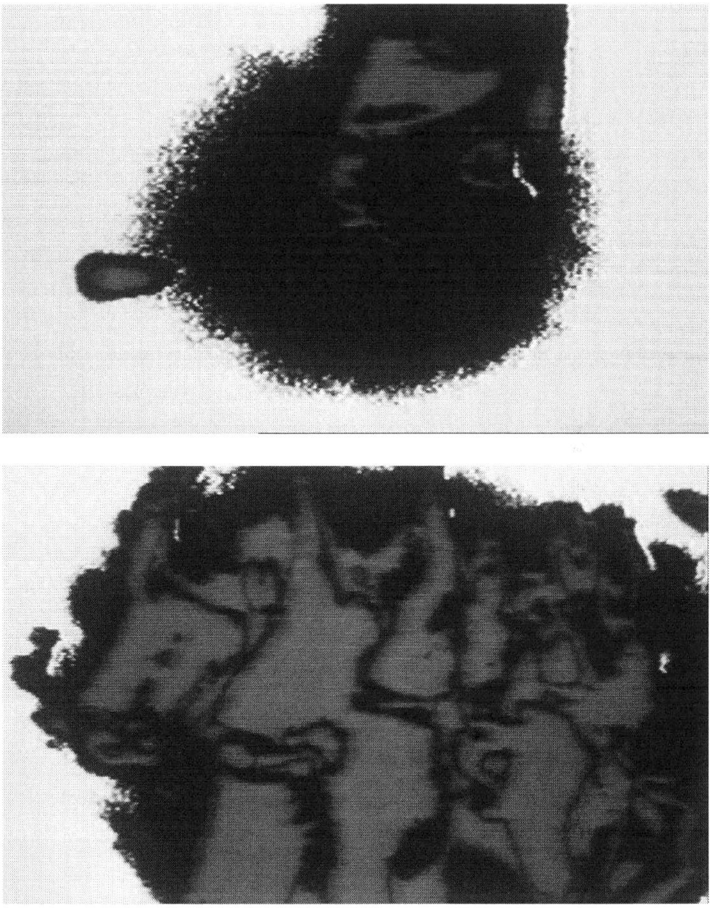

FIGURE 4.4. The same images (Figure 4.3) return as non-images later in the film, which are barely detectable (*Sans Soleil,* Chris Marker, 1983).

make explicit the operation of time and memory upon film images, by transforming them from mimetic representations of the world into shifting and manipulable fields of vivid pixellated colour."[41] The Zone foregrounds the transformation and mutations of image and sound in a scene or across scenes that increasingly become nonrepresentational and atonal. In the letter that is read in voice-over, however, Hayao also informs Krasna that "electronic texture is the only one that can deal with sentiment, memory and imagination." Taking the example of "Eta," a forbidden word that refers to low-paid workers, the letter reads: "They are non-persons; how could they be shown except in non-images?" From the density of obscured images of Eta, a feeling creeps up.

Depth is inexhaustibility, not ambiguity, according Dufrenne. And depth does not emerge from stylistic continuity of space and time. *Sans Soleil* hardly preserves the Bazinian spatial unity or homogeneity conveyed through the contiguity of physical space; rather, it emphasizes fragmentation and heterogeneity. A Bazinian would pay particular attention to the representation of a giraffe's death in the film. A short but powerful sequence is bookended by the images of Japanese people commemorating the death of an animal in the zoo, offering chrysanthemums to an altar. In an abrupt cutaway to a shot from an unspecified film, a man fires a rifle. In the shots that follow, we see a giraffe being hit, stumble momentarily, but continue to jump toward the screen left; the sound of two more shots is heard from off screen as the camera focuses in closer on the lower end of the giraffe's neck, which gushes with unrealistically red blood. Finally, the camera cuts to show in close the giraffe on the ground; as the camera zooms out from the animal's head to show a wider view, a man enters from off screen left to fire the last shot in the head, terminating the giraffe's life. This sequence of an animal's death is followed by another shot of a chrysanthemum being offered, then a cut back to the dead animal, now with birds poking its eyes. One may argue that the nonrealistic style here (the initial shot from a fiction film, Noh theater–style music, and the artificial sound effect of gunfire) leads the film to point to the ambiguity of the Bazinian phenomenological reality, but I offer an alternate reading. Against Dufrennian density and the materiality of sound/image, what is felt is not the obscurity or opacity of whichever reality but its expression—the feeling of mourning (and, further, the desire to cope with death).

Aesthetic feeling results from the interplays between density and depth in *Sans Soleil,* as well as between what is shown and said versus what is felt. But perhaps the feeling of its depth is neither "immediately intelligent" nor "singular," as Dufrenne assumes.[42] In one sequence, against the non-images of war footage of soldiers, children, and planes, the letter being read in voice-over quotes a few lines written by a kamikaze pilot, Ryoji Uebara, who reflects on the extreme duality of density and depth of his being; the kamikaze pilots are "machines. . . . In a plane, I'm a bit of magnetized metal that will plaster against an aircraft carrier. But once on the ground I'm a human being with feelings and passions. . . . I'm leaving you a rather melancholic picture, but in the depths of my heart, I am happy." What kind of feeling can the spectator detect and experience? To answer the question, I refer to the voice-over that accompanies the opening sequence with the black leader: "If they don't see the happiness in the picture, at least they will see the black." Marker constantly orients the spectator to the expressivity of the film, while disorienting him or her through its density (including non-images as in the sequence), and at the bottom of it all lies the power of expression, its inexhaustible depth. In fact, the film ends with computer-generated "non-images," the referents of which one can barely discern except some: girls dancing in the neighborhood ceremony (see Figure 4.4), emus, and a woman Krasna encountered in a market in Bissau, whose glimpse at the camera, the voice-over informs, lasts for one twenty-fourth of a second: one frame of stasis/eternity/time, in Dufrenne's term, "where representation gives way to expression" (411).

This essay has aimed to explore Dufrenne's idea of depth, which counterbalances a spatial notion of depth and reality that still dominates the film studies discipline. The relationship between aesthetic object and experience that Dufrenne proposes, for which feeling is the key, helps to analyze films with intricate temporality, where it is not duration through which a sense of linear time is undone and interiority emerges, but the film's fragmentation and density of both image and sound, which evoke in the spectator an acute sense of being and feeling—feeling-in-depth.

Notes

1. André Bazin, "The Evolution of the Language of Cinema," in *What Is Cinema?*, vol. 1, trans. Hugh Gray (Berkeley: University of California Press, 1967), 38.

2. Vivian Sobchack, "The Passion of the Material: Toward a Phenomenology of Interobjectivity," in *Carnal Thoughts: Embodiment and Moving Image Culture* (Berkeley: University of California Press, 2004), 286–318.

3. Mikel Dufrenne, *The Phenomenology of Aesthetic Experience* (Evanston, Ill.: Northwestern University Press, 1973), 398.

4. Dufrenne, 279–80.

5. Sobchack, "The Passion of the Material," 315.

6. Dufrenne defines aesthetic feeling as "being-in-depth," while feeling is the way that we can reach "the depth of aesthetic object"; Dufrenne, *The Phenomenology of Aesthetic Experience,* 398, 407. "Feeling-in-depth" in the title of this essay and in the rest of this essay is a phrase I devised to designate the reciprocity of the depth of both aesthetic feeling and object.

7. David G. Allen, "Aesthetic Perception in Mikel Dufrenne's *Phenomenology of Aesthetic Experience,*" *Philosophy Today* 22, no. 1 (Spring 1978): 50–64; Randolph M. Feezell, "Mikel Dufrenne and the World of the Aesthetic Object,"

Philosophy Today 24, no. 1 (Spring 1980): 20–32. These companion pieces on Dufrenne are some of the few scholarly articles in philosophy that I could locate on Dufrenne in English.

8. Dudley Andrew, *Concepts in Film Theory* (Oxford: Oxford University Press, 1984), 40; Sobchack, "The Passion of the Material," 300–301.

9. Daniel Yacavone, "Toward Theory of Film Worlds," *Film Philosophy* 12, no. 2 (2008): 97. He mentions "depth" once in his entire article, in relation to Tarkovsky's "expressive depth."

10. Dufrenne, *The Phenomenology of Aesthetic Experience,* 242–44.

11. D. N. Rodowick, *The Virtual Life of Film* (Cambridge, Mass.: Harvard University Press, 2007), 66.

12. Edmund Husserl, *Ideas,* trans. W. R. Boyce Gibson (New York: Humanities Press, 1931), cited in Dufrenne, *The Phenomenology of Aesthetic Experience,* 101.

13. Dufrenne, 406.

14. André Bazin, "The Virtues and Limitations of Montage," in Bazin, *What Is Cinema?,* 48.

15. Dufrenne, *The Phenomenology of Aesthetic Experience,* 398.

16. Diane Arnaud, "From Bazin to Deleuze: A Matter of Depth," in *Opening Bazin; Postwar Film Theory and its Afterlife,* ed. Dudley Andrew and Hervé Joubert-Laurencin (Oxford: Oxford University Press, 2011), 87.

17. Song Hwee Lim, *Tsai Ming-liang and a Cinema of Slowness* (Honolulu: University of Hawaii Press, 2014), 14.

18. Thomas Elsaesser "A Bazinian Half-Century," in Andrew and Joubert-Laurencin, *Opening Bazin,* 8.

19. Sobchack, "The Passion of the Material," 313.

20. Allen, "Aesthetic Perception in Mikel Dufrenne's *Phenomenology of Aesthetic Experience,*" 60.

21. Peter Kivy, *The Corded Shell: Reflections on Musical Expression* (Princeton, N.J.: Princeton University Press, 1980), 50–51, cited in Stephen Davies, *Musical Meaning and Expression* (Ithaca, N.Y.: Cornell University Press, 1994), 240.

22. Dufrenne, *The Phenomenology of Aesthetic Experience,* 470.

23. Allen, "Aesthetic Perception in Mikel Dufrenne's *Phenomenology of Aesthetic Experience,*" 59.

24. Dufrenne, *The Phenomenology of Aesthetic Experience,* 180.

25. Feezell, "Mikel Dufrenne and the World of the Aesthetic Object," 25. Feezell mistakenly attributes a unity of a work to the world of the actual creator and challenges such an equation as flawed, but does not interpret it as that Dufrenne confines the aesthetic quality manifest in a work of art as singular.

26. Gary Bettinson, "Partial Views and the Aesthetic of Disturbance," in *The Sensuous Cinema of Wong Kar-wai: Film Poetics and the Aesthetic of Disturbance* (Hong Kong: Hong Kong University Press, 2015), 58–59.

27. Stephen Teo, *Wong Kar-wai: Auteur of Time* (London: British Film Institute, 2005), 140.

28. Jean Ma, "Chance Encounters and Compulsive Returns," in *Melancholy Drift: Making Time in Chinese Cinema* (Hong Kong: Hong Kong University Press, 2010), 135.

29. Dufrenne, *The Phenomenology of Aesthetic Experience,* 401.

30. Dufrenne, 396.

31. Bettinson, "Partial Views and the Aesthetic of Disturbance," 58–59.

32. Bettinson, 60; Rey Chow, *Sentimental Fabulations, Contemporary Chinese Films* (New York: Columbia University Press, 2007), 76–77.

33. Teo, *Wong Kar-wai,* 150.

34. Carol Mavor, "Happiness with a Long Piece of Black Leader: Chris Marker's Sans Soleil," *Art History* 30 no. 5 (2007): 742.

35. Edward Branigan, *Narrative Comprehension and Film* (London: Routledge, 1992), 211; Catherine Lupton, *Chris Marker: Memories of the Future* (London: Reaktion Books, 2005), 150.

36. Mavor, "Happiness with a Long Piece of Black Leader," 748.

37. Similarly, recall the first image of Japan in the film shot on a ferry from Hokkaido to Tokyo: a hand of a passenger on the deck. When the camera cuts to passengers inside, most of whom are snoozing, with somewhat high-pitched ambient noise, the repetition and rhythm that underlie the montage of faces transfer their fatigue into what the voice-over states: "small fragments of war enshrined in everyday life." A similar pattern is found in the sequence of a commuter train, but there, it is through the editing between the tired passengers and the images from various horror films: turning the passengers' fatigue into the horror of Japan's apparent postwar economic prosperity or matching anonymous commuters to horror images with "faces and names."

38. Mavor, "Happiness with a Long Piece of Black Leader," 739, 744.

39. Mavor, 750; she comes up with a similar observation on meaning, characterizing it as "interpretation being postponed."

40. Dufrenne, *The Phenomenology of Aesthetic Experience,* 404.

41. Lupton, *Chris Marker,* 159.

42. Dufrenne, *The Phenomenology of Aesthetic Experience,* 471, 180.

PART II

Depth Hermeneutics and Surface Turns

As several essays included in part II suggest, concepts of depth are frequently, if not always, intertwined with their shifting antonyms—perhaps most notably concepts of surfaces. Without doubt, the ground for thinking differently about depth today has been prepared by late twentieth-century and early twenty-first-century scholarly work on surface. We ask how and when turning to depth might not function as a regressive or reactionary defense either of a singular depth or of the intellectual traditions, such as Western metaphysics, that have claimed depth's superiority. Although surface is often posited as the opposite of depth, particularly within Western philosophy, we see the essays collected here, almost paradoxically, as a continuation, but not a doubling, of these "surface turns."[1] As scholars of surface uncouple or "free" their term from a mandatory antonymic pairing with depth, we wonder with our contributors what then happens to depth, which is similarly unmoored by this move, yet sometimes neglected, or left in a static place, as its former partner (surface) takes off in all directions. For example, in the index for Rosalind Galt's *Pretty,* discussed in the Preface, there are fourteen subheadings under the category of "surface," while the entry for "depth" reads "*See* surface," as if the thinking of one automatically takes care of the thinking of the other.[2] But having uncoupled surface from depth in order to think differently about surface, film and media theory now needs to reflect on how depth functions—and has the potential to function—as an altered concept in our field. In expansive and evolving discussions of surface, depth often seems petrified, operating as something like a straw man standing in for the Western metaphysical tradition and its visual analogues, or obsolescent film theories collapsed into each other, when in fact there are more complicated and nuanced stories to tell about this other term. Just as recent work highlights that surface is often not singular but plural and layered (even deep!) in nature, we have become curious about modes of depth that confound conventional understandings and definitions of this term.

Here, we build on the work of a 2018 issue of *Film-Philosophy,* which starts by critiquing philosophy's general neglect and denigration of surface, superficiality, and depthlessness. The issue's coeditors—Catherine Constable, Matt Denny, and Timotheus Vermeulen—challenge the surface's "oppositional and hierarchical pairing" with depth, which, they point out, the Western European philosophical tradition has tended to charge positively, associating it with history, affect, contemplative thought, rigor, insight, authenticity, truth, complexity, and even freedom.[3] Tim Ingold, in a 2017 special issue of *Theory, Culture, and Society,* "Visualizing Surfaces, Surfacing Vision," suggests that this "revival of surfaces happened more or less spontaneously."[4] But, in fact, it is possible to sketch something like a timeline for the development of the renewed critical interest in surfaces, particularly as it pertains to the purview of cinema and media studies, and to summarize some of the major insights about surfaces. We hope that this will prove helpful in intellectually locating this volume's intervention. One could identify four, occasionally overlapping, areas where critical attention to surfaces has tended to coalesce: (1) postmodernist screenscapes, (2) skin and the haptic, (3) aesthetics of the decorative, and (4) reading practices.

Following swiftly in the wake of Fredric Jameson's 1991 account of late capitalism's "depthlessness" and what he identifies as its "weakening of historicity, both in our relationship to public History and in the new forms of our private temporality" (6), Anne Friedberg makes a crucial intervention into the discussion of cinema's place in the postmodern landscape, *Window Shopping: Cinema and the Postmodern* (1993). She pursues historically, and from a feminist perspective, some of the positions that Jameson had adopted on postmodern visual culture's relationship to depthlessness and time.[5] Through a sustained focus on the long history of the mobile and virtual gaze, which became ubiquitous with the rise of nineteenth-century technologies that changed "the measure of space and time," as well as on "the relation between sight and bodily movement," Friedberg highlights the general absence of cinema as an object of reflection in postmodern debates, the occlusion of historical female subjects as well as feminist voices, and the way in which the inclusion of all three would destabilize the modern-postmodern binary and allow a more nuanced way of thinking about spatiotemporal dimensions of life and ideologies of visual culture in the wake of industrialization.[6] Friedberg acknowledges Jameson as a rare theorist of postmodernism to take account in any detail of the role of cinema, but she notes nonetheless that the "jumbled relation to the historical referent that" he "finds exclusively in the 'nostalgia film'" (169) mirrors "the apparatus's inherent capacity to alter the spectator's relation to temporality" (168). This "temporal mobility" is accentuated in the age of the VCR, which she describes as "the age of easily replayable, accessible time-shifting" (169), but this quality of temporal mutability is, she insists, present from the beginning of film and television spectatorship, representing a new and still-evolving experience of spectatorship that has "produced" and continues to produce, as Friedberg would go on to explore in *The Virtual Window: From Alberti to Microsoft* (2006), "a new relation to the past."[7] Engaging the depthlessness that Jameson associated with postmodernism and the scrambling of historical time is not as simple as retrieving the old relation to the past, Friedberg argues, because our access to and knowledge of the past has been transformed over the temporal period we seek to understand through the phenomenon we call "history." And though this transformation of what history is entails some losses, it simultaneously makes visible experiences that had failed to register in the depth model of history, described by Kathryn Yusoff as being organized around "the imperial-colonial narrative tropes of character, place, and agency"—tropes that write out of history those who do not register as fully human.[8]

While Friedberg was calling the field's attention to the difference a feminist lens made to thinking about the interaction of time, space, and moving images on different platforms, another feminist scholar, Lisa Cartwright, demonstrates medical visual culture's crucial role in configuring a modernist sense of the body in a book whose primary epistemological frame might be understood as the dynamic between surface and depth. Cartwright's examples and arguments substantially enrich the terms we have at our disposal to think about images' relationships to the concepts of surface and depth, and the physical body of humans (and animals too—she notes that the frog is selected as a privileged specimen for experimentation because of its relative flatness, making it most suitable for microscopy).[9] Through close analysis of medical motion pictures, kymographs, microscopy, and X-rays, she tracks the way new medical imaging technologies transform how meaning is produced on and under the surface of the body, noting the medical imager's repeated "penchant for flatness" and the general "abhorrence and revulsion regarding the physical body in its complexity and depth."[10] The French scientist and chronophotographer Étienne-Jules Marey, for example, "eliminat[es] the factor of depth" in his images (36); the photomicrograph shifts the medical film's diegesis "from body surface to the blood cells" (81); the microscope produces the body as a "modernist text" and strips its object "of historical as much as spatial depth" (84). As Cartwright moves into the second part of the book, she describes her turn to medical images as an effort to "rough up the smooth modernist surface of the microscopic image in order to uncover a history encoded in the interstices of this complexly layered field" (84). Her mode of inquiry becomes increasingly formal, art historical, and spatial.[11] She demonstrates the medical imager's "abhorrence of dimensional form," the "operative force" that reconfigures the body's interior as "an endlessly divisible series of flat surfaces and mobile networks" (91), and asks about the microscope-generated images produced using "serial slices" of the human body in questions such as, "If not according to conventions such as perspective, object/space opposition, and overlap, how was this flat optical field organized? What was its historical context?" (96). While this important text is often cited in the context of medical imaging, its nuanced discussion of the wide variety of modes of spatial organization in medical images generated by and shown on a number of image-making and image-displaying technologies makes clear that our film-theoretical vocabulary for describing both surface and depth would be richer had the field's sense of what counted as "film" and "spectatorship" been wider, earlier.

The body's central role in troubling the surface-depth binary's shaping of our thinking about knowledge appears again when philosopher of religion Mark C. Taylor grapples in *Hiding* (1997) with Hegel's use of the language of phrenology—a science used to order humans hierarchically—to come to terms with human understanding. Taylor writes, "If comprehended speculatively, phrenology serves as a figure for the understanding of understanding. As the word itself implies, to understand is to grasp that which stands under. True knowledge, it seems, is never superficial or insubstantial but appears when surface gives way to depth."[12] The next paragraph, however, begins with a "But" as Taylor goes on to demonstrate how Hegel's phrenological language of surface/depth and outer/inner constantly folds in on itself, where the latter term of each binary is always more highly valued than the former. Taylor concludes: "If the principle of dialectical reversibility is applied to the binary surface/depth, then surface is depth and depth is surface . . . what appears at one level to be depth supporting surface turns out to be another surface. In phrenological terms, bone and even mind are invaginated layers of skin. Peel away skin and you always find more skin: . . . ectoderm . . . mesoderm . . . endoderm . . . mesoderm . . . ectoderm."[13]

The perhaps-too-ready alignment of skin and surface came under further pressure in 2011, when Anne Anlin Cheng questioned whether skin is actually as available to vision as theorists including Frantz Fanon, Mary Anne Doane, and Homi K. Bhabha have claimed it to be, suggesting, through close analyses of the films of Josephine Baker, that we might instead think of skin as "a discursive construct" and "a corporeal agent," one on whose surface "we have failed to see certain things."[14] Cheng points to the complex and multilayered surfaces in modernism as well as in contemporary design and architecture that reveal neither singular surfaces nor receding depths, but rather "skins that have depths," or surface upon surface upon surface.[15] Cheng's argument remains centered throughout her book on issues of skin, complicating how we think about the relationship between visuality and race, which frequently raises insights and even examples that overlap with Galt's concerns in *Pretty.* Both authors, for example, reproduce the same image of the house that Adolf Loos designed for Josephine Baker, and Galt argues that film theory's disdain for ornament and the superficial disguises—among other issues—histories of exclusion, questions of gender and value, and colonial-era ideas of racial and geographic inferiority. Margo Natalie Crawford both takes ideas about the relationship of blackness to surface and depth in new directions in her discussion of the Black Arts Movement and argues for giving historical specificity to the ways that depth and surface interact in particular times and places, exploring, for example, the difference between BAM's "radical use of surface to produce the substance of feeling black and empowered" and white people's appropriation of "black style and surface" in popular culture.[16] Citing Cheng's *Second Skin,* Crawford suggests, "The cultural nationalism of the BAM was also 'this tensile and delicate moment' when people, consciously and unconsciously, experimented with ways of letting surface remain surface so that black style is not reduced to shallowness and is also not frozen when it is given a fixed 'deep' meaning" (195). Cheng's and Crawford's work might both be viewed as making distinctive contributions to a heterogeneous constellation of critical arguments that offer ways of seeing surface and depth less as binary oppositions and more as always coextensive and variable, from those put forward by Gilles Deleuze and Ellen Rooney to Giuliana Bruno and even Karl Marx himself. As Raymond Williams once pointed out, in the "transition from Marx to Marxism," Marx's formulations of the relations between base and superstructure lost some of their nuance.[17]

This skin is also a medium of thought that haunts some of the most interesting interventions into twenty-first-century film and media theory. Just as Taylor and Cheng explore how the surfaces of skin mediate (or confound) the relationship between mind and body, inner and outer being in the world, Laura U. Marks developed a haptic theory of vision in 2000 that accesses the "non-visual knowledge" of "diasporan" and "intercultural" experience. Skins and surfaces, including those on and of film, are entangled in questions of legibility, knowability, difference, and relationality. Marks discusses films that draw vision up to the surfaces of eye and image, describing the operations of cinematic perception in the language of eye-touching and intense physical proximity between the viewer and the image: "I have been brushing the (image of the) fabric with the skin of my eyes, rather than looking at it."[18] She explains: "Haptic visuality is distinguished from optical visuality, which sees things from enough distance to perceive them as distinct forms in deep space: in other words, how we usually conceive of vision. Optical visuality depends on separation between the viewing subject and the object. Haptic looking tends to move over the surface of its object rather than plunge into illusionistic depth, not to distinguish form so much as to discern texture. It is more inclined to move than to focus, more inclined to graze than to gaze."[19]

Vivian Sobchack argues that while not all screens are the same, the surfaces of screens shape "our presence to the world, our representation in it, and our sensibilities and responsibilities about it."[20] In "The Scene of the Screen," first published in 2005, the difference between cinematic and electronic images turns on questions of depth, surface, and point of view. Without depth and point of view, Sobchack suggests, in a position that betrays some nostalgia for photography and cinema and leaves little room for variation within the multiple worlds of electronic screens, the body seems destined to fall away: "Electronic presence has neither a point of view nor a visual situation, such as we experience, respectively, with the photograph and the cinema. Rather, electronic presence randomly disperses its being *across* a network, its kinetic gestures describing and lighting on the surface of the screen rather than inscribing it with bodily dimension (a function of centered and dimensional intention)."[21] In comparison with her understanding of cinematic space, "an invested situation in which action counts rather than computes," electronic space, for Sobchack, emerges as "abstract, ungrounded, and flat"; as a result, this flatness, "a function of its lack of temporal thickness and bodily investment," offers a different aesthetic because it has to "attract spectator interest at the surface" (125). More than fifteen years after this essay was written, it is easier to nuance the stark distinctions Sobchack makes between cinematic and electronic images as thick and flat media. But one key issue to take away from this influential essay is Sobchack's insistence on the matter—both the materiality and the mattering—of the physical body as something vulnerable (mortal) that exists in a time and place within the world, a world increasingly mediated to us through screens.

In 2014, Giuliana Bruno reframed questions of matter in the virtual age not by considering how to get past the surface to the "real" body but rather by asking: "In this age of virtuality, with its rapidly changing materials and media, what role can materiality have? How is it fashioned in the arts or manifested in technology?"[22] Instead of determining whether images make space for the physical body by evaluating their representations of spatial depth and point of view, Bruno, in contrast to Sobchack, largely does away with the place of the spectator in relation to the image, deciding rather to seek out materiality in the space of contact between the image and the surface(s) on which it appears. Adopting, like Marks, a haptic approach, she states, "This is why I prefer to speak of surfaces rather than images: to experience how the visual manifests itself materially on the surface of things, where time becomes material space. Digging into layers of imaging and threading through their surfaces, my theoretical interweaving of materials will emphasize the actual *fabrics* of the visual: the surface condition, the textural manifestation, and the support of a work as well as the way in which it is sited, whether on the canvas, the wall, or the screen."[23]

By this moment, for Bruno at least, the digital is no longer a site of dimensional impoverishment, but rather the vehicle for the creative exploration and at times thickening of surfaces and screens, which can "hold multiple planes, host simultaneity, and foster combinatory patterns and virtual connectivity" (7). She pursues the way that "the surface contains depth" as a result of the "build-up of layers," giving rise to the concept of "surface thickness" that allows us to rethink "new forms of materiality with different materials, including the digital" (7). Arguing that "images have come to be manifested more and more as surfaces" (74), Bruno explores various artworks that allow the screen to take "center stage," suggesting that such works may require us to question and rethink film theory's "canonical notions of the screen," such as the window and the mirror, in order to make space for different types of images *and* thought (75). This thought space opens backward in time as well as forward, reanimating the multiform screens and expanded screen geometries of avant-garde cinema in ways that enable them to make a contribution—belatedly, as if theory has now caught up to the ahead-of-timeness embedded in the (by some deemed passé) avant-garde—to screen theory.

In the early twenty-first century, a number of literary scholars and new media theorists began more directly to confront questions brought on by digital transitions, energizing and shaping the discussion of depth and surface in important ways. As Lev Manovich postulates in *The Language of New Media* (2001), "the visual culture of the computer age" is "cinematographic in its appearance, digital on the level of its material, and computational (i.e., software driven) in its logic."[24] At the moment of heightened anxieties within film studies about the changes ushered in by the digital, in Manovich's model, the cinematic becomes one salient layer among many folded into contemporary visual culture. And so it could be said that now, rather than staging depth within the frame, the way to understand depth in relation to cinema is that cinema itself becomes buried within a new media landscape, acquiring depth *as* media—as a media form layered among others.

Paralleling the "death of cinema" debates dominant in film studies that found theorists, historians, archivists, and critics grappling with cinema's increasingly digital materiality, there was a widespread shift in reading practices that had for centuries relied on printed text. Just as cinema was increasingly displaced, or, as Francesco Casetti calls it, "relocated," from movie theaters and onto domestic screens, diverse opportunities to read literary text on screen suddenly seemed prime to eclipse the material specificity of the book's paper pages.[25] Calling for "media-specific analysis" of these new modes of electronic textuality, N. Katherine Hayles suggested in the title of an essay published in 2004 that "print is flat, code is deep."[26] Resonant with Manovich's awareness of the many layers of digital media, and contrary to claims about the superficiality of the electronic screen, Hayles's essay usefully describes how electronic screens, underwritten by invisible layers of computer code, in fact have more material depth than their predecessors. Building on her influential considerations of new modalities of reading, Hayles moves in her book *How We Think: Digital Media and Contemporary Technogenesis* (2012) from code's depths to deep reading, provocatively proposing that deep reading itself is perhaps overvalued. Instead, she suggests that we take skimming more seriously as a meaningful critical practice. This critical embrace of surface practices could be read in part as a measured response to a more popular paranoia, which finds some of postmodernism's claims fully synthesized, represented by a best-selling book like Nicholas Carr's *The Shallows: What the Internet Is Doing to Our Brains* (2010), which expresses concern that the internet has surreptitiously rewired our "massively plastic" brains, interfering with cherished practices of deep reading and deep thinking—"chipping away" one's "capacity for concentration and contemplation."[27] As Carr writes in his introduction, "Once I was a scuba diver in the sea of words. Now I zip along the surface like a guy on a Jet Ski."[28]

While Hayles's work is driven by technological changes and a focus on the materiality of texts, other recent scholarship stems from theoretical, political, and ethical arguments that have had the effect of bringing reading practices to the surface and explicitly challenging the value of depth.[29] In "Surface Reading: An Introduction" (2009), for example, Stephen Best and Sharon Marcus describe a skepticism of twenty-first-century humanists toward a too-easy equation of symptomatic readings and political activism, and question the tendency of symptomatic reading patterns to align three binaries: present/absent, manifest/latent, and surface/depth.[30] In "Close but Not Deep: Literary Ethics and the Descriptive Turn," Heather Love suggests that while many literary methods responsive to critiques of humanism's "founding exclusions" and roots in mystical divination have rejected close reading in favor of more remote methods, it is also possible and perhaps desirable to "develop modes of reading that are close but not deep," modes that not only decenter the human in the text but also do away with the "ethical heroism of the critic" by replacing reading as an act of divination with the more "humble" work of analyzing and observing.[31] These important interventions often formulate critiques of depth in line with a "hermeneutics of suspicion," which assumes that to truly understand something, one must understand the relation of surface countenances and activities to the deep, often less immediately visible, psychic or economic structures with which they are intertwined.[32] Mere description of surface phenomena, in this genealogy, falls short of true comprehension.

Such inquiry has generally centered around literary texts, but in this volume's second part, "Depth Hermeneutics and Surface Turns," cinema and media scholars consider, directly and indirectly, similar questions in relation to contemporary art cinema and documentary film and media. Each essay in its own way drives the reader to think twice about the hermeneutic paradigms we activate in studying film and how these intersect with broader modes of valuation.

Notes

1. Many of the reframings of surface as a site of meaning emerge from the 1990s on, but Hannah Arendt preempts this collective shift by two decades. In chapter I.3 of *The Life of the Mind,* vol. 1, first published in 1971, entitled, "The Reversal of the Metaphysical Hierarchy: The Value of Surface," Arendt asks, "Since we live in an appearing world, is it not much more plausible that the relevant and the meaningful in this world of ours should be located precisely on the surface?" Hannah Arendt, *The Life of the Mind,* vol. 1, *Thinking* (New York: Harcourt Brace Jovanovich, 1977), 27.

2. Rosalind Galt, *Pretty: Film and the Decorative Image* (New York: Columbia University Press, 2011), 389, 381.

3. Catherine Constable, Matt Denny, and Timotheus Vermeulen, "Introduction: The Surfaces of Film-Philosophy," *Film-Philosophy* 22, no. 2 (2018): 143–47.

4. Tim Ingold, "Surface Vision," *Theory, Culture and Society* 34, no. 7–8 (December 2017): 99–100.

5. Anne Friedberg, *Window Shopping: Cinema and the Postmodern* (Berkeley: University of California Press, 1993).

6. Friedberg, 3.

7. Friedberg, 7.

8. Kathryn Yusoff, *A Billion Black Anthropocenes or None* (Minneapolis: University of Minnesota Press, 2018), 16.

9. Lisa Cartwright, *Screening the Body: Tracing Medicine's Visual Culture* (Minneapolis: University of Minnesota Press, 1995).

10. Cartwright, 91.

11. Like Cartwright, Pansy Duncan uses the language of rough and smooth to grapple with the depth-surface paradigm, particularly in relation to the cross-implication of emotional and hermeneutic flatness. See Pansy Duncan, "Taking the Smooth with the Rough: Texture, Emotion, and the Other Postmodernism," *PMLA* 129, no. 2 (2014): 204–22.

12. Mark C. Taylor, *Hiding* (Chicago: University of Chicago Press, 1997), 16–17.

13. Taylor, 18.

14. Anne Anlin Cheng, *Second Skin: Josephine Baker and the Modern Surface* (New York: Oxford University Press, 2011), 7–8.

15. Cheng, 11.

16. Margo Natalie Crawford, *Black Post-Blackness: The Black Arts Movement and Twenty-First-Century Aesthetics* (Urbana: University of Illinois Press, 2017), 194.

17. Raymond Williams, *Marxism and Literature* (New York: Oxford University Press, 1977), 75.

18. Laura U. Marks, *The Skin of the Film: Intercultural Cinema, Embodiment, and the Senses* (Durham, N.C.: Duke University Press, 2000), 1–2, 127.

19. Marks, 162.

20. Vivian Sobchack, "The Scene of the Screen: Envisioning Photographic, Cinematic, and Electronic 'Presence,'" in *Carnal Thoughts: Embodiment and Moving Image Culture* (Berkeley: University of California Press, 2005), 111.

21. Sobchack, 126.

22. Giuliana Bruno, *Surface: Matters of Aesthetics, Materiality, and Media* (Chicago: University of Chicago Press, 2014), 2.

23. Bruno, 3.

24. Lev Manovich, *The Language of New Media* (Cambridge, Mass.: MIT Press, 2001), 180.

25. Francesco Casetti, "The Relocation of Cinema," *NECSUS: European Journal of Media Studies* 1, no. 2 (Autumn 2012): 5–34.

26. N. Katherine Hayles, "Print Is Flat, Code Is Deep: The Importance of Media-Specific Analysis," *Poetics Today* 25, no. 1 (2004): 67–90.

27. Nicholas Carr, *The Shallows: What the Internet Is Doing to Our Brains* (New York: W. W. Norton, 2010), 26, 3.

28. Carr, 3–4.

29. N. Katherine Hayles, *How We Think: Digital Media and Contemporary Technogenesis* (Chicago: University of Chicago Press, 2012). For an example of the material turn, see Peter Stallybrass, "The Library and Material Texts," *PMLA* 119, no. 5 (2004): 1347–52.

30. Stephen Best and Sharon Marcus, "Surface Reading: An Introduction," *Representations* 108, no. 1 (Fall 2009): 4.

31. Heather Love, "Close but Not Deep: Literary Ethics and the Descriptive Turn," *New Literary History* 41 (2010): 381.

32. Paul Ricoeur, *Freud and Philosophy: An Essay on Interpretation* (New Haven, Conn.: Yale University Press, 1970). See also Rita Felski, "Critique and the Hermeneutics of Suspicion," *m/c journal* 15, no. 1 (2012), http://journal.media-culture.org.au/index.php/mcjournal/article/view/431./0; and Jacob Golomb, Weaver Santaniello, and Ronald Lehrer, eds., *Nietzsche and Depth Psychology* (Albany, N.Y.: SUNY Press, 1999).

CHAPTER FIVE

Depth Effects

Citizen Kane, Citizenfour, and the Deep Time of Cinema

Jeff Scheible

Laura Poitras's 2014 Oscar-winning documentary *Citizenfour* takes its audience behind the scenes as Edward Snowden's revelation to journalists of mass surveillance by the National Security Agency (NSA) of American citizens' personal communications becomes headline news. Much of the film unfolds in Snowden's Hong Kong hotel room, where he meets with Poitras and journalists Glen Greenwald and Ewan MacAskill, to whom he discloses troves of classified documents. Some of the film's most captivating sequences are filtered through a metagaze, with Poitras observing Snowden observing himself as he engages in banal, quotidian activities that become imbued with unusual resonance: sitting on his bed watching TV as it broadcasts reportage about himself, or fixing his hair in the mirror as he prepares to leave the hotel room in which he has been hiding and to sacrifice himself to the coming media frenzy (Figures 5.1 through 5.3). *Four*'s intense captivation with looking at Snowden reaches a paranoiac crescendo in one of its penultimate sequences. Here, the film's metagaze becomes displaced by a window rather than mirrors and screens, structured by a camera voyeuristically peering in on the whistleblower from the outside, reunited with his wife in a kitchen, taking asylum at an undisclosed location in Russia (Figure 5.4). One of "multiple ironies of the Snowden affair" documented by Poitras, Lisa Parks notes, is "that an inside man could become one of the US's biggest threats and that he would end up, after his revelations, living freely in an even more authoritarian state, Russia."[1] Yet another irony layers this documentary sequence in terms of cinematic coding. We are provided narrative cinema's conventionally reassuring happy ending—the reunion of the heterosexual couple—but rather than offering relief, the surveilling gaze on the couple here is

FIGURE 5.1. Snowden in mirror. *Citizenfour* (Laura Poitras, 2014).

FIGURE 5.2. Snowden on TV. *Citizenfour* (Laura Poitras, 2014).

undeniably unnerving. Though Snowden is reunited with his wife, their partnership and future are strained, a reality Snowden concedes will be the most difficult price to pay for his actions more than once earlier in the documentary. This unsettling, voyeuristic gaze on the reunited lovers keeps in step with a queer reading of the film that the documentary's ongoing, arguably central, preoccupation with "outing" Snowden—if, how, and when to publicly reveal himself as the whistleblower—opens.[2]

FIGURE 5.3. Snowden on a public screen. *Citizenfour* (Laura Poitras, 2014).

FIGURE 5.4. Surveilling gaze on Snowden with Lindsay Mills in a kitchen in Russia. *Citizenfour* (Laura Poitras, 2014).

Snowden's asylum and its attendant geopolitical and gender dynamics in fact premediate a surprising number of the largest flare-ups to surround the 2016 U.S. elections, from WikiLeaks' release of private Democratic National Committee e-mails hacked by Russians and Trump's unapologetic support of Putin to the media's widespread fascination with Hillary Clinton's e-mails during her presidential campaign.

FIGURE 5.5. Young Charles Kane playing in snow in a deep-focus shot. *Citizen Kane* (Orson Welles, 1941).

Rotated ninety degrees to the right, the framing of this scene toward the end of *Four* visually echoes of one of the most scrutinized scenes in film history: when, toward the beginning of *Citizen Kane* (Orson Welles, 1941), young Charles Kane plays in the snow and the camera tracks backward to reveal his parents inside finalizing arrangements to send him off to boarding school (Figure 5.5). The uninterrupted shot allows the spectator to see and hear Charles in the distance through the window as he continues to play outside. Both scenes are unsettling, with symbolic framing that emphasizes familial strain. Inside and outside are separated, with the spectator positioned in one and the subject in the other, on the threshold of entering a future whose regulation rests in others' hands. The scenes' chronological placements in each film, however, lend them significantly distinct effects. In *Kane* distance and depth foreshadow a narrative about to unfold and the troubles the boy will encounter as a man, while in *Four* the image has more of a cumulative effect, arriving near the film's end, marking the uncertainty of the present, with the protagonist stripped of his naivete and weighed down by the consequences and ripple effects of his actions. The visually but also conceptually perpendicular difference between these two key moments provides a suggestive glimpse of the ways in which effects of depth technically operate within both films and more broadly in the media cultures of which they are exemplary, as I will further explore here.

Among the many points of return in discourse that has accumulated about *Kane* and this scene of young Charles playing in the snow is cinematographer Gregg Toland's sophisticated staging in depth. André Bazin admired and discussed Toland's depth of field at some length. Responding to George Sadoul's dismissal of *Kane* as not groundbreaking but instead an "encyclopedia of old techniques," which prompts him to lay out systematically earlier examples of everything *Kane* is claimed to have inaugurated, such as *Arrival of a Train*'s depth of field, Bazin concedes:

> Sadoul's comparisons are accurate except one, whose importance is in fact paramount: to equate Gregg Toland's special lenses with Louis Lumière's fixed lenses seems wrong to me. The depth of field in the shot of the train's arrival could easily be obtained in full sunlight by a simple reduction of the size of the diaphragm. The interesting thing about Welles's depth of field is that it is created *in the studio,* where lighting can vary tremendously depending on the scene. And it is the very sharpness of the deep-focus shots that contributes to *Citizen Kane*'s significance.[3]

Bazin champions the deep focus that allows *Kane*'s spectator to see narratively and semiotically significant material in multiple planes of the image at the same time, revealing the "ambiguity of reality" that shallow-focus images or quick cutting does not as readily afford the spectator. Being able to see deeply into the image is for Bazin connected to complexity and profundity; one could say that *seeing* deeply is intimately connected to *knowing* deeply. As Andrea Brighenti outlines elsewhere, "There is a deep *epistemology of seeing* in Western thought."[4]

Set side by side with *Citizenfour*, the relationship between visual depth and epistemological depth staged by *Kane* yields new questions. First, the very juxtaposition of these scenes shifts our focus from depth of field to what we might think of as *cinematic deep time*. Siegfried Zielinski suggests that deep-time methodology entails an "experiment": "Do not seek the old in the new but find something new in the old."[5] Zielinski enfolds a long, multi-millennial historical arc within his formulation of deep time; following his provocation, one could trace a trajectory of cinematic deep time all the way back to Paleolithic cave paintings, the allures of which are explored in Werner Herzog's *Cave of Forgotten Dreams* (2010).

Depth, however, is a relative concept, and one could just as generatively consider a smaller-scale idea of cinematic deep time, encompassing a span of a century's moving-image practices, enabling us to locate resonances between moments separated instead by the temporal distance of a human lifetime that lies between *Kane* and *Four*. Second, and more pertinently, their juxtaposition suggests the presence of an invisible vertigo effect of sorts. Bazin's privileging of depth of field represents a long-standing linkage between depth as a visual concept and depth as a metaphysical concept. The potency of this affiliation has come to be upheld by virtue of its presumed negation in contemporary media. Critical and popular discourses about postmodernity and digital media overwhelmingly emphasize the centrality of depthlessness as a descriptor of today's mediascape, conflating the proliferation of hypermediated surfaces with the loss of a more psychological sense of depth. Yet such claims fail to account for the fact that there are nevertheless more visual "depth effects" proliferating across media cultures than ever before: 3D screen-based media, photographic editing software that adds depth as an effect to images after they have been captured, the iPhone's multiplanar design, and much more.

From deep time to multiplanarity, the possibilities for critically apprehending depth I have referenced thus far are *temporal* and *visual,* which divert our attention from an altogether different modality of depth that is quantitative, datafied, and a dominant characteristic of computing technologies and epistemologies of the early twenty-first century: in short, what I would refer to as "informatic depth." Today's networked computers and smart technologies have become repositories of so much data that we talk about them in terms of informatic layers: Google's DeepDream software, for example, assists in facial recognition, using machine learning techniques to process large numbers of images, while the deep web accounts for the 90 percent of the internet that is not ever indexed by search engines. Meanwhile, scholars and corporations alike regularly use the (misleading) metaphor of "mining" to describe pattern apprehension of large datasets. *Citizenfour* is centrally *about* informatic depths (the thousands upon thousands of documents Snowden hands over to the reporters, far beyond any individual journalist's capacity to process—particularly in the timely way required by this profession). At the same time, its very material existence as a film *depends on* such depths: Snowden needed to communicate with Poitras and Greenwald through the deep web, and the film's files were encrypted using deep web technologies to evade state censorship.

I wish to entertain the idea here that despite the seemingly incongruous modalities of depth at play in both films—one is visual, presupposing the expansiveness of human knowledge, while the other suppresses visual logics, presupposing the limitations of human knowledge—*Kane*'s optic depth and *Four*'s informatic depth both bind them to epistemological depth. The very linkage of these depths, one could argue, is assisted somewhat paradoxically by a surface-level connection; the titular parallels between the films help us think them alongside one another, which feeds into an associative chain of linkages across different modalities of depth.[6] Surface connections that a model of depth hermeneutics might initially resist can in fact become catalysts for locating deeper resonances that one would otherwise never locate. But perhaps this is not so counterintuitive after all: surface and depth hermeneutically depend on one another. This symbiosis of depth and surface bears a resemblance to Ellen Rooney's critique of Stephen Best and Sharon Marcus's call for surface reading. No text, Rooney suggests, simply "self-mediates," and no mode of reading, such as the mode of description envisioned by surface reading, is ever neutral. Instead, the very act of reading enables a "disorienting doubleness of meaning *on a single plane*," Rooney writes, wherein the stable distinction between surface and depth no longer holds.[7] With this in mind, I explore how the paradigmatic concept of depth might afford an opportunity to consider these two films together. They individually rely on distinct techniques of depth but, when considered together, highlight cinema's multivalent relationships to media cultures, pertaining to questions not only of hermeneutics and mediation but also of power and control.

Four might initially seem worlds apart from *Kane*, and in many ways it is. *Kane* stands at the pinnacle of classical Hollywood narrative storytelling; *Four* is documentary. *Kane*'s narrative chronology is fascinatingly out of joint, while *Four*'s is adamantly linear, even though it was edited by Mathilde Bonnefoy, the editor of *Run Lola Run* (Tom Tykwer, 1998). On her collaboration with Bonnefoy, Poitras has explained, "My editor and I decided early that we would not mix up the timeline. In other words, what we filmed on the first day would be shown first, so we would be true to the chronology of how events unfolded and to try to give this ticking clock quality to it."[8] Adhering to cinema verité principles as much as possible, Poitras—with few exceptions, such as reading e-mails addressed from Snowden to her or glimpsed discretely in a mirror reflection holding her camera—keeps herself out of *Citizenfour*. (This is a strategy she controversially abandoned with the inclusion of production diary narration in 2016's *Risk,* her more recent documentary about Julian Assange, which bears a palimpsestic relation to *Four*.)[9] Meanwhile, even if Kane as a character is something of a structuring absence, Orson Welles as a physical presence is everywhere in his film. *Kane* came out at the beginning of World War II, while *Four* followed *My Country, My Country* (2006) and *The Oath* (2010) in Poitras's *9/11 Trilogy,* documenting the security state's expansion in the aftermath of September 11, placing it in a current, more indeterminately bookmarked, wartime context.

Despite these and countless other differences, there are nonetheless a series of resonances between the two works. *Citizenfour,* like *Citizen Kane,* is centrally about journalism and American politics. They both offer visions of how cinema hierarchically stacks up against—and offer implicit solutions to the limitations of—mainstream news media. The two films are critically revered and are themselves Oscar winners. They are often described with the same vocabulary: labyrinthine, genius, great, important, elusive, to name a few. *Citizenfour* shares with *Kane* a compelling and larger-than-life but simultaneously complicated and mysterious historical figure at its center. Both of these figures lend the films their titles, foregrounding the citizenry of their protagonists. Yet they nevertheless negate the "glamour effect" that Laura Mulvey has noted is given no room in *Kane* due to Welles's "towering presence on the screen," leaving, as she puts it, "little space for sexualized voyeurism."[10] One could certainly say the same of *Four,* despite its intense interest in looking—at an attractive man.

While *Kane* is notable for its use of innovative photography, *Four*'s cinematography is also significant, if less visually dazzling. Kirsten Johnson's captivating cine-memoir *Cameraperson* (2016) documents her work shooting for *Citizenfour* in addition to many other important documentaries. Credited alongside Johnson, another of *Citizenfour*'s cinematographers is accomplished media artist and photographer Trevor Paglen. Paglen is well known for documenting media infrastructure and what he refers to as manifestations of the "deep state," secret places that are "blank spots on the map," where the objects of the image—like secret military bases—are often nearly if not entirely invisible.[11] Early in *Four* we see images Poitras began filming in 2011 of the construction of the NSA data center in Bluffdale, Utah. Later, the film presents footage of the "Dagger Complex" NSA surveillance base in Germany and the undersea cables intercept site for TEMPORA at GCHQ Bude in the United Kingdom. Such images are generally only obliquely linked to the film's narrative threads, but they render

FIGURE 5.6. Infrastructural (in)visibility: Menwith Hill Station. *Citizenfour* (Laura Poitras, 2014).

visible the ubiquitous invisibility of the surveillance state, visually amplifying *Citizenfour*'s critique of the massive overreach of government-sponsored information gathering. Indeed, these infrastructural images' purposeful resistance of visual depth transports us to a contemporary mediascape affectively shaped by informatic depth. In one moment toward the end of the film, for example, Poitras cuts to a nighttime shot of the NSA surveillance base at Menwith Hill Station in the United Kingdom (Figure 5.6). The only way the spectator knows we are situated here is through text overlaid on the image that identifies and locates the base. The image itself is mostly dark, with a line of lights running across the bottom third of the frame, legible only as a nondescript nighttime scene. The shot is followed by a closer perspective on one patch of this area with white spherical structures, presumably the base itself. President Barack Obama's voice forges a sound bridge to the next image, as he expresses in a televised address that he does not believe Snowden is a "patriot." Given Obama's general affability and the film's sympathetic relation to Snowden, the effect is chilling—further driving home that the most familiar mediated images and sounds are impossibly entwined with the sinister reaches of state control.

In contrast to depth of field, informatic depth in sequences like this is imagined in terms of inscrutability and banality, as explored across much of Paglen's work, such as in *Autonomy Cube* (2014–18), a sculpture

FIGURE 5.7. Trevor Paglen, *Autonomy Cube,* 2015. Plexiglas cube, computer components, 14 × 14 × 14 in. (35.56 × 35.56 × 25.56 cm). Copyright Trevor Paglen. Courtesy of the artist, Metro Pictures, New York; Altman Siegel, San Francisco.

designed to be housed in art museums, galleries, and civic spaces, which is essentially a computer that reroutes museumgoers' Wi-Fi connections through the deep web, amplifying its claims to anonymity by including more people in the circuit (Figure 5.7). Although this sculpture makes the deep web seen, the object's mode of visualization stages a tension that lies in how the cube paradoxically foregrounds the network's technological opacity. As a physical artwork, it is simply some wires in a transparent box. If, as Bazin says, the "sharpness" of *Kane*'s deep-focus shots helps to form the film's "significance," to what extent does the inscrutability of deep web mediations contribute to *Four*'s?

David Bordwell's writing on *Citizen Kane* offers some direction here. Echoing Sadoul's critique referenced earlier, he notes that *Kane*'s privileged aesthetic status lies not in its innovative use of techniques, all of which had already been skillfully developed by many championed filmmakers, but in its fluid oscillation between two poles of filmmaking. We

might understand these "poles" through Siegfried Kracauer, who once referred to cinema's "two main tendencies," or perhaps through Bazin's own famous distinction between those directors who have "faith in the image" and those who demonstrate "faith in reality."[12] In other words, *Kane* both embraces the ability of depth of field to approximate the human eye's perceptual activity and also succeeds in fulfilling cinema's theatrical potentials of texturing realistically mediated space with symbols and enigmas. In this sense, *Kane* to *Four* maps a historical transition in the vicissitudes of the photographic image, from its contradictory ability in *Kane* to furnish epistemological command while simultaneously undermining the certainty of this command through to *Four,* where the image holds limited authority over knowledge in our current digital regime.

Citizenfour contains multiple sequences that display encrypted code on computer screens and the relay of messages among Snowden, Greenwald, and Poitras. Despite these visualizations, *Citizenfour*'s debts to the deep web are coded and never explicitly mentioned until its closing credits, when Poitras lists the free software projects that made the film possible. The first of these is TOR, the abbreviation for The Onion Router, the most commonly used deep web browser. In her discussion of the film, Lisa Parks points out that while "some critics have described *Citizenfour*'s structure as relatively straightforward, the film is one of the first documentary feature films to be born in digital encryption."[13] Indeed, the film—and Snowden's revelations—would not have come about had Snowden not been able to communicate anonymously with Poitras and Greenwald through the deep web, and had Poitras not relied on TOR's encryption of information to store and save the twenty hours of footage she recorded in Hong Kong.

A particularly engaging sequence comes toward the end of *Citizenfour*'s extended twenty-minute-long exposition, before we travel with Poitras and Greenwald to meet Edward Snowden in his hotel room in Hong Kong. In this sequence, Jacob Appelbaum delivers a talk about "linkability" at an Occupy Wall Street training session in New York City, sketching how metadata works. He explains to his audience that once one uses a credit card to buy a metro card, there is essentially a domino effect whereby entire narratives about one's life can be deduced and tracked by those with access to that information. This sequence is bookmarked by footage from Senate and judiciary hearings where national intelligence directors talk in circles and flatly lie under oath about collecting American citizens' personal information.

Upon first reflection, *Citizenfour*'s editing seems to lend Appelbaum's otherwise unprompted inclusion a rhetorical obviousness worthy of a Michael Moore documentary: Poitras prepares the viewer to sympathize with Snowden for his work in exposing the NSA's invasive and alarmingly unconstitutional tracking of personal data. Interestingly, though, we are not told who Appelbaum is, but he is well known for formerly being a leading director of TOR. In this context, it is worth reconsidering how Appelbaum's expository linkability speech is rhetorically doing more for *Citizenfour* than it first seems; indeed, it warrants a depth hermeneutics. Immediately following this collection of footage, the camera moves through a dark tunnel, echoing the beginning of the film but this time opening out into Hong Kong. Coupled with this tunnel, an evocative image of common metaphors figuring the internet as an information superhighway or even of Gilles Deleuze's "coils of the serpent" metaphor for the control society, this withheld contextualization of Appelbaum amplifies the deep web's hushed structuring of *Citizenfour,* justifying not only the documentary's political message but also the material means of production of Poitras's film.[14]

In this regard, one might note *Citizenfour*'s affinities not only with *Citizen Kane* but also with a landmark work of cinema verité about another, if very different, countercultural hero, *Dont Look Back* (1967), D. A. Pennebaker's portrait of Bob Dylan. While critics often claim Dylan comes off as harsh and unfriendly in the film, Jeanne Hall has demonstrated how Dylan is in fact always kind to fans and only ever appears antagonistic in the film in moments when he is being interviewed by reporters from the mainstream press.[15] The inclusion of these moments, as Hall explains, validates Pennebaker's decidedly nonintrusive observational style as a superior, more truthful mode of documenting Dylan than popular journalism, without ever having to make a direct case for it. Footage of Appelbaum's rousing speech included in *Citizenfour* serves a similar function for Poitras, relieving her of the burden of making the case for the film's mode of production, which uses the anonymity and encryption made available by the deep web to convey its messages about digital surveillance and the state's violation of privacy. Other acts of remediation, such as those bookmarking the Occupy Wall Street sequence that draw on courtroom testimony footage, emphasize the film's processes of remediation while paradoxically masking the arguably most essential process of remediation at play, through the deep web. (One could analogously follow Bazin's reading of *Kane,* with its masterful use of depth of field, sound, and mixed chronological narration, as suggesting the power of cinema's techniques over journalism's in accessing life's truths and complexities, which is indeed more explicitly critiqued in *Kane* by way of revealing the constructedness of newsreel and its restricted abilities to adequately narrate Kane's story.)

I am not only trying to decode *Citizenfour*'s indebtedness to the deep web but also applying pressure to how this debt to depth is entangled with what one might think of as the film's greatness—an overwhelmingly shared critical consensus—and in turn what Paul Ricoeur and, following him, Dudley Andrew would theorize as its own emerging "surplus value." This term suggests how a text continues to generate interpretations upon return and reexperience.[16] It signals the same idea Laura Mulvey refers to when she writes at the outset of her British Film Institute monograph on *Kane* that its "elusiveness is one of the qualities that makes it infinitely re-viewable, re-debatable."[17] Like *Kane,* this film is propelled by a technical depth that lends it a gravitas and an "ambiguity" (to borrow Bazin's phrase about *Kane*'s cinematographic deep focus) or an "elusiveness" (to borrow Mulvey's description of *Kane*'s psychosocial depths) or a "profoundness" (to borrow Parks's final appraisal of *Four*).

The two films share depth effects, mechanisms by which layered epistemological structures of visuality shape our critical reception and regard for works of art. What might we make of the ways in which these depth effects are inscribed onto notions of citizenship? Note the different ways the citizens of these film's titles are identified: Kane and Four. Kane is of course the main character's last name, while Four is a number Snowden uses to disguise his name, suggestive of the datafied nature of our identities today in the informatic depths of algorithmic, digital cultures, or what Matteo Pasquinelli has recently termed, following Deleuze and Félix Guattari, the "society of metadata."[18] Snowden's signature with this handle might also be read as a gesture to *not* be exceptional in the way that the word "citizen" counterintuitively implies, seeing himself not as the first or the last to come forward but as part of a small community committed to refusing to accept the state's abuse of power. Indeed, one of *Citizenfour*'s paradoxes is the way in which Snowden repeatedly emphasizes he does *not* want to be at the center of the story, yet ultimately and inevitably is—both in the press and in the documentary. In this sense, it is important to remember that although discourse about the film centers on Snowden, Poitras suggests how other figures were of course critical in helping the event unfold: from William Binney to Jacob Appelbaum to Glen Greenwald to, perhaps most important, Poitras herself. If Snowden is "four," these—or other NSA whistleblowers like Russ Tice, Mark Klein, and Thomas Tamm—could be interpreted as one, two, three, five, and more yet to come.

Or, might Kane be Citizenzero or one?

Cinema's Deep Time

I have considered how *Citizenfour*'s depth effects open up a feedback loop in which to critically locate—or perhaps displace—*Citizen Kane,* and vice versa. Let us return to the concept of cinematic deep time. The questions encompassed by cinematic deep time ask what we stand to learn when we consider older moving-image practices, films, film theories, and lessons they teach us in relation to newer contexts not contemporaneous to their production and reception histories. These questions already of course emerge across a range of critical writings in film and media studies, such as Paul Flaig and Katherine Groo's *New Silent Cinema,* which collects a variety of essays about digital anachronisms and returns to silent cinema in contemporary film and media.[19] It is also at least part of what is on D. N. Rodowick's mind in *The Virtual Life of Film* when he writes, "The old (cinematic) and the new (electronic and digital) media find themselves in a curious genealogical mélange whose chronology is by no means simple or self-evident."[20]

The single most influential and provocative return to earlier film to think about new media is surely Lev Manovich's extensive reliance on Dziga Vertov's *Man with a Movie Camera* in his canonical book, *The Language of New Media,* published in 2001. He declares at the outset of his twenty-page illustrated prologue that the "avant-garde masterpiece *Man with a Movie Camera,* completed by Russian director Dziga Vertov in 1929, will serve as our guide to the language of new media."[21] Each of these pages contains stills from Vertov's film accompanied by bits of text from the book to follow, creating what Manovich refers to as a "visual index to some of the book's major ideas" (xiv).

For Manovich, Vertov's silent film was always already new media. In one sense, it serves as a simple reminder that film was, in the early 1900s, a new medium whose possibilities and futures were not yet defined, and that artists and visionaries were putting cinematic technologies to creative uses and for new effects. At the same time, *Man with a Movie Camera* more precisely prefigures the specific form of the database that becomes an integral component to computer-based media. Beyond that, the film is multilayered or, as Manovich calls it, "metatextual," which is crucial for his description of how new media work. As Manovich later explains, "The visual culture of a computer age is cinematographic in its appearance, digital on the level of its material, and computational (i.e., software driven) in its logic" (180).

Alexander Galloway's more recent book *The Interface Effect* delivers a sympathetic reading of cinema's looming presence in Manovich's book, which was frequently taken up as a point of critique: for its formalism, for its ahistoricism, and for its heavy reliance on an older medium to explain new media. As Galloway observes, this mise en abyme model "shows how Manovich's methodology is implicitly historical, for the media landscape changed fundamentally after the invention of cybernetics in the late 1940s. Today all media are a question of synecdoche (scaling a part for the whole), not indexicality (pointing from here to there). This assumption is absolutely central in *The Language of New Media,* and it helps explain why Manovich is prompted to look *within,* to cinema, in order to look to the present."[22]

I mostly share the point of view articulated through Galloway's generous reappraisal of Manovich's turn to film. I think it would be more historically irresponsible if we did *not* turn to so-called older media such as film to help think about new media. I also agree that media work in a synechdochal—and, I would add, accumulative—manner, so that they build on and incorporate each other, and their histories, within them.[23] If Manovich saw in Vertov a revolutionary artist who was thinking about computer databases avant la lettre, Manovich's turn to Vertov nevertheless helped to describe new media at a *historically specific moment*: at the end of the first generation of web culture in the 1990s, in what is largely understood to be its more revolutionary and communal phase.[24] Today's internet culture looks very different—bolstered by high-speed broadband networks, trafficked by algorithms and status updates, and controlled by more systematic and pervasive state surveillance that has closed off many fantasies about the internet's utopian possibilities. It is thus the right time to ask once again which histories or earlier works of cinema offer opportunities to critically place the digital and political transitions facing us.

My suggestion in this chapter, then, is that Manovich's use of *Man with a Movie Camera* could be updated with *Citizen Kane*—with all the critical potentials and problems this move might entail. In Vertov's film, the modular logic of substitutability reigns supreme; this, after all, is a key formal feature, and indeed fascination, of the database. One could swap images and sequences for others in the film, and so long as they maintain a more or less equivalent syntagmatic function in the grammar of the film, the meaning conjured by Vertov's film would not really be very different. In fact, one version of such a project has already been realized, with Perry Bard's *Man with a Movie Camera: The Global Remake* (2007), where Bard developed an interactive website for users around the world to update the film shot by shot with new, contemporary footage. The website pulls from this new database of images daily to create a new remake, ensuring no single remake will ever be exactly the same. Through questions the project poses about authorship and digital versus analog images, Bard makes clear that Vertov's film corresponds fittingly to the digital dream of infinite substitutability.[25] *Man with a Movie Camera* celebrates the revolutionary dreams of the avant-garde, the merging of database and narrative logics, the energies of formalism, the radical newness of new media, and, even in its "global remake," the creative, emancipatory powers of participatory culture.

Citizen Kane, as film scholars know well, is a different beast. It stands for the achievements of but also the reactions to classical Hollywood style, the codified set of practices standardized through a well-developed industry, the deep ambiguities of realism, and the dark side of the American dream. This set of qualities forecasts, or even premediates, to borrow Richard Grusin's term, a more representative appraisal of the situation of digital media and culture today, which is to not even mention Donald Trump's own misogynistic musings on the film's greatness documented by filmmaker Errol Morris in unused footage for a short film that opened the 2002 Academy Awards.[26] And I would emphasize the term "digital media" over Manovich's "new media," because the group of technologies and practices that these terms generally refer to today (in 2021) have matured into a secondary, more standardized, phase. *Citizenfour,* a film made with and about digital media, displays the problems of how this current digital order has taken shape, especially when juxtaposed with the kinds of new media examples about which Manovich was writing, from CD-ROMs to CGI, which are now either obsolete or integrated and routine. The opportunities for enhancing knowledge and creative expression and developing new business models that were so integral to early web culture have largely been refashioned into a more deeply layered internet with more limited conditions of possibility at the participatory level of the interface. The urgent questions posed by digital media today are more about politics, control, global flows of power, and what I have discussed here as informatic depth.

Citizenfour reveals some of the labyrinthine processes that obfuscate informatic depth and makes a case for the difficulties and power of responsible journalism within a mediascape increasingly recognized to be littered with fake news. In these terms, both *Man with a Movie Camera* and *Kane* offer instructive media historical examples of the blurred boundaries between fact and fiction. *Man with a Movie Camera* is generally regarded as documentary, yet it is also recognized for indiscriminately collating footage of multiple Soviet cities (Kiev, Kharkkov, Moscow, and Odessa) into a composite metacity that Vertov almost deceitfully presents as a single city. The film's composite city anticipates the dilemma of the manipulable digital image, a concept whose theme of the lost promise of indexicality has dominated theorizations of digital imagery but, as Tom Gunning suggested more than a decade ago, does not necessarily remain the most fruitful way to think about the vicissitudes of cinematic realism in the twenty-first century.[27]

Kane pulls in the inverse direction. In addition to Kane's stylistic oscillation between cinema's documentary and spectacle-making tendencies, there is more than just a question of Welles's orchestration of cinematic technique at stake: this push and pull extends to the narrative's own relation to reality. Although, controversially, *Kane* was based on the real-life William Randolph Hearst, Welles always officially denied this connection to presumably avoid legal repercussions, and the film thus raises questions about Hollywood's fictionalization of the real, a practice that shows no signs of disappearing anytime soon. While Welles willfully denied the truth about his film's own relation to the real, *Kane* nevertheless thematically and fearlessly tackles the problem of truth and its contortion by the media; its protagonist's emergence as a ruthless newspaper tycoon serves as a cautionary tale about how the hunger for power and media coverage can override journalistic credibility. In this light, Kane's status as a citizen—perhaps most essentially characterized by an internalized sense of moral responsibility toward fellow citizens—is troubled, and his egoistic quest to maintain this role as a model citizen is ironically what undermines his ability to be a proper one.

Laura Poitras presents this argument too, but from the outside in—as in *Four*'s inversion of Welles's inside-looking-out view of young Kane through the window. Snowden, deemed a bad citizen by the state, was in fact acting out of his sense of responsibility, perhaps naive but nevertheless bold, to actualize his moral obligations as a good citizen. *Kane* and *Four* thus lay bare the irony of citizenship: the morally good citizen does not equal the state's good citizen. As Lauren Berlant notes, "Citizenship is a status whose definitions are always in process. It is continually being produced out of a political, rhetorical, and economic struggle over who will count as 'the people' and how social membership will be measured and valued. It must, then, be seen as more than a patriotic category."[28] The very term "citizen," in other words, and as both films highlight, is neither stable nor inherited but produced through social acts, necessarily always calling its own meaning into question. Snowden's own justification of his actions in a document he left for Poitras and journalist Glen Greenwald to read as they were on their way to meet him in Hong Kong foregrounds the responsibility to not take one's attachment to the category for granted:

"Citizenship carries with it a duty to first police one's own government before seeking to correct others."[29]

These words illustrate one key transformation around citizenship that is worth noting. Discursively, when the word "citizen" is uttered today in the twenty-first century, it by and large evokes the unevenness engendered by the failures of representational democracy, with leaders who do not represent constituents, voter suppression, social inequalities, and problems bound up with a working-class population whose interests have been abandoned. The term "citizen" arguably relates more to what Paolo Gerbaudo refers to as the anarchopopulist "'ideology of the indignant citizen,' a citizen outraged at being deprived of citizenship."[30] Far from being a conservatively patriotic concept that celebrates one's belonging to a state, today "citizen" more frequently invokes a set of aspirations that are in fact denied by those in power, and it is aimed to ideologically mobilize those who believe in standing up to protect the rights of the disenfranchised. A rich illustration of this shade of the term's meaning is Claudia Rankine's best-selling book *Citizen* (2015), which collects accounts of relentless racial slights in an inventive literary form that combines poetry, memoir, cultural analysis, and visual imagery. An even more thoroughgoing example can be seen to cohere around user-generated practices of digitally mediated "citizen journalism," where activists with personal technologies now have the tools in their own hands to document everything from social movements to localized injustices witnessed in everyday life.

The inherently indignant contemporary citizen clearly aligns with the libertarian, anarchist motivations behind Snowden's actions and self-categorization as citizen. The prescience of Kane as an inherently—indeed, supremely—indignant citizen in this current context only goes so far, as he is never deprived of the rights of citizenship or threatened by such an attack. He figures more as a stand-in for the state—in control of the media, hungry for power and money. If citizenship today cannot be conceptualized outside of a locus in which the neglect of citizen's rights is exacerbated, what has become of the state-conceptualized citizen? Here, Appelbaum's speech in *Citizenfour* and the number in the film's title itself provide insight: in the eyes of corporations and other state apparatuses, citizens are voters and consumers—largely numerical, digitized entities, aggregations of metadata, engaged in a series of statistically monitored and predictable behaviors. The drawback to this, of course, is the crystallization of the filter-bubble phenomenon that has been blamed for the results of the 2016 American elections and the United Kingdom's European Union membership referendum. As today's tech giants know, we

FIGURE 5.8. "No Trespassing" sign in the opening scene of *Citizen Kane* (Orson Welles, 1941).

remain more engaged when we have more personalized experiences, when our social media feeds are filled with news we agree with, rather than a balanced and diverse range of stories. An important historical precursor to such clickbait culture is "yellow journalism," the term describing the catchy headlines that was in fact coined in the 1890s precisely in order to describe Hearst's *New York Journal*. *Citizen Kane*'s opening and closing shots of the "No Trespassing" sign might as well mark digital space and the everyday realities with which it is entangled too; and we might learn a lesson from Welles's camera, like Poitras's, which refuses to comply with the restrictions written on the fence (Figure 5.8).

Notes

Special thanks to Alice Maurice for first prompting me to consider sustaining a comparison between *Citizen Kane* and *Citizenfour* and to Michelle Stewart for reading multiple drafts.

1. Lisa Parks, "Cover Your WebCam: Unencrypting Laura Poitras's *Citizenfour*," *Film Quarterly* 68, no. 3 (2015): 12.

2. I owe this observation to an insightful conference presentation related to *Citizenfour* delivered by Samuel Topiary, "The Anti-representational Mode," Visible Evidence XXII (Toronto, August 2015).

3. André Bazin, "The Technique of *Citizen Kane*," in *Bazin at Work: Major Essays and Reviews from the Forties and Fifties*, trans. Alain Piette and Bert Cadullo, ed. Bert Cadullo (New York: Routledge, 1997), 232.

4. Andrea Brighenti, "Visibility: A Category for the Social Sciences," *Current Sociology* 55, no. 3 (May 2007): 327.

5. Siegfried Zielinski, *Deep Time of the Media: Toward an Archaeology of Hearing and Seeing by Technical Means* (Cambridge, Mass.: MIT Press, 2006), 3.

6. Stephen Best and Sharon Marcus, "Surface Reading: An Introduction," *Representations* 108, no. 1 (Fall 2009): 1–21.

7. Ellen Rooney, "Live Free or Describe: The Reading Effect and the Persistence of Form," *differences* 21, no. 3 (2010): 116, 132.

8. Stephen Saito, "Interview: Laura Poitras on Finding Freedom through Filmmaking in 'Citizenfour,'" *Moveable Fest*, October 23, 2014, moveablefest .com/moveable_fest/2014/10/laura-poitras-citizenfour.html.

9. See Jeff Scheible, "*Risk*'s Fraught Mediascape," in *The Routledge Companion to Media and Risk*, ed. Bishnupriya Ghosh and Bhaskar Sarkar (New York: Routledge, 2020), 377–87.

10. Laura Mulvey, *Citizen Kane*, BFI Film Classics (London: British Film Institute, 1992), 17.

11. Paglen calls the "deep state" the "part of the state which is not democratic at all." See Alex Pasternack, "The Geography of Secret Places: An Interview with Trevor Paglen," *Motherboard*, February 11, 2014, motherboard.vice.com/blog /the-geography-of-secret-places-watching-the-watchers-with-trevor-paglen.

12. David Bordwell, "Citizen Kane," *Film Comment* 7, no. 2 (Summer 1971): 44.

13. Parks, "Cover Your WebCam," 15.

14. Gilles Deleuze, "Postscript on the Societies of Control," *October* 59 (Winter 1992): 7.

15. Jeanne Hall, "'Don't You Ever Just Watch?': American Cinema Verité and *Dont Look Back*," in *Documenting the Documentary: Close Readings of Documentary Film and Video*, ed. Barry Keith Grant and Jeannette Sloniowski (Detroit, Mich.: Wayne State University Press, 2014), 237–52.

16. See Paul Ricoeur, *Interpretation Theory: Discourse and the Surplus of Meaning* (Fort Worth: Texas Christian University Press, 1976); Dudley Andrew, "The Gravity of *Sunrise*," *Quarterly Review of Film Studies* 2, no. 3 (August 1977): 356–87.

17. Mulvey, *Citizen Kane*, 9.

18. Matteo Pasquinelli, "Italian *Operaismo* and the Information Machine," *Theory, Culture and Society* 32, no. 3 (2015): 51.

19. Paul Flaig and Katherine Groo, eds., *New Silent Cinema* (New York: Routledge, 2016).

20. D. N. Rodowick, *The Virtual Life of Film* (Cambridge, Mass.: Harvard University Press, 2007), 184.

21. Lev Manovich, *The Language of New Media* (Cambridge, Mass.: MIT Press, 2001), xiv.

22. Alexander R. Galloway, *The Interface Effect* (Cambridge, UK: Polity Press, 2012), 8–9.

23. This accumulation of course, as numerous media historians have illustrated, is not necessarily linear or all-inclusive, with trajectories shaped by failures, absences, and forgotten histories and figures as much as those that are successful and remembered.

24. See, for example, Fred Turner, *From Counterculture to Cyberculture: Stewart Brand, the Whole Earth Network, and the Rise of Digital Utopianism* (Chicago: University of Chicago Press, 2008).

25. For a more detailed analysis of Bard's project, see Jaimie Baron, "The Experimental Film Remake and the Digital Archive Effect: *A Movie by Jen Proctor* and *Man with a Movie Camera: The Global Remake*," *Framework* 53, no. 2 (Fall 2012): 467–90.

26. Richard Grusin, *Premediation: Affect and Mediality after 9/11* (London: Palgrave Macmillan, 2010).

27. Tom Gunning, "Moving Away from the Index: Cinema and the Impression of Reality," *differences* 18, no. 1 (2007): 29–52.

28. Lauren Berlant, *The Queen of America Goes to Washington City: Essays on Sex and Citizenship* (Durham, N.C.: Duke University Press, 1997), 20.

29. Glen Greenwald, *No Place to Hide: Edward Snowden, the NSA and the Surveillance State* (London: Penguin, 2014), 31.

30. Paolo Gerbaudo, *The Mask and the Flag: Populism, Citizenism and Global Protest* (London: Hurst, 2017), 7.

CHAPTER SIX

Bankers Dream of Banking, or Against the Interpretation of Dreams

Jennifer Fay

Taking stock of the new empirical dream research and cognitive studies of sleep today, it is hard to avoid the conclusion that we have become fully immersed in a neoliberal order in which the time for deep sleep and the mysteries of dream interpretation are a thing of the past. Long-form sleep and its REM dream cycles have given way to sleep deprivation, short-form napping, and "slow-wave" or NREM mentation, and the interpretation of dreams is now a much more descriptive affair. As a corrective to the "methodological pitfalls inherent to subjective interpretations of dream content employed by psychoanalysts," sleep researchers Erin Wamsley and Robert Stickgold insist on the empirical method and the "transparently obvious" and "straightforward . . . relationship between the dream content and everyday life."[1] Aggregated dream reports provide this rather startling demystification: "Skiers dream of skiing, surfers dream of surfing, and mountain climbers dream of climbing mountains. Teachers dream of classroom situations, bankers dream of banking activities, and nurses dream about their patients."[2] Sleep and its dream content are not a release of repressed thoughts or unexpressed wishes, but a weak rehearsal of a day at the office. We dream some version of our occupational selves, and we are told to take our dream reports at "face value": "There is little, if any, evidence that conscious experience during sleep is particularly more inaccessible, complex or symbolic than waking thought."[3] The work of interpretation, then, has been utterly transformed: we no longer require trained experts or analysts to decode the unconscious economies of the self and its irrational symptoms. The bizarre and hallucinatory content of our REM dreams, such that they are recalled, find easy, surface relation to rational waking life, even if the dreams are themselves irrational.

The demystification of dreams, in other words, does not involve hidden meanings nested within elaborate complexes; rather, what is available to the conscious subject is all the meaning there is.

Connecting dream research to "surface reading" in the spirit of Stephen Best and Sharon Marcus, these are, we might say, the "depthless hermeneutics" of interpretation that free the dreamer and the reader from the limited scripts of psychoanalysis, transforming the often "adversarial relation" between a reader and a recalcitrant or coded text (including a dream) into one of far more easy association.[4] The new modes of dream interpretation, like the descriptive turn in literary analysis, may help us to achieve a novel form of freedom (or recognize different limits to our freedom), to discover newly meaningful texts, and perhaps to focus on the complexities of the text rather than theorize what it represses, suppresses, or does not know about itself.

This essay considers the surface reading of dreams as a way to also interpret contemporary, neoliberal art cinema and its new sources of mystery. My primary example is Christian Petzold's *Yella* (2007). Petzold is associated with the Berlin School of filmmakers who explore postunification Germany and, in Petzold's case especially, the subjects, affects, and modes of existence that have been rendered obsolete by the country's turn to fully globalized capital culture and attendant precarity. Petzold refers to *Yella* as the last of his "Ghost Trilogy," a triptych of films in which unified Germany is haunted by both its divided past and its anachronistic citizens, like Yella (Nina Hoss) and her estranged and bankrupted husband, Ben (Hinnerk Schönemann), who may not have survived the former East's transition to capitalism. An accountant by training and a former partner in a failed business with Ben, Yella finds lucrative work in a venture capitalist operation after meeting Philip (Devid Striesow), a broker who skims from the profits to fund a start-up company of his own. Yella thrives in her new position even though, or perhaps because, she seems to be afflicted with sleep disorder. In this eighty-nine-minute film of corporate gains and losses, risky investments, and forced liquidations, more than half of the scenes involve Yella either falling asleep or waking with a start. Her public wakefulness is often disrupted by drowsiness and atonia in train compartments, unlocked hotel rooms, and moving automobiles, places where homey privacy has given way to insecure corporate areas and what Petzold refers to as the "transit spaces" in which so many of his films take place.[5] These instances of sleep are decidedly sudden and short in duration. Especially under extreme duress, Yella falls into an unbidden and defenseless sleep, or, in the midst of brokering high-stakes deals, she

FIGURE 6.1. Yella's unprotected sleep in a corporate hotel room. (*Yella,* Christian Petzold, 2007).

appears to be distracted, overwhelmed by phantom phenomena and hypnogogic images (Figure 6.1). As she travels between the depopulated spaces of postunification Germany—the former East (specifically Wittenberge, where Yella has recently moved back in with her father after separating from her broken and maniacal husband) and former West (where she hopes to work as an accountant in Hannover)—it is hard to know if the eerie quality of these locales is simply a fact of twenty-first-century Germany, or if they are projections of Yella's own investments and disinvestments in her world. The cradle of the Protestant Reformation, Wittenberge appears to be as empty of history as it is of residents. Indeed, there is only a slight difference between what we perceive as the film's objective world of corporate hotel rooms, executive offices, predatory men, and scenes of predatory lending, on one hand, and what may be Yella's subjective dreamscapes, on the other.

This film knows something about the new culture of sleep, and it opens itself up to the noninterpretation of dreams. The hallucinations and hauntings in the film are as unsettling and strange as the rituals of venture capitalism. And if we do, indeed, have access to Yella's dream life, it is one in which her need for sleep and her interest in venture capitalism are explicitly avowed and, in some ways, played on the surface of the narrative. One does not need to dig deep to arrive at these two desires, which do not appear to mask other hidden desires. Or, to put this within the framework of the dream research quoted earlier, in this film accountants dream about accounting. What, then, might it mean for us to read a movie of late capitalism and its sleep economy at the face value of its image? How might the new dream science help us to understand what it means to be living the neoliberal dream, a dream stripped of its metalanguage, no longer in need of interpretation, read "with the grain"?[6] What does the surface obscure? What is the connection between surface sleeping and surface reading?

Art Cinema and the Ends of Sleep

Before considering the new dream research and neoliberal art cinema, it is perhaps worth noting that the golden age of art cinema and auteurism presumed connections between film work, dreamwork, and the director's unconscious. As Peter Wollen wrote in 1972, auteurist interpretation calls on the theorist to mine the depths of the film's complexities by positing the director not in the role of the artist per se; rather, "it is through the force of his [the director's] preoccupation that an unconscious, unintended meaning can be decoded in the film." The theorist, like the professional psychoanalyst, is a master decoder of the "film *auteur* as an unconscious catalyst."[7] The spectator, aided by the theorist, puzzles out the status of each scene, as if sorting through the dream life of the director (or the film as a kind of unconscious dreamlike text), searching for latent social relations represented as symptoms on screen.

Yet, this dream life of cinema was possible in a liberal state of both country and mind in which the delusion of the unified subject was sustained by a good night of slumber and in which REM sleep was still part of the brain's nightly cycle. That is, the first wave of art cinema, which consolidated in the early 1950s, envisions dreams and perplexing subjective experiences in need of interpretation while presuming the habits and culture of sleep. Characters are of a piece with the psychoanalytic model of REM dreams whose remembered content is presumed to represent repressed desires and unconscious primordial drives that, once revealed, may threaten the entire ego formation. Such a cinema may also presuppose a spectator awake and attentive enough to do the difficult work of interpretation. David Bordwell writes of viewer protocol when watching art films that reads "for maximum ambiguity" between the play of subjective experience (including dreams that may not be signposted as such by "objective" images of sleep), objective complexity (the modern world as itself a kind of puzzle), and authorial commentary that the film sustains without clear resolution. The open-ended narrative "knows that life is more complex than art can ever be, and the only way to respect this complexity is to leave causes dangling, questions unanswered."[8] The art cinema viewer, drawing on the structures and meanings of modernist art and literature, is the active reader who works through the status of each scene, a person capable of appreciating something like objective boredom and modernist ennui while watching a film rather than falling asleep in the theater.[9] Boredom, one of the aesthetic categories of art cinema, to be sure, may turn out to be the privileged experience of a subject who is not only well-read but also sufficiently well-rested.

The liberal subject falls into sleep in the spirit of Jean-Luc Nancy's extended meditation on slumber: "I'm falling asleep, I'm falling into sleep and I'm falling there by the power of sleep. Just as I fall from exhaustion. Just as I drop from boredom. As I fall on hard times. As I fall, in general."[10] The gravitational pull of sleep on mind and body—a surrender to a conquering force, the becoming almost dead, "almost vegetable"—is "a nightfall" whose source emanates from the sleeper as he "descends from himself into himself" (6). In slumber, cut off from the external world, the subject "enters into the unraveling of plans and aims, of expectations and calculation" (3). Nancy contends that the state of sleep and that of death are also equally off limits to phenomenological experience or description: "This *I* that sleeps can no more say it sleeps than it could say that it is dead." The satiety of sleep sacrifices the *ipseity* of the subject. In deep sleep the philosopher finds himself "sheltered from knowledge," a nonself fully enveloped in the absence of consciousness (5). For Nancy, as with Jonathan Crary in his now-classic *24/7: Late Capitalism and the Ends of Sleep,* the daily retreat or fall from consciousness is perhaps the last bastion of self-preservation in the age of global, nonstop capital. "The restorative inertness of sleep," writes Crary, "counters the deathliness of all the accumulation, financialization and waste that have devasted anything once held in common."[11] Critiquing the neoliberal demands on the subject, Crary states that "sleep is the only remaining barrier, the only enduring natural condition that capitalism cannot eliminate."[12]

As we will see, *Yella* questions these norms in an age of global restlessness. In 2016, the Centers for Disease Control and Prevention reported that one in three Americans are chronically underslept, a deprivation that Gallup traces to 1990, when the average night of sleep dropped from 7.8 hours to the current norm of 6.8.[13] Big data suggest that Europe is also experiencing a sleep deficit in inverse relation to the rise of internet saturation and per capita GDP.[14] The "global sleep crisis" as evident through various self-reporting, smartphone sleep apps and measured—and likely caused—by online activity tell us that billions of people everywhere sleep fewer hours at night than their bodies require, leading to disease, depression, and, of course, chronic drowsiness and short-term (often unsolicited) napping, and even premature death.[15] The sleep epidemic is also connected to reduced employee productivity and to pernicious practices of neoliberal self-investment. The less an employee sleeps, the more likely this person is to engage in unethical workplace behavior, researchers tell us. From fabricating receipts for reimbursement and claiming credit for other people's accomplishments, to forms of "social loafing" when group effort is required, "sleepy employees," writes Matthew Walker, "choose the more selfish path of least resistance," while tired CEOs become more abusive and erratic: "Sound sleep is clearly sound business."[16] Employees steal not because they are inherently dishonest so much as because fatigue clouds their judgment.

While death and unethical behavior linger over the sleep-deprived in *Yella,* the film thematizes sleep itself as an externalized fallen state. Yella literally falls unconscious at the moment she should run, sleeps when she should leave, and hallucinates at just the moment she needs to focus. Yet her periodic slumber, which certainly makes her vulnerable, also makes up for lost sleep. She wakes seemingly unaffected by sleep inertia and extremely capable of managing the corporate wrangling of her new freelance job as a venture capitalist accountant. Her hypnogogic episodes do not detach her from the world of high finance and its largely virtual economy, however much *that* world is itself detached from humane relations. Her dreamy intuitions and postslumber sharpness grant her preternatural ability to detect overrepresented assets and tell the fortunes of companies on the brink of success and collapse. This is to say that rather than falling away from the world, Yella's sleep is a fall into financial figures.

In her first of many meetings, Yella accidentally knocks a glass of water onto the floor. Sound effects from earlier in the film are heard once again: water lapping, leaves rustling in the wind, a goose honking overhead. She appears to be lost in reverie—an awkward moment at the negotiating table when Yella, the only woman, drifts into dream. But these sound effects rivet her attention on a spreadsheet where assets for recently acquired technology are radically overvalued. The sound cues bring her back to prior knowledge, to another, earlier spreadsheet from which these very assets disappeared. Far from vanquishing sleep or turning it into passive or lost time, venture capitalism in this film incorporates rest into its economy. Indeed, over the course of the film, Yella masters the ur-form of corporate repose. This is not the "broker pose" as taught to her by her mentor Philip but the power nap as propounded by *Power Sleep* and *Sleep for Success* author Dr. James B. Maas. Among other tips, Maas encourages his readers to develop the habit of "prophylactic napping": "Napping makes it possible to deposit needed assets in your sleep bank account." Power naps "can quickly restore alertness, enhance performance, reduce mistakes and accidents, and positively affect profits."[17] Another researcher agrees in the vocabulary of neoliberalism: "By any metrics we use to determine business success . . . creating the necessary conditions for employees to obtain enough sleep at night, or in the workplace during the day, should be thought of as a new form of physiologically injected venture capital."[18]

In Petzold's film, however, one needs to make a cash deposit in order to accumulate sleep. When Yella arrives at a slick corporate hotel in Hannover following a harrowing accident, she is prevented from checking in because she failed to pay a room deposit for the six-week trial period of her new accounting job. Yella's bank card (her *Sparkasse* card from her local, nonnetworked, public bank) is rejected and she has no proper credit card, marking her as something of an economic refugee, or financial nonperson from the former East. Exhausted, she pleads: "I'll sort it out tomorrow. I just need to get some sleep." But the scoffing hotel clerk will not budge on the rental terms. Yella then finds a roll of Euros that her father surreptitiously slipped into her coat pocket that morning, and thus she is able to finalize the transaction. Yella satisfies the terms for sleep using the outmoded medium of cash. Her subsequent hypnagogic episodes, in turn, inform the terms of her venture capitalist meetings, which often have an eerie if not dreamy quality to them. This film explores a capitalist economy of sleep.

It is no coincidence that Petzold modeled the scenes of financial brinkmanship after—at times lifting exact dialogue from—Harun Farocki's observational documentary *Nicht ohne Risiko* (*Nothing Ventured,* 2004), in which representatives from a venture capital firm negotiate the conditions of investment with an entrepreneurial family business in need of ready cash. This is an ecology of what Farocki calls "locust capitalism," as investors want not merely to devour the fruits of someone else's ingenuity but to claim controlling interest in start-up companies.[19] The dynamic is almost a force of neoliberal human nature. As Jaimey Fisher explains, *Nothing Ventured* provides the structure for *Yella;* the two long negotiating meetings and a lunch in Farocki's film are parceled out into five shorter scenes in *Yella* inspiring both the cold realism of corporate mise-en-scène and the theatricality and literal posturing of exchange. The actors in Petzold's movie adapt from these real-life brutalists the limited repertoire of power moves, including the "broker pose" (leaning back in a chair with arms folded behind the head, a stretch of the body that signals exasperation and negotiation fatigue), and the strategic call for breaks, pauses, and even sleep. In this world of high finance, the experts know when to declare a meeting over so that everyone can sleep on the terms of the offer. Because this is an observational documentary, we have no access to the inner thoughts, dreams, or subjective experience of these people. Indeed, we should presume that everything that plays out in front of the camera, including what appear to be confidential asides between members of the venture capitalist firm when they are alone in the room, is a calculated performance. Everything we glean about the outward expressions and inner desires of people in this documentary is resolutely on the surface of what can be objectively seen and heard. What emerges is a portrait and a narrative, in Fisher's words, of "how venture-capital firms aim to intervene in and 'monetize' ambitious people's plans, fantasies, and dreams."[20]

Yella wants to monetize other people's plans, and she dreams about financialization. Yet, in the spirit of art cinema, events in this film have ambiguous origins in either objective or subjective experience, waking or sleeping states, depending on how we read a key scene—a car accident—toward the beginning of the film that Yella may or may not have survived. Yella returns to Hannover after securing "a good job" at a firm. Ben, the psychotic and estranged husband, stalks her as she walks from the train station back to her father's house. He comments on the confidence of her gait and from this presumes her new employment, pleads with her to return to the marriage, and threatens her with his menacing proximity. The next morning, Yella calls a cab after breakfasting with her father, but when she opens the front door she finds that Ben is waiting insistently to give her a ride. That she agrees may already be a sign that Yella has a death wish. For rather than chauffeuring her to the train station for her first day of work, Ben steers them both off of a bridge and into the Elbe River. Ben is driven to this suicide/murder because his own start-up company has been liquidated. While holding Yella hostage in a moving car, he forces her to look at his new investment plan based on the few remaining assets. It is from this report that Yella gleans the overvaluation of technology that will reappear as assets in her first venture capitalist meeting later in the film.

This deadly scene with Ben may indeed mark Yella's end. But Petzold presents an initial scenario that she survives the crash, pulls herself to the shore, passes out, and wakes with a start only to find Ben laid out next to her either passed out or dead. Wet and shaken, Yella leaves Ben behind, finds her soaked belongings, and boards the train to Hannover as planned. Once again, she falls asleep and wakes with a start in an empty train at the end of the line. It is telling that Petzold and Hoss decided that Yella would typically wake from sleep in the film as if awakening from a dream of drowning.[21] Thereafter, the scenes in which Ben haunts or stalks her may be dreamed or hallucinated, or perhaps they have an objective occurrence in the story world (he does have a habit of appearing out of nowhere). But the end of the film raises the possibility that Yella did not survive the crash. In the penultimate scene, Yella falls asleep in a long cab ride back to her hometown after disastrous negotiations with Dr. Gunthen drive him to suicide by drowning. Petzold cuts back to the scene of the crash. Rather than resisting the crash to come as in the first version of the scene earlier in the film, Yella accepts her violent end. And in short order we see the corpses of Ben and Yella laid out on the shore.

In one reading, the scenes following the initial fatal crash are Yella's dying wish: an extended hallucination or projection as she is drowning at the bottom of the river and dreaming of her life as a negotiator and spreadsheet analyst in Hannover who often falls asleep. Haunted by her homicidal husband who has been ghosted by the new economy, Yella realizes her financial personhood in a drowning fantasy in which she causes another suicidal death. Or, if she survives the crash, the episodes that follow have an objective yet uncanny status when the same music (Beethoven's *Moonlight* Sonata), the same sound effects (leaves rustling in the wind, the call of a crow), the same clothing (Yella's red shirt and black skirt) and same empty public spaces (East and West), the repetition of venture capital meetings (taken from a documentary), and themes of suicidal drowning speak to the limited and increasingly homogenized sensory experiences of postunification Germany and its economic arrangements. In this case, Yella's wish for death appears to us as a dream at the film's end. Or this final scene is simply Petzold's revision of the crash whose temporal status is left open. A flash-forward, a flashback, a repetition with a difference? All of these interpretations are equally viable and are finally small matters of interpretation. What is not ambiguous is that throughout the film—whether waking or sleeping, in life or in death—Yella finds herself torn between two explicitly stated desires: to sleep between bedsheets and to linger over spreadsheets.

Before her first day on the job in Hannover for a firm that turns out to have been forced into liquidation, Yella is having dinner in the hotel restaurant. She reads her water-damaged *Business English* textbook until her eye catches Philip at a nearby table just as he walks away from his

FIGURE 6.2. Yella spies the spreadsheet on Philip's computer. (*Yella,* Christian Petzold, 2007.)

FIGURE 6.3. The computer shifts into sleep mode. (*Yella,* Christian Petzold, 2007.)

laptop. Rather than following him, her gaze fixes on the screen. A flicker of a spreadsheet disappears when the computer, going into sleep mode, mesmerizes her with a screensaver image of a crashing, oceanic wave (Figures 6.2 and 6.3). Even the computer shares Yella's twin obsessions with financial figures and sleep, and conflates the state of sleep and company assets with that of oceanic drowning, or a dream of drowning. But the computer inverts the relationship between sleep and private experience; it sleeps both to save energy and to protect from prying eyes the information on the screen related to the financials of private firms. The image of sleep, in other words, is not a shift to a computing unconscious so much as an automatic image that hides private information. It may also be that this watery wave of a screensaver is a forecast of the corporate liquidation of a company whose assets in the form of devaluing technology just disappeared from view—an image that literalizes the liquidity of assets and the fungibility of computers. When he returns to his table, with a sneer, Philip reprimands Yella for her fixation on his screen: "Are you interested in balance sheets?" He immediately apologizes. But Yella confesses that she *is* interested in balance sheets. Inquiring after her English textbook, Philip utters in English the lingua franca of corporate seduction: "Forced to close a sale." This is as near a "meet cute" as one will find in a Petzold film, but it establishes up front, and on the surface, a deep connection between Yella's avowed desires and a relationship between sleep (as signaled through repeated shots and figurations of sleeping) and the power moves of financialization.

Dreaming at Face Value

What is the relationship between the dreamwork and the artwork, between the art of dreaming and the work of venture capitalism and the burden of interpretation? Sleep researchers Wamsley and Stickgold, referenced earlier, complain that "psychoanalytic approaches entrenched in the popular imagination" have produced the widespread misperception that dreaming is a "mysterious, symbolic form of mental activity" that is formally unique to every individual and that eludes "measured, classified, and quantitatively analyzed" data sets.[22] In a section of an article entitled "The Empirical Study of Spontaneous Subjective Experience," Wamsley and Stickgold aver: "Resurgent studies of such subjective concepts as emotion, mood, memory and belief, demonstrate the progress which can be made when one takes a simple and straightforward approach to subjective experience, casting obfuscating philosophical concerns aside" (9). Focusing on self-reported dream content and tracking brain physiology to explain "universal dream features," writes J. Allan Hobson, "the mystery of dreaming is largely stripped away, leaving the content nakedly open to understanding without complex interpretation."[23] The new dream science dispels such "deep-seated human need to believe that dreaming . . . has a deeply veiled meaning inscribed by a benevolent hand whose ways are known only to a few chosen mediators."[24]

Starting in the late 1960s, empirical dream researchers adopted the Hall/Van de Castle system of dream analysis, which pivoted away from Freudian/Jungian scenarios to more general and ordinary categories for coding thousands of dream reports. Ideally, writes one of the pioneers of cognitive dream research, G. William Domhoff, the categories arise "with no theoretical intentions in mind."[25] Easy to identify, the categories are thus also easy to quantify. Pencil in hand, the researcher counts and codes for such entities as characters, social interactions, objects, activities, striving, misfortunes and good fortunes, emotions, food and eating, elements from the past, and unrealistic elements. And within categories, the system codes more discrete differentiation. For example, the general category for social interactions can be further coded for aggressiveness or friendliness.[26] Assigning letters and numbers to each of these variables, Domhoff has created a complex symbolic system that is calculable using algebraic equations—symbolic, yes, but not in the humanist sense of complex meaning. A researcher can simply count the number of friendly interactions in the dream report against the aggressive interactions to see the trends in a dreamer's sleeping thoughts. Dreams then become the data for spreadsheets. Quantified and aggregated, the dream reports provide a baseline for the formal features of dreaming. Domhoff stresses that this mode of analysis yields "findings" but not "explanations."[27] The newer method of dream analysis is based on the test subject's self-reporting, including the subject's sense of the degree to which dreams may or may not reflect lived experience.

The relationship between the dreamwork and artwork has likewise undergone revision. A favorite example for empirical analysis is Franz Kafka's dream reports composed of the thirty-seven dreams he recorded in his diaries and letters. Suspicious of psychology in general and psychoanalysis especially, Kafka is a good subject both because he would not be inclined to find the repressed meaning in his dreams and also because, as Domhoff observes, "there is so much consistency" in his dream "from category to category" (163). In the 1970s, Calvin Hall (of the Hall/Van de Castle system of analysis) and Richard Lind applied the Hall/Van de Castle method to Kafka's dream reports (coded through the "mundane categories including 'activities' and 'objects'") comparing dreams to his biography and three of his novels, and against the norms of the aggregated dream data (163). The result was that Kafka's dreams reflected Kafka's everyday preoccupations and correlated much more closely with his life as a clerk who still lived with his family: a "quiet, passive person who preferred watching to doing" (165). Hall and Lind reported that it was "plainly evident that the interactions between the heroes and other characters in the three novels are much more complex than Kafka's social interactions in his dreams" and conscious experience.[28] Reflecting on this extended case study decades later, Domhoff concludes: "There is a connection between Kafka's dreams and his waking life, but not between his dreams and his literature. More generally, we suspect that the alleged close connection between dreams and artistic productions is a cultural myth."[29] So much for life being more complicated than art will ever be!

However disenchanted, sleeping and dreaming are necessary. They facilitate memory consolidation, emotional regulation, and even bodily repair; dreaming may provide unconscious preparation for (or processing of) threatening situations, and it may be instrumental for creative thinking and problem-solving. Dreaming is certainly essential to our physical and emotional well-being, and it enhances our waking performance. But, the *function* of dreams may bear no relation to their apparent *meaning*. And, more radical still, dreams, while interesting to discuss when remembered, may not have any meaning at all.[30] Domhoff reasons that because we remember less than 1 percent of our dreams and because there appears to be no measurable disadvantage to people with little or no dream recall, the manifest content of dreams matters less or not all.[31] Hobson reasons that dreams may be meaningful to the individual dreamer who is inclined to find connections between dreams and experience. But there is so much of our experience that never enters our recalled dreams. And dream reports, illogical and fragmented, are a challenge to scientific meaning. Or, science renders the forced causal logic of dream interpretation to be fallible if not altogether false: "We do not dream because our unconscious wishes or drives would, if disguised, wake us up. We dream because our brains are activated during sleep."[32] What we recall upon waking may be simply the night's residue, a vague awareness of the mind's self-management, its housekeeping, memory storage operations, and self-regulation during sleep. Dreams may be what comes to mind when the body is inhibited, sensory input eliminated, and the off-line cognitive processes take over clearing out space for new waking inputs.[33]

Baristas Dream of Muffins

The good news is that our dreams still hold just a little bit of mystery. The day's experience, such that it may be recalled, is not played out exactly in sleep, and the dream gives rise to "novel and sometimes bizarre scenarios."[34] Consider this oft-cited, real-life example of how remembered experience interacts with remembered dreaming:

> *Waking experience*: "When I left Starbucks, we had so many leftover pastries and muffins to throw away or take home. *I couldn't decide which muffins to take* and which to toss . . ."
>
> *Corresponding dream experience*: "My dad and I leave to go shopping. We go from room to room, store to store. One of the stores is filled with *muffins, muffins, muffins* from floor to ceiling, all different kinds, *I can't decide which one I want* . . ."[35]

What could this dream mean? Is the most memorable event in this employee's day the incapacity to choose which muffins to take and which to throw away? And by looping this indecision back into a prior experience with the father (or perhaps an imagined shopping spree with the father), does the dreamer thereby transform so many free leftover muffins into a proliferative commodity in a store full of "muffins, muffins, muffins"? Is this a wish to pay for the baked goods that are abundant and free in waking life? For Wamsley and Stickgold, the meaning of the dream is its *function* as memory consolidation, as indicated by the italicized words and phrases that carry over. From waking to dream recall, the mind interleaves select experience across a range of memories that share generalities. The gist of the day and its dream—what will lodge itself in this person's memory—is that there are many muffins in the world and it's hard to choose which one to eat.

Significantly, this particular muffin dream is recounted in at least three journal articles, the first of which provides just a bit more detail. For researchers interested only in overlapping content or categories, a shorter version may suffice. But a humanist interested in meaning may also want to linger over the repetition of the use of *this* dream, and how it morphs both from waking to sleep and also from article to article. The complete and original muffin story is as follows:

> Waking Element: When I left Starbucks, we had so many leftover pastries and muffins to throw away or take home. I couldn't decide which muffins to take and which to toss. I feel guilty letting food go to waste.
>
> Dream Element: My Dad and I leave to go shopping. We go from room to room, store to store. One of the stores is filled with muffins, muffins, muffins from floor to ceiling, all different kinds, I

> can't decide which one I want, but I do want one; what an opportunity.[36]

Interpreting this longer version of both experiences, we may speculate on a different relationship between waking judgment and sleeping content. This muffin dream does not manifest repressed guilt or, pace Crary, counter capitalist accumulation and waste. Instead, this dreamwork, or dream *of* work turned into leisure, transforms the conscious guilt of corporate abundance—so many wasted Starbucks muffins, "I feel guilty letting food go to waste"—into desire, appetite, and opportunity: so "many muffins, muffins, muffins. . . . I do want one." This example does not negate Freud's repression thesis so much as reverses it. The wakeful and conscious guilt of corporate waste becomes a dream of consumer opportunity; fretfulness at work becomes an eased conscience while dreaming of shopping. *This* is how we sleep at night and very likely how we soothe ourselves for another day of work at the coffee shop.

Deep REM sleep gives rise to dreams of commodities and work. But non-REM sleep, the sleep associated with twenty-minute power napping and the first three stages of sleep before REM onset, is likely the sleep we get *at* work (and the dream state of the underslept).[37] In NREM sleep, writes Matthew Walker, the dreamer possesses an enhanced "ability to form and retain nonemotional, fact-based ('episodic') memories" typically drawn from recent experience or task-related activities.[38] *Slow-wave* sleep, so called because it is driven by slow oscillations in the neocortex, is the domain of "emotion-free declarative memory."[39] Whereas REM provides the dreamer with emotionally charged, storylike (but illogical), hallucinatory dream content in more or less real time and with the brainwaves presenting more or less similar activity as waking (and hence referred to by Michel Jouvet as "paradoxical sleep"), NREM is associated with directive thinking, static images, logical arrangement, declarative (also called explicit) memory: events, facts, and figures.[40] The short-form sleeper may be doomed to dream about and then remember spreadsheets.

While the neoliberal power napper is hardly inhabiting a kinder, gentler, or more ethical world order, the presentation of the self in NREM sleep, such that it appears, researchers tell us, is friendly. As coded using the Hall/Van de Castle method, the REM self is by contrast far more often an aggressor. In these deep, vivid dreams we are more likely to experience fear, anxiety, and anger. Patrick McNamara writes that "the dreaming mind creates two dramatically different Selves" in REM and NREM sleep, even when experiencing negative social interactions.[41] The NREM self is "befriending" (NREM dreamers never report themselves as aggressors!), perhaps ready to strike a deal and to find an opportunity in hostile environments.[42] Aggregated dream reports, available for all to see at DreamBank.net, prove this trend to be virtually universal.[43] Are the power nappers enthralled by a dream self who is friendly with the brute facts of existence? Is there any real relationship between these dreamed selves and our waking self-conception? While the findings raise complex questions, the formal content of dream life itself offers few surprises: "Dream content, insofar as it is related to the self-representation, is not random. Instead it appears to be sharply constrained and relatively consistent."[44] We are repeatedly told by sleep scientists that dreams are not a "video-tape-like 'replay' of an event."[45] Yet the limited repertoire and recombination of characters, tasks, and feelings in dreams (whatever the medium or the dreamer's vocation) may be a bit like the genre of art cinema, or art cinema reduced to genre.

Decoding Spreadsheets

If we are no longer reading art or dreams as symptoms of an unconscious will or directorial desire; if what we need to know about a character and her world, including her dreamworld, is available to us in the image and explicitly avowed by the character, what is left for the task of interpretation? By asking these questions I do not mean to vanquish complexity or declare that what is there is not in need of reading. Surfaces are complicated. It is, rather, to ask what, if anything, still requires expert decoding, and where we should seek out obscured meanings and suppressed knowledge.

Yella does not dispense with the deep-reading practice; it usefully shifts attention to other signs and symptoms. Indeed, the mystery in *Yella* is not encoded as dream (and thus, I think, Petzold gives us the objective facts of sleep and the likely falling into death). What is hidden, what we, as viewers never get to see, but around which Yella's interest and fate pivot are balance sheets and investment plans. We see her and others read and scan them, but the spreadsheets are elusive to viewers of the film. Always these sheets are out of focus or off screen; or, as in the case when Philip leaves his laptop open in the hotel restaurant, the computer hides its information when it goes to sleep. Only then does Petzold track in for a closer view. These are the economic contracts that, in fact, require interpretation in order to discover hidden assets and undeclared devaluations, and to predict the return on investment. Nothing on the balance sheet is at face value, and she who surface reads these documents will certainly, in Nancy's words "fall into hard times." Economic reading in the time of power napping is a bastion for suspicious hermeneutics, to rephrase Paul Ricoeur.[46] What slow-wave, neoliberal art cinema gives us, in this instance, is not the unconscious mind unknowable to itself or a dreamworld in need of desublimation or even interpretation. Yella's desire for capital and sleep is articulated as explicitly, as such. We encounter a literal subject who must interpret the ever-more virtual, abstract, and above all phantasmatic economic order that is far from "transparently obvious." Art cinema may have reached "the limits of critique"—to borrow Rita Felski's phrase—but neoliberalism still requires its paranoid analysts.[47]

Notes

1. Erin J. Wamsley and Robert Stickgold, "Memory, Sleep and Dreaming: Experiencing Consolidation," *Sleep Medicine Clinic* 6, no. 1 (March 2011): 6.

2. C. Hall and V. Norby, *The Individual and His Dreams* (New York: New American Library, 1972), quoted in Wamsley and Stickgold, 6.

3. Wamsley and Stickgold, 9.

4. Stephen Best and Sharon Marcus, "Surface Reading: An Introduction," *Representations* 108, no. 1 (Fall 2009): 12. The phrase "depthless hermeneutics" is attributed to Benjamin Kahan.

5. Christian Petzold, "Interview with Christian Petzold," in Jaimey Fisher, *Christian Petzold* (Urbana: University of Illinois Press, 2013), 147.

6. This is Timothy Bewes's phrase quoted in Best and Marcus, "Surface Reading," 11.

7. Peter Wollen, *Signs and Meanings in the Cinema,* 3rd ed. (Bloomington: Indiana University Press, 1972), 167–68.

8. David Bordwell, "The Art Cinema as a Mode of Film Practice," *Film Criticism* 4, no. 1 (Fall 1979): 60, 61.

9. Falling asleep in a boring meeting or movie is a response not to boredom but to sleep deprivation. Boredom, from a neurological perspective, is a response to a nonstimulating environment. Sleep is a response to a body and mind in need of rest. For the correlation between sleep deprivation and falling asleep when bored (as opposed to experiencing what we might call aesthetic boredom, as such), see Olivia Petter, "How to Stop Yourself Falling Asleep When Bored," *Independent,* April 5, 2018, https://www.independent.co.uk/life-style/falling-asleep-when-bored-how-to-stop-at-work-class-during-day-tips-a8290641.html; and James

B. Maas and Rebecca S. Robbins, *Sleep for Success! Everything You Must Know about Sleep but Are Too Tired to Ask* (Bloomington, Ind.: AuthorHouse, 2011), 16. On aesthetic boredom, see Patricia Meyer Spacks, *Boredom: The Literary History of a State of Mind* (Chicago: University of Chicago Press, 1995); and Siegfried Kracauer "Boredom," in *The Mass Ornament: Weimar Essays,* trans. and ed. Thomas Y. Levin (Cambridge, Mass.: Harvard University Press, 1995), 331–34.

10. Jean-Luc Nancy, *The Fall of Sleep,* trans. Charlotte Mandell (New York: Fordham University Press, 2009), 1.

11. Jonathan Crary, *24/7: Late Capitalism and the Ends of Sleep* (London: Verso, 2013), 128.

12. Crary, 74.

13. Jeffrey M. Jones, "In U.S., 40% Get Less Than Recommended Amount of Sleep," Gallup, December 18, 2013, https://news.gallup.com/poll/166553/less-recommended-amount-sleep.aspx. In 2016 the CDC reported that one in three adults living in the United States were sleep deprived: "1 in 3 adults don't get enough sleep"; CDC press release, updated February 18, 2016, https://www.cdc.gov/media/releases/2016/p0215-enough-sleep.html.

14. "The Trillion Internet Observations Showing How Global Sleep Patterns Are Changing," *MIT Technology Review,* January 31, 2017, https://www.technologyreview.com/s/603541/the-trillion-internet-observations-showing-how-global-sleep-patterns-are-changing/.

15. Olivia J. Walch, Amy Cochran, and Daniel B. Forger, "A Global Quantification of 'Normal' Sleep Schedules Using Smartphone Data," *Science Advances* 5, no. 2 (May 2016), https://advances.sciencemag.org/content/2/5/e1501705.

16. Matthew Walker, *Why We Sleep: Unlocking the Power of Sleep and Dreams* (New York: Scribner, 2017), 301–2, 304.

17. James B. Maas with Megan L. Wherry, David J. Axelrod, Barbara R. Hogan, and Jennifer A. Blumin, *Power Sleep: The Revolutionary Program That Prepares Your Mind for Peak Performance* (New York: Quill, 2001), 127, 132.

18. Walker, *Why We Sleep,* 305.

19. Harun Farocki quoted in Anke Leweke, "I See Something You Don't See: Remembering Harun Farocki," Goethe Institute, October 2014, goethe.de/en/kul/flm/20440394.html?forceDesktop=1.

20. Fisher, *Christian Petzold,* 110.

21. Fisher, 112.

22. Wamsley and Stickgold, "Memory, Sleep and Dreaming," 9.

23. J. Allan Hobson, *Dreaming: A Very Short Introduction* (Oxford: Oxford University Press, 2002), ii.

24. Hobson, 6.

25. G. William Domhoff, *Finding Meaning in Dreams: A Quantitative Approach* (New York: Plenum, 1996), 9.

26. For a discussion of the Hall/Van de Castle method and its categories and nomenclature, see Domhoff, 9–37.

27. Domhoff, 12.

28. Calvin S. Hall and Richard E. Lind, *Dreams, Life, and Literature: A Study of Franz Kafka* (Durham, N.C.: University of North Carolina Press, 1970), 67; quoted in Domhoff, 166.

29. Domhoff, *Finding Meaning in Dreams,* 166.

30. For a recent overview, see Julian Mutz and Amir-Homayoung Javadi, "Exploring the Neural Correlates of Dream Phenomenology and Altered States of Consciousness During Sleep," *Neuroscience of Consciousness,* April 18, 2017, 1–2. See also Hobson, *Dreaming,* 136–39.

31. G. William Domhoff, *The Scientific Study of Dreams: Neural Networks, Cognitive Development, and Content Analysis* (Washington, D.C.: American Psychological Association, 2003), 158–59.

32. Hobson, *Dreaming,* 140.

33. Wamsley and Stickgold write: "Recent work suggests that dream experiences recalled from sleep are a direct reflection of concomitant memory processes in the brain"; Wamsley and Stickgold, "Memory, Sleep and Dreaming," 1.

34. Wamsley and Stickgold, 7.

35. Quoted in Wamsley and Stickgold, 7.

36. Dream quoted in Magdelena J. Fosee, Roar Fosse, J. Allan Hobson, and Robert J. Stickgold, "Dreaming and Episodic Memory: A Functional Dissociation?," *Journal of Cognitive Neuroscience* 15, no. 1 (January 2003): 3. The shorter form of the dream is also reproduced in Erin J. Wamsley, "Dreaming and Offline Memory Consolidation," *Current Neurology and Neuroscience Report* 14, no. 3 (March 2014): 5.

37. Walker, *Why We Sleep,* 45–46.

38. Matthew P. Walker, "The Role of Slow Wave Sleep in Memory Processing," *Journal of Clinical Sleep Medicine* 5, no. 2, suppl. (April 2009): S20.

39. Walker, S23.

40. J. S. Antrobus and E. J. Wamsley, "Sleep Mentation in REM and NREM: A Neurocognitive Perspective," in *Encyclopedia of Neuroscience,* ed. Larry R. Squire (Berlin: Elsevier, 2009): 1021. See also Michel Jouvet, *The Paradox of Sleep: The Story of Dreaming,* trans. Laurence Carey (Cambridge, Mass.: MIT Press, 1999).

41. Patrick McNamara, Dierdre McLaren, and Kate Duro, "Representation of the Self in REM and NREM Dream," *Dreaming* 17, no. 2 (June 2007): 3 of PDF, https://www.ncbi.nlm.nih.gov/pmc/articles/PMC2629609/pdf/nihms53729.pdf.

42. McNamara, McLaren, and Duro, 8–9.

43. Adam Schneider and William Domhoff's online dream databank: http://www.dreambank.net/.

44. McNamara, McLaren, and Duro, "Representation of the Self," 8.

45. Wamsley and Stickgold, "Memory, Sleep and Dreaming," 5.

46. Paul Ricoeur, *Freud and Philosophy: An Essay on Interpretation,* trans. Denis Savage (New Haven, Conn.: Yale University Press, 1979), 7.

47. Rita Felski, *The Limits of Critique* (Chicago: University of Chicago Press, 2015).

CHAPTER SEVEN

Blackness at the Heart

Extruding Sovereignty in Nancy's and Denis's *The Intruder*

Alessandra Raengo and Laurel Ahnert

Claire Denis's film *The Intruder* (2004) takes its inspiration from philosopher Jean-Luc Nancy's *L'Intrus*. In his very personal account, Nancy reflects on his experience with heart failure, transplant surgery, and subsequent cancer treatment after a severe autoimmune response to the transplanted heart.[1] Conversely, *The Intruder* is a detached narrative about a mysterious man, Louis Trebor, living in the forest along the French-Swiss border. Experiencing heart failure, Louis opts to have an illegal heart transplant on the black market. Rejuvenated, he abandons one adult son in search of another located somewhere in the Tahitian islands, before his health starts to decline once again. Denis describes the relationship between her film and Nancy's text using physiological language—as a "graft" onto the original—that Nancy later rephrased as an "adoption" borrowing the language of filiation.[2] Thus, what in traditional film studies would have been approached through the lens of adaptation theory occurs instead against the backdrop of a growing sense of "vitalism" in media theory where mediation itself is approached as a "theory of life."[3] We take seriously the complex interrelationship between mediation and life, but we also recognize that doing so necessitates an engagement with the fraught ontological and ethical implications of bodily mediation, which are inexorably tied to race.

When an unqualified and undertheorized concept of "life" becomes the conceptual support for an all-encompassing idea of mediation, as is the case in the work of Sarah Kember and Joanna Zylinska, it necessarily raises the ethical dilemma between exchangeability and exploitation Nancy articulates in *L'Intrus:* on the one hand, there is the "natural political economy" that underlies the very possibility of receiving a heart transplant (analogous to the "formal" equality of capitalism that underlies the possibility of organ exchange); on the other, there is the intrinsic violence and erratic quality of transplantation. "I will never ask the question," Nancy writes, "how does one decide, and who decides, when a single available organ is suited to more than one potential graftee?"[4] He expresses discomfort with his privileged first world access to this natural political economy and then, with a remarkable rhetorical move, challenges this unequal "network wherein life/death is shared out," wondering whether "my heart can be a black woman's heart."[5] Nancy's text offers a breathtaking exploration of the foreignness of the intruder but not of the blackness of this woman whose foreignness is implicitly given.

In his accounting, Nancy's malfunctioning heart becomes a "stranger" disrupting his previous illusion of carnal coherence.[6] Heart transplantation rends apart a stable notion of identity and embodied being, revealing a difference at the heart of the self, which he illustrates using the figure of a black woman. Denis's film, in contrast, unravels from the blackness of this hypothetical woman and, in so doing, advances an implicit critique of media vitalism from a position of deep mediation: not only the depth of the relationship between her film and Nancy's text but also their common sense of a negative ontology that connects the body, the transplanted heart, and a work of art.[7] In each case, Nancy's philosophy articulates an ontological fissure between materiality and meaning for which the withdrawal of the body from identity constitutes the primary model. Like the transplanted heart, the mediated text arrives as a stranger disrupting the stability of sense and sensation. Even more profoundly, Denis's film approaches the natural political economy of which Nancy is the beneficiary as a deep mediation, a very specific type of mediated life—not a metaphoric life but an actual mediated living—that is always already unavoidably racial.[8] For him to *live,* writes Nancy, "it was necessary to receive another's, an other, heart."[9] In the transnational postcolonial world of Denis's film, the space opened up by Nancy's negative ontology is haunted by the heart of the black woman.

To say *The Intruder* enacts deep mediation does not mean, however, that Denis ascribes to an aesthetics of depth. On the contrary, while we can say that Denis's film visualizes the invisible interior of the protagonist's body who, by her design, is the "flesh and heart" of the entire film, she characteristically never ascribes to narrative or psychological depth.[10] Instead, here perhaps more than in any other one of her films, she establishes an aesthetics of exposure or what Nancy has described as "exscription."[11]

Denis's idea of the "graft," in fact, speaks very powerfully not only to the gradual detachment or "gentle sliding" that separates Nancy from himself when the transplanted heart reveals the incommensurability at his core, but also to the "sensation of a void already open in my chest" when, confronted with his mortality, "the mind pushes against nothing: nothing to know, nothing to understand, nothing to sense. The intrusion of a body foreign to thought."[12] While autobiographical in nature, Nancy's text articulates the fundamental withdrawal at the center of being that defines his ontological thinking.

We suggest Denis's "ethos" of cinematic form in *The Intruder* shares this negative ontology.[13] But there is an important difference: while for Nancy this "void" or passage through nothingness is an ontological feature, Denis presents it as a by-product of colonial violence and the violence of racialization. Indeed, while the commonality of human physiology preconditions the heart transplant that saves Nancy's life, the heart is also where a profoundly unsettling difference is lodged, where the "intruder" is located. In revealing difference in the innermost space of human physiology and psychology—exposing himself and his reader to the untenable slippage between bodily substance and discursive thought—Nancy at the same time exposes interiority as always already cut through with the externalities of racial and economic difference. This figural blackness operates in Denis's film as what Fred Moten would describe as an "invaginative" supplementarity and, tellingly as a "stolen, transplanted organ, always eliciting rejection."[14]

The blackness of this woman functions in Nancy's account as a "fugal, centrifugal, fugitive ontological and epistemological disruption."[15] In the terms Moten has extensively addressed in the second volume of his trilogy *consent not to be a single being,* she is "stolen life," and this is precisely the way she appears in Denis's film. Yet, while both Nancy and Moten reject the fetishization of the sovereign subject, they do so from very different positions—the former through a process of divesting and the latter through the "refusal of what has been refused" to you.[16] The difference between them bears directly on how the concept of life itself has been mobilized in media vitalism, where it is evoked to advocate for increasingly more processual conceptions of mediation, yet never explained, as if there was such a thing as an equal life "we" all have in "common."[17] The exclusion of blackness from sovereignty is not an accident or even a historical tragedy, Moten argues, but rather sovereignty's very ground, the precondition for its normativity. Black social life is sovereignty's undercommon. Like the intrusive heart that demands to be extruded, black flesh comes before biology in the very space that separates bare life from its symbolic representation in the sovereign subject.[18] Moten describes blackness as what is always already "more-and-less-than single being."[19] In the Kantian system, it functions as the specificity, the sensible singularity that ultimately offers the instantiation of the supersensible: the limit case against which the universal subject erects both itself and the intersubjective validity of its own judgment of taste.[20] Seen through its relationship to the production of value, as the nonvalue(ed) object that nevertheless produces so much value, it becomes clearer how "Blackness is (in) common. Blackness is (in) universal exchange." Said otherwise, "What if embodiment enforces abstraction? What if the individuative limits of the body make the movements and relations of equivalence and the form of value possible?"[21]

This seems to be the role the black woman plays in Nancy's text, where she appears to convey his desire to distance himself from the brutal logic of a (natural) political economy of (organ) exchange by virtue of her gendered and racial embodiment and specific individuation. Far from reproducing the epistemology of depth and surface, although it is located in the innermost "depth" of Western thought—indeed as the object that not even Levinasian phenomenology is capable of "intending"—blackness, argues Moten, is more properly approached under the rubric of the "surround," as a thought of the *outside*, an *ecstatic interiority* of the ones "whose being is a refusal of what is refused."[22] Therefore, once Nancy's black woman's blackness is evoked in *The Intruder* and her invaginated supplementarity recognized, it cannot be taken back and, in the hands of Denis's equally strong commitment against the delusions of sovereignty, it will necessarily reconfigure how foreignness is approached in her film. This three-way conversation between Nancy, Denis, and Moten forced by the black woman in Nancy's text articulates a profound critique of the assumption of sovereignty that still underlies media vitalism.[23] Against Kember and Zylinska, this black woman makes the statement "we are all Facebook" utterly nonsensical.[24] Furthermore, as the "exception to the state of exception," in the parlance of Carl Schmitt, Giorgio Agamben, and Eric Santner, blackness always escapes being tied to sovereignty as its point of origin.[25] On the contrary, Moten claims, blackness is "present to its own making."[26] As the stolen life of "thingly things," it does not reside in the interior of Heidegger's empty vessel.[27] Rather, it resides in its brokenness and, more precisely, in the "vibratory echo" that escapes from it.[28]

Expenditure

"A beating heart has been found," writes Nancy, bypassing the question of donation; instead, in Denis's film, a beating heart is left/abandoned on the snow. Unusable, expendable, supplementary—it goes to waste. With this move, which assumes the orientation of the blackness Nancy evokes as a figure for utter foreignness and intrusion, Denis's film wraps itself around the Other's heart not only by building the diegetic recipient, Louis Trebor, as an intruder, but also by structuring the film itself as the recipient of Nancy's *L'Intrus* as well as the film's body as "closed open."[29] More radically, it does so by turning the threat of organ rejection into a deliberate expenditure—a move that, we believe, forces the viewer to encounter this heart as a profound refusal of white settlers' self-possession. Blackness features here as what, building on Saidiya Hartman's *Scenes of Subjection,* Sarah Jane Cervenak and Jay Kameron Carter describe as essential *outdoorsness,* as the un/fenced terrain on which whiteness builds the universalist pretense of its freedom discourse. Thus, as "property acting improperly," blackness is "that which asserts vitality in the resistance to incorporation, and with that, an outness that's ecstatic to settlement."[30] The abandoned/transplanted heart's refusal of incorporation enacts a similar resistance in our view.

The abandoned heart is found during the central sequence of the film, a sequence that is inserted as a wedge in the place where Louis's transplant surgery is supposed to have taken place. Louis, a man with a dubious past, is played by Michel Subor, an actor Jean-Luc Godard uses for *Le Petit Soldat* (1963) in the role of Bruno Forestier—another man with a compromised past in the Algerian war, whom Claire Denis resurrects in her own *Beau Travail* (1999), where he is a commander in the French Foreign Legion. Louis, who lives alone in a cabin on the French-Swiss border, is first seen lying naked with his dogs in the woods. Then he swims in a lake and experiences an arrhythmia. After one more heart failure, this time while in bed with his girlfriend, and after inexplicably taking the life of a migrant attempting to cross the border in the darkness of the night, Louis opts for an "emergency solution" and departs for Geneva, where the payment and the transplant surgery will presumably occur. There, the film leaves him waiting in a hotel room, clutching his hunter's knife underneath his pillow. The next time Louis appears, he is in Pusan, South Korea, where a blind masseuse makes a tactile discovery of the scar the transplant has left on his chest. The surgery itself, it is implied, occurs in between the two shots of Louis in bed. Importantly, the transition

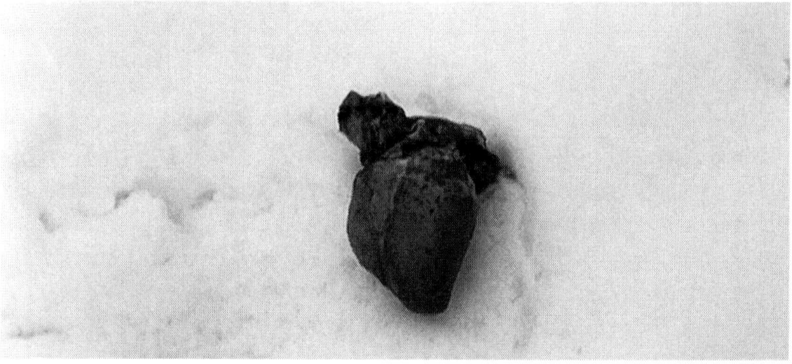

FIGURE 7.1. *The Intruder* (*L'Intrus,* Claire Denis, 2004).

between the two images (Louis falling asleep in Switzerland and then waking up in Pusan) is dilated by the insertion of a sequence in which a character referred to as the "forest girl" breaks into Louis's house and takes a bath surrounded by the two dogs Louis had to set free before traveling to Switzerland. In the next sequence, and without any transition, warning, or explanation, her blood-covered body is abandoned in the snow while a removed heart is left nearby (Figure 7.1). A handheld shot connects the two and, as the camera approaches the heart, the dogs enter the frame and begin to nibble at it.

It is in this obscene gesture of expenditure that we find the blackness that Nancy places in his text. With this move, Denis's film assumes the orientation of the woman's blackness (i.e., her utter foreignness and essential "outdoorsness") by turning the threat of organ rejection into deliberate wastefulness that refuses the very terms of exchange. In the film's economy it is important that the heart on the snow is approached through the close-to-the ground, handheld camera movement associated with the dogs. Often, in fact, the camera takes on the perspective of whatever is most vulnerable or closest to the ground, increasingly giving up its verticality as the consequences of the transplant wear on the protagonist and the film makes progressively unattainable the idea of the sovereign subject. This type of movement assumes the orientation of the black woman's heart, the perspective of the supplement that cannot be assimilated, reconciled, or absorbed. That is, this move enacts an intrusion of that same natural political economy, the deep life mediation, that would have allowed Nancy to hypothetically receive the heart of a black woman—not as a "passage through nothingness" that Nancy claims is experienced with a transplant, as the body is fully externalized and brought outside itself as it is kept alive—but rather as a passage through the amoral violence of physiological exchange: the implied killing to secure a black market heart and, even more obscenely, the expenditure of a heart seemingly procured in this way. Yet, by being abandoned in the snow and made unusable by the dogs, and thus removed from the very economy of exchange that triggered the forest girl's killing, this heart acquires an undeniable finality and demands to be approached on its own terms: not as a figure, stand-in, or substitute but rather something Other that irrupts into discourse, representation, aesthetics—"the intrusion on thought of a body foreign to thought," or, as Moten would say, as the "inappropriable ecstatics that goes along with the aesthetics."[31]

Negative Ontology: The Void

Here we note another point of tension this woman's blackness brings into focus. The failing heart intrudes upon the body's state of "normality" and forces the withdrawal of the illusory ground that once supported Nancy's sense and identity. The ground withdrawn, Nancy finds only a discomforting vacancy left in its wake. For him, Western philosophy is rooted in Christian religion and implicitly or explicitly rests on the desire to assert "this is my body (*hoc est enim corpus meum*)." The utterance insists *this* here *is* the body in its absolute presence. The body, he argues, gives metaphysical assurance to surface appearances, thus grounding the sovereign subject as singular embodied being. He writes, "*Hoc est enim* displays the body *proper,* makes it present to the touch, serves it up as a meal. The body proper, or Property itself, Being-to-itself *embodied.*" At the same time, the need to utter the phrase "this is my body" betrays a level of anxiety about the body's certitude. He continues, "Instantly, always, the body on display is foreign, a monster that can't be swallowed."[32] What is exposed is the strangeness of the Other inhabiting the self; paradoxically, the Other grounds the coherence of the self while simultaneously troubling it.

Blackness, argues Moten, cannot afford a body. There is no such thing as "my body," given that the "body," in the Western sense, is immediately stripped away from the black subject through the transatlantic slave trade, as Hortense Spillers has influentially argued.[33] Blackness, instead, is "animated flesh": an always-in-motion thinking *thing.* As such, in Moten's assessment of the phenomenological tradition, blackness is constitutively unthinkable and therefore un-*intended;* that is, blackness is literally outside of the purview of intentionality. In *The Universal Machine,* Moten insists in positing the thingness rather than the objecthood of blackness both to fully address the no-*thingness* of blackness in Western philosophy (i.e., Western philosophy's inability to "intend it," to *recognize* it as an object of knowledge) and to underscore its ecstatic internality to that same tradition of thought.[34] In other words, blackness might seemingly intrude into Nancy's own reflection on intrusion, but, in reality, it was always already there, agitating from within.

Perhaps we can read Nancy's negative ontology and profound divestment from the sovereign subject as already making a space for blackness to "intrude," but it is in Denis's film where we can see this fully taking place. Nancy sees this negative space, which is also an ectopic, fully externalized presence, exemplified in a work of art, which reflects a similar "coming of the stranger."[35] For Nancy, an image is primarily defined by the force of distinction.[36] Surrounded by a frame, an image is detached from its surroundings; the lines of the frame cut out the image, which produces an avisual underside.[37] At the same time, the viewer is invited to contemplate the spatial depth of the scene from a point of separation.[38] This voided "ground of the image" is a negative force that activates desire and draws the viewer into its imaginary depths. The image, in fact, remains a "threshold" because the viewer is neither inside nor outside the scene.[39]

This negative space "grounding" the image is figurally occupied in Nancy's text by the hypothetical black woman's heart and, in Denis's film, by a heart violently acquired and yet conspicuously left on the snow, in a sequence that is strategically placed at the "heart" of the film, in the place of the protagonist's substitute heart. What for Nancy is the force of negative withdrawal, and for Moten is "stolen life," becomes for Denis the violence of obscene expenditure: a life literally "stolen," subtracted to the demands of exchange as well as the logic of intentionality.

To read Denis's film as unraveling from the blackness of this heart is to read it from a position of life deeply mediated by race. The negative withdrawal of deep mediation can be seen in Nancy's description of film as a series of movements and interruptions that "discontinues continuously" like the diastole and systole of the beating heart.[40] In an interview, Denis remarked on the elliptical nature of the film, explaining, "I think it's important to cut before [starting in] the editing room. It's important to cut it already in the script."[41] The resulting film is characterized by discontinuous editing and negative space inviting "passage through the image, or to the image."[42] In an extreme example of this strategy of omission,

Denis told her cinematographer Agnès Godard that it was unimportant to include Subor in each shot because it is as if "every image came out of his mind."[43] Reading the film solely in terms of the protagonist's body would give in to Louis's obsession with his own sovereignty. Yet, this sovereignty is disrupted once the abandoned heart is left on the snow in the place where his own heart surgery is supposed to have been located.

In its editing and framing strategies, the film both offers a figuration of the hollow body Nancy describes in *L'Intrus* and enacts it through its discontinuities. The withdrawal, refusal, or force of negativity is further expressed through negative space on screen. After the film's title, a young Russian woman whose origin and identity remain unexplained emerges from the depths of a darkened cavern in the hillside. The cave, a visual rendition of Nancy's negative ontology, and an intrusion of the space where blackness is lodged, "opens an inside onto itself."[44] Instead of a window, the frame inside the frame is a black hole: "blackness as the un/fenced (fungible) terrain for whiteness's stately becomings."[45] A voice-over, which by many accounts does not belong to the character we see, warns the viewer and the protagonist that "your worst enemies are hiding inside, in the darkness, in your heart." The woman seen in the cave's threshold will haunt the film's protagonist throughout, appearing on every continent, at all important narrative points in the film, and even in a dream sequence in which his body is dragged by horses in the snow. "You'll never pay enough," she tells him, although he has already handed over the money that should cover his black market heart transplant.[46]

Most scholarship on Denis's film emphasizes how the fissure established at the film's opening is conveyed by the film's "closed openness" and the way its editing structure energizes the interval between frames. Martine Beugnet, in particular, calls attention to the motif of the double window used to introduce the viewer to Louis's first son as he is caring for his two young children.[47] Similar attention has been given to the alternation between lingering and contemplative wide-angle shots of still landscapes and moments of sudden internal kinesis within the frame.[48] Just as Nancy privileges films that are "making the gaze move, stirring it up, or even shaking it up, in order to make it carry further, close, more accurately," so too Denis uses long takes and shaky camera effects to "shake up" the gaze and transform visual perception.[49] Nancy admires such a gaze because it transports the viewer and enacts "a forgetting of the self, or rather: (de-)monstration that there will never have been a *self* fixed in a position of spectator, because a subject is never but the acute and tenuous point of a forward movement that precedes itself indefinitely."[50]

At the same time, these formal choices also offer a critique of Louis's predatory survival through his exploitation of stateless or un/fenceable bodies associated with brute mortality: the (female) nomad, the migrant, his own offspring—those with ambiguous ethnicities, nationalities, and parentage—in short, the people Moten would describe as "dispossessed" or the "refugee" (i.e., those who make a preferential option for radical displacement).[51] For Moten, these are the "dialecticians" who develop an "anaepistemology of passage," a "pedagogy of crossing," whose foundational moment is in the hold of the slave ship.[52] Nancy's black woman's blackness inhabits all instances of "transness" in the film: the insistence in transitional spaces, transient bodies seen in the fleeting glimpses of migrant bodies passing through the night, and the black market transactions, particularly their obscene expenditure. This latter category could be the film's deepest mediation, which, as Denis makes clear in a way that is not anticipated in Nancy's text, also involves different claims to sovereignty, including paternity and filiation. "The sovereign junkie is always high on his own supply and always in withdrawal," writes Moten, "which takes the violently antisocial form of the expansion of his territory."[53]

Filiation/Adoption

Nancy ponders this fact when he rephrases Denis's description of her film's relationship to his text as a graft—a concept that emphasizes supplementarity and rejection, including the unavoidable antagonism between competing immune systems—in terms of adoption. Writing about *The Intruder,* Nancy argues the heart transplant engenders "a disturbance that affects filiation."[54] From the point of view of the black woman's blackness, filiation is not disrupted by a sudden crisis of sovereignty but by a fundamental position of dispossession, although, in the slave economy, she is the only incontrovertible link to the reproduction of property and value.[55] True, in Denis's film Louis appears to have two sons, but his paternity is never conclusively established. The film does not fetishize legacy, inheritance, or blood relations, but rather "watches," so to speak, with a mixture of distance and contempt, as Louis does. Filiation is conveyed through a series of empty spaces, a negative ontology inhabited by an essential "outdoorsness."

In the film's diegesis Louis ends up in Pusan, South Korea, in order to purchase a ship that will take him to Tahiti to search for a son he fathered some thirty years prior. There, the Russian woman from the film's opening appears to remind him that although his heart might no longer be sick, it is certainly empty. Immediately after, the film cuts back to the Jura mountains, where Louis's French son, Sidney, breaks into his house and discovers a letter Louis had written to his son in Tahiti. Yet, once Louis gets to Tahiti, his son is nowhere to be found. Louis is told, "Your son belongs to us. He doesn't want to see you," a chosen invisibility that forces Louis to suspect that *any* young man he encounters *might* be his biological son. To fill this emptiness, Louis's local acquaintances arrange auditions to find a substitute son for him. Several local men are evaluated based purely on external appearances, but no one is found fit: too tall, too dark, looks "a bit like a white man," "too slanty-eyed," "looks Chinese." Eventually a man steps forward and under this pretense visits Louis in the hospital and eventually travels back to France with him. While this section of the film speaks directly to the "sovereign junkie," as we see with Louis enjoying the cosmopolitan mobility assured by his secretly amassed wealth and his multiple passports, the idea of paternity and filiation had been introduced much earlier, through Grégoir Colin's character, Sidney. He is the father of two young children and is shown feeding them, giving them a bath, and welcoming his wife at the door with attention, complicity, and desire. The film introduces Sidney even before Louis, yet the nature of their relationship is never conclusively established. The two meet only once. Louis is rude at first, but then eventually calls him *fils* (son), which in French, as in English, can be used figuratively as a paternal mode of address, not necessarily to refer to biological filiation. This connection places Sidney immediately in tension with the other "son," supposedly biological, for whom Louis is searching in Tahiti. Yet, at the end of the film, a handheld shot similar to the one that connected the forest girl to the heart abandoned in the snow connects Louis to Sidney's body—chest cracked open—which he identifies at the morgue in Tahiti. Underscoring filiation and perhaps attribution, this camera movement suggests that it is Sidney's heart that beats inside Louis's chest, although, from a temporal standpoint, this is suspicious, given that by this time Louis's scar has already healed (Figure 7.2). Yet, from the point of view of the invaginated blackness that already inhabits the natural political economy of which Louis is the beneficiary, *any* heart that beats inside his chest will necessarily be his son's.

Far from delivering closure, the unclear lineages between Louis, his son(s), and his transplanted heart enact a series of displacements and echoing resemblances that are never quite selfsame. As Louis searches for an abandoned son who is never found, the film cuts to grainy footage from *Le Reflux* (Paul Gégauff, 1965), an unfinished film featuring a young Michel Subor. Though the actor is the same individual, it is his younger self

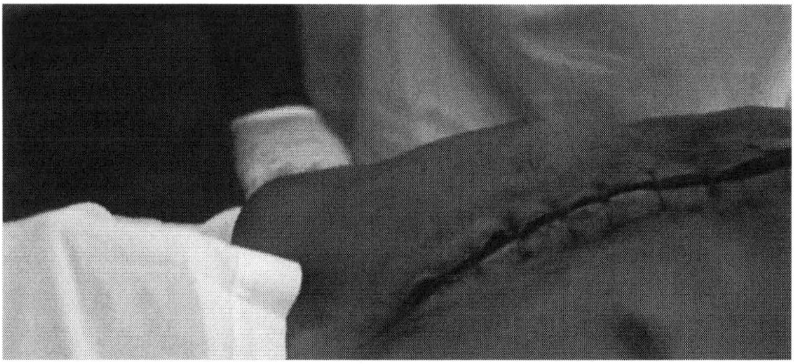

FIGURE 7.2. *The Intruder* (*L'Intrus,* Claire Denis, 2004).

displaced in time. This is a self that no longer resembles himself, a self playing another character (but in this case, the same character in *The Intruder*), that nevertheless doubles back on itself, tethered together even as these differences multiply. The deep mediation practiced by Denis emerges in the recurring beat of resemblances (and separations) in moments like this. Like the dubious parentage of the two sons in the film, as well as Tony, the third surrogate son, the cinematic images from 1965 and 2004 have ambiguous but unmistakable linkages to each other and to the world they (re)present. One passes on genetic material through biological reproduction, just as the photographic image passes on a photochemical imprint, but in both instances there is continuity marked by difference. When we are made to think the heart now beating in Louis's chest is that of the son he abandoned, there is the continuity of identity between father and son; earlier in the film, when Louis makes a request for a donor, he asks for a heart from someone who shares his "character," thus delusionally seeking an impossible consistency, continuity, and legacy all at once. But at what price? Louis is confronted with a fundamental fissure in the self, both as a physical cracking of the chest and as a breaking of the bonds of father/son in the separation of life and death. More deeply still, this impossible demand for a continuity of character, despite his callous willingness to resort to violence, has unavoidably exposed sovereignty's undercommon.

While the entire visual design of the film undermines Louis's own claims to sovereignty, the fact that the two missing hearts in the film are revealed by shots that both underline spatial and temporal continuity should not go unnoticed. At the morgue in Tahiti the camera moves along Sidney's body, from his feet, to the scar on his chest, to his face, and then tilts upward to

FIGURE 7.3. *The Intruder* (*L'Intrus,* Claire Denis, 2004).

show Louis standing over it. In the Jura mountains, the camera moves from the heart in the snow to the forest girl's lifeless body laying just a few feet away. Both hearts are unaccounted for. Even if it is Sidney's heart that beats inside Louis's chest, Louis's continued physical deterioration suggests it has gone to waste. His legacy, continuity, and bloodline have not been successfully secured. If racism is a structure of mediation "by bodies and bloodlines," as Paul Taylor has argued and W. J. T. Mitchell activates in his attempt to think of race mediatically, then here its implied epistemology of depth is fully evacuated and replaced with the ecstatically un/fenceable outdoors.[56]

At the end of the film, Louis boards a ship returning to France, with his surrogate son, while the coffin containing Sidney's body is loaded onto the ship. Yet the film proper does not end there, but rather comes full circle around the black woman's blackness with a scene of exhilarating kinesis and femininity featuring sonic and kinetic disruptions: the "wolf lady"—the dog breeder, played by Béatrice Dalle, who was Louis's neighbor in the Jura mountains—flies through the woods on a sled pulled by her dogs. The camera, mounted on the sled, alternates between her point of view onto the dogs and medium shots of her elated face as she urges her dogs to run faster and faster (Figure 7.3).

In terms of film form, this ending is reminiscent of the last scene in *Beau Travail* (1999), a film Denis made while already thinking about *The Intruder,* with which it shares a theme of expulsion/rejection of an "intruding" body. In the former film, Sergeant Galoup dancing alone in a Djibouti nightclub gains so much momentum that he rolls out of the frame.[57] In *The Intruder,* the energy of the sequence is assaulting to the fragility of

Louis's heart, threatening to tear it asunder. In both cases, the medium of film intervenes to mediate the ontological void in the self, but refuses to provide closure. "Very soon," writes Nancy, exhausted from his treatments, "you are just a wavering, a strangeness suspended between poorly identified states." He concludes, "The mediations are tiring."[58] Denis recognizes this fact, but in *The Intruder* she will not let the sovereign self stand: in the last scene her film becomes fully ecstatic in relation to Louis's imploding body, assuming the position of an inassimilable agitated flesh, a feminine outdoorsness that flaunts a radical refusal.

The idea of a "life" unmediated by race is a delusional fantasy only the sovereign subject can hope to hold on to. Nowhere as powerfully as in *L'Intrus* does the negative withdrawal of being coincide with the externality of "life," a life that even Nancy wonders why it is worth saving. Denis structures her film from the depth of racial mediation around the hypothetical black woman's blackness, her outdoorsness and invaginated supplementarity figured as an expendability that continuously haunts the sovereign subject. In doing so, she demands not only a qualification of the concept of life but also perhaps a critique of contemporary media theory's enduring attachments to sovereignty itself.

Notes

1. Throughout this essay, we will refer to Nancy's text using the French title and Denis's film using its English translation.

2. Jean-Luc Nancy, "*The Intruder* according to Claire Denis," in *The Films of Claire Denis: Intimacy at the Border,* ed. Marjorie Vecchio (London: I. B. Tauris, 2014), 147–62.

3. Sarah Kember and Joanna Zylinska, *Life after New Media: Mediation as a Vital Process* (Cambridge, Mass.: MIT Press, 2012), xv. See also Eugene Thacker, *Biomedia* (Minneapolis: University of Minnesota Press, 2004), and Jussi Parikka, *Insect Media: An Archaeology of Animals and Technology* (Minneapolis: University of Minnesota Press, 2010). Within adaptation studies, the film would fall within what Kamilla Elliott describes as the emerging "biocultural paradigm," in "The Adaptation of Adaptation: A Dialogue between the Arts and Sciences," in *Adaptation and Cultural Appropriation,* ed. Nicklas Pascal and Oliver Lindner (Berlin: De Gruyter, 2012).

4. Jean-Luc Nancy, *Corpus,* trans. Richard A. Rand (New York: Fordham University Press, 2008), 164.

5. Nancy, 166. Nancy advances the idea of a "natural political economy" in Nancy, "*The Intruder* according to Claire Denis," 149.

6. Nancy, 161.

7. We consider Claire Denis's relationship to her source texts—especially the more strictly philosophical ones, which would include *L'Intrus* as the inspiration for *The Intruder* and Roland Barthes's *A Lover's Discourse,* the inspiration for *Let the Sunshine In* (2017)—in terms of a profound entanglement complicated by the dynamics of investment and withdrawal, concealment, and unconcealment that can also be found in the original sources (Nancy and Barthes).

8. Nancy describes as *échotechnie* the originary technicity of being and complete medical-technologization of his "life," which both accentuates his ontological plurality and disperses him through time. He benefits from a transplant that twenty years prior would not have been possible and now lives with a heart that is twenty years younger than "him." His living is therefore both "out of joint" and a source of "disgrace." Stefanos Geroulanos and Todd Meyers, "A Graft, Physiological and Philosophical: Jean-Luc Nancy's *L'Intrus,*" *Parallax* 15, no. 2 (2009): 88, 92; and Laura McMahon, "Figuring Intrusion: Nancy and Denis," *Contemporary French and Francophone Studies* 12, no. 4 (2008): 466.

9. Jean-Luc Nancy and Susan Hanson, "L'Intrus," *CR: The New Centennial Review* 2, no. 3 (2002): 2.

10. Damon Smith, "*L'Intrus:* An Interview with Claire Denis," *Senses of Cinema* 35 (April 2005), http://sensesofcinema.com/2005/conversations-with-filmmakers/claire_denis_interview/.

11. Nancy, *Corpus,* 11.

12. For a discussion of the "graft" as a process of postcolonial critique, see Bishnupriya Ghosh, "Grafting the Vernacular: The Consequences of a Postcolonial Spectrology," *boundary 2* 31, no. 2 (Summer 2004): 197–218; Nancy, *Corpus,* 162, 163.

13. Nancy describes an "ethos" of looking in *Abbas Kiarostami: Evidence of Film* (Leuven: Exhibitions International, 2001), 16.

14. Fred Moten, "The Case of Blackness," *Criticism* 50, no. 2 (2008): 191, 186.

15. Moten, 191.

16. Fred Moten, *Stolen Life* (Durham, N.C.: Duke University Press, 2018), ix–xii.

17. See especially Kember and Zylinska, *Life after New Media.*

18. Moten, *Stolen Life,* 178–80.

19. Moten, xii.

20. Moten, 13. See also David Lloyd, *Under Representation: The Racial Regime of Aesthetics* (New York: Fordham University Press, 2019).

21. Moten, *Stolen Life,* 81.

22. Fred Moten, "There Is No Racism Intended," in *The Universal Machine* (Durham, N.C.: Duke University Press, 2018), 41.

23. Even more specifically, the black woman in Kant—and, we suggest, also in Nancy's account—occupies the space between two opposite fantasies: she is both a "regulative instrument" that provides the space for thought and also a "natural agent" enacting a profound bodily "deregulation." Moten, *Stolen Life,* 3.

24. Kember and Zylinska, *Life after New Media,* 158. Critiquing D. E. Wittkower's claim that "Facebook is people," Kember and Zylinska instead land on an equally reductive claim that "we are all Facebook" (159). As a biopolitical force, social media operates on the affective level, adapting, deforming, and re-forming relationships with the plasticity of a neurological network (160–61). Life, here, is treated as an unquestioned and universalizing concept without consideration for the biopolitical and geopolitical distinctions that produce the subaltern populations responsible for physically extracting the copper and silicon necessary for all of "us" to become "new media." Kember and Zylinka's concept of life does not stand up to Giorgio Agamben's biopolitical critique based on the concept of bare life, and even less to Moten's even more radical critique of Agamben.

25. Carl Schmitt, *Political Theology: Four Chapters on the Concept of Sovereignty,* trans. George Schwab (Cambridge, MA: MIT Press, 1985); Giorgio Agamben, *Homo Sacer: Sovereign Power and Bare Life* (Palo Alto, Calif.: Stanford University Press, 1998); Eric Santner, *On Creaturely Life: Rilke, Benjamin, Sebald* (Chicago: University of Chicago Press, 2009).

26. Moten, *The Universal Machine,* 185.

27. Martin Heidegger, "The Thing," in *Poetry, Language, and Thought* (New York: HarperCollins, 2001), 165–82.

28. Moten, "There Is No Racism Intended," 39.

29. We build and expand on McMahon's reading of Trebor's body as the intruder in McMahon, "Figuring Intrusion." Importantly, Nancy writes, "I am closed open. Through the opening passes a ceaseless flux of strangeness." And, as a result of the various medications and treatments, "my self becomes my intruder"; Nancy, *Corpus,* 168. See also Wim Staat, "The Other's Intrusion: Claire Denis' *L'intrus,*" *Thamyris/Intersecting* 19 (2008): 195–208.

30. Sarah Jane Cervenak and Jay Kameron Carter, "Untitled and Outdoors: Thinking with Saidiya Hartman," *Women and Performance: a journal of feminist theory* 27, no. 1 (2017): 47. Their essay builds on the second half of Hartman's field-defining *Scenes of Subjection: Terror, Slavery and Self-Making in Nineteenth Century America* (New York: Oxford University Press, 1997), as well as Fred Moten's work.

31. Fred Moten, *In the Break: The Aesthetics of the Black Radical Tradition* (Minneapolis: University of Minnesota Press, 2003), 201; cited in Cervenak and Carter, "Untitled and Outdoors," 46. The ecstatic possibilities of the aesthetic, and in particular of the surface, have been the subject of a growing art historical approach known as "surfacism." See Anne Anlin Cheng, *Second Skin: Josephine*

Baker and the Modern Surface (Oxford: Oxford University Press, 2011); Krista Thompson, *Shine: The Visual Economy of Light in African Diasporic Aesthetic Practice* (Durham, N.C.: Duke University Press, 2015); Uri McMillan, "Introduction: Skin, Surface, Sensorium," *Women and Performance: a journal of feminist theory* 28, no. 1 (2018): 1–15; Amber Jamilla Musser, *Sensual Excess: Queer Femininity and Brown Jouissance* (New York: New York University Press, 2018).

32. Nancy, *Corpus,* 5.

33. Hortense Spillers, "Mama's Baby, Papa's Maybe: An American Grammar Book," *Diacritics* 17, no. 2 (1987): 65–81.

34. Moten, "There Is No Racism Intended," 1–64.

35. Jean-Luc Nancy, *Muses,* trans. Peggy Kamuf (Palo Alto, Calif.: Stanford University Press, 1996), 76.

36. Jean-Luc Nancy, *The Ground of the Image,* trans. Jeff Fort (New York: Fordham University Press, 2005), 1.

37. Although Nancy does not use the term "avisual," which was introduced by Akira Lippit in *Atomic Light: (Shadow Optics)* (Minneapolis: University of Minnesota Press, 2005), it is still appropriate to explicate his negative ontology.

38. In *Ground of the Image,* Nancy writes, "What [an image] brings into such close proximity is distance" (4).

39. Nancy, *Muses,* 57.

40. Nancy, *Abbas Kiarostami,* 60.

41. Smith, "*L'Intrus.*"

42. Nancy, *Abbas Kiarostami,* 66.

43. Smith, "*L'Intrus.*"

44. Nancy, *Abbas Kiarostami,* 46.

45. Cervernak and Carter, "Untitled and Outdoors," 47.

46. On the theme of debt in the film, see Katrin Pesch, "Ecologies of Debt in Claire Denis's *L'Intrus/The Intruder* (2004)," *Studies in French Cinema* 17, no. 3 (2017): 236–51.

47. Martine Beugnet, "The Practice of Strangeness: *L'Intrus*—Claire Denis (2004) and Jean-Luc Nancy (2000)," *Film-Philosophy* 12, no. 1 (February 2008): 31–48.

48. Beugnet, "The Practice of Strangeness," 44–46; see also Pesch, "Ecologies of Debt."

49. Nancy, *Abbas Kiarostami,* 26.

50. Nancy, 66–67.

51. Moten, *Stolen Life,* 191.

52. Moten, 196.

53. Moten, 194.

54. Nancy, "*The Intruder* according to Claire Denis," 149.

55. See, at least, Spillers, "Mama's Baby, Papa's Maybe."

56. Paul Taylor, *Race: A Philosophical Introduction* (Cambridge, Mass.: Polity Press, 2004); W. J. T. Mitchell, *Seeing through Race* (Cambridge, Mass.: Harvard University Press, 2012).

57. See also Erika Balsom, "The Closing Sequence of Claire Denis's *Beau Travail*," *Frieze*, no. 200 (January–February 2019), https://frieze.com/article/closing-sequence-claire-deniss-beau-travail.

58. Nancy, *Corpus*, 169.

CHAPTER EIGHT

Inaudible Evidence

Counterforensic Listening in Contemporary Documentary Art

Pooja Rangan

This chapter concerns three documentary artists whose practices of deep listening make audible what documentary audiences may not notice about their own listening. Alison S. M. Kobayashi, James N. Kienitz Wilkins, and Lawrence Abu Hamdan all listen with forensic scrutiny to recorded voices as the basis of their artistic practice: a decades-old amateur wire recording, a downloaded transcript of a 2006 public hearing in a New York town, and cassette tapes of audio tests employed by immigration authorities. They listen for the material and medial conditions under which testimonial voices become audible or fade into obscurity, and employ speculative methods for attuning listeners to these conditions of audibility.

Kobayashi, Wilkins, and Abu Hamdan revive an epistemological stance that the critical documentary community regards as a relic of the past: objectivity. Objectivity has recently made a resounding return in what human rights scholars Thomas Keenan and Eyal Weizman have called the forensic turn in law, science, and popular culture: an epistemological shift that prioritizes the evidentiary value of objects over witnesses and the testimonial agency of experts over civilians in shaping what counts as scientific and legal evidence.[1] Forensics is, at its core, an aesthetic and rhetorical practice. Derived from *forensis,* the Latin term for "pertaining to the forum," that is, the place where the results of an investigation are presented and contested, forensics refers to the art of making a persuasive argument before a professional, political, or legal gathering.[2] This is why Keenan and Weizman call for artists to seize forensics from state control and democratize the forum of its interpretation, by devising speculative and daring practices for giving voice to—or making evident—testimony that eludes the forensic gaze and ear.[3]

The hybrid projects I discuss (Kobayashi's *Say Something, Bunny!*, Wilkins's *Public Hearing*, and Abu Hamdan's *The Freedom of Speech Itself*) do not simply "give voice" to that which is inaudible. They confront the vestiges of objectivity that inhere in conventional, acquisitive modes of documentary listening. Documentary listening is usually predicated on the placement of the listener at an objective remove from recorded sounds that permits an efficient transmission of their informational content. The three artists I discuss work with and against this forensic tendency in documentary listening. They employ speculative techniques such as performative narration, reenactment, animation, and essayistic digression for training audiences to attend to evidence that exists beneath the threshold of documentary audibility.[4] Rather than making their findings evident—that is, obvious, clear, and audible—they train audiences to become aware of the habits of documentary listening that actively shape what they hear as self-evident.

The active and reflexive approach to listening modeled by Kobayashi, Wilkins, and Abu Hamdan resembles what the composer Pauline Oliveros calls "deep listening." "Deep Listening," writes Oliveros, "is a practice that is intended to heighten and expand consciousness of sound in as many dimensions of awareness and attentional dynamics as humanly possible. . . . Deep Listening comes from noticing my listening or listening to my listening."[5] While their ultimate goals differ from those of Oliveros, Kobayashi, Wilkins, and Abu Hamdan are likewise critical of habitual and passive modes of evidentiary listening. Their works belong, I argue, within the long history of reflexive documentary practices that have troubled the insertion of documents into rhetorical and aesthetic frames that transform them into evidence. They model "engaged objectivity," a mode of knowledge production that, according to Weizman, reflects how the embodied and particular position of the knower actively shapes what can be known, rather than aspiring to neutral knowledge that "bears no trace of the knower."[6] Kobayashi, Wilkins, and Abu Hamdan listen for what forensic, democratic, and juridical modes of listening cannot hear about their own listening, employing tactics reminiscent of those that experimental musicians like Oliveros and Michel Chion have employed for disrupting grooved habits of listening. The engaged objectivity of their deep listening diagrams the counterforensic potential of documentary media, as a retrospective means of investigating the past, and as a projective means of building new languages for acting in the world.

Listening for the Unremarkable

"Alison should really be working for the F.B.I." These were the stunned words of Larry Newburge, upon learning that Kobayashi and her creative partner and cowriter, Christopher Allen, had put together an elaborate and uncannily accurate theater performance based on research into an amateur wire recording made by his brother David during family gatherings in the 1950s. Sold during an estate sale following David's death, a suitcase containing the broken wire recorder and a spool of wire found its way to Kobayashi through a friend of a friend. The contents of the suitcase included no identifying information, and only one name was uttered in full during the recording: Bunny Tannenbaum. Tracing a path from this name and other popular cultural references through census records, college yearbooks, and news archives, Kobayashi managed to reconstruct at least two different recording sessions separated by two years, down to the names of individual participants, who include the extended Newburge family, several neighbors, and even two family pets: a dog and a parakeet. Larry, then a young boy and now an elderly man in his seventies, is the only one still alive among those recorded. He is not alone, however, in wondering at the incongruous merger of performative and forensic impulses driving Kobayashi's process: as one critic comments, *Say Something Bunny!* (2016–present; henceforth *Bunny*) "falls somewhere between a less invasive version of Sophie Calle's conceptual forays into personal relationships and obsessive, forensic-minded podcasts and documentaries like *Making a Murderer* or *Serial*."[7]

If the lure of true crime documentary media lies in the promise of an encounter with the abnormal, deviant, or freakish, Kobayashi claims this frisson for the tedious, unspectacular matter of everyday life. Her video works often take discarded objects and media as a point of departure: a grocery list, a love letter, an answering machine tape. "I'm curious about representations of our experience that aren't memoir," Kobayashi has said of such objects. "The thing that interests me most is that it's both forgotten in some way and isn't necessarily prized by the maker as something that's relevant."[8] The forensic version of this documentary impulse will surely be familiar to readers. Recall, for instance, how filmmaker Andrew Jarecki pounces on the semiconscious confessional musings of Robert Durst, recorded onto the still "hot" microphone that Durst unwittingly wears into a bathroom during a filming break for the 2015 HBO miniseries *The Jinx*. Jarecki's quest for the aural "money shot" that would clinch the murder charges against Durst exemplifies a conventional, evidentiary mode of documentary listening that film scholar Irina Leimbacher describes as "acquisitive" and "inquisitive." In conventional nonfiction works, as Leimbacher notes, "Speech is chopped, elided, and reassembled by media makers to shape a message, emphasizing speech's referential function and minimizing, if not eliminating, digressions, paralinguistic expression, and reflection on vocalized speech itself."[9] Arguably, the true crime genre values paralinguistic expressions only insofar as they constitute a form of embodied proof that speaks louder than words: Durst's mutterings are a case in point.

Kobayashi found that the wire recording contained no shortage of potential money shots. The Newburges were evidently fans of musical theater: the recording is punctuated by impromptu musical performances, including a transporting rendition of the showtune "Yankee Doodle Boy" (made popular by the 1942 film *Yankee Doodle Dandy*) by Larry's grandfather Sam within the first five minutes. Kobayashi could easily have leveraged the nostalgic value of such a performance by shaping it into a short meme-worthy audio piece suitable for online circulation. Instead, she chose to craft an experience that would require an audience of twenty-five (the number of discrete voices she gleaned from the recording) to gather at a round table constructed specifically for this purpose and listen to the entire forty-five-minute duration of the wire recording, with the assistance of an illustrated transcript and performative commentary from Kobayashi (Figure 8.1).

Much of the recording consists of banter and overlapping conversations audible to different degrees, including, at one point, a barely discernible recording of a radio program that survived being recorded over. Self-conscious performances for the microphone give way to overheard discussions and lapses into silence as the attention of the Newburges and company drifts from the novelty of the recording device to the exigencies of everyday life: a forgotten turkey in the oven, a football game on television. Kobayashi describes the comfort of sitting with these silences as an earned intimacy that requires listeners to make time and space, "not only [for] the parts that are exciting to listen to but also the parts that are difficult to listen to and are challenging, and require patience . . . the parts that are poorly recorded, unintelligible on first listening."[10]

Kobayashi's commitment to sitting with sound that is not immediately legible models what Lisbeth Lipari calls "listening otherwise": an ethical attunement that, with practice, yields "an ability to *not* understand—to simply stay with something . . .—and just be with it, experience it, appreciate it, without having to fit it into some tidy box of 'understanding.'"[11]

FIGURE 8.1. *Say Something Bunny!* at Gallery TPW, February 2016. Photo credit Henry Chan.

Conventional documentary forms seldom reward listening that relinquishes control of meaning. Scholarly accounts of narrative cinema have tended to theorize spectatorial and textual mastery in connection with visuality and the depiction and perception of spatial depth (the placement of the viewer at a privileged viewpoint outside the image). In contrast, in the field of documentary, aurality has been linked with the quest for objective knowledge and mastery, or what Trinh T. Minh-ha once described as the "totalizing quest for meaning."[12] Documentary media appeal to their audience as masterful through the ear, using a range of testimonial forms and techniques of recording and editing that organize reality into a verbal explanation of itself. The listener is positioned at a privileged point of audition in deep auditory space, such that sounds resolve into intelligible information: voices emerge, noises recede.

After experiencing the performance twice, I have begun to think of *Bunny* as an ear-training exercise in which Kobayashi makes us confront the practiced forms of attention that permit such an auditory perspective. As she informs the audience, the transcript of the show (a work in progress) emerged from "hundreds of listens" that involved at least three discrete stages of listening: identifying sounds, identifying cultural references, and identifying characters and relationships. Every stage of listening led to new research; in turn, each new piece of information (such as census records) led her to hear differently. Kobayashi strategically withholds and releases such information to allow her audience to experience the frustrations and rewards of being immersed in a soundscape of raw, unedited material shot on location. Foreground and background blur. Crackling disturbances, blowouts, and tinny tones attest to the impression of voices on wire and to the vintage quality of the recording. Kobayashi's expansive embrace of this spectrum of sounds recalls "haptic listening," a noninstrumental attunement that Leimbacher has identified as a shared ethical commitment among recent experimental documentary makers. An unassuming counterpart of acquisitive and inquisitive modes of documentary listening, haptic listening redistributes attention from the informational content of sounds toward their sonorous *surface,* thereby creating a space for receiving melodies, tonalities, timbres, and rhythms.[13] Surface-listening thus paradoxically enables a profound openness to difference. Kobayashi's decision to "cast" each audience member as one of the characters heard on the recording has the effect of turning each listening individual into a vessel whose ears prick up at the dawning recognition of and identification with the grain of "their" assigned voice.

The distinctive timbre and grain of historical sound technologies and recordings are, for many listeners, a self-justifying pleasure: a fetish.[14] In addition to activating her listeners as readers of the artifactual past (a practice that filmmaker Irene Lusztig has, in a different context, called "embodied listening"), Kobayashi also situates the sounds of the wire recording as indexes of interlocking social relations and contexts.[15] Consider, for instance, the way she reads both presences and absences as interpretive windows onto the political and aesthetic history of sexuality. Despite giving the performance its name, twenty-year-old Bunny speaks only a few reluctant lines. David pushes Bunny to "say something" for the wire recorder, and her mother June adds, "Say your philosophy course," to which Bunny responds: "No" and "I'm mute." A few moments later, upon being teased to explain why she smokes Lucky Strike cigarettes, Bunny drawls: "pleasure." Here Kobayashi inhabits one of her many narratorial roles: providing psychological insight into character motivation. Adding to the repertoire of her predecessors in the performative documentary tradition (Michael Moore and Agnès Varda, for instance) who insert themselves into the diegesis to provide highly subjective and occasionally theatrical commentary, Kobayashi employs a different strategy: historical performance. She transforms, with the addition of a brown wig, a red turtleneck, a cigarette, and a copy of *The Second Sex,* into a moody, budding feminist. Peering up from Simone de Beauvoir's book with an attitude of youthful disdain, she reads aloud a passage on pleasure. Later in the performance, Kobayashi speculates that David's pursuit of pleasure, specifically the prurient pleasures of working in the adult film industry, may have strained his relationship with his family; this may have been one of the reasons the family recordings taper off after 1954. Despite their differences, Kobayashi discovers unexpected common ground among David, writer of the erotic video *Big Thumbs* (Richard Lipton, 1977) and his mother, Juliette, child star of the silent film *The Silent Master* (Léonce Perret, 1919): both films have all but disappeared from circulation. To paraphrase Jacques Derrida, their absence is the condition of archival presence. In her (ultimately successful) quest for *Big Thumbs,* Kobayashi traces a path through the ephemera in which its traces survive, from seventies-era adult video almanacs to present-day internet chat rooms. Faced with the complete disappearance of *The Silent Master* (the fate of the vast majority of silent films), Kobayashi employs the feminist strategy made famous by Cheryl Dunye in her film *The Watermelon Woman* (1996): she conjures it into presence through reenactment. In trademark amateur style, she performs every role with barely concealed and crudely costumed glee (Figure 8.2).

Weizman describes "forum" as "a shifting triangulation between three elements: a contested *object* or *site,* an *interpreter* tasked with translating

FIGURE 8.2. Re-creation of a scene from *The Silent Master* in *Say Something Bunny!* Image courtesy of Alison S. M. Kobayashi.

'the language of things,' and the *assembly* of a public gathering."[16] *Forensis* is, by extension, the practice of establishing "a relation between the animation of material objects and the gathering of political collectivities"—one that resembles what the Roman rhetorician Quintilian called *prosopopoeia,* or the practice of using the powers of aural demonstration to bring inanimate objects to life, by making them evident, credible, and persuasive.[17] This could just as easily be a description of Kobayashi's "documentary theater." Kobayashi convenes an assembly of people to assess a sound object from which she coaxes historical and political meaning, employing whatever means are at hand. Her reliance on performance, intuition, and speculation as persuasive means points to the theatricality of the forensic arts: indeed, *Bunny* makes it impossible to see *forensis* as anything *other* than a mode of performative documentary.

Listening to Democracy

It is an hour into the public hearing. So far, we have heard a team of three Walmart representatives offer in-house presentations and analysis on the impacts of a proposed expansion of the local Walmart in Allegany, New York, into a Supercenter. Then, following a lengthy explanation of the hearing process by the moderator, testimony for and against the proposed expansion is provided by seven townspeople (including four Walmart employees, who defend the corporation), each introduced by the chairman of the planning board. A sociology professor (bearded, neatly dressed) is now speaking in quiet but authoritative tones on the dire impacts of the proposed Walmart Supercenter on local jobs and the quality of life in the Allegany community. The camera frames his face tightly. As he speaks, it cuts away to anonymous close-ups of his audience: a pair of burly hands fidgets and knuckle cracks; another, more delicate, opens up a jar of Vaseline to moisturize; the moderator toggles his pen in his mouth. As the sociologist comes to the last sentences of his prepared statement, he turns around the room for dramatic effect, eyebrows knitted, then raised, enunciating each word as if to rouse a classroom of listless students: "In my own estimation, corporate Walmart is *not* a good neighbor. And a lot of people have already spoken to the quality of life in this community. And I think we *can* preserve the quality of life if we choose to. But if we go to a corporation that is *big, powerful,* and *not based in New York State* we stand the possibility of losing it. Thank you." He leaves the mic. More fidgeting. The moderator comes up and removes the mic from the stand, causing high-pitched feedback. He begins to speak: "Just a reminder, if you don't have time, and . . . we're trying to get to everybody . . . please submit in writing . . . uh, we'll take your comments in writing, it will have *just* as much weight as what was said here, just that it's . . . in writing." He puts the mic back.

I have just described a scene from James N. Kienitz Wilkins's 110-minute feature film *Public Hearing* (2012). A fictionalized reenactment based on a court transcript of a 2006 event in Allegany, New York, *Public Hearing* is one of several works that Wilkins has created by using standardized communication formats and forms (stock images, unedited BetaSP tape, blog posts, PowerPoint presentations, elevator pitches) as ready-made scripts and prompts. Wilkins's films are explorations as much of the narrative affordances of these mechanical and seemingly neutral forms as of their coded politics. The transcript of the Allegany public hearing is a case in point: the event was recorded in machine shorthand, "unpacked" by a stenographer or secretary, and made publicly accessible on the town's online archives as a PDF, a stable, circulable format.[18] Every verbal utterance and half-completed thought has been faithfully transcribed, yet the aura of the event has no archival trace. The conditions that shape *how* these utterances were spoken and heard—the architecture and atmosphere of the room; the twinned anticipation and boredom of waiting for one's turn; the nervousness that overcomes speakers confronted by an audience, dissolving prepared words into fragmented phrases; the digressive and magnifying focus that ennui can bring to the mannerisms, dress, gestures, and facial tics of speakers and to the furtive movements of listeners—are not part of the transcript. In the spirit of bureaucratic efficiency channeled by the moderator ("comments in writing will have as much weight as what is said"), they have been struck from the record. As data they have no weight, no information value.

Wilkins reanimates these structuring absences of the public hearing, using black-and-white 16mm film to extravagantly imbue this filed-away and forgotten event with material significance.[19] His process embraces the embodied and speculative bases of historical knowledge, as a process marked by losses in translation and transcription. Having downloaded the transcript, Wilkins retyped it into a screenplay program, inserted stage directions, and filmed a mixed cast of New York City–based professional and nonprofessional actors performing the "script." The process of filming, which took more than two months, required both the filmmaker and the performers to read between and around the words. For the performers, this involved filtering the text through their own physical and psychological experience, rendering it in a range of performance styles. As Wilkins

FIGURE 8.3. Sample close-up of speaker in *Public Hearing*. Image courtesy of Automatic Moving Co.

has noted, "Some of them attempted to memorize the lines, some of them just read the lines as they were, some slipped in their own thoughts . . . the movie is really a unique performance based on a close reading."[20] Wilkins's own interpretive and conjectural voice is palpable in the cinematography and editing. The film is shot entirely in close-ups, a choice that conjures the spatial disorientation that a reader of the transcript might feel (Figure 8.3).

Whereas the transcript registers presence only in the form of speech—"when you are done speaking, and if you are never referred to again, you are good as gone as far as the transcript is concerned"—Wilkins rematerializes the presence of auditors using reaction shots and cutaways to idle gestures that cumulatively construct a sense of audiovisual and temporal perspective.[21] These cutaways humorously capture the manner in which off-center details can expand and demand attention in a manner simultaneously consuming and mystifying: I cannot stop thinking, for instance, of a scene where the moderator inexplicably and with scrupulous care pours soda from his glass back into the can, weighs the two, then delicately pours some soda back into the glass to even them out.

Reenactment, for Wilkins, thus becomes a process of critically analyzing the archival record rather than reconstructing a linear story using the cinematic language of historical fiction or documentary realism. Wilkins is unconcerned with fidelity to the record: the challenge of containing the

FIGURE 8.4. Still from drone animation in *Public Hearing*. Image courtesy of Automatic Moving Co.

transcript within a feature-length narrative framework required him to cut participants from the original transcript if they repeated what someone else said for the third or fourth time. As he notes, "This editing is surely evidence of the authoritarianism of the self-appointed director, just like the moderators cutting people down to three minutes."[22] Instead, *Public Hearing* listens for and resuscitates the powerful narrative codes that determine democratic outcomes (in this instance, Walmart prevailed) but which the record chooses to ignore. The transcript tells us little, for instance, about the animated presentation that Walmart representatives assembled using the corporation's considerable resources. The staggering disparities between the power of Walmart's "testimony" and that of the townspeople, many of whom are working-class Walmart employees, are conveniently flattened. In place of the absent presentation, Wilkins inserts 3D animation that exaggerates this gap to the point of hilarity: ambient music accompanies a drone's-eye view that soars over crude renderings of trees and a parking lot to reveal an anonymous rectangular structure that slowly recedes from view as we pull away (Figure 8.4). The animation is as rich in irony as it is poor in information. Its function in Wilkins's film is purely rhetorical: to demonstrate how evidentiary value comes from elsewhere than the present moment of testimony.

The indifference of the transcript to these distinctions is evidence of a pseudodemocratic mode of listening that is oblivious to its habitual biases. Wilkins's investment in disrupting these habits aligns him with experimental musicians who have sought to attune listeners to what they habitually tune out. For instance, the sound theorist and composer Michel Chion has advocated "acousmatic listening" (colloquially called "blind listening") as a method for recognizing and overcoming common biases in listening habits, including causal and semantic orientations toward gathering information about the source of sound and its linguistic contents above all else. Inspired by his predecessor Pierre Schaeffer, Chion believes that "acousmatic sound draws our attention to sound traits normally hidden from us by the simultaneous sight of the causes."[23] Sightedness, in other words, can often have the effect of making us oblivious to what we look for, and how that seeing impacts hearing.

Wilkins listens for that which democratic listening renders inaudible by dint of what it makes audible. Hearing, he shows, can similarly have the effect of making us oblivious to what we listen for. His speculative approach to inhabiting the transcript's nonhearing as a point of audition reminds me of Anri Sala's *Intervista: Finding the Words* (1998), a film about speech and listening under communism. Sala discovers a soundless 16mm newsreel film from the 1970s that shows his mother, Valdete, giving a speech at a communist youth rally, flanked by Albanian party leader and dictator Enver Hoxha. Valdete is unable to recall what she said, and Sala's interviews with surviving members of the party leadership do little to help fill in the gaps, so Sala devises an unusual solution: he solicits the assistance of students and faculty from a school for the Deaf, skilled in sign language and lipreading, in reconstructing Valdete's speech, which he then inserts into the film as captions. The results, a series of doctrinaire slogans, shock his mother, who exclaims: "Those aren't my words!" Later, Valdete realizes that her new political reality has changed what she is capable of saying and hearing. She reflects: "We lived in a deaf and dumb system where all spoke with one mouth and one voice." Sala's use of lip-reading (or Deaf listening) enables him to subvert this ableist metaphor to arrive at surprising insights about how the communist consensus might have shaped the listening of so-called hearing subjects. Under so-called democratic circumstances too, Wilkins suggests, reconstructing what the ear of democracy cannot hear about its own listening may require unorthodox measures.

Listening with an Accent

What happens when the ear of the law operates not through the repression of free speech but rather its incitement and objectification? Artist and scholar Lawrence Abu Hamdan is propelled by this question. Since 2010, Abu Hamdan has developed a body of work spanning critical essays, essayistic documentaries, and installation art interrogating what Naomi Waltham-Smith has called a biopolitical turn in legal listening: a "perversion of the voice whereby what is meant to be the support of political representation, self-expression, and agency is turned against the speaking subject."[24] While this is in some ways the founding philosophical dilemma of speech, as Waltham-Smith notes, Abu Hamdan's research-based practice uncovers intensified attacks on free speech in late twentieth-century juridical practice. Much of his work traces and responds to the emergence of "forensic listening," a radically objective and scientifically specious mode of juridical listening that has found its widest application in the speaker profiling of asylum seekers via forensic speech analysis, also known as LADO (Language Analysis for the Determination of Origin) or, more colloquially, "the accent test."[25]

LADO weaponizes *prosopopoeia*, or the art of "giving voice" and making evident: human rights claimants are incited to speak in a manner designed to be comprehensible to their interlocutor for which they are then held culpable.[26] The protocol for LADO currently employed by immigration authorities across Europe and Australia for deciding on the asylum cases of undocumented migrants is as follows: a brief telephone interview is organized between the asylum seeker and professional interpreters, typically employees of commercial firms subcontracted by government agencies with translation skills but no formal training in linguistics. These nonspecialist interpreters, working from audio recordings of the interviews, are tasked with assessing whether the asylum seeker's accent corresponds to the typical features of speech in their claimed place of origin. Their assertions are then reworked by linguists and turned into forensic reports for use in court during deportation hearings.[27] LADO derives its legitimacy from forensic linguistics, the science that studies the molecular constitution of individual phonemes to glean information about the conditions of production (including recording conditions), and details such as the age, health, and ethnicity of a voice and the geographic origin of its accent. However, forensic linguists and phoneticians widely acknowledge that voices cannot be studied outside the social, cultural, political, and technical contexts that mediate their production, whereas LADO treats the voice as an objective *thing* that can be separated from the bodies of the speaker and listener and examined as evidence.[28]

Abu Hamdan's *The Freedom of Speech Itself* (2012) is a meditation on the biopolitical implications of objective listening in the contexts both of the law and of documentary.[29] Introduced by Abu Hamdan as "a documentary about the politics of listening," the thirty-four-minute audio essay unfolds, in fact, as an interrogation of *documentary* listening and its complicity with forensic modes of juridical listening. The essay is structured like an onion, with layers of "expert" interpretation enclosing the testimony of Mohammed, one among countless asylum seekers who has been marked for wrongful deportation as a result of LADO—in this instance, as a result of how he pronounced the word for another innocuous vegetable: tomato. Abu Hamdan mimics the LADO protocol in the way he narrates and analyzes Mohammed's experience. The click of a tape recorder materializes the mediating presence of an auditor, followed by Abu Hamdan's voice asking Mohammed the types of questions that Mohammed might have been asked by his interviewer: "Where are you from?" "Can you speak Arabic?" Abu Hamdan soon transitions to questions about Mohammed's experiences with LADO. Mohammed responds, alternating between English and Arabic, that he came to the United Kingdom as an asylee from the city of Jenin in the West Bank of Palestine. He was apprehended and detained by police and forced to undergo accent analysis to prove his origins after UK immigration authorities lost his Palestinian identity card. He was then asked to speak to an interviewer in Sweden who sounded, to Mohammed, like an Iraqi Kurd. The interviewer spoke an extremely formal version of Arabic so different from Mohammed's dialect that Mohammed had to shift his manner of speech and pronunciation in order to be understood by his interviewer. At the end of the twenty-minute interview, Mohammed's interviewee concluded that the way Mohammad pronounced the word for tomato (*banadora,* which the interviewer deemed more typical of Syria, instead of *bandora,* as Palestinians might be expected to pronounce it) definitively proved Mohammed's Syrian origin, even though the Palestinian city of Jenin is located merely twenty-two kilometers from the Syrian border.

Abu Hamdan sandwiches Mohammed's responses between translation from an interpreter who interjects when Mohammad speaks in Arabic, and critical commentary from forensic linguists and sociolinguists. These "experts" provide valuable insight into the various forms of prejudice built into LADO: we learn that interviewers are usually located in a different country than the asylum seeker; that they usually have no firsthand knowledge of the linguistic cultures or regional landmarks about which they quiz asylees; that they make their assessments without the crucial visual cues that body language and gesture can provide; that interviews can be as brief as fourteen minutes; that their reports offer opinion in the guise of certainty.

We learn, to paraphrase Emily Apter's reading of Abu Hamdan's work, that LADO treats the subjective impressions of lay listeners as objective proof of the difference between those who get to enjoy the liberties and privileges of citizenship and others who are marked for "misattributed citizenship, internment in holding pens, imprisonment, and deportation."[30] Abu Hamdan's decision to cut between expert voice and refugee voice adds another layer of commentary to these insights. It makes evident how documentary's vocal conventions shape distinct listening modes that affirm the difference between narrating voices that *simply speak* in a manner that seemingly requires no translation or mediation, and narrated voices that are *spoken about,* analyzed, interpreted, captioned, or subtitled.

Abu Hamdan's editing thus traces the traffic between the LADO interview and the documentary interview as medial sites where oral and aural difference are policed, reinforcing discriminatory habits of listening that are nonetheless made to seem neutral or unmarked. Listening to the audio essay, I am aware of how it redistributes my auditory attention. I hear not the *how* of Mohammed's speech, but *what* he has to say about LADO, and in the same movement, I notice myself listening not for *what* the experts have to say but *how* they say it. When Abu Hamdan follows the Mohammed sequence with a performative interview with Mohammed's London-based translator, my attention shifts again, this time, to *how my own accented listening* informs these perceptual shifts. The exchange among the two men illustrates how the answer to the seemingly simple question "Where are you from?" is contoured by Abu Hamdan's accented auditory expectations:

> So, where are you from?
> What do you mean, I'm from Hackney.
> Yeah Hackney, but . . . you're Danish, aren't you?
> No, I'm Palestinian. Well, I grew up in Denmark.
> I see, so you're from where in Palestine?
> I'm not from Palestine.
> So, where are you from?
> Well, we're Palestinians from a refugee camp in Lebanon, Al-Hilweh.
> Ah ok, so you were born in Lebanon?
> No, I was born in Dubai.
> Ok. So how come you have an American accent?
> What do you mean?
> Well, you have this like American twang to your English.
> Oh its just . . . you know . . . Eddie Murphy and uh, Stallone and all these guys y'know?

So you're from Hollywood?
Nah, nah, I'm from Hackney.

The Freedom of Speech Itself forcefully argues that accent can be located neither in the speaker nor in the ear of the listener but in the space between them. Abu Hamdan reflects: "The instability of an accent, its borrowed and hybridized phonetic form, is testament not to someone's origins but only to an unstable and migratory lifestyle, which is of course common among those fleeing from conflict and seeking asylum, often spending years getting to the target country and living in diversely populated camps along the way."[31] This could just as easily be a description of the inevitability—and instability—of accented listening in the age of mass migration. A case in point: Apter transcribes the very passage that I have transcribed here, but in a telling illustration of the point being made in it, Apter omits the name of the refugee camp Al-Hilweh, perhaps because she heard it as a sound rather than a noun, or did not hear it at all.[32] Abu Hamdan concludes his audio essay with a question: Should the freedom of speech not be expanded to include the ways in which we are heard? I hear in his work a different question and provocation: How can documentary forms be used not to "give voice" but rather to train audiences to listen differently, to listen (to how they listen) with an accent?

Coda

"[inaudible]," writes Abu Hamdan, "is how transcribers and stenographers categorize human speech or any other sound that cannot be heard or could not be made intelligible. A voice that is impossible to write, a sound that cannot be transcribed, speech that does not form part of the historical record, except in its very inaudibility. The threshold of audibility is the threshold of the political. Those [inaudible] voices and sounds, not yet intelligible to the political ear, are the site of struggle in the politics of listening."[33]

This statement framing Abu Hamdan's artist book of the same name not only articulates the stakes of his critical and creative practice but also offers a framework for understanding the political significance of the practices of deep listening that Kobayashi and Wilkins stage for and cultivate in their audiences. Abu Hamdan's emphasis on the ear as a site of struggle in the politics of listening highlights, for me, the *counterforensic* implications of the ways in which Kobayashi and Wilkins innovate new documentary forms to attune us to sonic events and experiences that conventionally remain beneath the threshold of documentary audibility. Each of these three artists confronts how documentary forms have been used to habituate us to modes of listening that are in turns acquisitive, bureaucratic, and discriminatory even as they are framed as natural or objective. These habitualized modes of documentary listening, they show, play a profound role in reinforcing the ways in which recorded speech is archived, mobilized, and politicized. For Kobayashi, Wilkins, and Abu Hamdan, documentary listening is anything but self-evident. It is a site, rather, of speculation, reflection, and research. Deep listening, for them, is reflexive listening: a listening that listens for how it represents reality to itself.

Notes

1. See Thomas Keenan and Eyal Weizman, *Mengele's Skull: The Advent of a Forensic Aesthetics* (Berlin: Sternberg Press, 2012), esp. 11–14.

2. See Keenan and Weizman, 28.

3. Weizman is the founder of Forensic Architecture, a research agency that brings together interdisciplinary teams of architects, filmmakers, artists, scientists, and lawyers to produce evidence for use in legal as well as quasi-legal contexts such as citizen-organized truth commissions and tribunals, and human rights and environmental protection agencies. In a recent book theorizing the work of this group (with which Abu Hamdan has frequently collaborated), Weizman notes that one of its central interventions has been to legitimize the use of speculative methods such as surveys, models, animations, videos, and other techniques borrowed from art and architecture as counterforensic arts of persuasion. See Eyal Weizman, *Forensic Architecture: Violence at the Threshold of Detectability* (New York: Zone Books, 2017), 64–71.

4. The artists have been exhibited and discussed in spaces and venues that have emerged in response to the growing range of work exploring the seam between documentary and art. These include exhibition venues such as Union Docs (Brooklyn-based center for documentary art), Nightingale Cinema (Chicago-based microcinema devoted to independent and experimental film), and Western Front (Vancouver-based artist-run center for contemporary art and media); festivals and series devoted to innovations in hybrid filmmaking such as CPH:DOX, Camden, and The Art of the Real; museums of contemporary and moving-image art such as MoMA and the Tate Modern; and publishing platforms for critical discourse on artistic practice such as e-flux and World Records.

5. Pauline Oliveros, *Deep Listening: A Composer's Sound Practice* (New York: iUniverse, 2005), xiii–xiv.

6. Weizman, *Forensic Architecture,* 74–75; Lorraine Daston and Peter Galison, *Objectivity* (New York: Zone Books, 2007), 17.

7. See Elisabeth Vincentelli, "The Detective Was a Performance Artist: The Evidence Is Now a Show," *New York Times,* June 26, 2017, https://www.nytimes.com/2017/06/26/theater/say-something-bunny-alison-s-m-kobayashi.html. Larry Newburge, as quoted, appears in this article.

8. Alison S. M. Kobayashi, interview with the author, August 31, 2018.

9. Irina Leimbacher, "Hearing Voice(s): Experiments with Documentary Listening," *Discourse* 39, no. 3 (Fall 2017): 295.

10. Kobayashi interview.

11. Lisbeth Lipari, *Listening, Thinking, Being: Toward an Ethics of Attunement* (University Park: Pennsylvania State University Press, 2014), 136.

12. Trinh T. Minh-ha, *When the Moon Waxes Red* (Bloomington: Indiana University Press, 1991), 29.

13. See Leimbacher, "Hearing Voice(s)," 293, 299.

14. As Jonathan Sterne notes, both the object and the sound it makes become part of the commodity fetish of musical and recording instruments. See Jonathan Sterne, "Spectral Objects: On the Fetish Character of Music Technologies," in *Sound Objects,* ed. James A. Steintrager and Rey Chow (Durham, N.C.: Duke University Press, 2018), 96.

15. See D. Andy Rice, "The Sense of Feminism Then and Now: *Yours in Sisterhood* (2018) and Embodied Listening in the Cinema Praxis of Irene Lusztig," *Senses of Cinema,* no. 89 (December 2018), http://sensesofcinema.com/2018/feature-articles/the-sense-of-feminism-then-and-now-yours-in-sisterhood-2018-and-embodied-listening-in-the-cinema-praxis-of-irene-lusztig/.

16. Eyal Weizman, "Introduction: Forensis," in *Forensis: The Architecture of Public Truth,* ed. Forensic Architecture (Berlin: Sternberg and Forensic Architecture, 2014), 9.

17. Weizman, 9–10.

18. See Paul Dallas, "Lost in Translation: Public Hearing," *Filmmaker Magazine,* May 7, 2014, https://filmmakermagazine.com/84869-lost-in-translation-public-hearing/#.XEjLZc9KgdU. Wilkins reports that the court stenographer undoubtedly took liberties while "unpacking" the shorthanded transcript, as evidenced, for instance, by the numerous errors and incomplete sentences with which the official transcript is littered. Nevertheless, "In the appendix of the original, there is a sworn statement attesting that what she typed is true." See Michael Guarneri, "Interview with James N. Kienitz Wilkins," *Bomb Magazine,* February 5, 2015, https://bombmagazine.org/articles/james-n-kienitz-wilkins/.

19. Wilkins additionally produced a 106-hour-long film documenting the making of *Public Hearing* called *Public Hearing in Progress.* Shot on discarded VHS tapes using a security camera that Wilkins installed on location during the production of his film, *Public Hearing in Progress* was streamed "live" by ACRE TV.

20. Guarneri, "Interview."

21. Guarneri.

22. James Wilkins, discussion with the author, May 15, 2019.

23. See Michel Chion, "The Three Listening Modes," in *Audio-Vision: Sound on Screen,* trans. Claudia Gorbman (New York: Columbia University Press, 1994), 32.

24. Naomi Waltham-Smith, "Excursus 2: Lawrence Abu Hamdan's Border Crossings," in *Shattering Biopolitics: Militant Listening and the Sound of Life* (New York: Fordham University Press, forthcoming 2021).

25. Abu Hamdan reports that the forced mass migrations that followed the War on Terror became the catalyst for the implementation of LADO by immigration authorities around the world and that Australia, Belgium, Germany, the Netherlands, New Zealand, Sweden, Switzerland, and the United Kingdom now rely on LADO. See Lawrence Abu Hamdan, *[inaudible]: A Politics of Listening in 4 Acts* (New York: Sternberg Press, 2016), 21; and Lawrence Abu Hamdan, "Aural Contract: Forensic Listening and the Reorganization of the Speaking Subject," in *Forensis,* 72.

26. See Abu Hamdan, "Aural Contract," 74–75.

27. See Lawrence Abu Hamdan, "Act 1: Listening to Yourself," in *[inaudible],* 21. Abu Hamdan reports that two Swedish companies, Sprakab and Verified, currently dominate this market. He also notes that in response to criticism from linguists, numerous governments now base their accent analysis on recorded monologues from asylum seekers in lieu of interviews. Abu Hamdan's account here updates his previous research on LADO; see Abu Hamdan, "Aural Contract," 72.

28. Abu Hamdan, "Aural Contract," 70, 72

29. I have chosen to focus solely on the audio essay portion of *The Freedom of Speech Itself.* The installation of this work at The Showroom in London (February 1 to March 17, 2012) also included sculptural forms of voiceprints (or voice-fingerprints) constructed from foam, illustrating the frequency and amplitude of two different voices saying the word "you." Emily Apter writes: "The cartographic rendering maps the origins of phonemes while the acoustically absorbent foam slabs become a listening agent; both give material form to the fusion of voice and territory." See Emily Apter, "Shibboleth: Policing by Ear and Forensic Listening in Projects by Lawrence Abu Hamdan," *October,* no. 156 (Spring 2016): 105. Apter's essay has been reprinted as the foreword to Abu Hamdan's artist book.

30. Apter, "Shibboleth," 111.

31. Abu Hamdan, "Aural Contract," 73.

32. See Apter, "Shibboleth," 106.

33. Lawrence Abu Hamdan, "Introduction," in *[inaudible].*

CHAPTER NINE

To Narrate or Describe?

Experimental Documentary beyond Docufiction

Erika Balsom

In her 2013 text "Art or Life? Documentary Jargons of Authenticity," artist and theorist Hito Steyerl asked, "Truthfulness instead of genuineness: can documentarism resign itself to being art and relinquish the jealously guarded property of genuine life? Can it relinquish its inherent 'passion for the real' and the paranoia of authenticity it engenders?"[1] Steyerl posed these as questions, but she knew the answers already. Countless critics, curators, art historians, film scholars, and artists—including Steyerl herself—have, over the last two decades, described the documentary turn in contemporary art in just such terms, or have made work in this vein. At least since Okwui Enwezor's Documenta 11 in 2002, documentary practices have been a prominent feature of contemporary art, with a spate of documentary-themed exhibitions occurring in the early years of the millennium alongside a more generalized embrace of artistic practices making a claim on actuality, both in gallery spaces and in film festivals such as CPH:DOX and FIDMarseille.[2] While the field is pluralistic, encompassing an array of aesthetic styles and topical concerns, notions of doubt, contamination, hybridity, and impurity recur repeatedly as critical preoccupations. Fictionalization is never far out of sight, viewed not as an unfortunate inevitability but as a quality to cultivate; according to this discourse, its presence is needed if the artist is to adopt a sophisticated approach to the representation of reality. As art historian T. J. Demos writes, "The deepest understanding of reality, particularly a traumatic one, necessitates *an engagement with the fictional and conflictual aspects of images*. This realization allows me to situate this work on the cutting edge of globalization's system of images, wherein *the representational link between sign and referent has been severed and truth must be reinvented on the grounds of uncertainty.*"[3] Accounting for documentary practices included in Documenta 11, art historian Linda Nochlin suggested, "Many of these works function in the documentary mode but transform and expand it, making it into *a kind of hybrid* that appeals not merely to curiosity, a quest for specific information about some topic, but to *imagination,* political consciousness, and *unconscious fears and desires.*"[4]

Art's infatuation with documentary is equally a critique of documentary, or at least of a certain kind of documentary. Lionizing fictionalization and imagination, the theorization of documentary in contemporary art relies on an implicit denigration of the observational mode, which accords primacy to the mechanical operation of the lens-based capture of physical reality.[5] To record and re-present the appearances of the phenomenal world, without injecting a charge of overt fictionalization, would entail being too taken with a "passion for the real" and the "paranoia of authenticity" Steyerl derides. It would be painfully uncreative, shackled to the legacy of a discredited scientism. As Paolo Magagnoli notes, artists typically recruit strategies very other than those associated with the automatism of recording: "The distinction between documentary and fiction is blurred by the works at issue here, which deploy a range of representational strategies conventionally associated with theatre, literature, and drama: re-enactments, artificial staging of the profilmic, non-indexical media (e.g. animation and drawing), essayistic and autobiographical narratives, repetition and the manipulation of archival documents."[6]

The vitality of the documentary impulse in contemporary art might be understood as a symptom of a fatigue with postmodernist textualism, as evidence that this paradigm has now given way to a new cultural dominant. While this is very persuasive and in some respects accurate, one must simultaneously take care to weigh how substantially postmodernist discourse continues to inform theory and practice in this domain. As documentary scholar Brian Winston put it in 1995, "Postmodernist concern transforms 'actuality,' that which ties documentary to science, from a legitimation into an ideological burden."[7] When Steyerl urges documentary to "resign itself to being art," she is calling for it to unload precisely this weight. Postmodernist thought launched an assault on concepts such as objectivity, authenticity, and neutrality in the name of a progressive politics, rightly problematizing their naturalization as profoundly ideological and showing them to be historically contingent social constructions. The referential power of lens-based capture did not escape unscathed. Art historian John Tagg assailed as mere mystification Roland Barthes's conviction that the *noeme* of photography is "that-has-been," that photography ontologically delivers "the confirmation of an existence." He argued instead that whatever power photography possesses is a matter of history rather than alchemy: the photograph "is not the inflection of a prior (though irretrievable) reality, as Barthes would have us believe, but the production of a new and specific reality, the photograph, which becomes meaningful in certain transactions and has real effects, but which cannot refer or be referred to a pre-photographical reality as to a truth."[8] If the image is conceived not as trace but as the product of representational conventions and social forces, a picture constituted by the play of codes, with the "representational link between sign and referent" severed, as Demos puts it, documentary's dependence on an indexical claim to reality becomes a liability. Documentary must instead reinvent itself on the new groundless ground of hybridity. As digitization raised the specter of invisible manipulation, weakening the image's testimonial value, and as Baudrillard prophesied the "fading of the real," the vanguard of documentary practice turned to artifice, reflexivity, and performativity, "blurring boundaries" and establishing a new critical paradigm that understood the observational mode as irremediably lured by the fata morgana of immediacy. As the new millennium began, critics would repeatedly point to precisely these characteristics as typical of contemporary art's documentary turn. For many, these strategies were evidence of a sophisticated approach to questions of truth that favorably differentiated them from that poor straw man, "traditional documentary," whose mystified beliefs in the apparatus's ability to capture reality were to be abandoned.

Steyerl's questions must be understood within the context of these theoretical debates. Although her queries are formulated in the register of ability, they are more properly situated in the domain of prescription, setting out an agenda for practice. Documentary should not take as its priority the tasks of observing, recording, or describing, for this would shackle it to the legacy of a bad scientism, a naive objectivity, a stupid artlessness. Documentary—to be sophisticated, which is to say, to be art (or perhaps it is the other way around)—must plunge headlong into the realms of imagination and subjectivity, fiction and emotion. Evidential claims to actuality are to be cast aside.

When Demos writes of the "deepest understanding" of reality and Nochlin of "unconscious fears and desires," both turn to a penetrative rhetoric, implicitly opposing the profundity of the practices they champion to the superficiality of others. In this they are not alone. Werner Herzog's widely known manifesto "The Minnesota Declaration: Truth and Fact in Documentary Filmmaking" (1999) also contains topographical thinking that aligns docufiction strategies with the inner reaches of human creativity, while condemning the observational mode as but mechanically skimming the surface. Herzog elaborates his critique of cinema vérité as "a merely superficial truth, the truth of accountants," writing, "There are deeper strata of truth in cinema, and there is such a thing as poetic, ecstatic truth. It is mysterious and elusive, and can be reached only through fabrication and imagination and stylization."[9] Faced with the appearances of the world, which may be chaotic, deceptive, or simply banal, the gifted filmmaker must penetrate this superficiality and uncover the fundamental truths that lie beneath it by deploying a contaminated docufictional form. Truth is the domain of subjectivity and emotion, to be distinguished from facts and surpassing them in importance.[10] In *Little Dieter Needs to Fly* (1997), Dieter Dengler reenacts his experiences as a Vietcong prisoner of war, accompanied by Herzog; in *Lessons of Darkness* (1992), images of burning oil fields in Kuwait in the aftermath of the first Gulf War are accompanied by the filmmaker's poetic, science fiction voice-over. The Minnesota Declaration provides a synoptic agenda for this vein of practice and contains an explicit articulation of three elements that appear as ubiquitous features of contemporary art's discourse on documentary: first, there is a claim to artistry; second, this claim to artistry depends on elevating a certain kind of contemporary practice over and above "traditional documentary," especially practices grounded in observation; and third, this is conceptualized as the triumph of subjective and imaginative creativity, producing a truth superior to the facticity of recording.

The denigration of surfaces also marks ideology critique. But whereas in that paradigm, the mistrust of appearances stems from their status as ideological fictions, here the problem is that appearances are too bluntly, too stupidly, factual. Replaying the Platonic phobia of appearances, this line of argumentation sees the capture of profilmic reality as unthinking mimesis, an uncreative copying devoid of the transformative power of art—an action that might even be involved in a dissimulation, or masking, of processes of mediation that should be foregrounded. In arguing for fiction and artifice, what one might term the "ecstatic truth" paradigm maligns one of documentary's primary tools—the descriptive power of lens-based capture—even as it often continues to depend on it.

Herzog's "Minnesota Declaration" gives this general position a name, "ecstatic truth," but he is by no means the originator of a rhetoric that opposes the duplication of surfaces unfavorably to the depths of human subjectivity and, therefore, to art. Indeed, this binary is strikingly present in foundational discussions of the relationship between art and lens-based capture. Charles Baudelaire's objection to the once-new medium of photography is well known and abides by a similar logic. In his account of the Salon of 1859, he famously held that the advent of photography signaled the defeat of poetry in the name of progress—the overcoming of man by machine—and saw it as leading indubitably to the impoverishment of artistic sensibility.[11] Baudelaire did allow some useful functions for the medium: presaging Herzog's talk of accountants, he wrote that photography could be "the secretary and clerk of whoever needs an absolute factual exactitude in his profession"—but as for art, photography was its "most mortal enemy."[12] In his text "The Birth of a Sixth Art" (1911), Ricciotto Canudo asked, "Now, it is necessary to ask of the cinematograph, is it to be accepted within the confines of the arts?" The answer: "It is not yet an art, because it lacks the freedom of choice particular to plastic *interpretation,* conditioned as it is to being a *copy* of the subject, the condition that prevents photography from being an art."[13] In subsequent writing, Canudo would outline ways that the cinema could transcend the duplication of appearances, trading objectivity for subjectivity, mimetic surface for creative depth, and thereby ascend to the status of art.[14] Both Baudelaire and Canudo conflate the lens-based capture of the world's surfaces with a spiritual superficiality because it depends on the automatism of the machine. This attitude is symptomatic of a widespread late nineteenth-century fear that the technological transformations of industrial modernity would trample all uniqueness and authenticity—especially the uniqueness and authenticity of the individual, of which the artist was a paragon and which was understood to rest on being true to the inner reaches of the self in the face of external pressures.[15]

The stratigraphic opposition between mimesis and artfulness constitutes a strong line of aesthetic thought throughout the twentieth century, taking on varying articulations across time, discipline, and orientation. For Theodor Adorno, the duplication of appearances merely reproduced and thereby affirmed the petrified surfaces of our capitalist lifeworld—a position that is rearticulated in canonical works of film theory such as Jean-Louis Comolli and Jean Narboni's "Cinema/Ideology/Criticism" editorial of 1969.[16] Though of a very different persuasion vis-à-vis questions of realism and abstraction than Adorno, Georg Lukács would, in his text "Narrate or Describe?" (1936), also spurn bad mimesis. He argued passionately in favor of narration over description, finding it better equipped to confront the action of social forces, the pathways of historical development, and emotional truths, owing to its emphasis on hierarchy, causality, and epic themes. Description, by contrast, levels hierarchies; it "debases characters to the level of objects," figuring as "the inevitable product . . . of the domination of capitalist prose over the inner poetry of human experience, the continuous dehumanization of social life, the general debasement of humanity."[17] Though the medium under consideration for Lukács is literature, not cinema, the association of description with a machinic inhumanity and superficiality, with unruly details run amok all over the surface, is quasi-filmic in nature. In anthropology, too, description poses a problem: as David MacDougall writes, in that discipline, explanation, description, and experience "have traditionally been arranged hierarchically, with explanation dependent upon, but ranked higher than description, and description ranked higher than experience. This is part of the legacy of a logocentric tradition. Film alters this hierarchy, favoring experiential understanding over explanation."[18] MacDougall traces some of the opposition to ethnographic film to the tendency to construe the medium as insufficiently explanatory, too experiential and descriptive.

If the theorization of documentary in contemporary art is in some sense a radicalization of the postmodern critique of documentary and its debunking of the testimonial power of lens-based capture, in aligning human creativity with fictionalization, the "ecstatic truth" paradigm offers a second stimulus for eschewing practices that prioritize the recording of what is. To be sure, a tension exists between these two positions. The notion of ecstatic truth, after all, depends on a continued attachment to a traditional conception of the artist, whereby creativity and truth stem from the deepest reaches of the authentic individual. It is marked by an implicit investment in subjective uniqueness and a fear of the machine—qualities determinedly at odds with the critiques of originality and celebration of surfaces associated with a postmodern sensibility. And yet both positions work together to offer a powerful disqualification of the observational mode. As the banal, artless "truth of accountants," it is cast as bad object, bad copy, as superficial recording lacking intelligence and creativity. Struck by a "passion for the real," it is deemed naive and insufficiently reflexive. It falls short twice over.

But as Lukács reminds us in "Narrate or Describe?," aesthetic styles must be considered in relation to larger sociohistorical circumstances. In 2008, curator Mark Nash declared it to be "certainly true that there is no longer any mileage to be gained from the opposition between fiction and reality."[19] If this were ever "certainly true," is it anymore? Today, truths are multiple, siloed, and subjective; evidence-based claims are given the same weight as speculative, conspiratorial fancy; the U.S. president deems real news fake, attacks journalists, and circulates falsehood, and many listen. Referring to postgraduate education in the humanities, but describing a situation that might equally apply to documentary practices, Bruno Latour writes, "Entire Ph.D. programs are still running to make sure that good American kids are learning the hard way that facts are made up, that there is no such thing as natural, unmediated, unbiased access to truth, that we are always prisoners of language, that we always speak from a particular standpoint, and so on, while dangerous extremists are using the very same argument of social construction to destroy hard-won evidence that could save our lives."[20] Contemporary art's documentary turn is now almost twenty years old; perhaps it is time to interrogate some of its idées fixes in light of this emergency.[21] Given how much has changed, in documentary practice and in the world at large, since the initial articulation of the crucial critiques of the observational mode, perhaps it is now time to rehabilitate the power of description as produced through lens-based capture—not to dispense with docufiction, nor to deem it reactionary or outmoded, but to see what can be salvaged in those observational strategies that have for so long been overshadowed by the orthodoxy of ecstatic truth.

In their introduction to a special issue of *Representations* on the subject of description, Sharon Marcus, Heather Love, and Stephen Best acknowledge all the objections leveled against "bad description": it is lacking in analysis, "reproductive rather productive," mechanical. Looking across the humanities and social sciences, the editors assemble charges against description that echo those leveled against the observational mode: "that description is impossible, because all knowledge is situated; that it is ideological, because objectivity always masks interests; and that it is insufficiently critical or even tautological, because it simply repeats what anyone can see or hear."[22] Nonetheless, they advocate for the importance of "a better description," one that would involve, among other things, an adjustment of the negative attitude toward literalism and tautology, and an embrace of stray details. They imagine that description "conceived of as honoring the object described might occasion a kind of ecstatic dispossession or pleasure in identifying with an object, being, or world. Such acts of mimetic description . . . can be creative, illuminating practices that produce forms, data, and insights keyed to the liveliness of worlds and works."[23] Here, the ideology of authenticity and individualism that underwrites the retreat into the depths of the self is rejected in favor of an opening onto an encounter with alterity. The authors' invocation of "ecstatic dispossession" as an escape from the bounds of oneself throws into relief the thorough irony of Herzog's naming of his concept: how strange it is that an understanding of truth so rooted in the profundity of the individual imagination is modified by an adjective designating self-transcendence.

Marcus, Love, and Best do not specifically address cinema in their multidisciplinary special issue, but their call for a "better description" offers a way of pushing back against the widespread denigration of observation in theorizations of the documentary turn in contemporary art. The *in*scriptions of lens-based capture can offer thick *de*scriptions of the surfaces of the world around us, precisely at a time when reality has supposedly collapsed, and precisely at a time when computer-generated images with little to no grounding in profilmic reality proliferate. The power of photographic detail is most often understood, following Barthes's notion of the punctum, in the singular: it is the lone shock of contingency that shoots out of the image to bruise the subject, exerting a centripetal fascination that binds her to the photograph and, through it, to the captured moment. Yet what of the power of the many, *many* details of the photograph, which is to say, of its capacity for description? Perhaps all those elements of the studium are not so banal, not so devoid of cathexis, as Barthes makes them out to be. Barthes writes that the studium belongs to "the order of *liking,* not *loving.*"[24] But what if photographic description were indeed a domain of love, a site for the Arendtian practice of *amor mundi?* Rather than revealing a truth hidden beneath the surface, capturing appearances and making them available to collective consideration might provide a scene for building the common world—a scene endowed with the possibility of reckoning with the complexity of actuality, unsettling received ideas, accommodating multiple points of view, and surpassing solipsism.[25]

The postmodern critique of photography's regime of truth as socially and historically constructed was a necessary and important scholarly intervention. Yet one must acknowledge that beyond whatever protocols and discourses come to determine the photographic image's capacity to testify to what passed before the lens, there is a significant ontological difference between those images produced with the wild participation of the world through the automatism of lens-based capture and those synthetic images created ex nihilo, cut from whole cloth without such existential referentiality. Rather than resigning oneself to the notion that "the representational link between sign and referent has been severed,"

FIGURE 9.1. *El Mar La Mar* (Joshua Bonnetta and J. P. Sniadecki, 2017).

and thereby relinquishing the lens-based image's capacity to capture traces of the world, one might reparatively reassert this bond, rebuilding it from the ruins by choosing belief over suspicion. Joshua Bonnetta and J. P. Sniadecki's *El Mar La Mar* (2017) does this: it provides some sense of what a "better description" in film might look like and why it might be important to undertake such a project.

This feature-length film is a collaboration between an anthropologist and an artist, in other words, between two individuals coming from disciplines that, as noted earlier, each have clearly articulated suspicions of surface appearances. And yet this is precisely the realm the film confronts. Shot on Super 16mm, *El Mar La Mar* moves through the necropolitical landscapes of the Sonoran Desert, crossed by individuals attempting to enter the United States from Mexico without papers. It is not a film of information or talking heads but a film of huge skies, changing light, rugged vegetation, thirst, and disorientation—a film in which the epic mythologies of the American West are invoked and overturned for an age of border walls and mass deportations (Figure 9.1). The sounds of the theme from *Johnny Guitar* (Nicholas Ray, 1954) echo across militarized territory, with none of Joan Crawford's glamour in sight; rather, bottles of drinking water hang suspended, inscribed with messages telling those lucky enough to find them to keep hope, that God is with them (Figure 9.2). In this land of heat and desperation, people get lost and are found as corpses, littering

FIGURE 9.2. *El Mar La Mar* (Joshua Bonnetta and J. P. Sniadecki, 2017).

the brush alongside crumpled, bleached-out backpacks and discarded mobile phones.

In *El Mar La Mar,* cinema and landscape alike are understood as surfaces of inscription that hold traces of encounters between the human and nonhuman, encounters that are sometimes symbiotic but often marked by hardship, state violence, and death. The film forgoes any direct depiction of struggle or suffering; few people appear. Instead, Bonnetta and Sniadecki inhabit the time of the aftermath, arriving later to see what has been left behind. With a careful balance of lyricism and precision, the filmmakers explore the entanglement of the diverse populations that traverse and inhabit the desert, probing the geopolitical specificities of the spaces we see and the sounds and voices we hear, with the presentation of traces taking precedence over explanation at every turn. The film largely avoids attempts at interpretation and makes no claims of total comprehension. On the contrary, almost from its opening sequence, *El Mar La Mar* stages a crisis of vision and understanding, foregrounding the immense difficulty—the impossibility, even—of grasping reality. A hand in close-up holds a small torch that has little effect against heavy cloak of night; the desert beyond remains dark (Figure 9.3). In voice-over, a man recounts seeing a "beast" that he cannot explain, one perhaps responsible for mutilating cows, one that might look like a kangaroo but is not. Language falters in the face of the intensity of

FIGURE 9.3. *El Mar La Mar* (Joshua Bonnetta and J. P. Sniadecki, 2017).

experience. Explanation falls from its perch atop the hierarchy of knowledge.

This sequence, with its retreat from the arrogance of easy understanding and emphasis on the limits of what image and sound may capture, serves as something of a tutor-text for what follows: Bonnetta and Sniadecki adopt a largely observational stance that attends to the complexities of the world without ever asserting mastery over it. Indeed, *El Mar La Mar* very much grapples with absence and blindness, both at the level of content, in that we frequently hear of people losing their way, and formally, in the film's relationship to the registration of reality. Sound is often severed from picture, as disembodied voices describe images never seen and images are presented without commentary, sometimes pushing at the limits of recognizability. The screen is frequently flooded with darkness, with nothing visible other than periodic flecks and scratches, imperfections stemming from the process of developing and printing photochemical film that draw attention to the surface of the image. And yet despite these clear gestures toward the insuperable chasm that separates reality from representation, *El Mar La Mar* demands belief in what we see, not suspicion or doubt. It seeks not to transcend fact but to collect evidence of life and death, staging a phenomenological encounter with the world as mediated through cinema.

A common critique of the observational mode is that it purports to be neutral and objective but of course is not. Yet if one takes seriously this argument and acknowledges that no description is ever simply "mere" description, we rescue the concept from the accusation that it is devoid of creativity and engaged in a masking of situatedness: subjectivity is *always* at play in the framing, selection, and combination of shots. In the images of *El Mar La Mar,* to borrow the words of Donna Haraway, "the world neither speaks itself nor disappears in favor of a master decoder."[26] The film does not propose a view from nowhere; it does not perform the "god-trick" of claiming the immediacy of a perfect objectivity through which the world would speak itself without intermediary. Yet neither does it understand the lens-based image as purely a product of representational convention, a condition in which the world would disappear in the face of coded messages. These images are co-constituted through a triangulation of forces, bringing into communion the agencies of the filmmakers, the world viewed, and the filmic machine. All are present in this encounter. The precise attention to the composition and selection of the images, the consistent gestures to the specific qualities of photochemical registration, and the insistence that the capture of reality will necessarily be partial all place *El Mar La Mar* thoroughly in the domain of what Haraway terms "situated knowledge," a practice of a reconceived objectivity that is bound to "particular and specific embodiment and definitely not about the false vision promising transcendence of all limits and responsibility."[27] *El Mar La Mar*'s attention to the transformative craft of image-making is palpable, whether in capturing vegetation in close-up, registering the bewildering colors of the open sky, or using smudgy monochrome for the film's closing sequence, in which a woman reads a poem in Spanish that speaks of "a landscape still unknown, yet certain."

Still unknown, yet certain: like *El Mar La Mar* itself, these words offer guidance for how one might approach worldly reality. The "ecstatic dispossession" that Marcus, Love, and Best associate with description is a matter of contact and implication without guarantee of a resolved meaning. As they write, "Description connects us to others—to those described, to the makers of what we describe, to other describers."[28] It takes us beyond ourselves; it is an ethics. For Lukács, description is a disturbing leveling that compromises the humanity of the human: the chatter of things bubbles up to bleed across the surface of the text, toppling hierarchies and creating a "kaleidoscopic chaos"; he argues that description renders people thinglike, suggesting a homology between the aesthetics of naturalism and the fate of the human under capitalism.[29] That Lukács would adopt a left anthropocentrism in the first machine age is understandable. But today, when individuality is everywhere a commodity for sale and anthropogenic climate change demands that we attend to the fraught relations between human and nonhuman life, the stakes are different. *El Mar La Mar* recognizes this. In the absence of individualist epic themes, the film illuminates the immanent entanglement of the diverse populations—whether human, plant, animal, or mineral—that traverse and inhabit the desert, and probes the geopolitical specificities of the spaces we see and the sounds and voices we hear. The issues here are environmental, structural, and juridical, so why reduce them to individual-driven narration? At the core of the film is a durational attunement to the facticity of reality—with its stray, nonsignifying details, its ability to testify to experience, and its capacity to connect us to a sense of a shared world.

In a 1993 text, Brian Winston suggested that in the wake of postmodernism, it was perhaps best for documentary practices to "roll with the epistemological blow, abandoning the claim to evidence."[30] In many cases, and especially in the domain of experimental documentary, whether situated within the art world or outside of it, this is more or less what came to pass. To conclude his *Artforum* article "Real Fictions: Alternatives to Alternative Facts" (2017), Hal Foster repeats the old truism that the task now is to mobilize artifice and "the utopian glimmer of fiction" in "the service of the real," "avoiding a simple retrenchment to [its] positivistic framing."[31] But is artifice necessarily the royal road to truth? In some instances, perhaps it is—as stated earlier, the aim of these pages is emphatically not to disqualify hybridity or malign those techniques associated with the ecstatic truth paradigm. But it is worth underlining the extent to which a film like *El Mar La Mar* points to a different way forward, one founded in reasserting the evidential status of the image and making use of the contingencies of recording to bind us to reality while recruiting the transformative powers of cinema to enable us to encounter it anew, and across time and distance. Whereas many theorizations of documentary in contemporary art have manifested a suspicion of surfaces, implicitly framing the lens-based capture of reality as a machinic stupidity to be overcome by individual creativity or as a mystified empiricism, *El Mar La Mar* is exemplary of a diverging trajectory. It is a path not only taken in Bonnetta and Sniadecki's collaboration but also found in the works of many other artists and filmmakers—to note only a few, Éric Baudelaire, Wang Bing, Maeve Brennan, Antje Ehmann/Harun Farocki, and Kevin Jerome Everson—for whom the automatism of lens-based capture is a powerful tool of revelation with the capacity to attest to shared, enworlded existence. In their work, a passion for the real meets a passion for form.

The history of film theory provides good resources to argue for the importance of attending to surfaces. Here, the salient reference is less Giuliana Bruno, whose interest in surface is bound up in tactility, decoration, and artifice, than Siegfried Kracauer, who makes persuasive claims for the power of surface effects, both in his Weimar writings and in his later *Theory of Film: The Redemption of Physical Reality.* In his Weimar writings, contra Lukács, Kracauer argues that it is precisely through surface phenomena that history becomes legible; later, in *Theory of Film,* he elaborates this more specifically in relation to the redemption of physical reality and writes, "The cinema seems to come into its own when it clings to the surface of things."[32] The value of clinging to the surface articulated in these pages is not grounded in a prescriptive pursuit of cinematic specificity. Rather, it is both a response to recent artistic practice and a hypothesis that emerges out of a consideration of what this medium—so lacking in innocence, so closely associated with imperial modernity and the domination of life—might offer to our contemporary predicament. Shorn of its problematic associations with immediacy and the "view from nowhere," observation harbors the possibility of a noninstrumentalized encounter with the alterity of the world we inhabit together—a hope for an ethics and politics of attunement.

Notes

1. Hito Steyerl, "Art or Life? Documentary Jargons of Authenticity," in *Truth, Dare, or Promise: Art and Documentary Revisited,* ed. Jill Daniels, Cahal McLaughlin, and Gail Pearce (Newcastle upon Tyne: Cambridge Scholars Publishing, 2013), 7.

2. Among the most significant of these are Mark Nash's *Experiments with Truth* (Fabric Workshop and Museum, Philadelphia, 2004); Jessica Morgan and Gregor Muir's *Time Zones: Recent Film and Video* (Tate Modern, London, 2004); Enwezor's *Archive Fever: Uses of the Document in Contemporary Art* (International Center of Photography, New York, 2008); Maria Lind and Hito Steyerl's *The Greenroom: Reconsidering the Documentary and Contemporary Art* (Hessel Museum of Art, Annandale-on Hudson, 2008); and Hila Peleg's biannual Berlin Documentary Forum (Haus der Kulturen der Welt, Berlin, 2010–14).

3. T. J. Demos, *The Migrant Image: The Art and Politics of Documentary during Global Crisis* (Durham, N.C.: Duke University Press, 2013), xxi (emphasis added).

4. Linda Nochlin, "Documented Success," *Artforum,* September 2002, 162 (emphasis added).

5. Bill Nichols aligns the observational mode with direct cinema and cinema vérité, characterizing it as stressing the nonintervention of the filmmaker, relying on an impression of real time, the "exhaustive depiction of the everyday," lacking retrospective commentary, and providing the "expectation of transparent access." See Bill Nichols, *Representing Reality: Issues and Concepts in Documentary* (Bloomington: Indiana University Press, 1991), 38–44.

6. Paolo Magagnoli, *Documents of Utopia: The Politics of Experimental Documentary* (New York: Wallflower Press, 2015), 55.

7. Brian Winston, *Claiming the Real: The Griersonian Documentary and Its Legitimations* (London: British Film Institute, 1995), 243.

8. John Tagg, *The Burden of Representation: Essays on Photographies and Histories* (London: Palgrave Macmillan, 1988), 3.

9. Werner Herzog, "Werner Herzog Reads His Minnesota Declaration: Truth and Fact in Documentary Cinema," *Crosscuts,* April 30, 1999, https://walkerart.org/magazine/minnesota-declaration-truth-documentary-cinema.

10. It is worth noting the similarity between this formulation and the definition of "post-truth" provided in the *Oxford English Dictionary:* "Relating to or denoting circumstances in which objective facts are less influential in shaping political debate or public opinion than appeals to emotion and personal belief." "post-truth, adj," in OED Online (Oxford: Oxford University Press, 2019), https://www.oed.com/view/Entry/58609044?redirectedFrom=post-truth.

11. Charles Baudelaire, "The Salon of 1859: The Modern Public and Photography," in *Modern Art and Modernism: A Critical Anthology,* ed. Francis Frascina and Charles Harrison (London: Open University, 1982), 20.

12. Baudelaire, 20.

13. Ricciotto Canudo, "The Birth of a Sixth Art," trans. Ben Gibson, in *French Film Theory and Criticism: A History/Anthology, 1907–1939,* vol. 1, *1907–1929,* ed. Richard Abel (Princeton, N.J.: Princeton University Press, 1988), 61.

14. See Ricciotto Canudo, "Reflections on the Seventh Art," trans. Claudia Gorbman, in Abel, *French Film Theory and Criticism,* 301. Classical film theory is by no means a unified discourse; other writers, notably Jean Epstein, praised the automatism of recording. However, it is significant that the emphasis during this period tends to be on the way cinema *transforms* the appearances of the world through devices such as the close-up and slow motion rather than on how it *duplicates* these appearances, revealing a latent discomfort with mimesis even in those authors invested in the medium's ability to capture physical reality.

15. For more on the relationship between mechanical reproducibility and authenticity as a moral value, see Erika Balsom, *After Uniqueness: A History of Film and Video Art in Circulation* (New York: Columbia University Press, 2017), 27–37.

16. Responding to Lukács, in "Reconciliation under Duress," Adorno writes, "The truth of the matter is that except where art goes against its own essence and

simply duplicates existence, its task vis-à-vis that which merely exists, is to be its essence and image. This alone constitutes the aesthetic; art does not become knowledge with reference to mere immediate reality, i.e. by doing justice to a reality which veils its own essence and suppresses truth in favour of a merely classificatory order. Art and reality can only converge if art crystallizes out its own formal laws, not by passively accepting objects as they come"; Theodor Adorno "Reconciliation under Duress," trans. Rodney Livingston, in *Aesthetics and Politics,* ed. Ernst Block (London: Verso, 1980), 159–60. For Comolli and Narboni, "The classic theory of cinema that the camera is an impartial instrument which grasps, or rather is impregnated by, the world in its 'concrete reality' is an eminently reactionary one. What the camera in fact registers is the vague, unformulated, untheorized, unthought-out world of the dominant ideology"; Jean-Louis Comolli and Jean Narboni, "Cinema/Ideology/Criticism," trans. Susan Bennett, *Screen* 12, no. 1 (1971): 30.

17. Georg Lukács, *Writer and Critic and Other Essays,* ed. and trans. Arthur D. Kahn (New York: Grosset and Dunlap, 1970), 133, 127.

18. David MacDougall, *Transcultural Cinema* (Princeton, N.J.: Princeton University Press, 1988), 84.

19. Mark Nash, "Reality in the Age of Aesthetics," *Frieze,* no. 114 (April 2008), https://frieze.com/article/reality-age-aesthetics.

20. Bruno Latour, "Why Has Critique Run Out of Steam? From Matters of Fact to Matters of Concern," *Critical Inquiry* 30 (Winter 2004): 227.

21. In 2017, at the invitation of the Walker Art Center, where the "Minnesota Declaration" was first delivered in 1999, Herzog returned to his manifesto, concisely adding six more points without altering his position. He admits, "Facts cannot be underestimated as they have normative power," but adds, "But they do not give us insight into the truth, or the illumination of poetry"; "Werner Herzog Makes Trump-Era Addition to His Minnesota Declaration," https://walkerart.org/magazine/werner-herzog-minnesota-declaration-2017-addendum.

22. Sharon Marcus, Heather Love, and Stephen Best, "Building a Better Description," *Representations* 135 (Summer 2016): 4.

23. Marcus, Love, and Best, 14.

24. Roland Barthes, *Camera Lucida: Reflections on Photography,* trans. Richard Howard (New York: Hill and Wang, 1982), 27.

25. On Arendt's notion of the "common world," see Hannah Arendt, *The Human Condition* (Chicago: University of Chicago Press, 1958), 50–58. Arendt considered using "Amor Mundi" as a title for the book that became *The Human Condition.*

26. Donna Haraway, "Situated Knowledges: The Science Question in Feminism and the Privilege of Partial Perspective," *Feminist Studies* 14, no. 3 (Autumn 1988): 593.

27. Haraway, 582.

28. Marcus, Love, and Best, "Building a Better Description," 14.

29. Lukács, *Writer and Critic,* 133.

30. Brian Winston, "The Documentary Film as Scientific Inscription," in *Theorizing Documentary,* ed. Michael Renov (New York: Routledge, 1995), 56.

31. Hal Foster, "Real Fictions: Alternatives to Alternative Facts," *Artforum* 55, no. 8 (April 2017): 174.

32. Siegfried Kracauer, *Theory of Film: The Redemption of Physical Reality* (Princeton, N.J.: Princeton University Press, 1960), 285.

PART III

Deep Space, Deep Time

So we have begun to scratch, rough up, the surface; but what of depth in this context? While canonical discussions of windows, mirrors, and depth of field both retain their value as historical debates and acquire renewed significance in relation to interfaces within new media environments, a growing body of scholarship in diverse fields in recent years would seem to suggest, to recall Thomas Friedman's words quoted in the Preface, that as we move into the twenty-first century's third decade, "everything is going deep."

In media studies, scholars like Lisa Parks and Caren Kaplan, along with architectural theorist-practitioners like Laura Kurgan, have been activating a vertical line of thought for more than a decade by drawing attention to what Parks calls "cultures of orbit" or, more recently, "vertical mediation," and the political, spatial, aesthetic and epistemological implications of the expanded role that satellite technologies and drones play in structuring the rhythms and sensory fields of our daily lives. These authors ponder the consequences of an all-encompassing view of the earth from above that delivers inescapable visibility, aspirations to omniscience, and the transformation of life into quantifiable data. All three scholars resist technological determinism and explore possible forms of political and aesthetic agency in the satellite age, including using the body as a politically charged drawing tool within GPS, using thermal tracking technologies to protect vulnerable migrant populations, and making self-reflexive artworks that heighten our vertical visual literacy. There is much to say about how our everyday and philosophical thinking about film and media is shaped by the upwardly oriented vertical line established between the surface of the earth and the satellite, not least because this extraterrestrial axis extends and counterbalances the downwardly oriented vertical axis that traces a type of thought often described by the extractive and perhaps exploitative language of burrowing and mining, a signature mode of thought in the modern European tradition.

For Macarena Gómez-Barris, vertically oriented work like that of Parks and her own "decolonial queer and femme episteme and methodology" offer important correctives to many Eurocentric theories of both visual power and planetary crisis, neither of which takes proper account of the violence of settler colonialism and extractive capitalism.[1] She argues, furthermore, that some vertically oriented media studies scholars—Parks is noted as an exception—have warned against digital or technological colonialism and systems of planetary control but without noting the "differential ways that this power is experienced," thereby reproducing what she calls "the extractive view" that renders Native people invisible as well as inaudible.[2] To counteract this recolonizing potential of vertically oriented scholarship, Gómez-Barris develops a "perceptual method" that draws on women of color feminism, working to "lift submerged perspectives that perceive local terrains as sources of knowledge, vitality, and livability" (1). Throughout her book, she seeks out ways to explore what it means to "see from below" (xiv), to adopt "submerged perspectives" (xiv), like the river caiman: "With its eyes positioned just above the line of water, its sight hovers above as easily as it dips below the shadowy, fertile water" (18). While the natural world and Indigenous knowledge systems may offer alternative temporalities to the "frenetic timescape of extraction" (17), as well as alternative ways of relating to the world, Gómez-Barris follows Linda Tuhiwai Smith, author of *Decolonizing Methodologies: Research and Indigenous Peoples,* in emphasizing the need for "an ethical perspective that mutually respects and engages Indigenous knowledge without extracting from these communities" (10).[3] Central to this nonextractive mode of engagement is a willingness on the part of non-Indigenous scholars to "reconsider what we thought we had known," "[untrain] the social," and emphasize "submerged perspectives as those that must be learned from rather than suppressed" (11). We find an earlier, similarly submerged perspective, mapped onto a vertical axis in Stefano Harney and Fred Moten's *The Undercommons: Fugitive Planning and Black Study* (2013). Here the work of the subversive intellectual in the contemporary university happens underground, undoes the contemporary university, and cannot be incorporated into the university if the work is to remain subversive: "The university needs what she bears but cannot bear what she brings. And on top of all that, she disappears. She disappears into the underground, the downlow

low-down maroon community of the university, into the *undercommons of enlightenment*, where the work gets done, where the work gets subverted, where the revolution is still black, still strong."[4]

In the past decade, a range of media scholars have extended lines of vertical thinking downward, to the ground we walk on, to the layers of earth below us, and toward the ocean seabed. Melody Jue, for example, demonstrates how seriously considering the ocean shores up, so to speak, just how terrestrial our epistemological orientations are. As she writes in relation to the popular BBC documentary series' presentation of an underwater lake, showing a

> unique "surface" *within* the depths, *Blue Planet* reveals both the pervasiveness of our land-based perspective of surface and depth and how it colors the terrestrial metaphors we live by. We expect a surface on top and depth underneath in both reality and in figurative language, but there may be other possible senses of these terms. The underwater lake example suggests a stigmatism, or misalignment of the figurative and the literal . . . , which produces a kind of cognitive estrangement similar to what we experience in science fiction about oceans and aquatic beings.[5]

Nicole Starosielski's extensive media-ethnographic research on histories of controlling and mediating the ocean in *The Undersea Network* (2015) draws needed materialist attention to the vast infrastructural network of undersea cables through which the majority of the world's internet traffic flows, making possible our everyday interactions on the ground that we often fantasize to be apolitical and immaterial. Tung-Hui Hu's *A Prehistory of the Cloud* (2016) similarly grounds and maps the terrestrial infrastructure of the dematerialized and clean fantasy of "cloud computing," challenging readers to consider the relationship between the physical earth and the seemingly immaterial worlds of communication networks and philosophical thought.[6]

Jussi Parikka's *A Geology of Media* (2015) likewise explores the underground substances that constitute the physical reality of our media technologies, part of the so-called material turn that is inseparable from the vertical turn. Parikka's attention to the materiality of media spotlights the imbrication of resource extraction with models of thought that have historically been privileged within the humanities. Importantly, Parikka's work builds on recent thinking in media archaeology, a vibrant subfield of new media studies predicated on the idea of "deep time" and named after a materialist historical method of digging through cultural records.

The concept of deep time has been especially prominent in German media studies, such as in Siegfried Zielinski's influential book *The Deep Time of the Media* (2006) and Bernhard Siegert's *Cultural Techniques: Grids, Filters, Doors, and Other Articulations of the Real* (2015), but also in American media studies, with imaginative rethinkings of media temporality like Shannon Mattern's *Code and Clay, Data and Dirt: Five Thousand Years of Urban Media* (2017). Zielinski, Siegert, Parikka, Mattern, and many other scholars on both sides of the Atlantic have opened up promising lines of inquiry that look to constellations of media arrangements and formations that often stretch back thousands of years to find patterns that suggest hypothetical arrangements that could have been and that posit new ways of understanding our current technological conditions and lived environments, in ways that are both historically grounded and understood as not necessarily inevitable. Attention to deep time is often accompanied by an ecological sensibility that reminds us of the relativity of the concept of "media," urging us to think about media in flexible and provocative ways from which the shiny rhetoric of the "new" can often distract us.

This third part of *Deep Mediations* contains a cluster of essays that are all characterized by downward, upward, and outward pulls that stretch us to think more carefully about spatial depths, questions of deep time and historicity, and how perceptions of deep time and deep space shape each other in sites of mutual encounter and audiovisual production.

Notes

1. Macarena Gómez-Barris, *The Extractive Zone: Social Ecologies and Decolonial Perspectives* (Durham, N.C.: Duke University Press, 2017), 4.

2. Gómez-Barris, 7, 6.

3. Linda Tuhiwai Smith, *Decolonizing Methodologies: Research and Indigenous Peoples* (London: Zed Books; Dunedin, NZ: University of Otago Press, 1999).

4. Stefano Harney and Fred Moten, *The Undercommons: Fugitive Planning and Black Study* (Brooklyn, N.Y.: Autonomedia, 2013), 26.

5. Melody Jue, "Churning up the Depths: Nonhuman Ecologies of Metaphor in *Solaris* and 'Oceanic,'" in *Green Planets: Ecology and Science Fiction*, ed. Gerry Canavan and Kim Stanley Robinson (Middletown, Conn.: Wesleyan University Press, 2014), 226.

6. For a related discussion, see Stuart Grey, "Deep Space and the Impact of Space Debris on Communication Networks," accessed December 20, 2019, https://www.stugrey.com/2019/12/03/deep-space-and-the-impact-of-space-debris-on-communication-networks/.

CHAPTER TEN

Sinkholes, GIFs, and Cinematic Ecocatastrophe

Karl Schoonover

A problem of scale plagues popular moving-image texts that try to visualize the environmental impact of humans: the harbingers of the earth's imminent ecological apocalypse occupy spaces and temporalities immeasurable within the idioms of conventional screen media. The vast reach and submicroscopic effects of the dioxins resulting from trash incineration are not, for example, easily rendered by the moving image.[1] Environmental catastrophe does not fall into discrete parameters and thus challenges visual media with various phenomena that cannot be narrativized in linear time-space trajectories. The limitless and the abyss collide in the Anthropocene.

In this context, a response to the problem of scale has opened up in the spectacle of the sinkhole. The contemporary anthroposcenic landscape seems to both produce sinkholes and fixate on them as images. Sinkholes pop up (or down) everywhere and anywhere, in dense urbanity and in tranquil suburbs. When the earth suddenly gives way under our streets and homes and in front of our cameras, the sinkhole opens a challenge to conventional ecological discourses and questions the capacity of those discourses to manage the magnitude of humanity's environmental footprint. The seeming limitlessness of the sinkhole is key not only because of its infectious nature as visual spectacle but also because it revises our sense of how to approach ecological collapse and its inevitability.

The sinkhole possesses the qualities that ecotheorist Timothy Morton assigns to "hyperobjects": viscosity, nonlocality, temporal undulation, phasing, and interobjectivity.[2] Thinking of sinkholes as hyperobjects allows us to resist the tendency to make recourse to the category of the sublime when attempting to describe phenomena whose scale or duration overwhelms human perceptual capacities. This bracketing of the sublime has a political edge. Ecological catastrophe guides Morton's inquiry, as does his commitment to disallowing depictions of disaster to play into what he calls "end of world discourse," which he feels does more to promote a nihilistic apocalypticism than it does to forward a meaningful awareness of the Anthropocene. Sinkhole footage may be helpful in this context for how it furthers Morton's aim "to establish what phenomenological 'experience' is in absence of anything meaningful like a 'world' at all."[3]

When sinkholes arrive to us on screens, they carry characteristic traits. A small chunk of time is often replayed on a loop—in the context of an otherwise linear temporality—depicting the sinkhole swallowing and swallowing again, the image framing and holding in place an endless visual abyss, a dark hole that admits no measure of duration or depth. This looping has meant that the GIF supplies one of the most prominent sites for marveling at sinkholes—that is, it is sinkhole footage's ideal venue. The GIF facilitated the sinkhole's aesthetic and its rise to prominence in our contemporary mediascape. Sinkholes are popular on sites that aggregate GIFs, such as GIPHY, reddit, Twitter, and Tumblr, which supply their users with thousands of sinkhole GIFs. I argue here that the GIF's affinity for the sinkhole tells us something about what it means to represent this phenomenon.

Of course, moving-image depictions of sinkholes, fictional and actual, occurred before GIFs. How did what we now know as sinkholes first appear to us on screen? Across the mid-twentieth century, a number of films demonstrate sinkhole visuality, anticipating the GIF's characteristic features. In looking for sinkholes in films from the period before the age of the GIF, we find a set of structural affinities shared among GIFs, on the one hand, and ecological disaster as depicted in mid-twentieth-century films, on the other hand. This essay asks why the GIF is today one of the preferred means of pursuing a sinkhole, even as GIFness can be found foreshadowed in the sinkhole's predigital depictions.

In a sense, we might say that the grim finale of *The Red House* (Delmer Daves, 1947) anticipates one of the most famous GIFs of sinkholes, the sudden devouring of a stand of trees in Louisiana's Bayou Corne.[4] After driving his truck into the eponymous red house, creepy father Pete Morgan (Edward G. Robinson) and his vehicle are sucked into and then completely swallowed by deep, dark water that exists where the house's floor should be. It is easy to say that *The Red House* links the unfathomable depths of moral depravity depicted in the narrative with this final encounter with an actual abyss, and yet the formal disruption that ensues exceeds any ethical allegory. We are shown this swallowing in a sequence of three shots. The second two shots, while alternating the framing and bringing us closer to Pete, restart the action shown in the previous shots. Thus, Pete's upper body gets enveloped by the black waters of the house three times. Repetition of his descent produces a spatiotemporal hiccupping that allows us to get closer to the event without adding reasoned explication to the exposition of the event. As time picks up an odd looping quality, classicism's "integrity" of narrative space dissolves.

Likewise, when we stare into a GIF of the Bayou Corne sinkhole, the ordering of time and space as we know it dissolves before our eyes in the earth's looping ingestion of its surface. Origin, occurrence, consequence, and aftermath become impossible to disentangle. The holes left by the earth's giving way and the ground's caving under an accumulated anthroposcenic weight challenge standard ecological discourses and the capacity of those discourses to manage the scale of humanity's environmental footprint. The sinkhole's vanishing vanishing points demand that we rethink how to represent end games and how we represent how we see. In what follows, I look at various visualizations of sinkholes as potential images of ecocatastrophe that do not contribute to an "end of world discourse." We could even say that the sinkhole GIF and its predigital precursors help to unsettle a human point of view, disrupting it with a geologic perspective.

In contemporary popular moving-image cultures, the sinkhole appears as a portal not only to the unknown but also to unknowability, exposing instabilities of both physical and epistemological infrastructures.[5] Sinkholes regularly appear on standard factual television: the National Geographic channel, PBS's *Nova* (1974–present), and the BBC have all produced at least one hour-long documentary on the subject. These programs purport that in their exploration of the sinkhole's nature they will explain the phenomenon, but they always resist deflating the sinkhole's mystery and horror. Sinkholes strike without warning or reason, these programs tell us. Their root causes remain unclear. The programs seem invested in the idea that sinkholes ultimately frustrate any assignation of blame or culpability (even if fracking, industrial agriculture, and quick-build projects offer otherwise logical explanations for their increasing prevalence). The voice-over commentary that accompanies the footage of sinkholes aims to maintain this unknowability to such an extent that this commentary should be classified as phantasmagoric. The episode of the BBC2 documentary series *Horizon* (1964–present) titled "Swallowed by a Sinkhole" continually refers to the sinkhole as a passage to the indefinite and infinite and as an event that captures our "fear of dropping into the underworld."

These late twentieth-century televisual representations of sinkholes seem infected by a GIFness even when not appearing on GIF platforms. The sinkholes featured in these conventional genres of nonfiction television bring the qualities of the GIF with them; they are prone to repetition and looping in ways that make the beginning and end of an incident difficult to establish. They replay the same amateur and surveillance footage in a pattern that parallels the endless looping of the GIF.[6] Hence, these programs carry the quality of secondary texts, admitting they are simply building off images we already know well. Even when framed by conventional documentary narration, sinkholes often defy ordered recollections of incidents. Churning and swallowing dominate the sinkhole's spectacle, infecting the conception of the event with alternate trajectories of time and space.

We are reminded of this sinkhole visuality when we read Anna McCarthy's contention that a key aspect of the visual pleasure of the GIF is that it "always start[s] *in media res*, so that a certain desire to understand what's going on keeps us looking. GIFS may be short loops, but sometimes it takes several viewings for the viewer to comprehend their subject matter."[7] From the perspective that knows the GIF is an excerpt of a larger event, there are a complementary set of demands that lead us to be pulled into its repetitions. Moreover, the GIF immediately compensates for its broken promise to see more (its fragmentation of an event) via its looping, repeatedly admitting its lack and trying to offset it.[8] Like Freud's fetish, the GIF denatures the flow of time, stalling it and rewinding, over and over again. As Graig Uhlin describes it, the GIF's "repetition indicates that a viewer is not guided along by a narrative structuring of time. The viewer is rather caught up in the GIF's temporal suspension: to view it is to be captivated[,] keeping what was previously an ephemeral moment suspended before [the viewer's] eyes."[9] If the GIF allows for the transformation of "an image into an object of play," it must also be said that the GIF's looping only teases us with wholeness rather than providing it.[10] This is the fetishistic magic of its seam, the seam between one repetition and the next that both seals the event in infinitude and marks the impossibility of a moment starting again. Part of the GIF's thrill is finding that seam over and over again and participating in its disavowal, feeling its seaminess and seamlessness at the same time. Some of the most graphically intriguing sinkhole GIFs not only seem to swallow groves of trees or kiloliters of lake water in a matter of a seconds but also ingest time's forward movement itself because they swallow and swallow again in never-ending loops.[11]

McCarthy calls the "endlessness" of the GIF a "fugitive temporality," suggesting that it is the repository for a meditative wasting of time, an exercise of self-soothing, or a mode for exploring visual pleasure.[12] If the GIF streams data neither to nor from the user, but rather provides small nuggets of animation in an infinite looping, could we say, then, that a GIF is a sinkhole? After all the GIF is a *sync* hole. It is an accumulation—even a stockpile—of artificial synchronizations. At the same time, the GIF is also a sync *hole,* as in a pit that absorbs the meaningful passage of time and/or space, and thus it banishes the engines of conventional narrative: happenstance, coincidence, and chance meeting. The GIF's looping is where the telos of momentous time goes to die. It is, in other words, "a swallow hole," where the event's exceptionality is devoured and then regurgitated in a manner that frustrates progress, evolution, and even causation.

The many contemporary films depicting sinkholes are less interesting to my discussion than are sinkhole GIFs and certain midcentury films, because contemporary cinema can render geologic distress without incurring much visual disruption. Even when announced narratively as sinkholes, the cavities of twenty-first-century movies do not swallow up the narrative's coordination of spatiotemporal relations as such holes do in earlier films. Recent cinematic sinkholes provoke none of the "deep shudders of temporality" that Morton associates with the "world"-banishing qualities of the hyperobject.[13] Vis-à-vis the agile representational capacities of digital effects, the sinkhole loses its disruptive nature and welcomes an "end of the world discourse." Thanks to CGI, a film like *2012* (Roland Emmerich, 2009) can create a long take of a crack opening up, as Jackson Curtis (John Cusack) drives his family down a road, narrowly escaping a series of earthquakes and sinkholes. Crosscutting between the panic inside the car and shots of the car dodging the hazards of a world coming apart, the film never loses direction. A traditional narrative look (and its anthropocentric tendencies) remains stabilized, oriented toward linearity and directionality (the progress of mankind).[14] In other words, the sinkholes of this century's cinema proceed differently from the sinkholes of mid-twentieth-century films or for that matter, from the regurgitations of the GIF.

Looking for sinkholes in films from before the late 1990s (the original epoch of the GIF) and before digital animation took over movie special effects reveals a wide inventory, including not only films explicitly referencing sinkholes but also ravenously hungry tremors, ground cracks, and earthquakes.[15] Tectonic disturbances often disorganize the conventional narration of the gaze in the disaster of midcentury films, proposing a hiatus in linear time and space.[16] From a preliminary investigation into the aesthetic turbulence caused by the moving image of the ground "giving way" emerges a nascent order of destabilized time-space relations, one that later finds perfect formal affinity in the medium of the GIF. Put another way, when depicting geologic disaster, many older feature films express the same structural ambivalences toward the certainty of progressive time and space as GIFs, disorganizing vision, defying the primacy of the anthropocentric look, and turning over the image's narration to geology.

A consonance can be found in how both GIFs and these older films use spectacle to disorganize the look. *Crack in the World* (Andrew Marton, 1965) follows a mad scientist who sends a nuclear warhead under the earth's surface to mine the magma for a renewable source of energy to replace conventional fuels. Despite the endorsement of world leaders, this mining project leads to mayhem and near apocalypse. The sequence showing the crack disorders the narration of our gaze. We do not know exactly where to look, except everywhere at once. The montage-like qualities of covering the event contort spatial continuity, frustrating any mental mapping of the diegetic space. The viewer cannot anticipate the sequencing of movement across shots, placing our look momentarily outside of causal time and space. Thus, the sinkhole operates as Laura Mulvey defines the aesthetic parameters of spectacle, as that which is outside narrative.[17] As in Mulvey's definition, spectacle here slows down narrative time and the naturalistic pacing of the image in relation to the event, and the image loses the narrative spatiality of consequential direction and meaningful depth. Helen Wheatley argues that the slowing of time and movement in front of the spectacular landscape should be understood as a formalized "hesitation." This hesitation becomes so staccatoed in *Crack in the World* that it feels like a mode of seriality or repetition, much like that of the GIF's apprehension of the sinkhole.[18] We might think of these as four interrelated modes of sinkhole visuality: repetition, double framing, swallowing, and fractured linearity.

Toward the start of the Japanese Godzilla spin-off *Chikyû Bôeigun* (*The Mysterians;* Ishirô Honda, 1957), land slips into an ever-growing crack in the middle of a countryside scene. A series of edits from different angles and a repetitive soundtrack of crashing noises depict the frenzy of catastrophe but also unleash an indeterminacy about how and where we are traversing time and space. At first this cacophony may appear far from the satisfying repetitions of the GIF. However, while this sequence is not the Lumières's *Demolition of a Wall / Démolition d'un mur* (Auguste and Louis Lumière, 1896), its turmoil intimates a looping structure rather than a linear account of eventful time in which the instantaneous would be inimitable and consequential. In striving to cover the sinkhole as an event, *Chikyû Bôeigun* performs a stuttering of time-space relations. Each new shot not only offers a new perspective on what is happening but also introduces a new arc of the event, as if this sequence were a collection of separate events. Disaster begins afresh in each shot. This repetition of the event's time runs counter to conventional narrative's linear temporality. The pacing of each shot does not accord with those shots that come before or after it. This mishmash of perspectives on space and time can also be found in the landslide sequence of *It Came from Outer Space* (Jack Arnold, 1953), which combines slow motion and various points of view in its depiction of the ground splitting apart. When menacing cracks (later sinkholes) open the ground on London streets in *Quatermass and the Pit* (Roy Ward Baker, 1967), a similarly compulsive, multiple-viewed coverage of a single event occurs.

These films offer an account of the space and time of the event akin to Michelangelo Antonioni's experimental demolition sequence in *Zabriskie Point* (1970), in which the Italian art house auteur purposefully snubs traditional narrative cinema's prohibition of repeating the same instant twice to create a meditation on planned obsolescence in which the slowed detonation of a "new build" modernist home transforms into a ballet of household objects, appliances, and consumer goods exploding. The film metonymically links the initial repetitions of the explosion to this dance of detritus from middle-class American life. Many critics have taken this sequence as an experimental short of its own that reflects on the logics of consumer capitalist culture. We should, though, acknowledge that Antonioni is simply playing here with how mainstream midcentury cinema depicts catastrophe. In other words, he riffs on the disruption catastrophe introduces into classical narration and then amplifies that disruption. In *Zabriskie Point,* Antonioni gives us a theory of how catastrophe alters conventional filmic storytelling: catastrophe makes the image and editing behave in less than classical ways.

Chikyû Bôeigun and *Crack in the World* enfold two modes of reiteration in their disaster sequences. First, and simply, the sinkhole triggers in conventional film form a repetition that anticipates the GIF's looping structure. Second, the looping of an event's forward movement in time feels not unlike the GIF's "fugitive temporality," which McCarthy attributes to its "endless small acts of reproduction."[19]

Another mode of doubling brings endlessness to the fore: the frame within a frame used to signal bottomlessness. In his seminal account of Abel Gance, Norman King writes: "We could define filmic spectacle as that which arrests the spectator's look at the surface of the frame as opposed to what is within the frame."[20] He describes our detachment from narrative as a formal feature of the image and how it adjusts our attention: in spectacle we contemplate surface and the surrounding border, as much as image content. The Jules Verne adaptation *Journey to the Center of the Earth* (Henry Levin, 1959) uses double framing to portray voids in the earth. Before these voids appear on screen, the film describes the declared aim of the voyage's participants as "total penetration," to reach "the world below, whatever it may be." It is after these anticipatory pronouncements that we catch a glimpse of the challenges of these aims: a large sinkhole appears at nearly fifty minutes into the film. In the first glance at the spectacle promised by the film's title, and elsewhere later on, the film introduces a deep hole with an emblematic shot. The voids of these holes appear framed within a frame. A tension forms between the ragged, random, dropped-off, quasi-circular contours of the abyss of nothingness and the sharp geometry of the rectangular frame of the image. If we follow King's description, to what does this double framing draw our attention?

Such double framing accompanies the sense that this hole is an infinite and unmappable void. (This same composition proliferates in contemporary sinkhole footage.) Its limitlessness confounds perception, its blackness swallowing up everything, while exhausting human resourcefulness. "There's not enough rope in the world to get down there," declares one character, peering over the hole's perimeter. The black, emptied-out center of these two frames suggests a refusal of the representational imperatives of the image, a suspension of its otherwise figurative priorities. The void also dispenses with depth cues and seems to swallow narrative time, if we accept that narrative time in cinema requires marked spatial progression. Things are dropped down the hole, but they disappear quickly, rarely to reappear. They leave functionality (diegetic and otherwise), never to return.[21] GIFs seem to inherit this double framing as a means of exploiting voids and their voidings. Attending to these framed voids highlights another key mode of sinkhole visuality: swallowing. This mode uses the frame-within-a-frame structure to ravenously pull the image inside out formally and reject the image as a source of specification. In fact, the older word "swallow hole" carries a sense of the sinkhole's sudden ferocity, its obliterating tyranny, the menacing deep blankness it exposes, its churning upheaval of what grounds us, what seems solid, or its upsetting of all that is sedimented or foundational. "Swallow hole" raises an alarm of a ravenous predatory gravity, and sinkhole documentaries use the word "hungry" to describe the action of this geologic phenomenon.

A note about framing provides a useful clarification here. At first, it appears as if the frame works differently in repetition than it does in double framing. In the former, that is, repetition, the frame appears unable to hold the event within the image. In the latter, double framing, the frame appears to hold it. This is not quite correct. While the frame may appear more dominantly delimiting in double framing, to overemphasize this delimiting would discount the unrest that the swallowing void brings to the image. Swallowing can clearly be seen not simply devouring space and time but also obliterating it altogether, at least for a moment. Any stabilization that double framing brings by foregrounding edges is undercut in that these edges do not serve as boundaries to stabilize that which is at their center. The swallowing that double framing foregrounds is a disruptive formal mode that refuses to let us turn away from the troubling bottomless holes, such as the one at the end of *The Red House,* discussed earlier. The form of the GIF is again instructive here. With the popular aerially shot GIFs of sinkholes, double framing provides no leverage against the constant swallowing of the (w)hole. These are images with and without edges.

Bottomlessness also comes via a fissure in the ground of a vacant lot in the British sci-fi Cold War panic film, *X—the unknown* (Leslie Norman, Joseph Losey [uncredited], 1956). This film is an example of what Susan Sontag identifies as a formulaic element of midcentury sci-fi disaster films: "poking around in a huge crater."[22] As in *Journey to the Center of the Earth,* this poking comes accompanied with a pondering of how to measure endlessness, such as this conversation earlier on between two investigators:

– You mean it is bottomless?
– We simply don't have the adequate equipment.
– It is bottomless.
– How deep do think the fissure really is?
– I don't know.
– It has to have a beginning.
– And an end, too.

The last two lines are spoken with an ominous uncertainty. This overt ambivalence in their exchange suggests the opening as an ultimately unmeasurable space. In other words, as we witness it, this crack has neither a beginning nor an end.

Once again, the threat of the void—its infinity, its lack of origin, its obliteration of any means of orientation or measurement—brings instability to the image. *X—the unknown* suggests another mode of sinkhole visuality: fractured linearity. Near the start of the film, during a routine military training exercise taking place on an open field in a semirural landscape, a trainee discovers a hotbed of radioactivity emanating from a series of cracks in the ground. In this sequence, the event's forward trajectory of movement is broken up. After a few moments, a large crack gives way and consumes large swaths of ground and some of the new recruits. The mode of depiction shifts when the crack begins its journey across the ground. The sinkholes in *The Mysterians* introduces a similar mayhem. Somehow this crack makes the durational long take impossible. The cracking's temporality, by contrast, is patched together in a barrage of images. The short sequence introduces an erratic explosion of vectors of action, screen direction, and horizon lines. These are also unleashed in the GIF, for whose seams we are always looking. As described earlier, the GIF is never about either just seamlessness or just the seam. Its pleasures lie in the repetition of a single event and an event's infinite ongoingness.

In both films, as well as in *Crack in the World* and the sequence describing Lois Lane's death in *Superman: The Movie* (Richard Donner, 1978), the movement of the crack appears to contaminate the formal binding of image to image with an erratic and staccatoed quality. Compositionally, little endures from one shot to the next. Suddenly, smooth continuity is suspended, and an erratic chasing of the event takes over. Spaces fall out of contiguity. Temporal directionality admits interruptions, a punctuation of intermittent intervals. The sinkhole in these mid-twentieth-century films shatters (if only for an instant or two) the myths of smooth spatial and temporal sequentiality.

Since little if any space is carried over (or lines up) from shot to shot, we cannot help but feel the imposition of the spatial limitations of the frame on the flow of movement. When it comes to the coverage of certain events, the midcentury film image admits its failures. One framing must constantly be exchanged for another framing, as though the phenomenon being observed (the crack) sets in motion the unsettling of time-space conventions in the depiction. When it comes to coverage—the apprehending of the event—the long take is deemed irrelevant. When it comes to chasing the event, the spaces shown in each adjacent shot are neither contiguous, continuous, nor sequential. The serial qualities of the images' relation to time and space reveal the brokenness of this chain.

The failure of cinema to provide the temporal or spatial plenitude associated with "the event" is not uniquely exposed by sinkholes, but cinema has always tried to compensate for or cover over its inadequacies in relation to time and space (continuity editing being only one such system). Sinkholes reveal and flaunt these failures as constraints to be taunted. In each of its modes of disorganized vision—including repetition, double framing, fractured linearity, and swallowing—the sinkhole reveals the sham of spatiotemporal coherence. The cinematic image always involves repetitions, unnatural arbitrary bracketing, and a quasi-serial rather than continuous relationship to the flow of time. But the appearance of a sinkhole in these midcentury films often makes obvious the inherent discontinuities of recording an event cinematically.

There is something afoot in film theory: an interest in the cinematic image as an archive of the Anthropocene, a knotty archive that needs untangling to understand how we got the planet to this point. As Jennifer Fay writes, "Insofar as cinema has encouraged the production of artificial worlds and simulated, wholly anthropogenic weather, it is the aesthetic practice of the Anthropocene. Or, to put it more forcefully, cinema helps us to see and experience the Anthropocene as an aesthetic practice."[23] Prompted by earlier polemics of media archaeology, these theorists have unbound themselves from contemporary apocalypticism as the site for understanding the collapse of a sustainable ecosystem. Fay and others recognize in the old medium of film a defining relationality to the planet, one that now threatens to extinguish life as we know it. In considering the possibility that the ecological apocalypse is not a dystopia of the far future but has already been set in action and is being experienced as a catastrophe by billions of beings (human and otherwise), our task as historians of the image must involve figuring out the aesthetic and ideological work that got us here.[24] This task is one of excavation or spelunking. Using his rich geologic language to describe the spatial and temporal complexity of the cinematic image, Bazin tells us, "One must pass beyond [the] first level of significance, where one soon reaches, beneath these social deposits, the crystalline mass of moral significance."[25]

Digital media and the web's moving-image genres (such as the GIF) teach about both what cinema is not and what cinema was, as well as what it could have been and what it can be.[26] The GIF and the cinema's non–digitally produced sinkhole share an odd historicity. This historicity comes into view when we encounter sinkholes in twentieth-first-century cinema, such as those in *2012, Geo-Disaster* (Thunder Levin, 2017), and *Sisters* (Jason Moore, 2015), which lack the formal disruptions elaborated in the disaster sequences of midcentury cinema and that continue to reside in the GIF. My point has not been simply to explain this odd historicity shared among some media and not others over the past sixty years. Instead, it has been to attend to what these images make clear when we stop seeing them as representational failures—to listen for what Morton calls a "being-quake" of which they may be symptoms.[27]

The GIF is itself a throwback to an earlier generation of digital imagery, namely, Web 1.0 animation. In this context, we might call it a "loophole" or even a "wormhole" to the capacities of an earlier, apparently lesser mode of depiction. Obviously, some of the disruptions that interest me could be seen to simply index the limitations of the period's special effects relative to our current moment. These spatiotemporal hiccups can easily be dismissed as compromises, work-arounds, or ways of guaranteeing maximum visual payoff for a production's investment in expensive pyrotechnics. In this essay, however, I have ignored these seeming inadequacies of midcentury special effects. I have done this to avoid participating in a teleology of ever-increasing realism aided by technological advancement. Seeing earlier films as notches on an evolutionary path toward perfect realism prevents us from understanding the aesthetic lures and embedded knowing of older media practices. If we were able to encounter earlier cinema's holes as a measure of more than technological inadequacy, we could resee the predigital-era cinema of catastrophe as a complex representational mode of negotiating with the ecological, a lost way of seeing that disturbs the outlook of Anthropos. What if these sinkholes unearthed something disordering about the Anthropocene that the new blockbusters can too easily forget or even cover over?

Notes

This essay has benefited from the invaluable insights and critiques of Eugenie Brinkema, Thomas Elsaesser, Ivan Girina, Aya Nassar, Marijn Nieuwenhuis, Michael Pigott, Karen Redrobe, Jeff Scheible, and the audience at the University of Nagoya.

1. Certain ecocatastrophes are not mappable, or easily given a scale, and thus challenge us with phenomena that cannot be narrativized in linear time-space trajectories. For a discussion of these issues and the question of animation in

ecodocs, see Karl Schoonover, "Documentaries without Documents: Ecocinema and Toxins," *NECSUS: European Journal of Media Studies* 2, no. 2 (Autumn 2013): 483–507.

2. Timothy Morton, *Hyperobjects: Philosophy and Ecology after the End of the World* (Minneapolis: University of Minnesota Press, 2013). In descriptive passages (115, 192), he mentions sinkholes twice in the book but does not treat them as hyperobjects head-on.

3. Morton, 3.

4. Footage of the sudden devouring of a stand of trees in Louisiana's Bayou Corne footage provides the basis for one of the most popular GIFs of a sinkhole, accessed June 6, 2019, https://giphy.com/gifs/xKhCnEOPmErCw.

5. The ubiquity of sinkholes in contemporary culture has meant that these ground-swallowing events are no longer associated with specific genres. We can see sinkholes supplying a venue for comedic denouement in *The Good Place* (NBC, season 1, episodes 4 and 5, 2016) and *Sisters* (Jason Moore, 2015) or allowing an art house documentary's oblique commentary on the Ma'ale Adumim settlements in the West Bank (*Salarium,* Sasha Litvintseva and Daniel Mann, 2018) when a geographer states, "A sinkhole opens up when the surface collapses." The organizers of a symposium at the University of Warwick entitled "Losing Ground: On Holes and Other Absences," where this essay was presented, produced a list of art projects on sinkholes, which can be found at https://sinkholesworkshop.wordpress.com/related-links/, accessed June 6, 2019.

6. Claiming to be "the world's largest collection of sinkhole images and video," the site thesinkhole.org provides another rich source of footage on this phenomenon; updated July 14, 2017.

7. Anna McCarthy, "Visual Pleasure and GIFs," in *Compact Cinematics: The Moving Image in the Age of Bit-Sized Media,* ed. Pepita Hesselberth and Maria Poulaki (London: Bloomsbury, 2017), 116.

8. For more on how GIFs relate formally to the looping found in experimental cinema, see David Bering-Porter, "The Automaton in All of Us: GIFs, Cinemagraphs and the Films of Martin Arnold," *The Moving Image Review and Art Journal* 3, no. 2 (December 2014): 178–92. A related discussion of looping bodies can be found in Akira Mizuta Lippit's "Digesture: Gesture and Inscription in Experimental Cinema," in *Migrations of Gesture,* ed. Carrie Noland and Sally Ann Ness (Minneapolis: University of Minnesota Press, 2008): 113–31.

9. Graig Uhlin, "Playing in the Gif(t) Economy," *Games and Culture* 9, no. 6 (November 2014): 4–5. DOI: 10.1177/1555412014549805, accessed July 10, 2018.

10. Uhlin, 8.

11. For more on the GIF's cut and its edges, see Peter L. Galison and Caroline A. Jones, *Invisibilities: Seeing and Unseeing the Anthropocene* (forthcoming).

12. McCarthy, "Visual Pleasure and GIFs," 114.

13. Morton, *Hyperobjects,* 16.

14. *Sisters* is another useful example of contemporary mainstream cinema's depiction of sinkholes. This time a sinkhole opens up below a pool in the midst of a fight between the film's two main characters, the sisters. The hole sucks the pool down into the ground across several shots. At first, cracks open up around the edge of the pool. Then there is an intercutting of the ground opening up and a series of reaction shots of characters from around the pool. Yet, we are granted full view of the hole in a full aerial framing that allows us to see the pool caving in. Also, there is no reversal or hesitation of time or space: with each progressive shot the sinkhole grows markedly deeper.

15. In this essay, I bracket two adjacent phenomena—quicksand and the black hole—since both have independent valences. As a trope, quicksand has a historical particularity, in its formal capacity to reverse the teleology of colonialism within the mise-en-scène. In this sense, it is more about revenge than it is about the infinite. The black hole has a specificity in 1970s and early 1980s sci-fi films, functioning as an escapist wormhole from the period's bankrupt geopolitics and poisoned ecology. For a popular perspective on quicksand in cinema and its fans ("sinkers"), see Radio Lab's episode "Quicksaaaand!," WNYC, October 10, 2013, https://www.wnycstudios.org/story/quicksand. This episode was based on Daniel Engber's article "Terra Infirma: The Rise and Fall of Quicksand," *Slate,* August 23, 2010, http://www.slate.com/articles/health_and_science/science/2010/08/terra_infirma. Engber directs our attention to fan lists of quicksand scenes. See, for example, the very inclusive list, updated November 24, 2005, http://www.quicksandmovies.net/scenes26.html.

16. From this perspective, we could say that the sinkhole appears as the ultimate manifestation of Mary Douglas's definition of "dirt," which she famously claims "is essentially disorder." Could it be that in our contemporary pollution-saturated and toxic world, virtual engagements with the sinkhole (moving images) have become a repository in which we explore the ultimate destiny of filth? Douglas writes, "The reaction to dirt is continuous with other reactions to ambiguity or anomaly," words that Kristeva took as a means of facilitating her canonical discussions of abjection so productive to scholars working in a variety of areas, not the least of whom being Judith Butler. But rather than banishing the ambiguous or anomalous, the sinkhole's cinematic intervals revel in the indeterminate.

17. Laura Mulvey, "Visual Pleasure and Narrative Cinema," *Screen* 16, no. 3 (October 1975): 11–12.

18. Helen Wheatley, "Beautiful Images in Spectacular Clarity: Spectacular Television, Landscape Programming and the Question of (Tele)visual Pleasure," *Screen* 52, no. 2 (July 2011): 243–44.

19. McCarthy, "Visual Pleasure and GIFs," 114, 113.

20. Quoted in Helen Wheatley, *Spectacular Television: Exploring Televisual Pleasure* (New York: I. B. Tauris, 2016), 17.

21. This space of the unrecoverable operates as spectacle and antispectacle. On the one hand, as spectacle it proposes a slowing of the narrative to take in the exceptional and menacing presence in the image, here frustrating any teleological impulses of the film's adventure narrative (its investigatory and revelatory promises). On the other hand, as antispectacle this void refuses to provide a space (venue) in which the viewer can revel in the pure splendor of the unknown, the sublime, and so forth (as can be found elsewhere, such as in the crystal shower sequence).

22. Susan Sontag, "The Imagination of Disaster," *Commentary,* no. 40 (October 1, 1965): 43.

23. Jennifer Fay, *Inhospitable World: Cinema in the Time of the Anthropocene* (New York: Oxford University Press, 2018), 4.

24. As Jennifer Peterson and Graig Uhlin write, "Film and media texts trace a cultural history of the Anthropocene, charting the ways of living and thinking that have led to this crisis"; Jennifer Peterson and Graig Uhlin, "Film and Media Studies in the Anthropocene," *Journal of Cinema and Media Studies* 58, no. 2 (Winter 2019): 142–45.

25. André Bazin, "The Great Diptych: Geology and Relief," in *Orson Welles: A Critical View* (New York: Harper and Row, 1978), 65.

26. Dudley Andrew, *What Cinema Is! Bazin's Quest and Its Charge* (Malden, Mass.: Wiley-Blackwell, 2010).

27. "The discovery of hyperobjects and OOO (object-oriented ontology) are symptoms of a fundamental shaking of being, a being-quake. The ground of being is shaken"; Morton, *Hyperobjects,* 19.

CHAPTER ELEVEN

Underground Film

Thinking Vertically across the *and* of Cinema and Media Studies

Karen Redrobe

My title suggests a paradox in its invitation to think simultaneously in vertical and horizontal ways. This giddy mode emerges at the intersection of two forces operating within the hybrid field of cinema and media studies at a moment that can feel disorienting and limitless. On the one hand, a generation of younger and midcareer scholars is reflecting anew on the geopolitics of the field and calling for methodological and theoretical approaches, as well as objects of study, that are less Anglo- and Eurocentric than the canon of cinema and media studies has often been. These voices highlight the need for greater collaboration and horizontal exchanges and reject models of expansion that are additive but not transformative. On the other hand, media studies scholars have expanded our objects in ways that demand new thinking about environment, infrastructure, and materiality, often turning away from image analysis and toward explicitly vertical, infrastructural modes of thought. These pulls—horizontally across the globe and vertically toward new infrastructural objects—often emerge in conjunction with each other, yet they can feel like both an intellectual responsibility and an impossibility, certainly for the solo researcher. This vertical space and the often-horizontal infrastructures that it organizes and renders visible have become vitally important to contemporary media paradigms. But what, if anything, does the analysis of individual films have to offer when our scale is planetary or even universal, and how do we move among these shifting scales? I will consider these questions by entering into the subterranean space of the cinematic mine, which mentally and visually moves us along both vertical and horizontal paths into and across the earth's terrain.[1]

Global Film Theory and the Cinematic Mine

I first began thinking about the theoretical potential of the underground cinematic mine as a node of thought when I noticed a proliferation of early twenty-first century films, both fictional and documentary, about Chinese coal mining, as well as an increased press interest in Chinese mining conditions. These films included *Blind Shaft* (Li Yang, 2003); *The Shaft* (Zhang Chi, 2008); *San Li Dong* (Lin Xin, 2007); *Land of Black and Gold* (Kai Jia and Xiaofeng Li, 2011); *To the Light* (Yaunchen Liu, 2011); *A Touch of Sin* (Jia Zhangke, 2013); *In the Underground* (Zhantao Song, 2015); and *Behemoth* (Zhao Liang, 2015).[2]

In China, as in other parts of the world, mining conditions are dangerous and often underregulated, and these conditions feature in many of these films. But the films and their reviews, often created for a Western festival audience, rarely consider the international context for or implicatedness of "the West" in the conditions being descried.[3] As Danielle Wu writes of *Behemoth,* "This singular perpetuating narrative of China [as 'inherently wicked'] incubates existing xenophobia and resentment for Communism, which reaffirms the 'successes' of democracy. These tired viewpoints often conveniently omit Western democracy's own complicity in creating hazardous environments."[4] In part because of my own scholarly limitations, and in part to bring the West's history of mining and mining films into dialogue with these recent Chinese mining films, this essay will move backward in time and will shift geographic contexts to focus on earlier cinematic examples taken from Europe and North America, places where coal mining is now seen as a dying industry.[5]

But I want to pause briefly on the images that first drew me down into cinema's mines. The formal qualities of the contemporary cinematic images of the mine repeat across time and space in part because generic codes are being followed, but in part because the node of the mine enforces certain types of cinematography. The darkness of the mine gives it a quality of anonymity and fungibility, a "non-place" hard to distinguish from other similar places.[6] These qualities combine to make mining films prone to comparative and analogic modes of thinking that establish, at times too easily, similarities and solidarities between humans underground.

Emerging contemporaneously with and as a counterpoint to digital cinema's vertical turn as described by Kristin Whissel, a turn that primarily engages the space between the earth's surface and the universe above, privileges aerial and omniscient perspectives, and posits the body as immortal and unbound by gravity, the mining films I have mentioned "underground" (rather than "ground" or "elevate") twenty-first-century cinematic vision, minds, and methods.[7] *Into the Light* opens by juxtaposing the extraction of a horizontal miner's corpse and the vertical descent of living miners in a shaft elevator, confounding the axes along which we understand humans and precious resources to travel. This, like the camera's lingering on the naked and dirty flesh of miners in cramped tunnels and shower scenes, or the collapse of the mine roof onto miners within, is one of many visual tropes familiar from earlier mining films that repeats into this century, asserting generic affiliations across national boundaries, historical periods, political differences, and film cultures. The British film *A Day in the Life of the Coal Miner,* for example, establishes as early as 1910 some of the key locations and tasks that persist throughout the genre, which cuts across the categories of fiction and nonfiction film: the miner's cottage, the pithead, the distribution of lamps, miners descending and working the coalface, miners getting trapped and rescued, and the removal of tubs (Figure 11.1).

Mining cinema is and has always been a vertical cinema of gravity, and it exerts a downward pull. Shooting inside of real mines generates images and viewing positions that are partially sighted, limited, fumbling,

FIGURE 11.1. Miners descending. *A Day in the Life of the Coal Miner* (1910).

precarious, claustrophobic, and dependent.[8] The mining film often performs a certain incompatibility or tension between different types of depth. Shooting deep in the earth, for example, dramatically infringes on depth of field, as we learn from John Sayles when he describes the filming of the West Virginia mine scenes in *Matewan* (1987) with skilled cinematographer Haskell Wexler: "We were forced to work in truly low light levels, with a depth-of-field of inches or less. With this little depth, even slow movement, like a miner crawling toward the camera, becomes an extremely critical focus problem . . . we were determined to capture the claustrophobia and discomfort of working in 'low coal,' crawling through muck puddles on your hands and knees with the top only three feet above you."[9]

Whether documentary or fictional in nature, mining films shot inside of mines (and even some of those that are not) also almost inevitably participate in some level of community coproduction, making use not only of the authenticity of miners' bodies shaped by underground work but also of their expertise in navigating the precarious space of the mine. The pocket-like physical structure of the mine generates on film a type of visual sameness that operates like a narrative force within the genre. This sameness, produced in the image by the factors of both light and space, encourages viewers and readers of coal narratives, often in problematic ways, to make comparisons and draw connections across cultural differences and historical periods. For example, in the edited collection *Caverns of Night: Coal Mines in Art, Literature, and Film,* William B. Thesing universalizes what he calls the "aesthetics of coal," reminding readers that "coal is found on every continent on earth." Of the collection's geographic reach, he writes, "The focus of this study is on the coal-mining enterprise in Western Europe and America in the nineteenth and twentieth centuries. Nevertheless, the aesthetic and social issues examined in these essays have an applicability to the universal human condition."[10] Coal-mining narratives frequently assert a sentimental humanistic sameness among people, an assertion visually undergirded by the fact that coal dust and low light levels make the distinguishing features of individuals difficult to perceive. As George Orwell writes of the "fillers" who shovel all day on their knees in his essay, "Down the Mine" (1937), "You can hardly tell by the look of them whether they are young or old. . . . [W]hen they are black and naked they all look alike."[11] This assertion has the potential to give rise to meaningful solidarity, but also violent fantasy, or perhaps something entirely more nuanced than a scenario of pure sameness or difference allows.

Here Anne Anlin Cheng's intervention into the way we conceptualize the intersection of race, vision, and freedom is useful. Counterintuitively resisting the binary that posits surfaces as being superficial in contrast to the authenticity of depth, she introduces numerous modern examples, often mediated by cinema, in which skins "reveal and conceal" and "have depth, complexity, and their own behaviors and identities."[12] Josephine Baker's cinematic performances become privileged examples, and the first of those Cheng discusses involves Baker's racialized encounter with coal. In *La Sirène des Tropiques* (Henri Étiévant, 1927), a narrative structured around the intersection of transgressive desire and extraction economies, Baker plays Papitou, a woman identified as being from "Down There—in the Tropics." Papitou stows away on a ship bound for France, and while being chased by the passengers, she falls into the ship's coal pit and disguises herself with coal dust. Soon after, she transforms herself from black to white with the help of the ship's flour bin. Cheng discovers in these scenes a sense of "blackness" as ambivalent, an underscoring of "the unreliability of presumed racial legibility," as well as Baker's delight in playing with her body's malleable materiality, and for Cheng, the stakes of this rethinking of surface and depth are high. She writes, "If what we deem to be immutable is in fact mutable and what we believe to be surface may be profoundly ontologically structuring, then we would need to rearticulate the very assumptions (authenticity, identity, shared universal humanity, etc.) on which the rhetoric of freedom is built."[13]

Yet we find a wariness that is related to the mutability Cheng highlights in Baker's performance in an essay by Ina Rae Hark that reflects carefully on the utopian visions of sameness and solidarity to which mining—and, to be more specific, coal dust on faces on film—gives rise in John Sayles's film *Matewan* (1987). Hark argues that Sayles takes a story about the "historical oppression of miners" and tries to fit it into a "liberal ideology of the brotherhood of man and the impossibility of fighting violence with violence."[14] Sayles's conflation of the history and legacy of American slavery and the exploitation of white miners, Hark suggests, operates in part through a visual rhyme or resonance specific to the mining context that encourages a mode of analogical thinking that represses difference by conflating poverty and racial oppression.[15] Hark's concern about the unstable political effects of coal-blackened faces on film recalls Eric Lott's discussion of "the contradictions in blackface performance," and his recognition that, although in the United States "capitalism was the ultimate enemy" of both African American people and the white working class, "racial feeling" was "the immediate obstacle; energies directed against the state apparatus might too easily join those focused on black people."[16] Lott tries—via Marx—to end his book on an optimistic note, "a visionary conception of human collectivity" (238). But if the concept of the human, and by extension humanism and the humanities, can take on meaning only through the existence of a racially charged category of the nonhuman, we may have to do our thinking inside this tense and contradictory node, acknowledging the violence and discomfort it simultaneously works to resist and generate.

As we try to consider local and historical specificities without completely fragmenting or atomizing the field and making a global conversation impossible, to think comparatively while avoiding what Gayatri Chakravorty Spivak describes as "varieties of sameness" that "give in too easily to the false promises of a level playing field," mining films are interesting because they have repeatedly foregrounded, visually and narratively, the arguments for, as well as the potential violence of, forging alliances across difference.[17] This narrative tension results in part from the fact that, as Timothy Mitchell has powerfully argued, because coal mining depended on the relatively autonomous expertise and presence of miners underground, miners experienced unprecedented levels of mass collective agency, or what C. Goodrich in 1925 called "the miner's freedom," a freedom derived from "the extraordinary concentrations of carbon energy whose flow they could now slow, disrupt, or cut off."[18] But the new forms of democracy and mass political agency that arise as a result of the increasing dependence on coal are also intertwined, Mitchell points out, with "the concentration of population in cities and in manufacturing, enabled in part by the control of colonized territories and enslaved labour forces."[19] This fact should prevent this unprecedented collective power of workers from being idealized in oversimplistic ways.

Here, it might also be helpful to introduce Macarena Gómez-Barris's recent observation that Eurocentric theories of visual power rooted and invested in paradigms of modernity, as Michel Foucault's theories are, for example, often ignore what Gómez-Barris calls "the weight of colonial seeing" and tend to "render invisible the enclosure, the plantation, the shop, and the reservation." She develops a method that brings forward "submerged perspectives," calls for deeper efforts to "move decolonial theory into fuller engagement with scholarship on race, sexuality, and Indigenous studies," and critiques non-Indigenous scholars for actually repeating extractive logics on an intellectual level.[20] Mining films from the first half of the twentieth century represent an important site both for contemplating how cinema engages extraction and submerged perspectives, and for registering and negotiating this complex imbrication of changing forms of energy, power, and modes of collective political expression with various markers of identity, including nationality, class, and race. But while mines and miners on film can become almost indistinguishable from each other, leading to reductive alignments, many mining film narratives also draw attention to what Bhaskar Sarkar calls the "ongoing truck between difference and sameness."[21] For example, Humphrey Jennings's drama documentary/propaganda film *The Silent Village* (1943) establishes an analogy between the people of the mining village of Lidice, Czechoslovakia, who perished in a Nazi massacre in 1942, and the people of the Welsh mining village of Cwmgiedd, who agreed to improvise daily life, and reenact the Nazi occupation and destruction of Lidice, for Jennings's film.[22] By acting *in the place of* the mining village of Lidice, the Welsh mining community brings the war home, heightening the audience's affect around the threat of fascism in the service of mobilization. But in spite of this strategic goal, the film carefully prevents analogy from falling into identity, as when, near the beginning of the film, a title asserts, "Such is life at Cwmgiedd in the Western Valley of Wales—and such too was life in Lidice until the coming of Fascism." And by avoiding the conflation of different groups of people that frequently occurs within the space of the cinematic mine, *The Silent Village* communicates not only the suffering undergone by the people of Lidice and the potential for ordinary British people to suffer in the same way at the hands of the Nazis, but also the existing English oppression and cultural marginalization of the Welsh. At minute 16:50 in the film, the Nazi occupiers declare "NO MORE WELSH" to the inhabitants of Welsh "Lidice," instigating an underground resistance movement that urges children to speak Welsh in order not to forget their native tongue. Though mining here, as in other films, invites comparative thinking, the two struggles being compared remain distinguishable, in part through the stark difference between the living and the dead; as a result, more complex understandings of the relationship between nationality and oppression begin to emerge.

G. W. Pabst's French-German coproduction *Kameradschaft* (Germany 1931; United States and France, 1932) offers an early example of the more common pattern of erasing difference by entering the mine. *Kameradschaft* is based on the Courrières mining disaster of 1906 in which 1,099 miners died, and where German miners assisted in the rescue of French miners trapped by fire. While, as Mitchell underscores, the historical Courrières disaster resulted in a massive general strike that "paralysed Paris," Pabst shifts his narrative away from collective struggle and toward the theme of transnational cooperation.[23] He also moves the setting from 1906 to the postwar year of 1919, and adds to the story a gate marking the Franco-German border within the mine, which has to be broken through in order for the rescue to occur. Having rendered the border visible, Pabst then underscores the potential power of cross-border solidarity among miners through a lengthy tracking shot made possible only by the fact that, rather than filming in an actual mine, he built what James Steffen notes is a "massive, authentically detailed reconstruction of a mine interior, designed by Erno Metzner and Karl Vollbrecht" (Metzner and Vollbrecht may have been inspired by the reconstruction of a mine that has been on display in Munich's Deutsches Museum since 1925).[24] The reconstruction allows Pabst to bypass the mine's usual cinematographic constraints and to create the illusion through the tracking shot of a limitless underground horizontal mobility rarely seen in this genre. Pabst gives exaggerated visual form to a utopian desire to transcend national differences through a camera mobility, depth of field, and clarity of vision that the light constraints and nodal structure of the mine usually prohibit. But if the camera's freedom of movement posits a transnational optimism and an overly rosy vision of peacetime at the level of human interactions, this view is held in check by the fact that the camera's path is doubled by the equally nimble but deadly path of an underground fire. The tension in this scene between utopian and devastating, and volitional and nonvolitional versions of unchecked mobility provokes thought about how the mine's geologic underground structure takes on geopolitical meaning in different films at different moments.

Gavin Bridge, a British economic geographer, describes the mine shaft as a "discrete, molecular point of access rather than a contiguous territorial claim" and argues, "The punctuated, discontinuous geographies of extraction do not coincide well with notions of national territory or development."[25] On the one hand, the mine emerges as a space of political solidarity and resistance among workers, as Mitchell makes clear. Striking miners halt not just the production of coal but all capitalist production that depends on coal. But on the other hand, Bridge stresses, the mine's strained relationship with the nation guarantees nothing: "Land ceases to be part of national space and becomes instead a series of miniature corporate states: a modern mirror of feudal fiefdoms, with the corporate concession holder as sovereign."[26]

These questions about the mine's relationship to nationality, race, and economics can be usefully considered in the context of *The Proud Valley* (1940), a British Ealing Studio film directed by Pen Tennyson, the great-grandson of the renowned Victorian poet Alfred, Lord Tennyson, starring Paul Robeson, and set in 1938.[27] Made just as Robeson's communist and anticolonial politics were coming under increasing scrutiny in the United States, *The Proud Valley* would ultimately become his favorite film, and one could argue that Wales catalyzes Robeson's transnational approach to civil rights.[28] He claims that it was in Wales that he "first understood the struggles of the Negro people, or of any people, cannot be by itself—that is, the human struggle."[29] Yet like *Kameradschaft, The Proud Valley* gives audiovisual form to the violence that can exist within, or perhaps more precisely, be generated by, a politics of sameness and solidarity, in spite of the film's overt message, which celebrates the triumph of harmony in the apparently transnational and colorblind environment of the Welsh mining community. To notice and think about this aspect of the film is not to disregard the alliances, both fictional and historical, that existed between Robeson and the miners, but rather to pay attention to the question of who pays the price of solidarity within this fictional mining film, and what role the spaces of deep earth and the language of depth play in this realm.

Reviews of Robeson's singing, the press descriptions of his body, and the roles in which he was cast combine to suggest that Robeson essentially embodied the depth and the materiality of the earth, reminding us, as Kathryn Yusoff does, that "the energy regimes that structure material extraction were forced into black material and psychic life—of being energy for others, of putting sugar in the bowl, and in the muscles of white labor; as an 'object' of geochemical energy and the rationalization of the black body."[30] Robeson played characters possessing special knowledge of mines (Umbopa in *King Solomon's Mines* and David Goliath in *The Proud Valley*), and one journalist described him as "the huge black rock of a man who happens to be one of the world's most famous singers."[31] "Deep River," the 1905 version of which is the first entry in the Library of Congress's copyright files under the word "Deep," became Robeson's signature song and was one of his three favorites.[32] A 1924 article in the Rutgers *Targum* celebrates the "emotional depth" of Robeson's voice before a performance (that included "Deep River") in the university's gymnasium.[33] In 1940, Robeson described his songs as "simple little tales put to music, meaningless unless they come from deep inside"; a *New York Times* review from the same year discusses Robeson's "deep singer's breath"; and in 1941, Max de Schauensee declared, "Mr. Robeson is admirably suited to the spirituals of his own race, the deep and velvety vocal quality providing an ideal medium."[34] As a baritone, Robeson had a vocal range that was also marked by its depth or lowness, but the architecture of the concert hall, which Robeson had transformed into a space open to black musical traditions, prevented him from being able to hear his own deepest notes. Initially, he responded to this inaccessibility of his vocal depth by transposing his songs into higher keys, in spite of the fact that, as one article noted, "the richest part of his scale [was] in the bottom register."[35] But in 1940, with the help of a scientist from Rutgers, he pioneered at Carnegie Hall a sound-control technology called "the Robeson Technique," which had the effect of "shrin[king] the room way down" to create a "tonal envelope" around the singer imperceptible to audiences that allowed Robeson to hear his full range and to sing even lower than usual.[36]

Robeson's affinity with depth, then, was long-standing and often essentialized and racialized; but it was consolidated in a new way by a lifelong and particular affinity—one that was partly musical—with Welsh miners. He went down into the Welsh mines and sang with the miners, finding that "the Welsh people sing very much like we do—the Negro people—in many of our songs—beautiful songs."[37] He twice marched in solidarity with the Welsh miners, in 1927 and 1928, and again addressed the Miners' Eisteddfod in Porthcawl, Wales, in 1957, albeit by telephone because of the restrictions of his travel ban.[38]

In *The Proud Valley,* the name of Robeson's character, David Goliath, invokes a biblical drama and prefigures both the character's strength and his ultimate self-destruction. At the film's opening, we meet David, a black sailor and a vagrant who is consistently associated with mobility, has previously worked in the U.S. mines, and is now, the script tells us, on his way to look for work in a new armament factory in the Darren Valley, a fact that reminds us of the imbrication of energy and war. He hops what turns out to be a coal train and discovers he may be able to find work in a Welsh mine. The white vagrant already in his car is one of only two characters in the course of the entire film to explicitly comment on David's blackness. When David asks if he might find mining work, the man muses, "Well, maybe—there was a colored bloke, Blackie Ellis they called him." It is the beauty of David's disembodied voice as he fills in a missing bass part in the choral music from the street below the choir rehearsal room's window that gains him entry, sight unseen, into the ambitious miners' choir, which hopes to win the Eisteddfod competition (Figures 11.2 and 11.3).[39]

This musical belonging in turn gains him access to the miners' homes as well as, after some resistance, to the mine itself. When the choir master,

FIGURE 11.2. David's voice comes through the rehearsal room's open window (*The Proud Valley,* Pen Tennyson, 1940).

FIGURE 11.3. David sings from below on the street, with the choir above (*The Proud Valley,* Pen Tennyson, 1940).

Dick Parry, brings David to work, Seth, another miner, objects to a black man being brought to the pit. As David leans in to defend himself, Dick diffuses the tension by declaring, "Why, damn and blast it, man, aren't we all black down in that pit?"; he is supported by Evans, who says, "aggressively towards those with blackened faces," "Aye, take a look at yourselves."[40] As if to support Dick's argument about the universal blackness distributed by coal, the film offers numerous moments where either the white miners' skin tones become indistinguishable from Robeson's or Robeson's body fuses with that of a white miner in silhouette shots that create the illusion of a single organism, most noticeably when Robeson recovers Dick's body from a fire. Dick ultimately dies from this accident, and though the Eisteddfod has been postponed so that the Blaendy choir can compete, the choir abstains, replacing its entry with a performance of the song that David claims he used to sing for Dick when the two men were alone: "Deep River."

The film's narrative toys explicitly with Robeson's alignment with communism as David seems to transmit his own capacity for spatial and political movement to the miners when the mine is threatened with closure due to depletion.[41] He shows the miners that they can march on foot to London and accompanies them there, although he waits outside the door when they speak with the mine owners, stating, "This isn't Blaendy where everyone knows me. . . . I know what's best for you and your people. I'll wait here." Now on the brink of war, the owners agree to let an exploratory team search out passageways to other resource-rich nodes in an effort to save the mine. The off-screen voice of Sir John declares, "The government urgently needs coal," while Ned establishes an analogy between the pit and the trench, stating, "Coal in wartime is something worth taking risks for and our pits are an important part of the defense. Ay, as much as the front-line trenches are." Once back at the mine, David joins this high-risk expedition, but disaster strikes underground, and the men become trapped and oxygen-deprived. Dick's son, Emlyn, draws the straw to be the one to detonate the dynamite that might open an exit, but David knocks the boy out in order to detonate the blast himself (Figures 11.4 and 11.5). We see him momentarily blasted out of existence in a shot that places the black body at the intersection of the earth's material resistance to, and the human desire for, the limitless extraction of energy resources. This heroic action saves the Welsh miners, restores an economic future to the town, and energizes the community of song, but it does so at the expense of David's life (Figure 11.6).

FIGURE 11.4. David saves Emlyn (*The Proud Valley*, Pen Tennyson, 1940).

FIGURE 11.5. David initiates the suicidal blast and sacrifices himself (*The Proud Valley*, Pen Tennyson, 1940).

FIGURE 11.6. Miners celebrate renewed coal production under the Union Jack after David's death (*The Proud Valley,* Pen Tennyson, 1940).

Though this underground film is in some ways a labor film that dramatizes the plight and dignity of Welsh mining communities, it overcomes the miners' problems not by any structural economic change but by the displacement of mining's risk, the finite nature of energy resources and oxygen, and even Welsh marginalization within the United Kingdom, onto a foreign black body that is exploded into nothingness while seeming to live on in the same immaterial form in which that body was first encountered. As "Mam" leads the community in singing Welsh songs, the final shots of the film dissolve the posthumous voice of David accompanied by the Welsh choir into the Welsh mountains, fusing the miners back into their proper rural location, far from the city and the center of power. The final scenic shot of the shooting script states, "The camera swings onto the crest of the hills, then past the hills into the sky. David's voice rises supreme." But what is the effect of this transcendent ending, and does it transform the miners, through the sacrifice of David, from a potentially radical political collective into a culturally (i.e., musically) distinct but ultimately politically compliant and economically viable community vis-à-vis the imperial power of the mine-owning state?

Sergio Mims suggests, "You can rightly argue that Robeson plays one of the earliest examples of the 'Magical Negro' in the film; as in the black man who gives/uses his own life, if necessary, to improve and better the lives of white people in the film without any consideration for his own." And yet Robeson's star persona, the intertextual resonance and afterlife of his performances of "Deep River," which appears in the film, and Robeson's continued solidarity with Welsh and Scottish miners throughout his life suggest that the film's devastating closure fails fully to contain the more radical energy node that *The Proud Valley* opens up when it audiovisualizes the intersection of black subjectivity, the white working poor, and underground extraction economies.[42] Yusoff, following the caution of many Black Studies scholars, including Saidiya Hartman, to avoid reproducing the spectacle of black suffering and "the genre of black (social) death through geologic means," turns to black poetics.[43] She writes:

> In a corollary to geology's inhuman/inhumane modes of description, black poetics is epoch making in its redirection of the racial logics of extraction through new energetic modes and understandings of relation, desedimenting the forms of inhuman historicity that are established through colonialism. Hartman comments that these practices and poetics forged in the terror of slavery were necessarily subterranean: "For this opacity, the subterranean and veiled character of slave song must be considered in relation to the dominant imposition of transparency and the degrading hypervisibility of the enslaved. . . ." (Hartman 2007, 36). In the forged alliances with the inhuman, a different mode of subjective relation is forged, where Blackness is a name for nonnormative subjectivity (Moten 2003, 2016), or, in Césaire's ([1972] 2000, 55) words, a "communistic materialism." (19)

The energy, then, of which I speak here is not that contained in coal, but rather in Robeson, in his activism, his refusals, his songs, his audiences, and his friendships. Jacqueline Rose describes it in her discussion of the revolutionary fighter Rosa Luxemburg and women in dark times as "aliveness" or "the energy and potential of the people as a form of life."[44] Among the other things that cinema can do perhaps better than other media, it records, even as it often simultaneously works to contain, this potential of the people as a form of life, with the simultaneity producing what Cheng calls "visual pleasure in the contaminated zone."[45] The existence and complexity of the nature of this pleasure offer one argument for keeping film analysis and history in the picture, even as we try to think about the intertwining of energy with global media and political infrastructures and our pedagogical pasts, presents, and futures, all of which wrap themselves along the vertical axis from coal seams to satellites.[46]

Writing about the Chinese mining film *Blind Shaft,* Rey Chow warns against viewing such a film "from the domain of the West" and urges us to resist "the temptation of readily deciphering the film's message as simply an other-culture-speak (or a kind of third-world-speak), with the kind of neoliberal, egalitarian (but in fact discriminatory) undertone that comes across all too often in influential publications such as the *New York Times.*"[47] As we think about the role of the intellectual in this conversation that takes place at the intersection of mining and cinema and media studies, film history offers another interesting node for thought: *The Stars Look Down,* directed by Carol Reed and released in 1940, the same year as *The Proud Valley.* While both films struggled to establish new levels of realism in British filmmaking, they did so on different grounds. Publicity materials for *The Proud Valley* emphasized an authenticity derived from the involvement of Welsh people, including the use of "native talent," the fact that scriptwriter Jack Jones had been a miner, and that art director William Shingleton had been permitted to make on-site sketches for the underground scenes by the Rhondda Colliery Company.[48] By contrast, Reed's film established all kinds of precedents in British filmmaking. The set for the underground scenes was the largest (at six hundred square feet) and most expensive ever constructed in the history of the Twickenham Studios, with the mine construction costing 6,000 pounds.[49] A complete row of cottages was built based on photographs of Great Clifton, near Workington, which also provided authentic miners' clothing and pit ponies. A working cage was constructed for the mine shaft, and fifty tons of coal were delivered to the studio for the construction of a coal face from which the art department then took cast impressions. This cast impression was added to the back of the pit whenever Reed needed to transform the pit head into the bottom of the pit. As *The Birkenhead News* astutely observed, "The whole scene is dropped by a thousand feet into the earth without being moved."[50]

The Stars Look Down explores the attempt to align politically engaged academically informed work with the underground labor of mining, but reviews highlight the ambivalence of the film's political message. One announcement notes, "With *The Stars Look Down,* the newly awakened social conscience of the film world has reached England. The democratic moral is not so pointed as it is in some American films and the Trade

FIGURE 11.7. Superimposed image of a miner in *The Stars Look Down* (Carol Reed, 1940).

Unions are treated rather shabbily."[51] This ambivalence seems to have been shared, and perhaps cultivated, by Reed himself. When the shooting script describes a moment in the film that "extols the virtues of miners and reminds the public that the entire industrial system and wealth of the country depends on the hazardous work these men do," Reed's pencil notations state simply, "Oh. God."[52]

Davey Fenwick (Michael Redgrave) leaves his Lancashire mining town on a university scholarship in the hope of becoming a political advocate *for* miners fighting against privatization. He is soon asked to appear in the houses of Parliament to propose the first reading of the Coal Miners' Bill, and when he does, Reed does something rather unusual. When trying to establish identification between miners and nonminers, most mining films either plunge the camera below the surface of the earth or create the illusion of doing so, as if taking spectators down into another world. *The Stars Look Down* was renowned for its authentic re-creation of the underground mine, so this was certainly within Reed's grasp; but at the moment of Davey's speech, Reed instead decides to superimpose stock footage of a working miner over Davey's academic talking head (Figure 11.7).

But what is the effect of this aesthetic decision? As noted earlier, Reed's marginalia suggest that he was more interested than the scriptwriter in maintaining rather than resolving the tension between working miners and education-infused political action. While the scriptwriter describes Davey's mother, Martha, as "looking down on [Davey]" from the Ladies' Gallery in Parliament, "with tears running down her face," Reed scribbles, "Martha, this lovely character—who is disgusted with her son at having left the pit and not continuing in the family tradition—would never appreciate that her son had done good—to her, he is a Bolshi," underscoring Reed's reluctance to resolve the two worlds.[53] In the superimposed shot, those above and those below the earth appear in the same frame, yet they are not conflated. Reed seems both to recognize and to want his audience to recognize that solidarity among miners, university graduates, and politicians may be something of a spectral conjuring act, one that perhaps leaves the vertical hierarchies the film depicts relatively unchanged, not unlike the film's set, which created new levels of realism by cleverly "dropping" the whole scene by a thousand feet without any actual movement taking place. This is not to say that it is pointless for scholars to try think our way into or across the mine (or indeed other such spaces of extraction, like the quarry), but simply to be aware that the heady, underground thinking that emerges as part of the material turn, my own included, may allow us to see and think more deeply into our cultural objects, but without relocating any of the primary actors. Further, as Gómez-Barris suggests, such intellectual work may ultimately reenact extractive logics rather than "lift[ing] submerged perspectives"; as *The Proud Valley* shows, submerged perspectives do not all come from the same place, and they may not necessarily be in alignment with each other, even if they can look the same from above ground.[54] In the United States of America, rural, white, poor high school graduates, many of them from defunct mining, farming, and manufacturing communities where it used to be possible to make a living without access to higher education, are now the least likely of all populations to go to college, and as we can see all around us, the stakes of this immobility are high. But the mobility that higher education offers has also got its own problems, with its logics of extraction and its discourses of lifting up, finding gems, unearthing finds, penetrating, breaking through, digging deep, and, if we are honest, looking down. I am interested in how mining films help us think about such things.

Notes

This essay was inspired by the call for papers for the June 2016 Shanghai conference on the topic "Film Theory in Media History: 'Nodes' and 'Edges,'" organized by the Shanghai Film Academy, Shanghai University, Shanghai-Berkley Film and Media Research Center, *Dianying yishu* (*Film art*), and the Permanent Seminar on Histories of Film Theories. Thanks to Weihong Bao. Thanks also to the Penn History of Art and Cinema and Media Studies colloquia, the Yale Film and Media Studies program, and to the Penn Department of History of Art for research support.

1. American film critic Manny Farber first used the term "underground film" in print in his 1957 essay "Underground Films," in *Negative Space: Manny Farber on the Movies* (New York: Da Capo Press, 1998), 12–24.

2. Thanks to Ling Zhang for drawing some of these films to my attention.

3. Responding to an early draft of this paper at Peking University, Daoxin Li distinguished between this contemporary group of frequently censored Chinese mining films, which critique the lack of government oversight of the mines, and an earlier history of Chinese mining films in the 1930s and 1940s, where worker struggles are aligned with nationalism. Thanks to Professor Li and his students, and also to Professor Wangli Huang and her students at Shanghai University, for their comments.

4. Danielle Wu, "A Documentary about China's Coal Mining Industry Fuels Western Biases," *Hyperallergic*, February 7, 2017, https://hyperallergic.com/356989/a-documentary-about-chinas-coal-mining-industry-fuels-western-biases/.

5. While female miners appear in contemporary mining films, as well as in Émile Zola's *Germinal* (1885), women tend to play the secondary role of wives and daughters in the films I discuss here. For a fuller discussion of this issue, see Juliana Starr, "Coal Miners' Daughters: Representations of Women in *Germinal, Matewan,* and *Harlan County, USA,*" *Excavatio: Emile Zola and Naturalism* 22, no. 1–2 (2007): 73–86.

6. See Marc Augé, *Non-places: Introduction to an Anthropology of Supermodernity* (London: Verso, 1995).

7. See Kristin Whissel, *Spectacular Digital Effects: CGI and Contemporary Cinema* (Durham: Duke University Press, 2004).

8. When not shot on location, the realism of mine scenes often involves mimicking the shooting constraints of the actual mine.

9. John Sayles, *Thinking in Pictures: The Making of the Movie* Matewan (1987; Cambridge, Mass.: DaCapo Press, 2003), 74.

10. William B. Thesing, ed., *Caverns of Night: Coal Mines in Art, Literature, and Film* (Columbia: University of South Carolina Press, 2000), xii.

11. George Orwell, "Down the Mine," first published in *The Road to Wigan Pier,* pt. 1, chap. 2 (London: V. Gollancz, 1937), accessed July 15, 2019, http://www.george-orwell.org/Down_The_Mine/0.html.

12. Anne Anlin Cheng, *Second Skin: Josephine Baker and the Modern Surface* (New York: Oxford University Press, 2011), 11.

13. Cheng, 171.

14. Ina Rae Hark, "Blackfaced Rednecks: The Problem of Backcountry Whites as Victims in John Sayles's *Matewan,*" in Thesing, *Caverns of Night,* 261.

15. Hark, 259.

16. Eric Lott, *Love and Theft: Blackface, Minstrelsy, and the American Working Class* (New York: Oxford University Press, 1993), 234, 237.

17. Gayatri Chakravorty Spivak, "Rethinking Comparativism," *New Literary History* 40, no. 3 (Summer 2009): 611.

18. Timothy Mitchell, "Carbon Democracy," *Economy and Society* 38, no. 3 (August 2009): 399–432; C. Goodrich, *The Miner's Freedom: A Study of the Working Life in a Changing Industry* (Boston: Marshall Jones, 1925), quoted in Mitchell, "Carbon Democracy," 403–4. Mitchell argues that after the Second World War, the coal miners of Europe constituted a "militant threat to corporatist democratic politics," and he traces how U.S. planners engineered a shift from coal to oil because oil could be extracted by pressure rather than by people; transported by pipelines, not railways (thus breaking the potency of collective strikes); and transported across borders by sea, where workers were beyond the "territorial spaces governed by the labour regulations and democratic rights won in the era of widespread coal and railway strikes" (406–7). The recent wave of coal-mining films should be considered within this longer, entangled, and transnational history of the relationship among workers' rights, underground energy nodes, and changing forms of state and nonstate power. Thanks to Lisa Mitchell for this reference.

19. Mitchell, "Carbon Democracy," 403.

20. Macarena Gómez-Barris, *The Extractive Zone: Social Ecologies and Decolonial Perspectives* (Durham, N.C.: Duke University Press, 2017), 2, 5.

21. Bhaskar Sarkar, "Plasticity and the Global," *Framework* 56, no. 2 (Fall 2015): 452.

22. Thanks to Katie Trumpener for directing me to this film.

23. Mitchell, "Carbon Democracy," 405.

24. James Steffen, "Kameradschaft," Film Article, Turner Classic Movies, accessed March 17, 2017, http://www.tcm.com/this-month/article/107411%7C0/Kameradschaft.html.

25. Gavin Bridge, "The Hole World: Scales and Spaces of Extraction," *Scenario* 05, "Extraction" (Fall 2015): 3.

26. Bridge, 3.

27. I regret that this manuscript was completed before the publication of Shana L. Redmond's excellent book *Everything Man: the Form and Function of Paul Robeson* (Durham: Duke University Press, 2020) as her discussion of Robeson's voice and the concept of vibration is most relevant to this discussion. Robeson withdrew from public life in his final years for health reasons. While Simon Callow describes Robeson's refusal to acknowledge Stalin's crimes as "the tragedy of his life," it is worth noting that in his testimony of July 13, 1956, before the House Un-American Activities Committee, Robeson refused to discuss Stalin's crimes with Richard Arens as a representative of a government attempting to use Stalin's actions to assert its own morally superior position. Robeson states: "I have told you, Mister, that I would not discuss anything with the people who have murdered 60 million of my people, and I will not discuss Stalin with you. . . . I will discuss Stalin when I may be among the Russian people some day singing for them, and I will discuss it there. It is their problem." See Simon Callow, "The Emperor Robeson," *New York Review of Books,* February 8, 2018, 11; Philip S. Foner, ed., *Paul Robeson Speaks: Writings, Speeches, Interviews, 1918–1974* (New York: Citadel, 1978), 429.

28. See Thomas Cripps, "Paul Robeson and Black Identity in American Movies," *Massachusetts Review* 11, no. 3 (Summer 1970): 482.

29. Paul Robeson, "Pacifica Radio Interview, San Francisco, March 15, 1958," in Foner, *Paul Robeson Speaks,* 453.

30. Kathryn Yusoff, *A Billion Black Anthropocenes or None* (Minneapolis: University of Minnesota Press, 2018), 16.

31. Richard Davis, "World Will Never Accept Slavery, Robeson Asserts," *Milwaukee Journal,* October 20, 1941, n.p., Paul Robeson Archive, Special Collections, Rutgers University, Box 2, Folder 1, Newspaper clippings 1940–43.

32. Wayne D. Shirley details how "Deep River" retroactively becomes "a *famous old* spiritual." See Wayne D. Shirley, "The Coming of 'Deep River,'" *American Music* 15, no. 4 (Winter 1997): 513. Shirley notes that the first copyright file to be found in the Library of Congress under the word "Deep" is the Afro-British composer Samuel Coleridge-Taylor's (1875–1912) 1905 version of the song. Although the song is now strongly associated with African American history, Shirley demonstrates how it has been associated with timelessness, all-Americanness (rather than a "particularly black" identity), globally shared feeling, and the fusion of black American and classical European musical traditions, a fusion strongly on display in *The Proud Valley.* See Shirley, 498, 494, 518, and 504

33. "Robeson to Sing in Gym on December 17," *The Targum,* December 9, 1924, n.p., Paul Robeson Archive, Special Collections, Rutgers University, Box 1, Folder 1, Newspaper clippings 1916–24.

34. "Robeson 'Makes His Debut' at Princeton in Stage Role," *Daily Home News,* August 13, 1940, n.p.; "Several Ovations Welcome Robeson," *New York Times,* October 7, 1940, n.p.; Max de Schauensee, "Great Negro Singers of Our

Day," *Philadelphia, PA Evening Ledger,* July 12, 1941, n.p. All found in Paul Robeson Archive, Special Collections, Rutgers University, Box 2, Folder 1, Newspaper clippings 1940–43.

35. *Daily Home News,* November 15, 1940, n.p., Paul Robeson Archive, Special Collections, Rutgers University, Box 2, Folder 1, Newspaper clippings 1940–43.

36. The *Daily Home News* reports, "In the first concert in which the technique was tried at Carnegie Hall, Robeson was able to sing 'Water Body' in a lower key than he had ever used for that number in a concert"; *Daily Home News,* November 15, 1940, n.p., Paul Robeson Archive, Special Collections, Rutgers University, Box 2, Folder 1, Newspaper clippings 1940–43.

37. Paul Robeson, "Pacifica Radio Interview," in Foner, *Paul Robeson Speaks,* 453. For Robeson's favorite songs, see "Music of Today Is in Keeping with American Way—Robeson," in *Wichita, Kansas Eagle,* February 14, 1941, n.p., Paul Robeson Archive, Special Collections, Rutgers University, Box 2, Folder 1, Newspaper clippings 1940–43.

38. "Paul Robeson at the Miners' Eisteddfod, Porthcawl," 1957, BBC Radio Wales, http://www.bbc.co.uk/programmes/p00plvqw. For an in-depth discussion of Paul Robeson's relationship to Wales, see Mark Rhodes, "'They Feel Me a Part of That Land': Welsh Memorial Landscapes of Paul Robeson" (master's thesis, Kent State University, 2015), https://etd.ohiolink.edu/.

39. The shooting script repeatedly emphasizes David's disembodiment in this scene, describing him as "carried out of himself by the strength of his song," and his voice as "floating through the window," and highlights the verticality of the scene. David is "gazing up . . . as he sings" while the choir are "looking down to the pavement," with the shot being offered "from Dick's eyeline." *The Proud Valley Shooting Script,* August 11, 1939, S14892, 18, Special Collections, British Film Institute National Archive.

40. *The Proud Valley Shooting Script,* August 11, 1939, S14892, 31, Special Collections, British Film Institute National Archive.

41. *The Proud Valley* was written by Herbert Marshall, who studied filmmaking in the Soviet Union with Sergei Eisenstein before returning to Britain, where he cowrote *Tinker* (1949), a semidocumentary about the training boys receive before entering the mine. The film's associate producer was the Soviet filmmaker Sergei Nolbandov, who, five years after the release of *The Proud Valley,* was appointed as production supervisor on the British documentary *German Concentration Camps Factual Survey* (1945), which the British government shelved without showing to the public. The film had its premiere in 2014. See Manohla Dargis, "Revisiting Concentration Camps in Shattering Clarity," *New York Times,* January 5, 2017, https://www.nytimes.com/2017/01/05/movies/german-concentration-camps-factual-survey-review.html?_r=0.

42. Sergio Mins, “More Paul Robeson—His Favorite Film Proud Valley Coming to Blue Ray in January,” in *Shadow and Act: On Film, Television, and Web Content on Africa and Its Diaspora,* November 25, 2016, http://shadowandact.com/2016/11/25/more-paul-robeson-his-favorite-film-proud-valley-coming-out-on-blu-ray-dvd-in-jan/.

43. Yusoff, *A Billion Black Anthropocenes,* 17.

44. Jacqueline Rose, *Women in Dark Times* (London: Bloomsbury, 2014), 42. Peter Pickering’s short *A Star Drops In* (1949) documents Robeson’s interest in this energetic potential of miners. This film was part of a series of mining films made at DATA Film Productions for the *Mining Review.* See *Mining Review* 2, no. 11 (July 1949), http://www.screenonline.org.uk/film/id/474544/index.html. See also Patrick Russell, “Memories from the Mine: The Day I Filmed Paul Robeson,” British Film Institute, January 24, 2017, https://www.bfi.org.uk/news-opinion/news-bfi/interviews/paul-robeson-coal-mine-peter-pickering. In “Carbon Democracy,” Timothy Mitchell invokes Luxemburg, noting her departure from Engels in believing that workers could organize a revolution without a unified movement. Luxemburg invokes river networks to describe this possibility, but Mitchell argues that “her use of a fluvial metaphor missed the fact that it was railways and canals, more than streams and rivers, and the coal and coal-based products they carried that assembled workers together into a new kind of political force” (405).

45. Cheng, *Second Skin,* 167.

46. For two examples of work that explores the intertwining of mining histories with other forms of structural violence and exploitation, see the oeuvre of filmmaker Steve McQueen and artist Cameron Rowland’s installation, “Birmingham,” Galerie Buchholz, New York (April 23–June 24, 2017), https://www.galeriebuchholz.de/wp-content/uploads/2017/01/PT_Cameron_Rowland_ENG-4.pdf. While it is beyond the scope of this essay, the work of these two artists exemplifies how to use the visual arts to begin to imagine a transnational, complex, implicated, and enmeshed politics of depth.

47. Rey Chow, *Sentimental Fabulations, Contemporary Chinese Films: Attachment in the Age of Global Visibility* (New York: Columbia University Press, 2007), 173.

48. See “Here’s a Real Life Picture of the Welsh Coalfield,” *Daily Film Renter,* December 30, 1939, 5; and “Powerful Drama Which Cannot Fail to Thrill,” *The Stars Look Down* press book (1940), PBM-264444, Special Collections, British Film Institute National Archive.

49. See “The Stars Look Down,” *Daily Film Renter,* August 18, 1939, n.p.; and “The Stars Look Down,” *Aberdeen Evening Express,* August 7, 1939, n.p. Both in *The Stars Look Down* press book (1940), PBM-264444, Special Collections, British Film Institute National Archive.

50. "Black Faces in 'The Stars Look Down,'" *Birkenhead News,* August 16, 1939, n.p., *The Stars Look Down* Press book, Carol Reed Collection, Item no. 25, British Film Institute National Archive.

51. "'The Stars Look Down' at the Odeon," n.d., *The Stars Look Down* press book, Carol Reed Collection, Item no. 25, British Film Institute National Archive.

52. *The Stars Look Down,* script outline, 21, Carol Reed Collection, British Film Institute National Archive.

53. *The Stars Look Down,* script outline, 21. The Ladies' Gallery was nicknamed "The Cage"—also the name of a mineshaft elevator—until 1917 because of the grilles that were designed to prevent men from seeing the women in the gallery. The grilles were removed in response to suffragette agitation, but in the context of this film, the gallery's nickname established a link between the women who were hidden aboveground from view and the miners belowground whose needs the government neglected. See https://www.parliament.uk/about/living-heritage/transformingsociety/electionsvoting/womenvote/parliamentary-collections/ladies-gallery-grille/ladies-gallery/. Accessed August 14, 2020.

54. Gómez-Barris, *The Extractive Zone,* 1.

CHAPTER TWELVE

Transparency at Depth

Dark Mediation of the Deep Seabed

Lisa Han

What if human beings could make the deep ocean transparent? What would we discover? What could we gain, if we could see through the sea? These questions form the premise of a 2016 article in the *Economist,* which speculates, "The ability to peer unhindered into the deep would reveal a host of wonders—and have huge practical consequences."[1] The aspiration to create a transparent ocean is a defining piece of rhetoric within ocean science, perhaps a consequence of the extreme physical challenges involved in observing and traversing the deep sea. Water absorbs light; below one thousand meters, also known as the midnight zone, the ocean floor is pitch-black, under high pressure, and difficult to penetrate with conventional imaging tools.[2] It is also impossibly vast—only about 5 percent of the ocean floor has been mapped and imaged.[3] As one group of deep-sea researchers put it, "The fantasy of every marine geologist is to 'pull the plug' on the oceans—to drain the water from 70% of the Earth's surface hidden beneath the waves and have a direct view of the seafloor's myriad shapes and structures."[4]

In popular media representations of the deep sea, technology is inevitably seen as an antidote to the darkness of the ocean bottom, giving human beings the ability to bring benthic mysteries to light. Documentaries such as *DeepSea Challenge* (James Cameron, 2012), *The Silent World: A Story of Undersea Discovery and Adventure* (Jacques Cousteau, 1956), and *New Explorers: The Underwater Volcanoes* (1993) refer to the deep seabed using phrases such as "more foreign than the surface of the moon," "the last great frontier," a "silent world," "deeper than life itself," and an "empty abyssal desert."[5] These descriptions contribute to the cliché of a mysterious and unknowable abyss that must be occupied and subdued by media technology. The introduction to Paolo Favali, Laura Beranzoli, and Angelo de Santis's volume entitled *Seafloor Observatories: A New Vision of the Earth from the Abyss* reflects this belief: "The development of our understanding of the ocean has been hampered by our terrestrial existence as a species. . . . However, as we enter the 21st century, this is changing as a series of technological advances enables continuous virtual presence in the ocean, with sufficient power and bandwidth to operate a broad range of instruments."[6] Here, technology solves the problem of our remoteness from the deep, acting, as Marshall McLuhan would put it, as an extension of man. Deep-submergence vehicles have been described in similar terms, enabling man to "answer the mysteries of the deep," "become an intimate part of the ocean environment," and open a door to a "secret garden."[7]

Today, ambitions to sense, sample, observe, and occupy the seafloor are multiplying and evolving at breakneck pace. From the building of seafloor observatories to remote sensing, from large-scale mapping projects to state-of-the-art underwater vehicles, mediation at depth has become a progressive goal for oceanographic science and engineering. With undersea telegraph cables (and later fiber-optic cables) in particular, the seafloor became more than just a new spatial frontier—it was also the basis of a new media frontier. Similar to the rhetoric around networked media in terrestrial contexts, in current deep-diving projects, references to openness, visibility, immersion, and shared knowledge are pervasive. Nevertheless, humankind's pursuit of total ocean transparency begs the question: To what extent is a see-through sea actually achievable? What are the factors that feed such developments in the first place?

In this chapter, I push back against the idea that technology can or will create a transparent ocean. Instead, I contend that the emphasis on seafloor transparency chafes against a long history in which the deep ocean's obscurity and remoteness have played a central role in the development and management of underwater technological futures. Beyond the anxieties about the vastness and unknowability of this enormous swath of water, I consider how the history of deep-sea observation and sensing has consisted of both building infrastructure to learn and communicate through seawater, and of disrupting communications—a *dark mediation* that limits and controls signals across a vast expanse. This framework of dark mediation serves to decouple the associations of underwater mediation with light, visibility, and more knowledge to point out the manifold ways in which mediation amplifies darkness, cover, and opacity.

Dark mediation is part of a critical media studies tradition of thinking about communication, culture, and social interpretation alongside the development of media technologies that together serve as a precondition to thought and knowledge about the seafloor. In addition, this chapter builds on a critical infrastructures perspective, thinking of the ways in which underwater technological development is beholden to social arrangements and backstage legal and rhetorical work. Scholars of infrastructure like Nicole Starosielski have noted that existing undersea global communications networks are notoriously invisible and disconnected from public perception. I add that this disconnection is true for technologies developed to monitor and map underwater environments as well.

On a physical level, darkness also usefully points us toward the depths, as it is in deep waters that literal darkness reigns. The condition of extreme depth, pressure, and darkness presents special challenges to mediation and thus produces unique solutions: sonar, explosives, strobe lights, sensors, autonomous function, and so on. My use of this term importantly builds on Eugene Thacker's initial mobilization of the term "dark media" as a way of addressing communication with the inaccessible and the absent—"the mediation of that which cannot be mediated."[8] For Thacker, dark media both seek to illuminate that which is "in the dark" and to point to the incompletions, blind spots, excesses, and absences that precede all mediation; as he puts it, dark media describe the "seeing something in nothing" and "finding nothing in each something" (loc. 1239). My mobilization of "dark mediation" maps onto Thacker's to the extent that deep-sea technologies attempt to see or make transparent something that is opaque and nearly impossible to see in a conventional sense, and indeed, are shadowed by a specter of failure and the horror of the unexpected.

A medium, as discussed by Thacker and others, is inclusive of a broad spectrum of acts of mediation, both material and immaterial, that includes the use of bodies, environments, technologies, and texts as channels for communication and discommunication.[9] However, my first departure from Thacker's theorization of dark media involves the choice to speak of mediation as opposed to media. This theoretical adjustment comes from Sarah Kember and Joanna Zylinska, who offer mediation as a means for articulating a process of becoming with the technological world. To Kember and Zylinska, mediation involves "temporarily stabilizing the world into media, agents, relations, and networks."[10] This framework for mediation directs attention toward the media apparatus as not just representing the real but conditioning its possibilities through a co-constitutive, fluid relationship between humans and nonhumans within an assemblage. Echoing this and other new media perspectives, media scholar Alexander

Galloway has asserted that informatic modes of mediation, particularly those involving computers, create worlds as they strive to reveal them: "The promise is not one of revealing something as it is, but in simulating a thing so effectively that 'what it is' becomes less and less necessary to speak about, not because it is gone for good, but because we have perfected a language for it."[11] Galloway's theorization of media stresses a transition from revelation to simulation through the capture of particular forms of information.

My framework for mediation, however, emphasizes also the work of screening that produces this simulation: what is included and what is not included depends not only on the various techniques and technical process for mediating the seafloor but also on social mediations between people seeking both to expose and to hide. In this regard, dark mediation as an intervention points to something beyond Thacker's focus on desiring communication or fearing its failure. What is missing in Thacker's discussion is an explicit linking of dark media to institutional and environmental arrangements—that is, the relationship between media infrastructure and the deliberate decisions that accompany mediation within complex sociopolitical worlds. To speak of dark mediation requires acknowledging the military and state relationships that have funded and supported ocean research since the early twentieth century. This context serves as an entry point into understanding a central friction in the field, in which scientific impulses to know and understand more are undercut by proprietary data and politically motivated fears of others knowing too much. The inclusion of a sense of translation and occlusion across social worlds within this discussion of mediation takes its cue from science studies, which focuses on the often frictive, complex networks of cooperation and negotiation that shape (scientific) meaning.

As such, an overarching theme in the dark mediation of the deep seabed is the contestation over transparency. While the notion of transparency is often conflated with visibility in its practical use, my use of the term "transparency" offers a more capacious framework for collecting information about the ocean—particularly given that deep ocean mediation can also be sonic, thermal, chemosensory, or indirect. Beyond thinking about the capacity to see through dark waters, I am also considering transparency in terms of the sociopolitical ideal of information availability that is built, maintained, and thwarted by a network of participants. These two transparencies revolve around one another, but they do not always operate in tandem. As technological capabilities for sensing and imaging improve, new barriers to public visibility emerge.

In the pages that follow, I examine both the development of physical techniques for observing the seafloor, and the ethical ideal of sharing information about the seafloor. First, I discuss the historical development of deep-sea imaging by the U.S. Navy in relation to the notion of a transparent ocean. Next, I discuss seabed exploration and research efforts done in the service of deep-sea mining in order to explore contemporary ethical debates around data transparency. By including both, I aim to show that the military, industrial, and scientific rhetoric around deep-sea imaging and data collection espouses certain utopian ideals of visibility, and yet are also shadowed by dark mediation, a viewpoint that sees total transparency as either a liability or an impossibility. What stands out about this bipolar vision of the sea is that it sustains itself. The discursive acknowledgment of one extreme tends to amplify, rather than inhibit, the other. That is, fears of an unknowable abyss are accompanied by calls for total panopticism, and not something in between. I argue that the explanation for this dissonance lies in the fact that the development of seafloor media technologies speaks to more than a desire for simple sensory immersion or visual cohabitation. Rather, it attests to the role of deep-sea mediation in the strategic capture of futures, whether for risk management or for economic speculation. Ultimately, this speculative mindset drives the dark mediation of the deep seabed.

Naval Pursuit of a Transparent Ocean

Historically, the desire to mediate the seafloor has largely been associated with wartime naval endeavors and with the laying of undersea cable. In her book *Fathoming the Ocean,* Helen Rozwadowski dates the first major efforts to attempt deep-sea measurement to the mid-nineteenth century, when deep-water measurements became a regular part of hydrographic missions.[12] Media scholar Starosielski has also focused on the building of these network infrastructures, linking undersea cable construction to terrestrial politics and political ties.[13] Both Starosielski and Rozwadowski note the ways in which competitions to dominate seafloor space acted as a mode of flag planting, demonstrating national superiority through technological and scientific prowess.[14]

Early oceanographic research on the deep seabed was primarily understood through "sounding" techniques that involved lowering rope or wire into the depths and retrieving samples. Cable surveys captured the imaginations of early hydrographers, who were able to translate the craggy, varied constitution of the seafloor into pictures and develop an understanding of the seafloor that transcended previous notions of an abyssal desert. When the HMS *Challenger* first explored the depths of our oceans from 1872 to 1876, laying the infrastructure for modern oceanography, it conducted 133 bottom dredges and 492 deep-sea soundings.

It was only with the wartime invention of sonar that ocean "sounding" took on a new, sonic register. At the turn of the century, ocean research transitioned from study within independent disciplines (as with the *Challenger* expedition) toward comprehensive oceanography driven by political and economic aims. As Gary Weir explains, the U-boat menace "provided the catalyst that accelerated American naval oceanographic studies, dramatically altered scientific practice, and profoundly affected the selection of new subjects for investigation."[15] The U.S. Navy had a keen interest in understanding how sound travels through seawater and sediment to meet the U-boat threat, and thus funded much of the research on sound imaging technologies. As many have acknowledged, "the technologies which have done most to make the ocean transparent have come from the armed forces."[16] The story of dark mediation and transparency in the deep sea thus necessarily begins with the U.S. Navy's involvement in developing seafloor and deep-sea technologies.

John Shiga's scholarship on naval sonar underscores the emergence of distinctly active, directional forms of detection from this wartime competition in subocean dominance, wherein the transmission of acoustic pulses and the recording of echoes became the principle mode of perceiving marine objects.[17] There have been many iterations in the development of such ocean sounding techniques. For instance, early on, war efforts led to the development and use of the Reginald Fessenden oscillator, which allowed researchers to determine ocean depth through echo ranging. In the 1920s, U.S. Navy physicist Harvey Hayes subsequently developed the sonic depth finder (SDF), which used oscillator technology to make the first bottom profiles of the ocean. At last, sound "began to reveal what years of work with rope and wire sounding lines had only suggested."[18] Weir adds, "Although it did not make the ocean transparent, to a remarkable degree it freed the scientific community from severe physical constraints. . . . Hayes's SDF turned on a sonic light in a very dark room" (30). The invention of the SDF cemented the relationship between the U.S. Navy and ocean exploration at large, fusing state and scientific epistemologies for ocean exploration. During the Second World War, research on underwater sound developed further to include not only methods for communication and detection but also evasion. This included research into the noise created by ship and submarine wakes, as well as the distortion of sound by temperature and depth. Through the use of tools like the bathythermograph, navy researchers discovered that transition zones to cold water in deep water, called thermoclines, could allow submarines to disguise their positions and escape from enemy sonar.[19] Thus, early naval war efforts set the stage for a distinctly strategic and politically oriented perspective on deep-sea mediation.

Years later, in 1964, Allyn Collins Vine, an oceanographer at the Woods Hole Oceanographic Institution, presented a talk entitled "Project SEA-BED" to the U.S. Navy, introducing technologies that he correctly deemed to be a pivot point in human knowledge of the deep ocean. The purpose of the talk was to show off his new development, *Alvin,* an eponymously named, innovative deep-tethered vehicle that could give humankind access to a view of the ocean from the bottom up. In addition to being able to collect samples with its manipulators, the *Alvin* can measure heat, magnetism, conductivity, temperature, and depth, as well as take photographic stills and video at depths of forty-five hundred meters. Vine made an appeal to the navy that vehicles like the *Alvin* would offer more than just an opportunity to control and observe a new space of strategic interest. As he noted, the deep sea was also "the only medium left to man (perhaps in the entire universe) in which we can conduct military operations without the omnipresent observer in the form of the TV camera, newspaper reports, friendly or unfriendly bystanders, not to mention enemy reconnaissance."[20] It was a place of darkness and cover, outside the realm of mass media. It is thus instructive to note that already depth in the original context of deep-submergence vehicle development is associated with a productive blind spot—a space in which invisibility offers political sanctuary and military power. This military and political pushback against sharing information has thus always shadowed the development of tools that aimed to physically illuminate the deep.

Of course, sanctuary was and remains a relative idea; blind spots were also perceived as dangerous. As one might expect, eliminating blind spots when it comes to players from other nations has been a top priority. Rear Admiral Charles Richard, the current commander of the U.S. Strategic Command and former commander of the U.S. Navy's Submarine Forces, said as much in a navy blog post entitled "The Mirage of a Transparent Ocean." He references the Malaysian Flight 370 and EgyptAir Flight 804 tragedies as evidence that "the oceans are anything but transparent." Richard acknowledges that much of the difficulty associated with finding wrecks and attacking subs is attributed to the distorting physics of underwater environments and the complex processes of translation, classification, and localization. Ultimately, however, he expresses ideals of evolution and progressivism, insisting that human ingenuity and technology will make up for humanity's terrestrial existence and eventually help us become amphibious. Richard's parting words are perhaps the most instructive: "We will continue to find and we will continue to hide."[21] As with Vine's speech, undersea power for the navy remains contingent on the interplay between both of these aims, and on the continued development of technologies for both.

Today, sounding, imaging, chemical and temperature sensing, and physical retrieval of cores and samples all continue to be major techniques for understanding the seafloor. Even the relatively low-tech process of marine coring and sampling remains highly valued, as repositories with material collected from the 1950s on continue to grow and improve over time in their preservation and digitization efforts.[22] As the years have passed, however, the mandate for oceanographic research in the United States has shifted, and such techniques have largely moved away from military interests toward civilian research. Still, ship time and funding infrastructures in the United States remain closely linked to the navy and to industry. The high costs of underwater equipment and vessels further sustain an uneven power dynamic between state and science that limits the type and scope of oceanographic research questions.[23] As a result, relationships between state, scientific, and industrial actors continue to produce limitations on the nature and quantity of data that can be gathered about the seabed.

In the past decade, exploration of unknown areas of the seafloor has been vastly more difficult to fund than research that seeks to understand places that have already been studied and published on. According to several of my interviewees at Woods Hole Oceanographic Institution, Oregon State University, and Scripps Institution of Oceanography, funding agencies like the National Science Foundation increasingly prefer to have concrete deliverables and practical results over research done purely for the sake of increasing knowledge (Figure 12.1). Joe Stoner, a paleomagnetist and principal investigator of the Oregon State University Marine Geology Repository, calls it the "art of the doable." He elaborates: "Even though we have much better mapping and we can see things, and better targets for coring should be much more obvious than they were, it is hard to do anything explorative . . . the cores that already have the most information become the most valuable."[24]

FIGURE 12.1. Marine geologic core repository at Scripps Institution of Oceanography. Photo by author.

This funding structure underscores the speculative manner in which dark mediation is sustained. It is not the will or curiosity of scientists, nor is it technical capability that drives deep-sea exploration; rather, what propels novel seafloor research is the availability of funds and the statistical likelihood of acquiring data that will be meaningful within existing knowledge infrastructures. Finally, much of the scientific value of geologic databases is still locked up as what is aptly termed "dark data." That is, much of the data that oceanographers collect languishes on old forms of media and does not get published because their original experiments were abandoned.[25] In a nutshell, it has become arguably more difficult to collect data about unexplored areas of the seafloor, and the mere collection of data does not equate to knowledge or understanding of that data.

The privileging of less risky, pragmatic oceanographic research (applied science) over new discoveries (pure science) is exacerbated by the fact that a major driver of deep-sea research today is industry—both the well-known offshore oil and gas industry and the emergent industry of deep-sea mining. In the next section, I consider the emergence of seabed mining and the ethical debates around data sharing and availability, further problematizing the assumption that better technology leads to greater oceanic transparency.

Data Transparency and Seabed Mining

The idea of mining the seabed was first seriously debated in the mid-1980s and 1990s, when ocean researchers operating submergence vehicles discovered several sulfide deposits, including the Okinawa Trough near southwest Japan, the Clarion-Clipperton Fracture Zone (CCFZ), and the Woodlark Basin east of Papua New Guinea.[26] Later, mud samples revealed that elements like yttrium, neodyminium, lanthanum, and other rare earth minerals accumulate in the thick layers of marine mud from the eastern South and North Pacific seafloor.[27] In the last decade, global interest in deep-sea mining has skyrocketed, especially around areas like the CCFZ. This is thanks to a surge in metal demand in the Asian Pacific, in addition to automobile manufacturing in the United States, Germany, and Japan, which drives demand for metals like copper, gold, platinum, and nickel.

The International Seabed Authority (ISA), based in Kingston, Jamaica, currently regulates the distribution of minerals in the "Area," a zone that covers most of the ocean floor and is traditionally viewed as a global commons. This responsibility is shared with fourteen United Nations member states, excluding the United States (the U.S. regulatory body is the National Oceanic and Atmospheric Administration). They distribute mining and exploration licenses according to the doctrine of the Common Heritage of Mankind, and thus act explicitly "on behalf of mankind as a whole." This principle embodies ideals of international unity in order to waylay the environmental and social threat of what Garrett Hardin termed "the tragedy of the commons."[28] The ISA has thus far issued twenty-eight exploration permits from twenty countries. Notable contractors include Global Sea Mineral Resources; Japan Oil, Gas, and Metals National Corporation; and Nautilus Minerals.[29]

With deep-sea mining operations quickly becoming a reality, the ISA and industry contractors have come to rely on scientists to learn about the ecologies of potential mining sites and help put together regulations for environmental impact. Geologists are also actively working with industry contractors to evaluate metal concentrations in the deep seabed and help refine economic evaluations and technical models. All of this scientific work is pressing, as many independent researchers and environmentalists warn that a deep-sea gold rush could lead to the next great extinction.[30] As a result, industry growth and its increasingly entangled political landscape have driven efforts to map and understand the seafloor further. As Thomas Peacock, an engineer and deep-sea mining researcher, noted in a 2018 paper, "A great deal of what is known about ecosystems and resources in the CCFZ has come from contractor-related studies."[31] Moreover, due to the fact that much of this information about the seafloor is novel and expensive to replicate, the ISA mandates that the physical resources at the deep seabed and the data collected about these regions of interest should be centralized. Having a large, centralized repository of seafloor information would be highly valuable to scientists in their own research outside of mining aims, and particularly to those struggling to find funds for their own ship time.

However, the sharing of this newly collected data remains a major challenge, especially because contractors have strong incentives to hoard the information that they find, both to mitigate concerns from their investors and to limit competition. Under current ISA rules, mining contracts and contractor environmental data and compliance reports are treated as confidential. Moreover, they are submitted to a small group of thirty delegates who form the Legal and Technical Commission, which withholds information from the ISA's policymaking body and member state assembly.[32] The ISA's lack of data transparency was criticized in a 2014 report to the ISA on the implementation of environmental management of one of the major prospective mining areas, the CCFZ: "The online central data repository of the Authority only contains data on the form and availability of data from 18 institutions worldwide. The database was last updated in 2008, and the most recent data set in the cruise section is a cruise that took place in 1988. It does not offer access to any data from any contractor. The reason for this is not clear. Environmental baseline data should not generally be regarded as confidential, especially since the Area is defined as being 'the common heritage of mankind.'"[33] Two years later, in May 2016, an independent review committee was equally critical, pointing to the ISA's closed meetings, and recommended that improvements were needed in data transparency, enforcement, and oversight, particularly for data management and sharing as well as confidentiality regulations. According to the report, full access to data was limited to only a few privileged actors, and contractor reports with valuable biological and geologic information had not been consolidated into a public database. The Legal and Technical Commission also came under fire: "The review of contractors' annual reports is onerous, lacks transparency and its effectiveness in improving performance is questionable . . . no significant work has been carried out by the Authority to effectively monitor the development of marine technology relevant to activities in the Area."[34]

These critiques demonstrate a new chapter in the dark mediation of the deep seabed: while more novel information than ever is being gathered about the seabed by contractors, this information is fractured and in the dark, largely hidden from public view. The reasons for this dark mediation are political and economic. Contractors see their mining operations as highly valuable and crucial to national interests, and therefore requiring of privacy and security. As mentioned previously, withholding pieces of information about the seabed becomes a way of maintaining a competitive edge as well as a means to keep wary investors in the dark about potential environmental drawbacks and costs. As a result, concerns about disruptions to seafloor ecologies and scientific calls for open networks of information are constrained by economic and political motives.

Industry and state actors also prioritize the top-down, logistical management of a supply chain that seeks to maximize efficiency and minimize disruption. Too much observation becomes a barrier to the efficiency of this system, as well as a security risk. For instance, member states of the ISA have varying ideas of how much transparency and regulation is needed. Nations that hold mining contracts, like Japan, China, and South Korea, have advocated against excessive regulation or regular environmental inspections. Japan's representatives have stated, "To minimize the burdens of states, contractors and the Secretariat of the ISA including financial burdens, Japan is of the view that it is appropriate not to have inspections by inspectors on a regular basis but to have them only when deemed necessary."[35]

Meanwhile, delegates from states without licenses like New Zealand and South Africa advocate for strong enforcement and a "transparent and credible environmental impact assessment process."[36] Higher-income contractors who have the monetary and mechanical means to find minerals seek to hide it away and leave potentially obstructive environmental information in the dark, while lower-income nations that lack resources and capabilities to mine prioritize transparency and the sharing of knowledge. For a country like South Africa, increased transparency fulfills both environmental and political aims, leveling the playing field between nations. The intertwining of state and political interests within mining thus adds fuel to the strategic value of withholding newly discovered information about the seabed, reinforcing, as Rear Admiral Richard stated, the idea that power stems from the ability to both hide and find.

"If You Can See It, You Can Change It"

For both industrial and scientific participants, deep-sea mining is all about the calculus of risk and profit. How might access to these valuable resources impact political relationships? How much will it cost to mine a field with fees, fines, and equipment taken into account? How do we minimize or offset biological losses from mining waste? How do we predict the movement of toxic plumes? What will biological recovery look like in a decade, or in a century? The need to mediate environmental, economic, and political risk conditions the possibility for a patchy form of mediation, characterized both by an increasing need to know more about the ocean floor and by the desire to limit the sharing of this information.

There are some, particularly scientists, who have sought to bring this dark mediation to light. The Benioff Ocean Initiative, a nonprofit organization affiliated with the University of California, Santa Barbara, has recommended that as part of its mining code for the deep seabed, the ISA should require mining vessels to be equipped with tracking devices called Automatic Identified Systems (AIS), so that their movements can be monitored in real time. Carolyn Jablonicky, who works at Benioff with Douglas McCauley, a marine biologist at UCSB, explains, "What we're trying to do now is reach out to the ISA to encourage them to increase transparency overall in what's happening out there, such as creating cruise reports and making them public."[37] Under the direction of McCauley, Benioff partnered with an organization called SkyTruth, which uses views from space to monitor environmental threats—its tagline is "If you can see it, you can change it"—to create Deep Sea Mining Watch (Figure 12.2).[38]

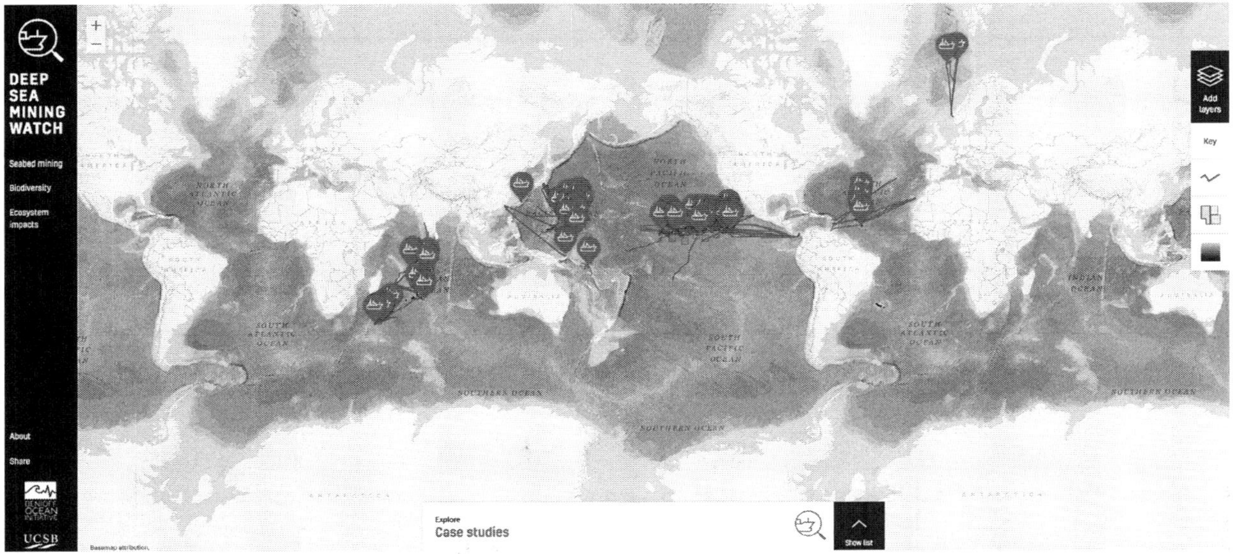

FIGURE 12.2. The main interface of the Benioff Ocean Initiative's Deep Sea Mining Watch. Image courtesy of Benioff Ocean Initiative, UC Santa Barbara.

This transparency in regard to the movements of vessels is ultimately meant to empower the public and raise awareness. Jablonicky explains that her goal is to provide "tangible proof" of mining activities to the public and prevent an "out of sight, out of mind" situation, which would allow for environmental abuses. Here, the availability of more information is thus associated with a minimization of environmental risk.

Adding to this idea, McCauley explains that the process of making mining exploration visible is a measure that will prevent the industry from creating an environmental catastrophe: "We have to make sure that what we're doing in ocean science isn't just an obituary that's being written with increasingly high resolution."[39] McCauley's use of a visual metaphor here is interesting, demonstrating both the value and the limits of visualization. High resolutions implicitly do not prevent environmental abuses, but other forms of visualizations can indeed be used to police. The AIS map created by Deep Sea Mining Watch is panoptic, attributing a bird's-eye view scopic regime to the operation of discipline. Mining Watch correlates AIS data with patterns of size, speed, and other available evidence to identify mining vessels. The use of AIS data in this way seeks to provide a form of vertical surveillance that would ideally produce norms in regard to the movements and operations of mining vessels. Ultimately, the very lack of aesthetic depth and detail on the interactive map surface of the Deep Sea Mining Watch tool points us toward deeper invisibilities and blind spots—implicit here but absent in spectacular, hyperreal images of the deep as seen in popular documentary, live camera feeds, or other forms of public outreach. It flips the script on dark mediation, aiming for an ideal of democratic access to information even while its interface remains relatively opaque.

Other researchers and antimining activists point to a lack of environmental impact information as the justification for delaying mining activity, arguing that industry must adhere to the Precautionary Principle. The Precautionary Principle, proposed at the UN World Charter for Nature in 1982, is the rule that currently informs the ISA regulatory framework for mineral exploitation of the deep sea.[40] It argues that in the event of uncertainty and scientifically determined risks to human safety or the environment, preventative actions should be taken, prioritizing social responsibility and the protection of communities.[41] The push for transparency and further scientific mediation of the seabed is thus seen as an important step toward responsible treatment of the environment, as well as a way of ensuring that local communities are given a seat at the table.

The idea behind needing to increase the industry's overall visibility ultimately acts as a strategy for limiting the risk of abuses in both environmental and political realms. As Deborah Cowen reminds us, the invisibility of supply chains to the public frequently goes hand in hand with violence both physical and discursive: "The entire network of infrastructures, technologies, spaces, workers, and violence that makes the circulation of stuff possible remains tucked out of sight for those who engage with logistics only as consumers."[42] Cowen signals the way in which the life of the supply chain is valued over human rights, but this critique extends to nonhuman life as well. Like gray goo, the production of logistical media and their facilitation of pipelines for mineral-rich "slurry" rely on a violent homogenization of living, nonliving, fluid, and solid. Integrated into a supply chain, these slurries come to signal virtual, transferrable value, leaving complex ecological relationships at the seafloor in the dark. Transparency is thus a bulwark against bad industry behavior, and a way of keeping the environment as well as lower-income nations and coastal communities in mind.

Practically speaking, however, much of the resistance against mining activities merely advocates for a delay, which creates a situation in which scientists must race to gather more information about the seabed and publish it, before industry actors can make their own discoveries and hoard them. Transparent mediation ends up competing against dark mediation. Yet none of these actors acknowledge that seafloor data transparency also conditions the possibility for a potentially toxic industry in the first place, as contractors come to learn about the viability of exploiting seafloor resources through science. In a world of dark mediation, data collection is thus what Jacques Derrida has called a *pharmakon*: a necessary measure "which acts as both remedy and poison."[43] Multiple forms of risk management—political, economic, and environmental—are thus deeply connected and often, although not always, come into conflict with one another, as extremes of total transparency and deregulation are alternately seen as desirable. Ultimately, the defining step of seafloor mediation, the resolution between poison and cure, is the interpretation of these data by a network of people, not merely their collection.

Living in the Shallows

In *Program Earth,* sociologist Jennifer Gabrys contends that in contrast to visual epistemologies that celebrate the power to unveil, unconceal, or make transparent, sensory data streams like those from the seabed are not self-evident but are rather translated across human and nonhuman participants within a network. According to Gabrys, such networks amplify the chatter of an always "talking" planet and its human audience.[44] But while the planet may always be "chattering," its translators are not; much of our sensory data is lost before it can be amplified. We might infer the existence of "chatter," of fluid flows, U-boats, sedimentation, and mineral extraction without hearing or seeing anything directly. We may know of an industry gathering on the horizon, without knowing the full extent to which such anthropogenic activity has taken place. Deep-sea media technologies are powerful actors within a system that have the capacity to both capture and mold perception of reality, and they operate through regimes of seeing without being seen.[45] This mediated capture is complicit in the construction of the seabed as alternately a media frontier, a military hideout, a thriving ecosystem, or a fragile environment in need of protection.

In some ways, the darkness, depth, and even vastness of the seafloor stands in metaphoric relation to the digital sphere. Dark mediation might include a larger realm of digital culture that regularly contends with questions of transparency, secrecy, and ambivalence even as information becomes more abundant. Modern computational systems decouple seeing from knowing and interpreting. Information collection capabilities—from tracking and data capture to seafloor sampling—are decoupled from the processing of that information. Even as our technologies travel deeper and wider to collect data about the world, our digital culture increasingly facilitates shallower depths of knowledge. Ultimately, this dark mediation paradox stems from a shared imperative for extraction. Digital media today are characterized by molecular and distributed extractions of data about everyday life, from location data, to facial recognition features, to website visits, to the steps we take, made through processes that are inaccessible to us.[46] We give more and understand less because of capitalist acts of enclosure, from black-boxed algorithms to the formation of proprietary databases.

Much like the quotidian production of data bodies, the value of deep-sea data extends beyond representation; data produce and define the rocky, dark, and sediment-strewn depths of the ocean itself, becoming their own reservoir of potential discovery, future evidence for future policy justifications, and a form of insurance in the event of disaster or disagreement. These data are metonymical, mere pieces of the deep dark sea that come to stand in for the rest. Regardless of their origin, underwater media technologies produce surrogate environments for an ocean that is unfathomably vast and largely unknown. Yet, these digital aquariums are also fallible and are at risk of being lost or hidden from public view. Whether they take the form of satellite maps, documentary footage, sonar images, or sediment libraries, ocean media are not smooth, glacis-like structures that reflect, but rather have themselves become inhabitable environments—layered, and penetrable to varying degrees. As techniques of capture grow alongside global interest in seafloor resources, we must ask questions regarding not only their representational accuracy but also the neoliberal policies and structures that exploit and shield knowledge from the public. Deep-sea mediation can be a profoundly hopeful practice that opens up new avenues for human environmental knowledge and kinship. As we venture deeper, we have the choice not just to control and occupy but also to acknowledge and live with the unknown.

Notes

1. "If the Ocean Was Transparent: The See-Through Sea," *Economist,* June 7, 2016, http://worldif.economist.com/article/12151/see-through-sea.

2. "How Far Does Light Travel in the Ocean?," Ocean Facts, National Ocean Service, accessed May 17, 2019, https://oceanservice.noaa.gov/facts/light_travel.html.

3. Kyle Frischkorn, "Why the First Complete Map of the Ocean Floor Is Stirring Controversial Waters," *Smithsonian Magazine,* July 13, 2017, https://www.smithsonianmag.com/science-nature/first-complete-map-ocean-floor-stirring-controversial-waters-180963993/.

4. Jeffrey A. Karson, Deborah S. Kelley, Daniel J. Fornari, Michael R. Perfit, and Timothy M. Shank, *Discovering the Deep: A Photographic Atlas of the Seafloor and Ocean Crust* (Cambridge: Cambridge University Press, 2015), 1.

5. *DeepSea Challenge 3D,* directed by James Cameron (Washington, D.C.: National Geographic Entertainment, 2012); *The Silent World,* directed by Jacques Cousteau (France: FSJYC Production, 1956); *New Explorers: The Underwater Volcanoes,* January 1, 1993, Media Tape 6058, Videocassete (VHS), WHOI Audiovisual Collection, Data Library and Archives, Woods Hole Oceanographic Institution; "The Deep," *Blue Planet II* (London: BBC Natural History Unit, 2017), https://www.bbc.co.uk/mediacentre/mediapacks/blue-planet-ii/the-deep.

6. Paolo Favali, Laura Beranzoli, and Angelo de Santis, *Seafloor Observatories: A New Vision of the Earth from the Abyss* (Heidelberg: Springer, 2015), 5.

7. *New Explorers: The Underwater Volcanoes; Flying at the Bottom of the Sea,* January 1, 1991, Media Tape 9196, New Office, WHOI Audiovisual Collection, Data Library and Archives, Woods Hole Oceanographic Institution.

8. Eugene Thacker, "Dark Media," in *Excommunication: Three Inquiries in Media and Mediation* (Chicago: University of Chicago Press, 2014), loc. 1178 of 3596, Kindle.

9. Several people have articulated this broad perspective on media, including Thacker himself, who discusses mediation through physical space, as well as scholars of environmental media such as Stefan Helmreich and John Durham Peters, who see environments as also performing mediatory functions. See Stefan Helmreich, *Alien Ocean: Anthropological Voyages in Microbial Seas* (Berkeley: University of California Press, 2009), 32; John Durham Peters, *The Marvelous Clouds: Towards a Philosophy of Elemental Media* (Chicago: University of Chicago Press, 2015).

10. Sarah Kember and Joanna Zylinska, *Life after New Media: Mediation as a Vital Process* (Cambridge, Mass.: MIT Press, 2012), xv.

11. Alexander Galloway, *The Interface Effect* (Cambridge, UK: Polity Press, 2012), 13.

12. Helen M. Rozwadowski, *Fathoming the Ocean: The Discovery and Exploration of the Deep Sea* (Cambridge, Mass.: Belknap Press of Harvard University Press, 2005), 33.

13. Nicole Starosielski, *The Undersea Network* (Durham, N.C.: Duke University Press, 2015), Kindle.

14. Rozwadowski, *Fathoming the Ocean,* 32; Starosielski, *The Undersea Network,* loc. 866 of 9506.

15. Gary Weir, *An Ocean in Common: American Naval Officers, Scientists, and the Ocean Environment* (College Station: Texas A&M University Press, 2001), 6.

16. "If the Ocean Was Transparent."

17. John Shiga, "Sonar: Empire, Media, and the Politics of Underwater Sound," *Canadian Journal of Communication* 38, no. 3 (2013): 357–77.

18. Weir, *An Ocean in Common,* 14.

19. Weir, 127, 152; Robert Derencin, "Counter Sonar Measures—A Bathythermograph," uboat.net, June 24, 2002, https://uboat.net/articles/45.html.

20. Allyn Collins Vine Papers, July 24, 1964, MC-01, Box 3, "Project SEABED: 'Deep Ocean Technology,' final presentation, Monterey, Calif., P. Fye," Data Library and Archives, Woods Hole Oceanographic Institution.

21. Rear Admiral Charles Richard, "The Mirage of a Transparent Ocean," *Navy Live,* July 29, 2016, http://navylive.dodlive.mil/2016/07/29/the-mirage-of-a-transparent-ocean.

22. See Shannon Mattern, "The Big Data of Ice, Rocks, Soils, and Sediments," *Places Journal,* November 2017, https://doi.org/10.22269/171107.

23. Chanda Mukerji, *A Fragile Power: Scientists and the State* (Princeton, N.J.: Princeton University Press, 1989). Mukerji's volume importantly explores both applied and pure research on the deep sea and concludes that scientists in both camps relate to the state as a reserve labor force.

24. Joseph Stoner, interview with author, August 16, 2018.

25. Kim Martineau, "Contest Aims to Bring 'Dark Data' into Digital Archives," *State of the Planet,* Columbia University Earth Institute, accessed August 28, 2018, https://blogs.ei.columbia.edu/2013/04/29/contest-aims-to-bring-dark-data-into-digital-archives/.

26. "Polymetallic Sulphides" (Kingston, Jamaica: International Seabed Authority), https://www.isa.org.jm/files/documents/EN/Brochures/ENG8.pdf.

27. Yasuhiro Kato, Koichiro Fujinaga, Kentaro Nakamura, Yutaro Takaya, and Kenichi Kitamura, "Deep-Sea Mud in the Pacific Ocean as Potential Resource for Rare-Earth Elements," *Nature Geoscience* 4, no. 8 (2011): 535–39.

28. The language from the Third UN Conference on the Law of the Sea (UNCLOS III) in 1974 reads: "All objects of an archaeological and historical nature found in the Area shall be preserved or disposed of for the *benefit of mankind as a whole*"; quoted in Lowell Bautista, "Ensuring the Preservation of Submerged Treasures for the Next Generation: The Protection of Underwater Cultural Heritage in International Law," *LOSI Conference Papers* (2012), https://www.law.berkeley.edu/files/Bautista-final.pdf. See also Marta Chantal, "What Is the Area and the International Seabed Authority?," *Institut Océanographique,* May, 2013, http://www.institut-ocean.org/images/articles/documents/1367593542.pdf.

29. Thomas Peacock and Matthew H. Alford, "Is Deep Sea Mining Worth It?," *Scientific American,* May 2018, 73–77.

30. Embodying this gold rush mentality, UK Prime Minister David Cameron, sponsoring the Lockheed Martin subsidiary, UK Seabed Resources, referred to deep-sea mining as a "global race" with the potential to "create specialist and supply chain jobs," as well as bring in "up to £40bn to the UK economy over the next 30 years." This quote is from a press release that is no longer on the Lockheed Martin website: Lockheed Martin, "UK Government Sponsors Lockheed Martin UK Subsidiary for License to Harvest Polymetallic Nodules," Lockheed Martin Press Release, March 14, 2013, https://www.lockheedmartin.com/uk/news/press-releases/2013-press-releases/uk-government-sponsors-lockheed-martin-uk-subsidiary-for-licence.html. For more information, see Shreema Mehta, "The Dangers of Deep Sea Mining," *Earthworks,* September 28, 2015, https://www.earthworksaction.org/earthblog/detail/the_dangers_of_deep_sea_mining.

31. Peacock adds, "Our expedition from San Diego, for example, was a joint program funded by the Massachusetts Institute of Technology and the Scripps Institution of Oceanography, in collaboration with the ISA, the U.S. Geological Survey and the GSR [Global Sea Mineral Resources]. In 2019 Europe's JPI Oceans

program will conduct a study with the ISA and GSR in the CCFZ"; "Is Deep Sea Mining Worth It?," 77.

32. Todd Woody, "European Parliament Calls for a Moratorium on Deep-Sea Mining," *News Deeply,* February 1, 2018, https://www.newsdeeply.com/oceans/articles/2018/02/01/european-parliament-calls-for-a-moratorium-on-deep-sea-mining.

33. Seascape Consultants Ltd., *Review of Implementation of the Environmental Management Plan for the Clarion-Clipperton Zone* (Kingston, Jamaica: International Seabed Authority, May 20, 2014), 10, http://isa.org.jm/files/documents/EN/20Sess/LTC/CCZ-EMPRev.pdf.

34. David Johnson, Philip Weaver, Vikki Gunn, Wylie Spicer QC, Sara Mahaney, Dire Tladi, Angel Alvarez Perez, and Akuila Tawake, Seascape Consultants Ltd., *Periodic Review of the International Seabed Authority pursuant to UNCLOS Article 154, Interim Report* (Kingston, Jamaica: International Seabed Authority, May 15, 2016), 1, https://www.isa.org.jm/files/documents/EN/22Sess/Art154/Art154_InterimRep.pdf.

35. Government of Japan, *Comments on Draft Regulations on Exploitation of Mineral Resources of the Area* (ISBA/23/LTC/CRP.3), (Kingston, Jamaica: International Seabed Authority, December 20, 2017), https://www.isa.org.jm/files/documents/EN/Regs/2017/MS/Japan.pdf.

36. In light of these disagreements, the European Parliament called for a moratorium on deep-sea mining. Yet Conn Nugent, director of Pew Charitable Trust's Seabed Mining Project, was skeptical of this proposal: "There is no evidence (so far, at least) that any national government is prepared to endorse what [they] said in this regard"; quoted in Woody, "European Parliament."

37. Caroline Jablonicky, interview with author, January 18, 2018.

38. "Deep Sea Mining Watch," Benioff Ocean Initiative and UCSB, October 2016, http://deepseaminingwatch.msi.ucsb.edu/#!/intro?view=-14.9448/-159.9609/2//1124/576.

39. Becky Ferreira, "The Marine Biology Using Big Data to Protect Ocean Life," *Vice Motherboard,* December 8, 2017, https://motherboard.vice.com/en_us/article/kzgbpx/the-marine-biologist-using-big-data-to-protect-ocean-wildlife.

40. A recent piece of ISA draft regulation reads, "All persons engaged in activities in the Area shall apply the Precautionary Approach, as reflected in Principle 15 of the Rio Declaration, to the assessment and management of risk of harm to the Marine Environment from Exploitation Activities in the Area and where scientific evidence concerning the scope and potential negative impact of the activity in question is insufficient but where there are plausible indications of potential risks of Serious Harm to the Marine Environment"; *A Discussion Paper on the Development and Drafting of Regulations on Exploitation for Mineral Resources in the Area (Environmental Matters)* (Kingston, Jamaica: International Seabed

Authority, 2017), 26, https://ran-s3.s3.amazonaws.com/isa.org.jm/s3fs-public/documents/EN/Regs/DraftExpl/DP-EnvRegsDraft25117.pdf.

41. "The Precautionary Principle," Deep Sea Mining Campaign, A Project of the Ocean Foundation, accessed September 18, 2018, http://www.deepseaminingoutofourdepth.org/what-is-the-precautionary-principle/.

42. Deborah Cowen, *The Deadly Life of Logistics: Mapping Violence in Global Trade* (Minneapolis: University of Minnesota Press, 2014), loc. 145–46 of 6330, Kindle.

43. Jacques Derrida, "Plato's Pharmacy," in *Dissemination,* trans. Barbara Johnson (Chicago: University of Chicago Press, 1981), 70.

44. Jennifer Gabrys, *Program Earth: Environmental Sensing Technology and the Making of a Computational Planet* (Minneapolis: University of Minnesota Press, 2016), 275.

45. Philip Agre, "Surveillance and Capture: Two Models of Privacy," *Information Society* 10, no. 2 (April 26, 2010): 108.

46. Trevor Paglen, "Invisible Images (Your Pictures Are Looking at You)," *New Inquiry,* December 8, 2016, https://thenewinquiry.com/invisible-images-your-pictures-are-looking-at-you/.

CHAPTER THIRTEEN

Depth Mediators

Undersea Cables, Network Infrastructure, and the Deep Ocean

Nicole Starosielski

The ocean is a powerful conceptual model for understanding depth in contemporary culture. Popular songs from Irving Berlin's "How Deep Is the Ocean" (1932) to Belinda Carlisle's "Deep Deep Ocean" (1989) use the depth of the ocean to describe the extent of love and hidden emotions. Motivational posters encourage their readers to find joy and meet challenges as deep as the ocean. Even the dictionary definition of depth, specified as "the distance down from the top surface of something to the bottom," offers an aquatic example: "They were scuba diving at a depth of 22 meters."[1] In a philosophy of matter, *Water and Dreams*, Gaston Bachelard describes standing at the sea: "In my own reverie, it is not infinity that I find in waters but depth."[2] Bachelard argues that it is only by spending time near the ocean's surface that we can "understand the value of depth."[3] Across these cultural imaginations, whether popular, informational, or philosophical, the ocean's apparent distance from terrestrial forms of life makes it a powerful inspiration for articulations of the inaccessible, the unconscious, and the deep.

As this chapter will show, the ocean did not always have depth or volume in the popular imaginary. Its bottom was not always figured in opposition to a surface. While biblical and literary references had historically mentioned the depths of the sea, depth as a specific, relative, and meaningful distance between two planes (a surface and a bottom, for example) emerged in the mid-nineteenth century with the need to lay communications cables on the ocean floor. Although all forms of depth are mediated in a general sense by cultural forces and specifically by instruments and representational technologies, I argue that the depth of the ocean was critically mediated by network infrastructure in both of these senses. Laying cables was an economic motivation for assessing oceanic depth, and their representation offered visions of the seafloor *as* deep. The mid-nineteenth century, when submarine cables were being laid on the ocean floor, was also the period in which a science of oceanic depth originated. This science, which sometimes emerged on the same ships that were conducting cable surveys, involved extending lines of connection—a form of cabling—between surface and bottom. As Sylvia Earle, famed ocean explorer, describes: "Much of the information that forms the basis of modern oceanography has been literally dragged, hauled, hooked, and pulled, one data point at a time, from the depths of the ocean."[4] The cable's distinct structure rendered it particularly effective as what I describe as a "depth mediator": like the lines fishermen cast into the ocean and the twine used for soundings, the cable offered a linear bridge beneath two planes, allowing ocean depth to be figured in relation to length and as height. It was a volumetric technology and an infrastructure of depth.[5]

Even after the nineteenth century, media about cable systems would help to construct and reconstruct a sense of oceanic depth. In the early years of cabling, articulations of oceanic depth were often present in cable discourse: this discourse simultaneously defined humankind's technological accomplishment in the mastery of depth (the occupation of another axis of space) and positioned the deep sea as critical to cable security (it was depth that prevented disruption). Even as surveyors assigned a numerical distance to the ocean's depth, images of cabling the seafloor tended to represent the depths as a negative extension of height and portray the subsea world as a version of the terrestrial world. The ocean depths were represented as a foreign territory, a zone of otherness to be explored, charted, and colonized. The representation of ocean depths thus mirrored the colonial relationships that undergirded cable construction itself.

This early understanding of the ocean's depth, even as it persists in contemporary representations, multiplied with the transitions in the ocean's depth mediators. In the second section of this chapter, I move to a series of cable repair texts from the 1920s and 1930s, in which the cabled ocean was reframed not in terms of its distance from the surface but in terms of its relative accessibility. Depth was flattened in the interest of portraying cables and the deep ocean as *close to* the surface. This focus on cables' and the seafloor's accessibility was both a historically specific reaction to competition with new wireless technologies and the result of new forms of mediating depth via sonar, submarines, and subsea exploration.

In this transition, even as the depths were rendered closer, they remained a key form of what Lisa Parks describes as "vertical mediation," material processes of articulating, communicating, and organizing the world as a vertical field.[6]

Over the following decades, the cable would be joined by a multitude of other oceanic depth mediators: underwater cameras, scuba equipment, and remote-operated vehicles. Alongside these technologies, cable representations continue to visualize the ocean as having depth. For example, although I do not describe their development in detail here, industrial and educational films about undersea cables, which were screened publicly in the 1950s and 1960s, often focused on the cable repeater—an amplifying technology that rested on the seafloor. They revealed cabling as a way for humans to inhabit the deep sea and dovetailed with cultural fantasies of submarines, scuba diving, and sea stations.[7] The chapter concludes by turning to a recent media example, *Deep Down Tidal* (Tabita Rezaire, 2017), which offers an alternative model of depth to the cable imaginaries of the late nineteenth and early twentieth centuries. In this video essay, Rezaire powerfully connects the internet and its aquatic infrastructures to colonial networks. Here, depth is not an extension of negative verticality into the ocean, or a neutral projection of the global South into the sea, or an envisioning of the deep as a resource frontier. Instead, the video essay offers an orientation to temporal depth: the surfaces here are not surface and bottom, but rather past and present. To dredge the depths, in *Deep Down Tidal,* is to pull the histories of networked power into the current digital age.

Collectively, the examples described here from the late nineteenth, early twentieth, and early twenty-first centuries reveal how undersea cables, infrastructures that stretch across the seafloor, serve as a means of publicly mediating the deep sea. They are a site for the transmission and transformation of knowledge about depth: a form of depth mediator. In many cases, they index broader cultural imaginaries of the ocean, but they also offer a particular and nuanced mode of such representations: depictions of cabled depths reveal the imagined role of the depth mediator itself. In early cable discourse, the cable was depicted as a site for connecting surface and bottom as well as colonizers with their colonies. In the 1920s and 1930s, the cable was portrayed as a material form that could grasp ethereal communications and yet still be easily accessed. Today, as *Deep Down Tidal* illustrates, the cable is being tapped as a means of both connecting to and illustrating the deep structures of power that remain embedded in digital networks.

FIGURE 13.1. "Carta Marina," by Olaus Magnus (1539). The Lionel Pincus and Princess Firyal Map Division, The New York Public Library, "Americae nova descriptio," New York Public Library Digital Collections, http://digitalcollections.nypl.org/items/510d47da-ef53-a3d9-e040-e00a18064a99.

Another World

Although it provides a spatial model for contemporary imaginations of depth, the ocean was not always conceptualized as a three-dimensional entity. On medieval and Renaissance maps, monsters emerged from or simply laid atop the ocean's flat surface, the only indication of the unknown that existed beneath (Figure 13.1). Through premodern history, Philip Steinberg observes, while some societies saw the ocean as a landlike resource for connection and others saw it as an arena of competition, all saw the ocean first and foremost as a kind of transport surface.[8] In the late eighteenth century, the deep was a "great void that was empty and featureless, the antithesis of civilization."[9] As Helen Rozwadowski describes in her seminal text *Fathoming the Ocean,* before the nineteenth century "the deep sea hardly made an impression on most people, even citizens of maritime nations."[10] Even as it offered a medium for transportation, a site for imagining the antithesis of civilization, and a resource-space filled with potential food, the early ocean was not perceived as having depth, nor was it subject to volumetric measurement.

Between the 1840s and 1880s, there was a dramatic increase in the awareness of the ocean as a place for work, leisure, adventure, and scientific study. This was in part due to the fact that many more people were working at sea, and global migration and travel had brought even more across the ocean. It was also a result of new media practices, including the widespread expansion of the voyage narrative as a genre of oceanic writing. Maritime novels, from *Moby Dick* to *20,000 Leagues under the Sea,* included not only commentary on ships' voyages and travelogues about the locations they connected but also speculations about the ocean's depths. Rozwadowski argues that it was during this period that the "deep sea" entered the conceptual and discursive arena of Western cultural production, sometimes even as a "sales tactic" for advertising ocean-related products, from fish to leftover submarine cable (4).

While the expansion of activity on the ocean prompted speculation about "an almost unimaginably vast three-dimensional scale," the challenge of conceptualizing the ocean as having depth—a directional gradation of distance between planes—was a problem of media technologies (5). Rozwadowski points out that in 1823, the *Encyclopedia Britannica* entry for "sea" read: "Through want of instruments, the sea beyond a certain depth has been found unfathomable" (5). Access to the ocean "below a few feet underwater," Sylvia Earle argues, "will always rely on harnessing technologies."[11] Connective technologies, especially ropes, twine, and wire, were the primary instruments through which the ocean gained its depth. In this process, according to Sabine Höhler, "Depth became a matter of scientific definitions, systematic measurements and graphic representations."[12]

The particular form of this measurement was the *line*. Up until the 1920s, soundings involved attaching lead or instruments to a long line (made of twine, rope, silk, or steel wire) and lowering it to the seafloor for "single spot soundings."[13] A line into the ocean, whether extended by the men who began to hunt sperm whales in the deep sea during the nineteenth century or for the first set of "soundings" that were taken in the 1850s, became a means of capturing depth. In 1851 and 1852, the first transatlantic deep-sea soundings were taken aboard the USS *Dolphin* for navy officer Matthew Fontaine Maury's ocean studies. He collected both deep-sea temperature and depth measurements, the latter of which would eventually be assembled into a "bottom profile." In these profile images, depth was represented on a graph, translated to the y-axis. In such images, the viewer is not positioned above the ocean, looking down at it. Depth became height. Submarine topography became undersea plateaus, mountains, and valleys.

One of the prime motivations for these depth studies was the construction of submarine telegraph cables, which were also beginning to be laid in the mid-nineteenth century (Figure 13.2). Matthew Fontaine Maury, sometimes described as the "father" of oceanography, would provide consultation and technical advice for cable projects and viewed the ocean's depth contours as a cable bed. Following one line of readings, Maury described a submarine "plateau" that seemed "to have been placed there especially for the purpose of holding the wires of a submarine telegraph."[14] Depth was a critical cable epistemology. It was not sufficient to simply unwind a cable overboard, letting it fall to the bottom of the ocean. Without proper measurements, the cable would string between submarine mountains, resulting in an increased risk of cable disruption: whales and other marine creatures might get caught in the line. To make the cable safe, it needed to unravel such that it would align precisely along the ocean's depth contours. In cable laying, depth became *operational:* it was integral to the determination of both cable length and boat speed.

Submarine telegraph cables were key instruments through which the ocean would be given depth, not simply through the generation of an economic and technical motivation for soundings but as sites for the transmission of the idea of the deep ocean to a broader public. Cable surveying and laying were newsworthy events that helped to circulate the significance and knowledge of the ocean's depth. As one of a number of examples, during the survey for the transpacific cable in 1899, the USS *Nero* discovered a previously unknown trench. A newspaper in Guam recounted the history of the survey: "One of the most interesting results of the Nero's survey was the discovery of a submarine abyss between the Midway Islands and Guam, which at the time was the deepest known in the world." The author goes on in extensive detail, describing the contours and depths of the seafloor:

> From Midway to Guam for about a thousand miles there is a plane a little more than three thousand fathoms (almost 3½ miles deep), broken occasionally by submarine reefs and mountain ranges; then suddenly, a short distance to the eastward of the great submarine volcanic range of mountains running north and south, which, rising above the surface, forms the chain of the Ladrones or the Marianas, and near the latitude of Guam, this plane sinks into the valley known as the Nero Deep, lacking only sixty-six feet of depth of six statute miles. The southern limits of this deep are not yet known.[15]

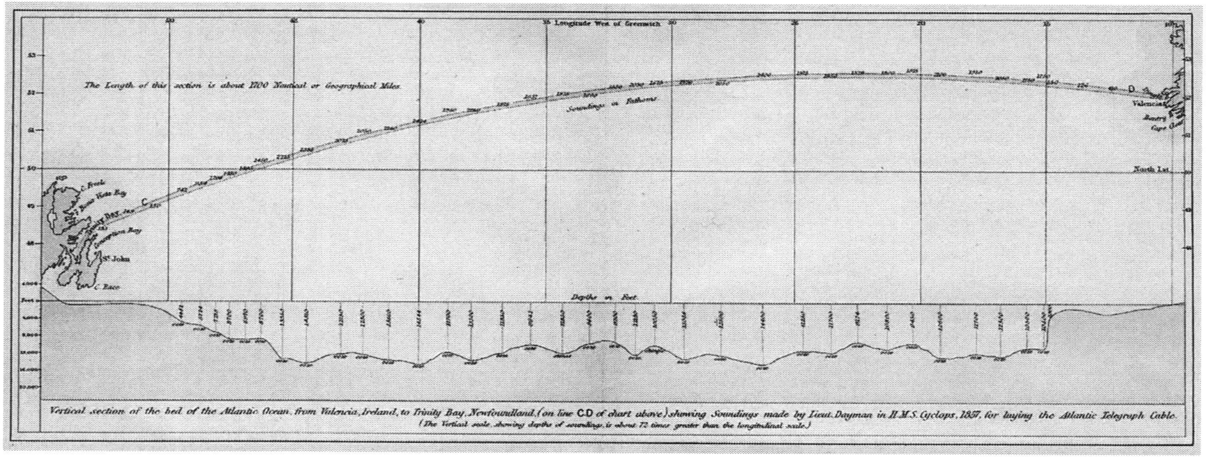

FIGURE 13.2. “Vertical section of the bed of the Atlantic Ocean, from Valencia, Ireland, to Trinity Bay, Newfoundland,” made by Lieut. Dayman in HMS *Cyclops*, 1857, for laying the Atlantic Telegraph Cable. AtlanticCable.com.

Here, as in the bottom profile, the ocean comes to have depth: there is a floor that is a discrete numerical distance from a surface. The reader is positioned on the floor, looking up to mountain ranges and volcanoes. Depth is made sense of as height, and the viewer is encouraged to adopt a submerged viewpoint, albeit one located distinctly on the ocean's floor.

While cable surveying would slip into the background as a technical practice, the cable remained a means of communicating the ocean's composition and dimensionality. The distance between the surface and the seafloor was often commented on, sometimes as a means of articulating the safety of the cables (they would be far from any source of potential human disruption). In the arguments to establish support for the transpacific cables, its proponents claimed: "In the depths of the Pacific Ocean, the cable would be absolutely safe from interference."[16] At other times, the deep was articulated as a strange home for the cables. Rudyard Kipling's poem "The Deep-Sea Cables" (1893), written from the perspective of the cables, also emphasizes the verticality of the ocean's depths:

> The wrecks dissolve above us; their dust drops down from afar—
> Down to the dark, to the utter dark, where the blind white
>   sea-snakes are.
> There is no sound, no echo of sound, in the deserts of the deep,
> Or the great grey level plains of ooze where the shell-burred
>   cables creep.
> Here in the womb of the world—here on the tie-ribs of earth
> Words, and the words of men, flicker and flutter and beat . . .

Here, the cables are described as "sea-snakes," an inhabitant of the ocean floor that "creep[s] on the plains" and "tie-ribs of earth." Terrestrial metaphors and creatures help to transpose the familiar world onto the seabed, while casting the words of men—transmitted through the cable—as a kind of foreign visitor.

Visual representations of the cables in the nineteenth and early twentieth centuries similarly grappled with the depiction of the ocean's depth. Take, for example, a cartoon created by H. Treby Heale, "Prehistoric Cable Repairing," which features a boatful of prehistoric men evading sea monsters and saving one another from drowning while attempting to catch a cable with a grapnel (they catch a sea serpent instead) (Figure 13.3). Part of the humor of the cartoon, especially for those in the cable industry, was that cable repair seemed to many akin to a prehistoric activity: with no visibility of the seafloor, it entailed dragging a grapnel back and forth in the zone of a cable, hoping to catch it rather than another occupant of the

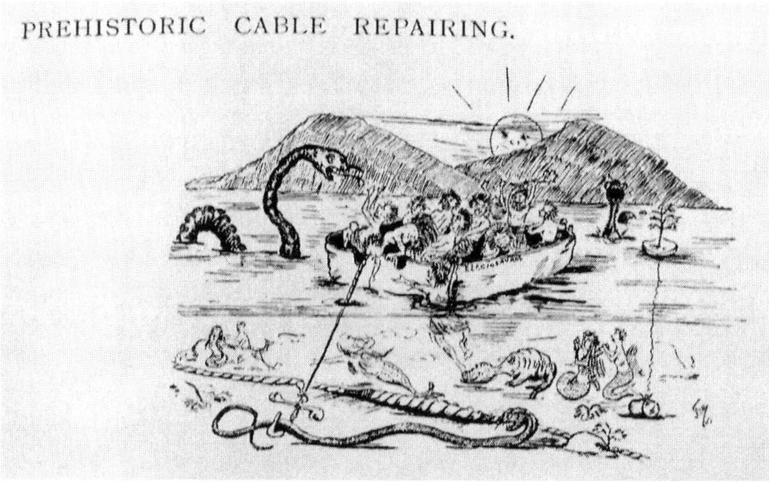

FIGURE 13.3. "Prehistoric Cable Repairing," by H. Treby Heale. *The Zodiac: The Submarine Cable Service Paper* 3, no. 26 (1908–9).

deep. Visually, this image is divided into thirds, with mountains in the background, the men on the ocean's surface in the center, and the seafloor occupying the bottom third. Here, as in Kipling's poem and the surveying notes, the depths are not striated into zones, as they would be in future representations. Telling is Heale's clarification of the image: "I am afraid I have rather failed to give the impression I wanted, viz., to make the mermaids, etc., appear as the Lord's wonders at the *bottom* of the sea, and not on the *beach*."[17] The image, Heale intuited, might incorrectly lead them to believe that the deep-sea occupants were closer than they appeared. In other words, in this image, the bottom of the sea mirrors the directionality and dimensionality of the ocean surface and activities on land. And the two technologies, each a depth mediator—the cable and the buoy (which ties a floating mark on the surface to the seafloor)—allowed the vertical connection of these different realms.

This imaginary can be traced across many of the cable representations of the late nineteenth and early twentieth centuries. Cartoons from this era show mermen using the cable as a rope for a tug-of-war and, in another image, a jump rope (Figure 13.4). In such images, like Heale's cartoon, the deep made legible through cabling is a mystical, invisible, and uncontrollable zone, and yet one that largely conforms to the spatial dynamics of surface activities. These cartoons depict cabling as a way of

FIGURE 13.4. Jumping rope with a cable on the seafloor. *The Zodiac* 3, no. 26 (1908–9): 250.

engaging with the inhabitants of the depths and imagines their responses to cable intrusion. In other cartoons, sharks take a bite out of a cable and flee, and a sawfish cuts the cable (Figure 13.5). Counter to the bottom profiles and the survey reports, the depths are not depicted in terms of their numerical distance from the surface but are a rendering of surface activities as Other and as foreign. Scientific publications about cables, such as the article "How Submarine Cables Are Destroyed" (1878), often lifted undersea disruptors from the ocean altogether.[18] Laid onto a flat canvas, there is no depth of field. As is true for the drawn images of the bottom of the sea, there is no z-axis through which the ocean can be oriented. A few pages after one of the cartoons, however, is a full-page spread of photographs in which a fishermen's trawl net has been hooked on a cable. Fishermen in this period were snagging cables regularly—and yet few commented on the conflict between those who used the deep as a resource and the cable companies to which it remained a pathway. Collectively such images presented the depths not as a site of struggle between humans but as an arena of imaginative and fantastical connections between oceanic Others and man.

Across these representations, illustrated and narrated, there are a number of key patterns. First, in these descriptions the cable is a depth mediator—a material means through which distance was organized along

FIGURE 13.5. Sharks and sawfish are imagined as threats to cables. *The Zodiac* 2, no. 33 (April–May 1907–8): 427.

a directional, dimensional axis. In some cases, it mediated the depth of the ocean by providing a set of economic and technical incentives to measure seafloor topography, for instance, in the generation of depth profiles. It also mediated the ocean's depth in the proliferation of discourse about the ocean's specific depths and the distance of the "deep." In other cases, the seafloor is strangely reminiscent of terrestrial geographies, with a bottom that one can walk on, mountains rising up, and cultural activities. There is no attention to the specificity of the subsea environment or to the differences between far and near depths. Even as it mirrored the dimensionality of terrestrial orientations, cable descriptions tended to translate the seafloor as a mystical realm. It was a world "beneath" ours, connected only by cable, the southern limits of which, even if not yet known, were grounded on an imaginary floor.

Given the context of early cabling, these images and descriptions framed the ocean's depths not only as a kind of negative verticality, a distinct world beneath the ocean's surface, but also as a colonial territory. Telegraphs that were being laid around the world during this period were connecting Western colonizers with the colonies. The cable was the material infrastructure that enabled ongoing communication between Europe and the global South. The ocean, in such images, is depicted as one more Other territory: like the representations of the colonies that also pervaded cablemen's magazines, there are here angry natives, hostile forces, and seductive mermaids. The visual and textual cultures of the cables not only generated imaginations of the ocean as having depth but also reflected an anxiety about how distant and deep locations might be the means of connecting Western listeners, speakers, and communicators. In turn, the representation of the deep ocean here inflected the Western imagination of colonized peoples: as animals, as not quite fully human, and as inhabiting a completely Other world.

The Close Depths

In the 1920s, there was a shift in cable representation and, as a result, a corresponding shift in the mediation of the ocean depths. During this period, following the advent of the wireless telegraph and radio communications, the cable industry and its operators faced a new rival, one that challenged their domination of global telecommunications. At the same time, the cable industry was facing regular disruptions of its systems from trawlers and fishermen, both of which compromised the sense of safety that the otherworldly depths had seemed to provide. These industrial and material conditions prompted a shift in cable discourse, one that generated a new articulation of the bottom of the ocean: as closer and more manageable than ever before.

In this new cable imagination, the ocean was much less frequently a domain of a foreign and oceanic Other and more often coded in domestic terms. In 1925, in the submarine cable magazine *The Zodiac*, one article title claimed, "The Bed of the Ocean Is the Dormitory of the Cables" and described the seabed as an inhabitable space.[19] A 1928 poem, published in the magazine of sea travel *The Blue Peter*, begins like Kipling's "Deep-Sea Cables": "Three thousand fathoms deep I lie; And went my way across the ocean bed."[20] This poem, however, eventually transitions into a story of care: "Well cared for by the mariners above, no stress nor storm can daunt my soul," continues the author. This exemplifies one pole of the new cable discourse: the deep ocean is made familiar as a home, a dormitory, a bed, and a place of rest.

Even as cables were described as resting in their bed, the new discourse of this period simultaneously foregrounded the vertical manipulation of cables and cablemen's technical ability to master the ocean surface.

FIGURE 13.6. Men working to repair an undersea cable (1924). *The Zodiac* 15, no. 182 (August 1923–July 1924): 106.

Numerous media examples from this period featured cable repair, including images of ships from which cables were laid, poetic lamentations about broken systems, narratives and drawings of divers working on subsea cables, and photographs of cables covered with marine growth. One essay, "The Interrupted Long Splice," described for those in the cable industry a story of cable repairing events that occurred more than forty years prior.[21] A story from *The Zodiac* in 1924 featured an image of a man poised on a buoy, reaching out to catch a line from sailors on a dinghy (Figure 13.6). There is no undersea in this depiction of the undersea cable. More than half of the frame is occupied by the rolling waters of the ocean's surface. The submarine cable is in the control of men, linking two boats. Instead of the negative verticality of the ocean's depths, the focus of the image is on the buoy itself, whose architecture visually parallels the wireless towers that were being put up during this same time period. Instead of showing the cable resting on the seafloor, the image focuses attention on the buoy's reach to the top of the frame, signifying cable infrastructure's vertical reach. Unlike many cable images prior, here the depiction of cable repair, which is marked by its expansive depth of field, features a large cable ship on the horizon and locates the supporting infrastructure for cabling at the center of the frame. The mark buoy was often depicted in images and stories of cable repair (Figure 13.7). Other vertically oriented images included photographs from the ship's deck, with the cable (caught in a trawl net) tracking down the hull of the ship (Figure 13.8).

One of the most notable cable representations of this period was a film made by the Eastern Telegraph Company (later to become Cable & Wireless), *The Romance of the Submarine Cable,* which was also circulated free of charge to educational institutions as a series of lantern slides. The short film chronicles the manufacture, laying, repair, and operation of undersea cables. While there are many photographs of the cable ship and the labor of repair that echo the broader discourses of cabling at this time, there are also a few key underwater scenes. In them, the intact cable is first depicted on the "bed" of the ocean, and then a second drawn image indicates how a grapnel would pick up the cable from its bed (Figure 13.9). The environment is neither mystical nor threatening. The features of the subsea landscape are clearly marked, and the action includes pulling the cable from its resting place on the seafloor. The film also features extended coverage of the management and negotiation of mark buoys as they sit on deck, are lowered into the water, and float on the ocean's surface.

With this shift in imagery and focus, there was also a shift in tone. These discourses largely adhere to a scientific and factual understanding of the ocean. In one article written in the mid-1930s, entitled "Sea Serpents!," the author begins by recounting a moment of cable repair. The cablemen are grappling to retrieve a cable, but instead, to the surface comes an "enormous snake-like head with some 6ft. to 8ft. of neck quickly followed by two great arms, widely extended, all grisly black and menacing." The author goes on to tell the reader, however, that the "monster, on examination, was found to be an enormous tree with roots."[22] Another story, also from the mid-1930s, describes the teredo worm's former ability

FIGURE 13.7. The January 1924 cover of the cablemen's magazine features a man on a mark buoy. *The Zodiac* 16, no. 186 (January 1924): cover.

to "slay" submarine cables, which had been stopped by the tactic of binding the cables in brass tape.[23] Still other articles during this period describe how cablemen found a "river" under the seabed and detail "portraits" of the teredo worm.[24] In these accounts, there is a shift from the description of the ocean depths as a wonderous and mystical space to a knowable, predictable, and scientifically manageable environment.

In an era in which broadcast radio was permeating households, wireless telegraphy was expanding around the globe, and cables were being

FIGURE 13.8. Photograph taken during the repair of a cable for the Western Union Company's 1880 cable off Valencia (May 25, 1925). "Davy Jones' Lost Property Office," *The Zodiac* 17, no. 205 (August 1925): 80–81.

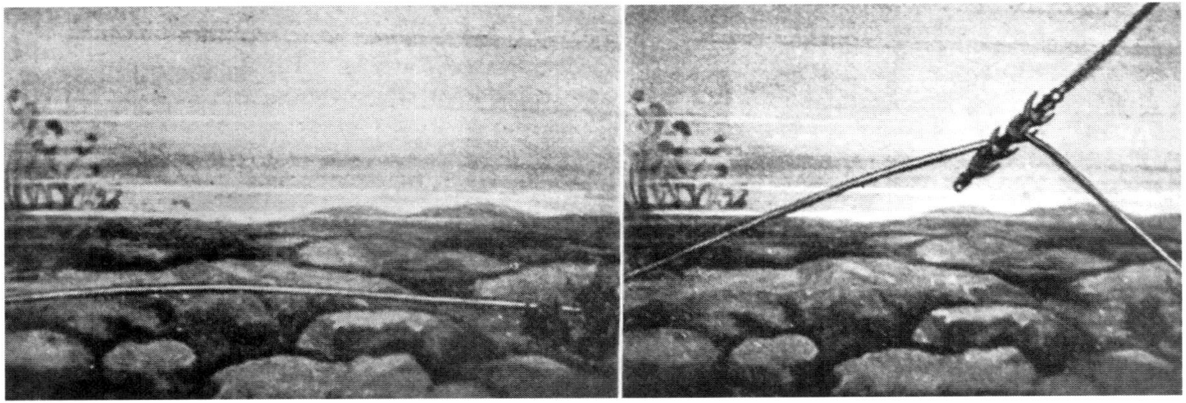

FIGURE 13.9. Still from *The Romance of the Submarine Cable*. Printed in *The Zodiac* 17, no. 210 (August 1927–July 1928): 92.

regularly damaged by fishermen, the use of imagery—and especially repair imagery—performed a critical function. It showed how cables were *accessible* and could be concretely marked, harnessed, and drawn to the surface. At the same time, it was permeated by vertical imagery that clearly evoked wireless communications: the vertical lines of a boat's hull, the standing towers of the mark buoys, and the masts of ships. One advertisement, featured in the *West Coast Leader* (Lima, Peru), boasted: "The future of the cable is assured. . . . The cable, with its world-wide organization, its freedom from atmospheric disturbance, and its privacy of transmission, remains an essential feature of modern life."[25] In this period, cables—and by extension the ocean depths, were brought closer in the interest of marking them as accessible as wireless and yet free from atmospheric problems. The ocean's depths often disappeared from the frame altogether. The transition in cable discourse also followed a proliferation of the practices of seeing and measuring subsea spaces. Submarines were widely used during World War I, sonar was developed as a means of subsea detection, and John Ernest Williamson's 1912 photosphere enabled the cinematic capture of subsea spaces. This cultural imaginary of the ocean as closer, more immediate, and accessible was part of a larger shift in the ocean's depth mediators.

Deep Down Tidal

Neither of these ways of seeing subsea environments—as a fantastical zone of a colonized Other or as an easily manageable habitat—disappeared in the years that followed. As described elsewhere, even some of the earliest films of the ocean's floor produced using Williamson's photosphere projected it as a colonial space.[26] Such imaginations were not limited to cable discourses. But cable representations serve a particular function in giving the ocean depth, as they offer a reflection on the cable's role as a mediator of that depth. While images and descriptions in the nineteenth and early twentieth centuries cast the cable as a line to an Other world, a means of bridging a discrete surface and a discrete bottom, in the 1920s the cable portrayed the depths as a safe home for the cables, and the cables themselves as an easily extractable communications resource. As a final example, I describe how one contemporary cable representation, the short video *Deep Down Tidal* (2017), reconstitutes the ocean's depth, offering an alternative model of what cable connection might look like.

Produced by French Guyana–based artist Tabita Rezaire, *Deep Down Tidal* is part of a larger body of work that, recalling the mode of early net.

art aesthetics, is characterized by collages, juxtapositions, pixelated imagery, and tropes of interconnection. The video, along with Rezaire's other works, uses superimposition to bring together a range of images—of environments, systems, technologies, and bodies that typically inhabit different representational domains—onto the same plane. This, Rezaire argues, is a mode of Afro Cyber Resistance. Articulated on Rezaire's website, these "cross-dimensional practices envision network sciences—organic, electronic and spiritual—as healing technologies."[27] Across this work, there is an ongoing reconfiguration of dimensionality, especially depth.

The reorganization of depth is particularly powerful in *Deep Down Tidal*. The video begins with a woman sitting on a cloud and describing the problems with Facebook via a cell phone call. The video then cuts to text: "This phone call was brought to you by ELECTRONIC COLONIALISM." Across the screen, Rezaire superimposes browser search windows with racist autofills of Google searches ("why are black people . . . ," "when will africa . . . ," "why do black lives matter") over the surface of a body of water and against a colorful sky. These constitute the plane of contemporary digital life: internet searches are separate neither from the environments that they traverse nor from the people who receive them. "The west urgently needs new spaces to conquer and when they don't actually exist, they must be created," the text of *Deep Down Tidal* reads. Cyberspace is this space. But the internet is not decentralized or universal or in the clouds, the narration tells us. "It lies on the sea floor." The video's animation moves us from above the surface to below and describes the submarine cable infrastructure that supports internet traffic (Figure 13.10). In these images, the bottom of a seafloor does not serve as the relational plane for contemporary digital surfaces. The cables themselves are not depicted as resting on the seafloor at all. The ocean in this vision is composed of mountainous topography, overlaid with silhouettes of a fish and a brain, through which the viewer can glimpse images of fiber-optic cable laying. In the corner of Rezaire's wide screen, an animated fiber cable sends off wireless signals. *Deep Down Tidal,* while drawing attention to the cables that cross the ocean, refuses either of the traditional models of its depth—either fantastical or managed—just as it refuses to organize these activities in Western dimensionality.

Later on in the film, while giving us a glimpse of cable maps through a porthole, the text narration tells us, "Cables are spaces where labour, knowledge and capital sunk into the sea," and that these systems are an architecture of violence, exploitation, and exclusion. "Don't these triangular routes look familiar?" the text asks, drawing a direct parallel

FIGURE 13.10. *Deep Down Tidal* (Tabita Rezaire, 2017).

between cable maps and the slave trade: these are the internet's "genocidal routes (roots)." *Deep Down Tidal* exposes how laying communications cables is explicitly a neocolonial project: "Cables are the hardware of the new imperialism." If the ocean's depth in traditional cable representations is established through a relationship between surface and seafloor, here depth is constituted differently: cables serve as a way to link the contemporary play of digital surfaces with histories of violence, exploitation, and exclusion. Beyond the simplistic binaries of software and hardware, content and infrastructure, and surface and depth, the video offers a different kind of relational scale: one in which the plane of the present is linked, via cables, to the oppressions of the past.

With its science fiction and afrofuturist aesthetics, *Deep Down Tidal* both draws parallels to and departs from what Stefan Helmreich calls the "alien ocean," the figuring of aquatic space as a zone of an extraterrestrial other. "Alien oceans," Helmreich writes, "are oceans formed of already mixed-up lineages of those outside, beyond, or within known oceans."[28] Although the imagination of the ocean in relation to outer space took hold in the 1960s in the context of the space race, the comparison of outer and submarine space remains critical in popular discourse. "A dozen astronauts have walked on the moon," Sylvia Earle writes, "but only two people have ventured and safely returned from the deepest crack in the ocean."[29] While the rhetoric of exploration dominates such descriptions, these zones remain particularly important as imaginative sites for those who have historically been marginalized in terrestrial worlds: as Mette Bryld and Nina Lykke write, "The difference of both spaces from the current terrestrial abodes of 'civilized selves' . . . makes them a perfect match for contemporary desires for a 'truly' wild and vast elsewhere."[30] In *Deep Down Tidal*, the ocean is a space for reimagining both culture and media, through water itself. "Water remembers," *Deep Down Tidal* narrates, "water copies information," "water carries data," "water records and circulates." In the world of this video, the "deep" of the ocean is not the seafloor (it is neither distant, nor Other, nor accessible and managed). Rather, the ocean's depths are its histories carried forward into the present and future both through water and in the bodies that traverse it.

Notes

1. "Depth," in Cambridge Dictionary Online (Cambridge: Cambridge University Press, 2019), https://dictionary.cambridge.org/us/.

2. Gaston Bachelard, *Water and Dreams: An Essay on the Imagination of Matter,* trans. Edith R. Farrell (Dallas, Tex.: Pegasus Foundation, 1982), 8.

3. Bachelard, 11.

4. Sylvia A. Earle, "Foreword," in Helen Rozwadowski, *Fathoming the Ocean: The Discovery and Exploration of the Deep Sea* (Cambridge, Mass.: Harvard University Press, 2005), x.

5. Franck Billé, "Introduction: Speaking Volumes," *Fieldsights,* October 24, 2017, https://culanth.org/fieldsights/introduction-speaking-volumes.

6. Lisa Parks, *Rethinking Media Coverage: Vertical Mediation and the War on Terror* (New York: Routledge, 2018).

7. Nicole Starosielski, "Beyond Fluidity: A Cultural History of Cinema under Water," in *The Ecocinema Reader: Theory and Practice,* ed. Salma Monani, Stephen Rust, and Sean Cubitt (New York: Routledge, 2012), 149–68.

8. Philip E. Steinberg, *The Social Construction of the Ocean* (Cambridge: Cambridge University Press, 2001).

9. Helen Rozwadowski, *Fathoming the Ocean: The Discovery and Exploration of the Deep Sea* (Cambridge, Mass.: Harvard University Press, 2005), 6.

10. Rozwadowski, 4.

11. Earle, "Foreword," ix.

12. Sabine Höhler, "Depth Records and Ocean Volumes: Ocean Profiling by Sounding Technology, 1850–1930," *History and Technology* 18, no. 2 (2002): 119.

13. Höhler, 121.

14. Henry M. Field, *The Story of the Atlantic Cable* (New York: Charles Scribner's Sons, 1892), 19–20, quoted in John Steele Gordon, *A Thread across the Ocean* (New York: HarperCollins, 2003), 38.

15. W. J. Kealy, "Surveying for the Pacific Cable," *Guam Recorder,* October 1928, 154.

16. Pacific Cable Board, "Telegraph Cables (Further Papers Relating to) No. 13," Papers Presented to both Houses of the General Assembly by Command of His Excellency, New Zealand, 1914, New Zealand National Archives, Wellington, New Zealand.

17. H. Treby Heale, "Prehistoric Cable Repairing," *The Zodiac: The Submarine Cable Service Paper* III, no. 26 (1908–09).

18. "How Submarine Cables Are Destroyed," *Scientific American,* February 2, 1878, 2.

19. "The Bed of the Ocean Is the Dormitory of the Cables," *The Zodiac* 17, no. 205 (August 1925).

20. "The Submarine Cable," *The Blue Peter,* December 1928.

21. A. E. Kennelly, "The Interrupted Long Splice," *The Zodiac* 17, no. 210 (January–July 1926): 328.

22. "Sea Serpents!" *The Zodiac* 26, no. 306 (August 1933–July 1934): 290.

23. "The Teredo," *The Zodiac* 26, no. 306 (August 1933–July 1934): 405.

24. "River under Sea Bed," *The Zodiac* 27, no. 306 (August 1934–July 1935): 335; "Scientific Research," *The Zodiac* 28, no. 306 (August 1935–July 1936): 413.

25. "Cable West Coast," *The Zodiac* 17, no. 205 (August 1925): viii.

26. Starosielski, "Beyond Fluidity," 149–68. Ann Elias, *Coral Empire: Underwater Oceans, Colonial Tropics, Visual Modernity* (Durham, N.C.: Duke University Press, 2019).

27. Stefan Helmreich, *Alien Ocean: Anthropological Voyages in Microbial Seas* (Berkeley: University of California Press, 2009), 17.

28. Helmreich, 17.

29. Earle, "Foreword," x.

30. Mette Bryld and Nina Lykke, *Cosmodolphins: Feminist Cultural Studies of Technology, Animals and the Sacred* (London: Zed Books, 1999), 19.

CHAPTER FOURTEEN

From Planetary Depth to Surface Measure, or How to Read the Future from an Image

Jussi Parikka

If You Can See It

Planetary surfaces record traces of geologic depths as well as geographic changes.[1] These surfaces run deep, and they are constantly observed, analyzed, and measured but also calculated. Surfaces should be approached as nothing like superficial, a realization that echoes Gilles Deleuze's observation that any binary of surface versus depth is a false juxtaposition.[2] Indeed, the volumes of planetary depths have been constantly turned into image surfaces, and discussing surfaces is one way to expand the scope of visual analysis, as Giuliana Bruno has demonstrated in her work that speaks to spaces and architectures, fabrics, and materials of surfaces.[3] Furthermore, to speak of surfaces becomes much more spatially complex than one would at first imagine. Surfaces are always mediated, and they are mediating in ways that also enfold depths. In the midst of the nineteenth-century obsession with depths that produce geology and archaeology, a complementary form of mediation emerges as well: diagrams, maps, and other visualizations that record in two dimension the existence of the underground. Furthermore, the planetary surface as a record of physical, biological, and ecological dynamics contains depths, and the media inscription of a surface becomes what Bruno Latour would call "immutable mobile" on flat surfaces: "All these charts, tables and trajectories are conveniently at hand and combinable at will, no matter whether they are twenty centuries old or a day old; each of them brings celestial bodies billions of tons heavy and hundreds of thousands of miles away to the size of a point on a piece of paper."[4] But instead of being merely a record of a planetary surface and its spatial dimension, these immutable mobiles are full of unfolding potential for transformation of that surface. In other words, as geomedia—a term used by Sean Cubitt—such mechanisms from diagrams to real-time operations such as seismographs but also contemporary financial metal markets offer a varying set of temporalities that feed back into their constitutive conditions.[5]

"What does this represent?" might be a relevant question when it comes to interpretations of images of geography, geology, and aerial images. But particularly important is also the question: What can we *do* with these images? To which ends are they mobilized as forensic insights about the surface that tells stories of the depths that lie beneath them? What potential implications, potentials of actions, does the image contain and condition? Hence, surfaces—and, in our case, planetary surfaces of geography and geologic formations—are constantly mobilized as objects of visual culture but also, as I argue, as objects of future-oriented calculation that takes a particular intensive temporal turn in contemporary contexts. Here the surface takes the place of depth, as a privileged epistemological entry point to depth understood spatially (extraction industries and the planetary deposits) and to depth as temporal. A track record of the long-term changes is recorded on surfaces, which then are mobilized for the future-oriented predictions in, for example, machine learning environments that process aerial images. So, what is it to see the surface as an image, and the image as one of movement and a record of changes? What is it to see the geologic and geographic aspects of planetary materials as surfaces that are images, and hence "flattened" from their deep times to algorithmic material and through datasets such as Google Earth Engine and the European Commission Global Human Settlement? The standard verticality of this mode of observation—from down below the underground infrastructures to the view from on up of aerial imaging or satellite-based media—shifts in current contexts into one of surface calculation. It is this calculated surface that is the focus of this chapter and its take on depth and media that meet at the point of the image of the surface. Depth has become part of media studies vocabulary in how aspects of geophysics and geology are articulated both as part of the material supply of media technologies and as part of the expansion of the temporal horizon of media into the planetary durations of metals and minerals. I am interested in picking up on these expanded senses of media cultural discussion to engage with how the question of surface is part of both "reading" those depths and also "predicting" their current valuations in the financial sense and in the sense of forensic-driven predictive mechanisms. Reading depth from the surface also becomes inserted into a "futuristic" framework of machine learning mechanisms of prediction. The chapter will outline some key aspects of aerial imaging and geomedia before connecting these with the Surface Value workshop. The artistic workshop led by Abelardo Gil-Fournier addressed questions of machine learning becoming part of the calculatable image surfaces that also are one backbone of future predictions.

It is in this context apt, then, that many contemporary forms of vertical imaging have a particular use not merely as techniques of seeing but as techniques of processing the recorded data. Besides the usual suspects of institutions of military and surveillance, less malicious forms of imaging are also part of this production of planetary surfaces as images. What connects different discursive and institutional uses are that images are seen in terms of their potentials. Consider how the motto of the environmental monitoring company SkyTruth sounds in the context of the discussion so far: "If you can see it you can change it" rings somewhat like a utopian liberal promise as to the power of visibility and transparency, and it echoes a belief in powers of imaging as one already halfway there to manipulation.[6] In uses such as satellite imaging not only is what you see what you get, but what you see is what you can manipulate and change so that every observable thing, object, or surface turns into possible transformation. In other words, one is dealing with operations that start—even if perhaps not end—as aesthetics: surfaces that are observed to reveal their depths and their secrets. Their lines and their patterns reveal all sorts of truths, and their surface is the interface to both the political geology and the political geography of the landscape.[7] SkyTruth's work encompasses gathering data from satellites in order to track and analyze fracking sites, oil spills, and similar large-scale incidents and operations that transform the earth's surface but also its wider habitability. Such work exemplifies the sort of remote sensing–enabled forensic analysis as well as collective projects that allow environmentally destructive extractive practices—from mining to oil drilling, fracking to fishing—to be effectively mapped and brought to contexts of visibility.

Of course, there is a distinct media historical irony in play when you start to consider how SkyTruth's motto about visibility is merely one form of tweaking the meaning of aerial vision in military terms: if you can see it, you can target it, to refer to Rey Chow.[8] Seeing or vision are not solitary techniques but, echoing Paul Virilio's words, are about the "logistics of perception on all fronts" that has become more important than "the logistics of weapons targeted along a particular front."[9] Hence, over the extended wars—and the slow wars of environmental destruction—the operations of visuality as they are bundled into a range of other techniques of calculation retain their centrality.[10]

In other words, logistics of perception do not merely operate along the axis of visibility and hiding, or observation and camouflage. They also operate along an extensive line of cultural techniques that make things visible in the first place and connect those visibilities to various other forms of operations.[11] The history of aerial imaging and observation is also dependent on various forms of techniques, even infrastructures that are not at first instance always considered *visual* technologies: as Caren Kaplan reminds us in her work, techniques of motility from air balloons to drones are part of an infrastructure of observation of the earth's surface.[12] In this sense, the X and Y of the vertical field surveying landscapes is a logistical environment that includes the underground as much as the surface level as part of its map. Lisa Parks writes about the drone view in such terms as a vertical field that "extends from the earth's surface, including the geological layers below and built environments upon it, through the domains of the spectrum and the air to the outer limits of the orbit."[13] In addition, as we will see, besides such spatial sets of logistics of depth and its surface the contemporary technologies of calculation of spatial sets in machine learning become a way to extend from the x- and y-axis to the z-axis—the temporal manipulation of images—both as movement and as prediction. It is important to see how these techniques (also geomedia) relate to the earlier traits of bureaucratic media of domination. In Sean Cubitt's words, "That trinity of fundamentally bureaucratic media—databases (filing cabinets), spreadsheets (ledgers) and GIS (maps)—still operates, not least at the level of companies and institutions, where it continues to provide the backbone of a residual early-modern biopolitics. A history of the types of mediation evolved since then indicates a new turn in modernity."[14]

Surface readings are part of the historical techniques of media recording and analysis (e.g., aerial imaging and composite photography), but I want to address contemporary forms of data culture that relate to this lineage of analysis, logistics as well as bureaucratic media expressed as visual culture. Hence engaging with surfaces—planetary surfaces to be exact—becomes a way to expand on some of the topics that relate to forms of data analytics—often branded as artificial intelligence (AI)—that works with geographic surface data. Images of the earth and its surface have for a long time been part of the production of various forms of observational power that SkyTruth encapsulates in its techniques of identification that are part of "geospatial intelligence"—a network of practice and remote sensing that combines satellites and "optical, thermal, radar, and radiometric remote sensing tools."[15] Images function nowadays primarily as data, and in extensive quantities as "operational images," a term used by Harun Farocki and adopted by Trevor Paglen to refer to the regime of images that are less the focus of (humans) looking at pictures than about a functional part of operations from the military to other large-scale infrastructures, such as in finance or environmental monitoring.[16] In other words, besides the usual military focus of operational images, it is important to ask in which ways are data images about geographic surfaces operational images, and in which ways do they participate in the aforementioned other regimes of mapping, observing, and, indeed, governing the earth as a surface that claims to speak on behalf of its depth? Before I turn my attention to Google Earth Engine Datasets later in this chapter, I first want to elaborate key aspects of the media techniques of surfaces, depth, and geology. In other words, I want to elaborate questions of mediation of depth through elaborating some of the cultural techniques of surfaces through which depth becomes analyzable and as flat surfaces of images—or as flat images of data. This relates to the argument I am developing that instead of a binary of surface and depth the two are entangled and in machine learning environments also include the futuristic side of prediction, exhibiting parallel temporal aspects through images of surfaces, and surfaces as images.

Techniques of Depth

In my book *A Geology of Media*, the question of depth becomes a central thread for the analysis of the material aspects of technical media.[17] I wanted to extend the media archaeological discussions about the deep times of media to a more environmental arts and humanities approach, which also meant that geology was carried forward from what it designates as a scientific discipline to a cultural marker that speaks of depths and materialities of technical media. In this manner, it relates both to the spatial aspects of depth as a central historical theme from modern cultures of extraction (mining, minerals, and energy) and to the centrality of those materials in the contemporary computational culture and infrastructure. While *A Geology of Media* already speaks of the particular extension of the media theoretical timescale from human media to the deep times of the materials of media, it also relates to a larger shift in media and the humanities. Whether or not we use the term "Anthropocene," this topic has become a vehicle for discussion about the technical changes that affect the vast scales of planetary habitability from the soil to the atmosphere. And it has become one reference point for the work on large-scale landscapes that become transformed as part of the long tail of urban infrastructures visualized in work such as Unknown Field Division's, discussed in art projects such as Geocinema, and also brought into speculative contexts as generative imagery by artists such as Grégory Chatonsky.

Besides the visual arts, the entry of environmental and geologic concepts into media theory has been one of the most interesting discussions over the past years, and it has complemented the otherwise often urban focus of media studies.[18] Earth arts had emerged as post–studio art practice that dealt with the expanded vocabularies, practices, and landscapes of contemporary art.[19] In media studies a parallel extension has happened by way of both artistic work and theoretical arguments that addressed concepts such as deep time, media paleontology, and the elementals of technological culture.[20] Many of these media studies approaches have brought to the fore that not all of media culture happens above the ground, while I want to continue this line of thought about deep times of the media or geomedia by arguing, alongside Giuliana Bruno, for a thorough understanding of the usefulness of the surface.[21] In many uses, the surface remains a privileged object of analysis, from screen surfaces to, as argued in this chapter, the geographic surfaces of the planet.

Surfaces are interfaces not only between depth and what lies above but between the underground and its inscription. Furthermore, surfaces are where the human-modified underground emerges as what Matt Edgeworth terms the "archeosphere": the modern underground not merely in terms of the spectacular holes that define it but as a supporting carpet for the visible surface structures. In his words, this sphere is "a giant carpet covering large areas, on which the furniture of the human world (its buildings, monuments, pylons, oil-rigs, telegraph poles, roads, railway viaducts, shanty towns, parks, airports) stands and is supported, and into which it will eventually crumble. Deep layered in places, threadbare and patchy in others, this carpet of near-global extent provides the surface on which people carry out their lives."[22] To address the surface as a carpet helps to understand how depth becomes surfaced: this carpet mediates undergrounds and surfaces; it mediates technological infrastructures and their multiple modern uses. The carpet is both a material modification and an operation of knowledge. The surface—and its relation to depth—becomes part of operations of knowing (such as through technical media), and this knowing is constantly operationalized in various institutional contexts.

The way in which we speak of the centrality of extraction industries as a crucial feature of contemporary capitalism is here evident on a wider logistical level that relates to the transformation of space and its connection to media.[23] While concepts such as the Stack outline the intensive transformation that is material and informational, political and geopolitical, it also means how the visual and data-enhanced ways of mapping those carpets mobilize a new dynamic sort of earth engineering.[24] Observing transforms into mapping potentials of change; visual culture entangles with engineering of those visibilities. This, then, has effects for the governance of space and its movement, as material soil and deposits, landscape and its mutations, as well as data about those materials. These data and the data visualizations turn into key parallel assets on top of the materials that are extracted. Hence the discourse about planetary capitalism as one form of stratification of the already stratified technological sphere of extraction is important for understanding the links among materials, data, and their operationalized uses. This does not mean that I would see the data aspects of analysis of planetary depths and surfaces as "extraction" in the exact same sense as extracting limited resources, but there is a link between the two. In any case, both the property regimes and the financialization of depth is one way of approaching the deep time of planetary resources as they are handled and mobilized as data units whether on the market or in other institutional contexts. The vertical angle to contemporary material politics of architecture, urbanization, and control including aerial images finds another form of stratification in how data about the vertical become operated across a surface of a screen of patterns.[25]

In a related manner, Sean Cubitt refers to this assemblage of operations as "geomedia," a term briefly mentioned earlier. It refers to the operations that both mediate the earth and establish a relation between time and value.[26] Cubitt contextualizes more recent digital versions of data visualization as part of a longer history of techniques that also establish how planetary materials and dynamics are recorded as data—as "immutable mobiles," to use the Latour term with which we began. These techniques include both analog and digital ones, recording changes in surface, tectonic, soil, and other conditions. The seismometer is an apt example of a historical medium that functions, according to Cubitt, both as a stand-alone analog instrument that records a vector image of the earth's tectonics and subsequently as part of a network of seismographic data, the Global Seismographic Network that connects instruments and their data relative to their locations. Hence, individual techniques relate also to infrastructures of measurement and governance, and as such they also have an institutional aspect that allows data to be compared, distributed, actioned, and made operative. River monitoring and various techniques such as spectrometric analysis that extends data visualization to chemical reactions on and of the planetary surface are also examples of geomedia. Cubitt, however, points out that river monitoring also can be seen as "mirroring the complex of meteorological instruments and translations in the concatenation of observational devices used to track the consequences of an environmental crisis shifting minerals through watersheds towards the ocean."[27] Besides being useful in extending the various technologies and operational aspects of media history to environmental questions, these techniques have, according to Cubitt, an inherent relation to time. "The seismograph tells time as it occurs; river monitoring establishes a history," against which one is able to demonstrate patterns of change. Both are time-based media that are central to the technological culture that produces and mediates forms of space (as planetary dynamics) and forms of time. Furthermore, they already include potentials for an elaborated set of temporalities that emerge through forecasting. In other words, data are not only directly measured and registered but become dependent on the various distributed mechanisms that circulate data through simulations and other means of synthesis: "Such phenomena-to-data translations no longer deal exclusively in real time or the accumulation of records: more typically, we use the accumulation of data to predict."[28] The various earth transformations—even of geographies and geologic deep times—that we witness are also mobilized as data and, as such, become oriented toward the future at least as much as the past that is only the record of changes.

Concerning prediction, Cubitt's third example complicates things in most fruitful ways. These predictive forms of data visualization detach from a direct recording of planetary material dynamics—tectonic or, for example, atmospheric—and are more directly related to the "registering" of the abstractions of the financial transactions of the metal market. As such, Cubitt's example presents a creative twist on geologies of media by way of including the media of finance and futures trading, a key part of contemporary financial capitalism. Here geomedia becomes one form of data-intensive and algorithmically driven governance of planetary materials: price fluctuations, predictions, and derivatives are at once part of the speculative sphere of finance and in a constant feedback loop with various material operations such as mining. Any location and its cost analysis, then, can include speculative data about the possible value of particular minerals, whether for the technology sector or some other industrial use.

The massive amounts of data processing that feed through institutions such as NASDAQ and the London Metals Exchange represent an algorithmically determined form of the temporality of metals as data. The deep times of planetary geology that have presented one trope of natural history—the temporality of extraction and infrastructure of modern capitalism—shift gear to become part of the ultrafast circulation of data-as-speculation. The sort of "immutable mobiles" that in the earlier phases were most accurately described as the two-dimensional paper-based media about, for example, planetary materials are now dynamically multidimensional sets of data both dynamic *and* mobile, expressing one key facet of capitalism of futures trading. Planetary (slow) deep time is massively accelerated so that most of it becomes machine-to-machine communication. High-frequency trading is a prime example.

The metal futures market concerns not only the scale of operations but also a scale of time that relates to a financial premediation.[29] It is a future-present that is a financialized version of Cold War operations research: from the operations room to the business consultants and, in this case, the algorithmic machine-to-machine operations produce an odd sort of a time that is meant to run ahead of the present. Is this an advanced form of probability theory, the branch of mathematics that emerges at the back of the Enlightenment and becomes one form of statistical thinking that captures much of modernity's key forms of organization since the nineteenth century?[30] It fundamentally functions as creation of manageable little futures by way of calculation. As John Beck writes: "Probability theory is thus a way of dealing with uncertainty by mediating between knowledge and mere opinion; the calculus offers a way to be uncertain without being irrational. A fictional probability can be wrested away from the impossible and placed in relation to the present that is a version of the real: probability provides a rational means of accounting for decision-making that is not necessarily a continuation or repetition of the past but is not entirely at the mercy of chance."[31] This is also the point where it becomes evident that the sort of depths I am dealing with in this chapter do not concern merely underground as a site of deep time and the usual sort of geologic evidence of a past but enter into the realm of calculated probability: the sort of futures that might come about when these deposits and deep times enter the algorithmic realm in machine learning.

This bureaucratic media of accounting for presents and futures is characteristic of the geomedia of surface calculations. In other words, the mediations of depth (i.e., geologic materials and, as we will soon see, geographic surfaces) becomes embedded in a further layer of time. Such operations complexify the question of what exact "time zones" current deep times are in—a question that sounds oxymoronic but is at the center of contemporary forms of manipulation of planetary materials. What happened to the slowness of the planet? What happened to the depth of planetary materials and the weight of the ground? What surfaced? How are the deep times of planetary materials, metals, and such constantly circulated as part of both a current media culture of finance and the forms of prediction that emerge in such contexts? In the final section of this essay, I turn to one particular example I have been working with, namely, machine learning and geographic datasets.

The Predicted Image

The arguments in this chapter are closely tied to practice-based work and a workshop that artist Abelardo Gil-Fournier and a team of scholars from Winchester School of Art organized at the transmediale festival in February 2018. Titled "The Surface Value," our project engaged with the question of the geographic, the geologic, and the planetary surface from the perspective of aerial vision since the early twentieth century.[32] Furthermore, we inserted these questions into contexts of contemporary practice with geographic datasets and technological images, as well as forms of operating with the images extending from their representational status to their operational functions. However, instead of assuming that the aerial observation of surfaces is reducible to the visual component, we wanted to look at how the use of such images expands as part of operations of data. Verticality gives way to infrastructures of data.

The workshop's practice-based aspect was organized by Gil-Fournier, who linked our theoretical discussions with a crash course on machine learning. He offered a tutorial on the basics of machine learning, from installing the necessary software and plug-ins to a discussion of the Google Earth Engine platform. One emphasis was on the question of what sorts of moving images are those we watch in the model case studies and time lapses that the site offers.[33] We also considered how those image sequences of movement and change can be produced via means of machine learning, focusing on the temporality of the time lapse, but in ways that move the sequences forward.

Some of the examples of the datasets are listed on the website of the workshop as case studies (see Figure 14.1). They mostly deal with

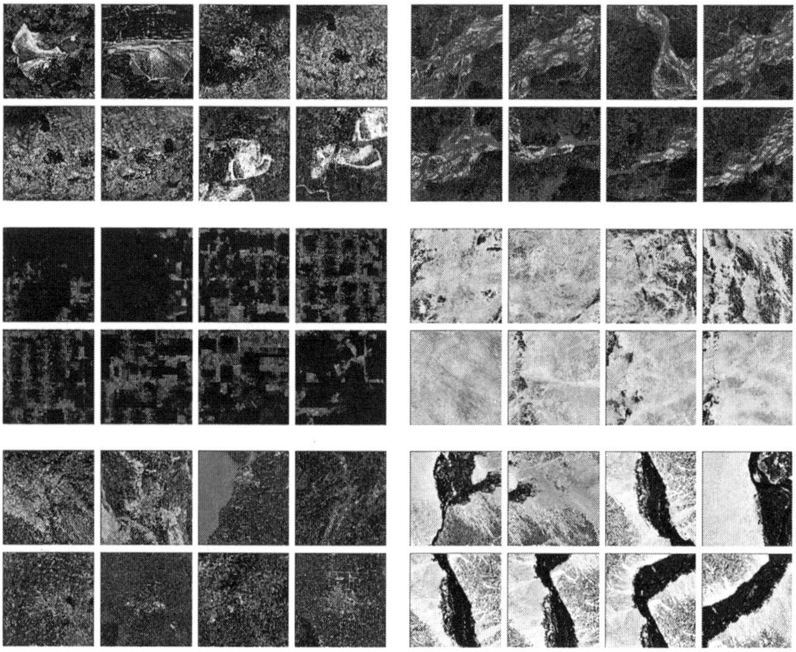

FIGURE 14.1. A collection of samples of some of the datasets of planetary surface behaviors used in Abelardo Gil-Fournier's workshop. Clockwise, starting top left, they show brown-coal mines, meanders of the Ganges, dunes in the Sahara Desert, the agricultural lands by the Nile riverside, cities in China, and deforestation in the Amazon. Courtesy of the artist.

different monitoring and research uses, with a special focus on forest and water coverage changes, agriculture and urbanization, and animal habitats. With the available satellite data and the relevant application program interfaces (APIs), projects such as "Global Forest Cover Change" and "Disease Surveillance and Risk Mapping" are good examples of how data are used for prediction. Historical change across years and decades was visualized through time-lapse images; the mobilization of near real-time data enabled a different type of analysis that also provides a feedback loop in terms of possibilities of intervention. It is clear that for situations that require more accuracy, a massively distributed set of computing power is the only viable way of engaging with the predictions that can potentially be read out of the datasets. But Gil-Fournier's focus was to investigate these techniques themselves as test cases concerning the media operations working with surfaces as forms of geomedia.

What kinds of audiovisual and calculated entry points to the world of planetary images are part of this engagement that then, besides the corporate, military, financial, and such operational uses, becomes integrated into an artistic research platform? Besides historical time lapse, what are predictive images—or prediction as a way of *forming* images for analysis—in this set that aims to measure the earth *as it might become?* And how do these images mediate concerns that are part of environmental monitoring, financial culture, geologic matter, and also, in this case, artistic forms of research?

In Gil-Fournier's brief, the participants were tasked to consider what to do with a planetary image that is contextualized as a video image. As the workshop explained it:

> Next Frame Prediction names the experimental set of Machine Learning techniques aimed to algorithmically produce the frame that follows a video stream of images. This approach to video-prediction makes use of convolutional neural networks that, relying on large databases of videos, are able to identify temporal patterns and behaviours within a sequence of frames. This analysis provides them with the capacity of generating future movement and, in consequence, of extending videos with plausible futures.
>
> This project is conceived as a platform to research on the application of techniques of video prediction to sequences of historical satellite data. Starting from the available timelapses of archived aerial images, this platform aims to generate future visions of the surfaces of the Earth where, flattened as video sequences, terraforming activities such as deforestation or urbanisation might be scrutinised as visual feeders for predictive algorithms.[34]

Gil-Fournier uses next frame prediction as the example of a particular technique for the production of ensuing imagined images (Figure 14.2). This technique mobilizes video-prediction and convolutional neural networks as forms of temporal pattern creation that then start to resemble simple abstract forms on screen that can still be connected to the operational sense of an image: they are meant to speak of plausible futures (urban growth, deforestation, basically any identifiable surface-level change).

There is already a range of operations mentioned in the description: aerial images and flattening (as one part of imperial power), terraforming (as one aspect of contemporary geoengineering), predictive algorithms (as mediated governance), and then, of course, video too. Video becomes part of the discussion of AI and data, terraforming opens up as a visual activity,

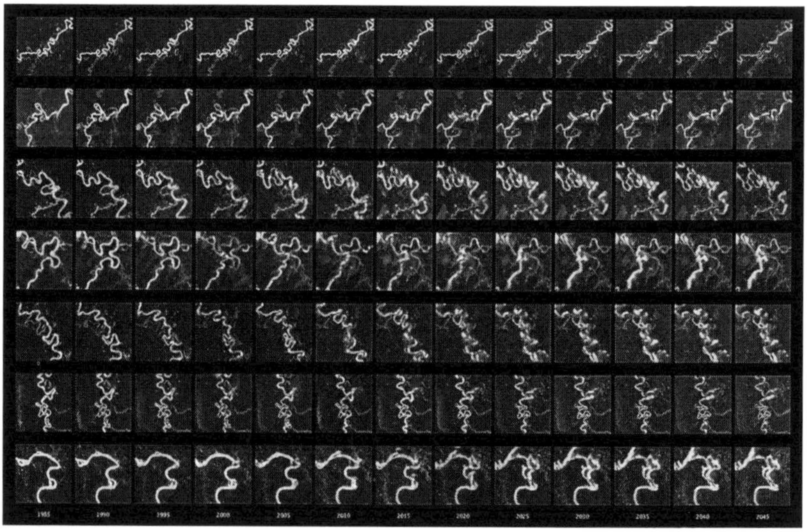

FIGURE 14.2. A series of predictions of the movements of Ucayali River in Peru as part of Gil-Fournier's experimental workshops that test how geographic datasets can become visual experiments. Some of these sequences display predictions that clearly "fail" as the river seems to dissolve itself. The failure, however, is visually interesting: a visual accident becomes a reminder of aerial images of flooding and rivers out of control. Courtesy of the artist.

and the operational loop between visuality, geologic operations, urban developments, landscape changes, and what can be coined as the planetary-scale image factory. What is particularly interesting in the context of both this chapter and the book, *Deep Mediations,* is how this generation of planetary-scale images involves a mobilization of the often-perceived slowness of earth's durations into a calculated platform of other temporalities. It can be seen as one example of geomedia, but also as the micro-temporality of calculation that itself introduces a further layer of time onto the operational surface that does not so much represent but operates on and with data.[35]

Gil-Fournier also raised the question as to what sort of mechanisms create *plausible* futures that emerge from the historical set of data about depths, geographic and geologic patterns, and the surfaces through which these are analyzed. However, what rationality decides on plausibility concerning something that by definition should be contingent? In this case, plausibilities can be seen, for example, as part of the futures that are useful for the futures market and various value mechanisms. Besides its use for environmental monitoring, prediction stands at the center of various mechanisms or techniques of speculation that act upon a future already now. There is a long history of how speculation becomes a technique to pin down futures—firmative speculation, as coined by the uncertain commons collective.[36] But in the short remaining space of this chapter, I just want to point to how the temporal aspect of working with the surfaces of images, datasets about surfaces, and surfaces read as analytics of a future come together in the context of machine learning. Furthermore, the predictions based on machine learning readings are already becoming a service. In other words, the mechanism for this data-landscape prediction is already becoming fine-tuned as one aspect of input into the turbulent financial machine. Here the deep time of planetary materials is merely one input for the processing of possible (even plausible) futures.

These operational images mobilize geospatial intelligence about the earth and its historically recorded dynamics. The various techniques demonstrate how data, including uncertain and predictive data, play a central part in the aforementioned speculative sense of futuring. The temporal nature of the financial market is inextricably bound to forms of algotrading, in terms of both its speed and its futuristic turbulence. Complementing Cubitt's sense of the geomedia of algotrading as the algorithmic angle to what earth materials, metals, and other resources are in contexts of financialized trading, Melinda Cooper argues that the sort of futures methodologies that we recognize from climate change research share a temporal emphasis that is familiar from finance: "the multiple future worlds attendant on alternative actions in the present."[37] This deep time of the media measures earth's surface changes while itself participating in transforming those surfaces: the images are potential avenues to intervention—whether environmentally focused policy changes or capital investment that terraforms regions in its own image. Multiple times coexist in these techniques of media: historical, even deep time data, the microtemporal processes of processing that data, and the future-oriented promises of prediction.

Furthermore, the importance of probability persists. As noted earlier, there is a particular institutional basis for the techniques of probability and statistics as they are rolled out as part of financial/futuristic techniques, and they come out as one essential part of this speculative context. To quote uncertain commons: "These social and analytic technologies become generative places for knowledge production: knowledge about economies, bodies, and globalities as effects of unknown and unknowable futures. Economic, medical, and political regimes are increasingly organized around statistical calculations of possible futures, a probabilistic accounting of the present in terms of an always-deferred assessment of whatever might come."[38]

In many ways, I want to think of the methods Gil-Fournier employed as forms of artistic interventions into the logistical imaginary of images as they persist as part of the governance through data.[39] The artistic research platform can be understood through Keller Easterling's words, emphasizing how "design also vividly anticipates and materializes change, using tools found in many forms of cultural persuasion."[40] For the purposes of understanding such technical media practices as Gil-Fournier's, this insight to design can relate to art too: anticipating and materializing change instead of merely ornamenting cultural processes at a distance, and in this way trying to establish both pedagogical and aesthetic platforms for engagement with the new normal of AI and other techniques of data-defined culture.[41]

Such experimental planetary moving images clearly relate to the turbulent financial environment, but they are also speculative images in other ways too. These little snippets of data images gleaned and cleaned from satellite and remote sensing services are like image experiments that test out both what the neural network can do and how moving images can be created not by traditional forms of recording the world in movement but as found-data footage. Hence, the site of the automated predictive imaging is also a site of creative practice. Images are part of training sets for neural networks, for priming and optimizing those functions of both identification and accuracy of predictions. But besides optimization, the images start to live a life of their own. They form landscapes that could be; they form imageries of the planetary surfaces that might take place. Gil-Fournier's workshop was one form of a stage that operated as artistic research into surfaces—but, as argued in this chapter, these surfaces are part of a longer media history of "immutable mobiles" that includes both the administrative, bureaucratic visual culture of diagrams, graphs, and statistical visualizations and the sort of surface readings that participate in datametric culture. This is indeed one form of imperial power where images—even moving images—about planetary surfaces remain useful for that speculative sense of future capture. These images operate as interfaces to reading the deep times of the planet, and the constant fluctuating of those times as they are expressed in large-scale events: deforestation; desertification; urban planning; and planetary-scale infrastructures paving the way for the extended urbanization that itself is becoming one way of layering, accessing, and terraforming the archeospheres of the planetary skin. It is also one version of the story of the climate disaster to which we are too slowly reacting.

Notes

1. The research for this article has been supported by Czech Science Foundation funded project 19-26865X "Operational Images and Visual Culture: Media Archaeological Investigations."

2. Gilles Deleuze, *Logic of Sense,* trans. Mark Lester with Charles Stivale (New York: Columbia University Press, 1990).

3. Giuliana Bruno, *Surface: Matters of Aesthetics, Materiality, and Media* (Chicago: University of Chicago Press, 2014).

4. Bruno Latour, *Science in Action* (Cambridge, Mass.: Harvard University Press, 1987), 227.

5. Sean Cubitt, "Three Geomedia," *CTRL-Z,* no. 7 (2017), http://www.ctrl-z.net.au/articles/issue-7/cubitt-three-geomedia/.

6. "SkyTruth" website, accessed May 13, 2019, https://www.skytruth.org/.

7. On political geology, see Adam Bobbette and Amy Donovan, eds., *Political Geology: Active Stratigraphies and the Making of Life* (Basingstoke: Palgrave, 2019).

8. Rey Chow, *The Age of the World Target: Self-Referentiality in War, Theory, and Comparative Work* (Durham, N.C.: Duke University Press, 2006).

9. Paul Virilio, *Strategy of Deception,* trans. Chris Turner (London: Verso, 2007), 24.

10. For slow environmental wars, see Rob Nixon, *Slow Violence and the Environmentalism of the Poor* (Cambridge, Mass.: Harvard University Press). See also Jussi Parikka, *A Slow, Contemporary Violence Damaged Environments of Technological Culture* (Berlin: Sternberg, 2016). On the operations of visuality, see Caren Kaplan, *Aerial Aftermaths: Wartime from Above* (Durham, N.C.: Duke University Press, 2018).

11. On cultural techniques, see Bernhard Siegert, *Cultural Techniques: Grids, Filters, Doors, and Other Articulations of the Real* (New York: Fordham University Press, 2015); Abelardo Gil-Fournier, "Seeding and Seeing: The Inner Colonisation of Land and Vision," *ARPJA* 6, no. 1 (2017), http://www.aprja.net/seeding-and-seeing-the-inner-colonisation-of-land-and-vision/.

12. Kaplan, *Aerial Aftermaths.*

13. Lisa Parks, *Life in the Age of Drone Warfare* (Durham, N.C.: Duke University Press, 2017), 136.

14. Cubitt, "Three Geomedia."

15. Jacques Leslie, "Eyes in the Sky. Green Groups Are Harnessing Data from Space," *Yale Environment 360,* January 11, 2016, https://e360.yale.edu/features/eyes_in_the_sky_green_groups_are_harnessing_data_from_space.

16. See Trevor Paglen, "Operational Images," *e-flux* 59 (November 2014), https://www.e-flux.com/journal/59/61130/operational-images/.

17. Jussi Parikka, *A Geology of Media* (Minneapolis: University of Minnesota Press, 2015).

18. Nicole Starosielski, *The Undersea Network* (Durham, N.C.: Duke University Press, 2015).

19. Rosalind Krauss, "Sculpture in the Expanded Field," *October* 8 (Spring 1979): 30–44.

20. See, for example, Siegfried Zielinski, *Deep Time of the Media,* trans. Gloria Custance (Cambridge, Mass.: MIT Press); and John Durham Peters, *The Marvelous Clouds: Toward a Philosophy of Elemental Media* (Chicago: University of Chicago Press, 2015). On recent technological earth arts, see Jussi Parikka, "Earth Forces: Contemporary Land Arts, Technology and New Materialist Aesthetics," *Cultural Studies Review* 21, no. 2 (September 2015): 47–75, http://epress.lib.uts.edu.au/journals/index.php/csrj/index.

21. See also the recent volume edited by Yeseung Lee, *Surface and Apparition. The Immateriality of Modern Surface* (London: Bloomsbury, 2020).

22. Matt Edgeworth, quoted in Stephen Graham, *Vertical: The City from Satellites to Bunkers* (London: Verso, 2016), 292.

23. See Imre Szeman, "On the Politics of Extraction," *Cultural Studies* 31, no. 2–3 (2017): 440–47; and Brett Neilson and Sandro Mezzadra, "On the Multiple Frontiers of Extraction: Excavating Contemporary Capitalism," *Cultural Studies* 31, no. 2–3 (2017): 185–204.

24. Benjamin H. Bratton, *The Stack: On Software and Sovereignty* (Cambridge, Mass.: MIT Press, 2015).

25. On verticality, see Graham, *Vertical.*

26. Cubitt, "Three Geomedia."

27. Cubitt.

28. Cubitt.

29. On premediation, see Richard Grusin, *Premediation* (Basingstoke: Palgrave, 2010).

30. Ian Hacking, *The Taming of Chance* (Cambridge: Cambridge University Press, 1990).

31. John Beck, "The Future: RAND, Brand and Dangerous to Know," in *Cold War Legacies: Systems, Theory, Aesthetics,* ed. John Beck and Ryan Bishop (Edinburgh: Edinburgh University Press, 2016), 45.

32. Part of transmediale 2018, theme "Face Value"; see https://2018.transmediale.de/program/event/surface-value-landscape-prediction-an-amt-workshop-day-1, accessed May 13, 2019.

33. For Google Earth Engine, see https://earthengine.google.com/, accessed May 13, 2019. For Abelardo Gil-Fournier's Github page for the Surface Value images and methodology, see https://github.com/abe-/landscape-prediction, accessed May 13, 2019.

34. Landscape Prediction, Gil-Fournier's Github page.

35. Wolfgang Ernst, *Chronopoetics: The Temporal Being and Operativity of Technological Media,* trans. Anthony Enns (London: Rowman and Littlefield, 2016).

36. "This specifically modern form is what we call *firmative speculation,* a firming (from the late Latin *firmā*) or solidifying of the possibilities of the future. It is a speculative mode that seeks to pin down, delimit, constrain, and enclose—to make things definitive, firm. The ur-image of such agency is the *firm,* a type of business house (emerging in Germany in 1744) that capitalizes on market conditions, working toward an optimal level of production that will ensure maximum profit and minimum cost while always on the lookout for fresh opportunities for expansion—aggressively pushing its products through advertising, shaping new needs, and consuming publics"; uncertain commons, *Speculate This!* (Durham, N.C.: Duke University Press, 2013), chap. 1, https://speculatethis.pressbooks.com/chapter/chapter-1/.

37. Melinda Cooper, "Turbulent Worlds: Financial Markets and Environmental Crisis," *Theory, Culture and Society* 27, no. 2–3 (2010): 170.

38. uncertain commons, *Speculate This!*

39. On logistical imaginary, see Ned Rossiter, *Software, Infrastructure, Labour: A Media Theory of Logistical Nightmares* (London: Routledge, 2016).

40. Keller Easterling, "Rumor," in *Dirt,* ed. Megan Born, Helene Furján, and Lily Jencks (Cambridge, Mass.: MIT Press, 2012), 31. In terms of art methodologies, we should be aware of the role of artist-run workshops as part of "a new culture of learning and working together, supported by models like master classes, seminars, and workshops for audiences eager to learn and act," as Daphne Dragona writes. Dragona, "What Is Left to Subvert? Artistic Methodologies for a Post-digital World," in *Across and Beyond: A transmediale Reader on Post-digital Practices, Concepts, and Institutions,* ed. Ryan Bishop, Kristoffer Gansing, Jussi Parikka, and Elvia Wilk (Berlin: Sternberg, 2016), 186.

41. See Benjamin H. Bratton, *The New Normal* (Moscow: Strelka Press, 2017).

PART IV

Deep Networks

Many of the essays across this volume suggest ways in which contemporary technological systems and media regimes are reconfiguring or are reconfigured by practices of depth—from Jeff Scheible's discussion of the deep web and "informatic depth" to Jussi Parikka's consideration of the reading of planetary surfaces by way of aerial imaging and machine learning. As we signal in the Preface, part of the impetus to take stock of depth's changing status in relation to contemporary culture is motivated by media studies' infrastructural turn, which could be seen to correspond to a distinct historical phase wherein the social world is embedded with and recursively shaped by media to an unprecedented degree. Nick Couldry and Andreas Hepp identify this "latest wave of digitalization and datafication" as "deep mediatization," corresponding to a "much more intense embedding of media in social processes than ever before."[1] As they explain, "digitalization involves a further deepening, both in the *connectedness* of the infrastructures on which media-related practice depends, so, for example, the digital is now dependent on the development of Wi-Fi and other mobile services—and in the *layering* of connected media practices in which individuals or groups are now routinely engaged" (52). Depth, for Couldry and Hepp, then registers not only a vertical layering and a horizontal interconnectedness of media but also a magnitude of operations of enfolding that have formed a distinctly identifiable—and indeed felt—transformation in the social world, much as they are right to acknowledge that such transformations are more acute in some parts of the world than they are in others. They choose to name this suite of shifts "mediatization" over "mediation" to emphasize that this is a high-order transformation "at every level of interaction" (35). While we are ambivalent about the need for a more complex term than mediation (we believe it is already possible to say mediation is pervasive and structural), their observations about the reorganizations underway through the multidimensional computerization of society that they use the term to describe are worth taking heed of and certainly aligned with ideas explored throughout this volume, and particularly in this final section.

The book's closing part, "Deep Networks," contains two essays and a conversation that take as a central concern the consequences and cultures of machinic operations. Moving us away from human-centered practices of visioning and sensing the world, this part reflects on how in today's mediascape, "deep learning"—the training of computers to process large datasets—reshapes or offers an opportunity to rethink components and practices of visual culture that only a few years earlier we might have taken for granted. This part takes seriously the ways in which contemporary media formats might render earlier modes of visual analysis and critical thought practically impossible, and considers what the field of cinema and media studies might have to offer, or learn from, those moments where we encounter new epistemological blocks.

Taylor Arnold and Lauren Tilton's essay identifies a quality of impenetrability in deep learning models, something that, it is worth noting, one also finds in other "deep" sites (from consciousness to the oceanic to outer space), and these scholars root the impossibility of interpretation and decipherment in the layered structure of such models. If layered, impenetrable deep learning algorithms are increasingly impacting human lives, they ask, how can humanists evaluate the merit or biases of the algorithms in question? And if they cannot, what does this reflect to us about the (ir)relevance of hermeneutically oriented models of the humanities, especially ones that have not methodologically adapted to this altered discursive landscape? James J. Hodge's *Sensations of History: Animation and New Media Art* similarly begins from the premise that we need to rethink some of the fundamental terms of the humanities as we recognize that the computer, and more specifically what he, quoting Bernard Stiegler, calls the "deep opacity of contemporary technics," has outrun our ability to think about it and its operations analytically.[2] Rather than throwing up his hands in despair, however, Hodge turns to the realm of animation in new media art as "both a symptom and a critical response to the opacity of digital experience," as a form of art making that "creatively articulates and expresses the widening chasm between lived experience and the insensible technical infrastructure that makes so much of it possible" (1). Just as such art "holds itself critically proximate to the furious pace of the ever-updating present" while "resisting any simple promotion of the 'new'" (2), according to Hodge, so this volume attempts to grapple with the critical questions that arise in response to altered experiences of impenetrable depths, even when that involves being "critically proximate" in uncomfortable, implicating ways with bodies of knowledge and methods that overlap with the militaristic; that depend on undesirable collaborations with nonstate actors like Google and Facebook, or on learning languages, including the languages of algotrading and spreadsheets, which exceed those languages that have tended to be prized by the humanities.

One of the most prominent conversations concerning machine learning and contemporary culture in recent years has been around the phenomenon of "deepfakes," whereby computers work with large datasets of images to "doctor" existing moving images and deceptively make it appear that people are engaging in behavior in which they have actually not participated. Deepfake software relies on a technology called a "generative adversarial network" (GAN), which is composed of two machine-learning neural networks working in tandem: one network generates fake audiovisual content modeled on source data, and the other, the "discriminator," tries to detect it. The content is volleyed back and forth, improving each time until it passes for real, in a twist on the classic Turing test paradigm. The system seems as challenging to defeat as a mythological Hydra: built into it is a troubling paradox, whereby the better the network gets at detecting the fake, the better it becomes at generating fakes based on any defects (such as the absence of blinking) that might have signaled the fake in the first place. This has been especially alarming in the realms of politics and pornography, where various platforms and people would of course like to ensure that deepfake content does not circulate—to uphold whatever remnants there are of distinctions between "real" and "fake." Anticipating the central theme of his feature-length 2019 horror film about evil doppelgangers, *Us*, filmmaker Jordan Peele released a one-minute video, "You Won't Believe What Obama Says in This Video! 😉" online in 2018 in which a photo-audio-realistic Barack Obama declares, "Our enemies can make it look like anyone is saying anything at any point in time." The video went viral, as did British artist Bill Posters and Daniel Howe's video simulation of Mark Zuckerberg, repurposing footage used in a previous address about Facebook's role in Russia's interference in the 2016 U.S. presidential election. This time, Zuckerberg directly speaks to his digital audiences: "Imagine this for a second. One man with total control of billions of people's stolen data. All their secrets, their lives, their futures. I owe it all to Spectre."

Spectre was an installation created by Posters and Howe for the Sheffield Doc/Fest in 2019, which they advertised as "poised to reveal the secrets of the Digital Influence Industry." These videos serve as unsettling, reflexive warnings about the potential threats of artificial intelligence–assisted disinformation, taking us further down into the recesses of "uncanny valleys"—perceptual phenomena stemming from robotics that, appropriately, mobilize a metaphor of geologic depth.

The final chapter of *Deep Mediations* stages a conversation among three experts on media and sexuality who discuss the significance of deepfakes, particularly insofar as they raise questions related to pornography, gender, shame, and pleasure. They give credence to a claim that pornography scholars know well: that most key questions about film and media, from popular culture to genre to materiality to copyright law, often play out first in the realm of pornography. The rise of deepfakes seems to be no exception. While we should be vigilant about knowing sources and suspicious of the veracity of the information and videos streaming through our everyday feeds, we ought at the same time to be wary of how "fake" and "real" delimit the terms of debate about deepfakes in popular media. To what extent does a fixation on these terms derail attention from more pervasive and insidious slippages between real and fake, which trouble the production and dissemination of content in today's information economy? What might it mean, for example, to orient the conversation around responsibility rather than fakeness? The case of deepfakes is just one of many indices explored in this volume of both the prevalence and the shifting terrain of where discourses and conceptualizations of depth reside in the media environment of the early twenty-first century.

Notes

1. Nick Couldry and Andreas Hepp, *The Mediated Construction of Reality* (Cambridge, UK: Polity, 2017), 34.

2. James J. Hodge, *Sensations of History: Animation and New Media Art* (Minneapolis: University of Minnesota Press, 2019), 1.

CHAPTER FIFTEEN

Depth in Deep Learning

Knowledgeable, Layered, Impenetrable

Taylor Arnold and Lauren Tilton

Over the past decade, research in machine learning has made remarkable progress in the processing of text and image data. Computational models are now able to outperform human experts in certain classes of well-defined tasks. These improvements have come in part through advances in computer hardware, as well as access to larger public datasets for training models. Perhaps the largest contributing factor, however, has been the refinement and application of so-called deep learning models. The incredible accuracy achieved through these models has led directly to real-world applications, including automated medical imaging diagnoses and machine translation software. Deep learning models have also been employed in troubling ways as tools for the security state, as justification for heavily policing minorities, and in the resurgence of a computational study of eugenics.[1] The prevalence of deep learning demands that we take seriously the study of their structure and impact in society. The unmatched predictive power of these models in certain critical domains guarantees that deep learning will continue to inject algorithmic logic into critical decisions affecting everyday lives.

Deep learning models are a class of algorithms that find latent hierarchical structures within large datasets. They are constructed by chaining together layers of smaller transformations. Taken together, these layers transform input data—raw text, images, sound files, and other unstructured formats—into predictive outputs that capture semantic features detected in the original data. While the internal structures of deep learning models make them ideal for certain tasks, these benefits come at a significant cost. State-of-the-art models contain dozens of layered models and billions of numerical parameters. This complexity makes their inner workings impossible to fully understand, even for experts in the field.

In order to understand what exactly is meant by "deep learning," we argue that the "depth" explicit in the term has a triple meaning: *knowledgeable,* the accuracy displayed in the model's ability to excel in certain image process tasks; *layered,* a visualization of the learned hierarchical structures; and *impenetrable,* the inherent lack of interpretability and understanding (such as in the "deep sea" or "deep space") of their algorithmic operations. In this chapter, we interrogate these three meanings and then argue that all three are intricately linked to each other. There is no way to achieve the observed levels of accuracy without constructing layered models and introducing black-box methods. Further, there is an intrinsic depth to the tasks in domains where deep learning models are applied. That is, depth is not just an instrumental feature of working with text and image data. The deepness is inherent in the tasks themselves. Meaningful computational results in these domains require a deep learning approach. Finally, we relate the essential deep nature of certain computational tasks to implications for future study in the humanities and social sciences and to the proliferation of deep learning models throughout society. We will limit our analysis to the task of processing image and text data, as they are particularly well suited for deep learning and also are a primary object of study for humanists and social scientists.

Knowledgeable

Deep learning techniques are now used in nearly all subfields of machine learning but are most well known for their application within predictive modeling. Predictive models make use of tagged datasets to algorithmically discover patterns that can be used to predict tags for new objects outside of the original collection. A classic example consists of starting with a collection of e-mails tagged as being "spam" or "not spam" and finding patterns that can be used for automatic spam detection on new messages. Several classes of powerful, general-purpose predictive models that are frequently used in machine learning have been shown to produce reliable predictions within a wide range of applications.[2] The majority of models struggle, however, on some important classes of problems, most notably when applied to tasks involving the processing of text and image data. Processing unstructured inputs such as raw text and images is precisely the type of problem where deep learning models excel.

The inherent difficulty of building predictive models with text and image data can be understood from two related perspectives. First, the way that text and image data are stored digitally does not directly capture semantic meaning. Consider, as a point of contrast, the task of predicting the sale price of a work of art. Features that may be available to determine the price include who created the work of art, the medium of the object, the original date of creation, and its overall size. Each of these values measures real-world quantities that directly impact the value of the work. Compare this with the task of building a model that detects sarcasm in a corpus of text or determines the identities of people depicted in a collection of photographs. What features will be available for these tasks? Machine-readable text is stored as a stream of characters. Digital images are represented as three rectangular grids of pixel intensities (red, green, and blue). Unlike the semantic variables describing the sale price of works of art, individual characters and pixels are essentially meaningless in isolation. It is only in context that we comprehend the significance of the textual or visual message. Further, there is no obvious alternative representation that would map directly onto a semantic meaning.[3]

A second, closely related, challenge of working with text and image data concerns the machine learning concept known as "dimensionality." Textual data are represented as a stream of characters; however, the converse does not hold: many streams of characters are not (understandable) textual documents. In fact, only a very small proportion of randomly constructed streams of characters will result in readable text. Similarly, almost no random constructed rectangular grids of pixels will resemble a recognizable image. Most will look like static noise. This creates a challenge for predictive models because the majority of possible inputs, random streams of characters or grids of pixels, fail to be sensible objects for consideration in the first place. Therefore, a predictive model must simultaneously detect the hidden structures within text and image data while also predicting the specific tag of interest. This task turns out to be very difficult but well-suited to deep learning approaches, the specifics of which we discuss in the next section.

Text and image processing, in addition to being difficult objects of study in machine learning, share another common feature: the human brain seems particularly well-designed for both tasks.[4] The power of billions of interconnected neurons firing signals to one another inspired the neurophysiologist Warren McCulloch and logician Walter Pitts to design a computational model in which signals are passed between independent nodes using a threshold potential similar to the biochemical functioning of neurons.[5] The approach of McCulloch and Pitts, applied to predictive modeling tasks, is considered the genesis of the class of models known as "neural networks," the earliest example of a deep learning algorithm.[6] Early work on neural networks was heavily integrated with neurophysiology. Modern developments have diverged sharply from biological motivations to the point where "state-of-the-art deep learning algorithms rely on mechanisms that seem biologically implausible."[7] Despite this disconnect, the language of neurology—*neurons, neural* networks, *potential,* long-term *memory, activation* functions, *developmental* networks—remains dominant within the machine learning community. Partially this is a result of momentum from the earliest research, but today it also serves as a strong cultural signal that deep learning represents, more than alternatives, "real" humanlike intelligence.[8]

Interest in neural networks has varied over time. Early excitement was dampened by the negative results of Marvin Minsky and Seymour Papert, and the inability to train large networks with the computational resources available at the time.[9] Advances in the 1980s and 1990s addressed some of these concerns and led to several well-known examples, including Yann LeCun's classification of handwritten digits.[10] However, continued computational challenges and lack of strong empirical motivations for neural network models held off general interest until very recently.

The ImageNet Large Scale Visual Recognition Challenge (ILSVRC) is an image classification contest held annually since 2010 in which teams compete to build algorithms that classify images into one of one thousand categories.[11] In 2012, building off of nearly a decade of work refining neural network architectures, Alex Krizhevsky, Ilya Sutskever, and Geoffry Hinton produced a winning neural network model—commonly known as AlexNet—that had a top-5 error rate of only 16 percent, compared with the 25 percent top-5 error rate achieved by the second-place team's model.[12] In 2017, for example, a neural network model achieved an error rate of only 2 percent on the ILSVRC dataset.[13] Early and continued success on ILSVRC is largely seen to have launched the deep learning "revolution in computer vision," which continues with no sign of slowing down anytime soon.[14] Today, the vast majority of research in predictive models for computer vision is built on neural networks. Text analysis had at first been slower to adopt deep learning, but neural networks have recently become popular in the processing of text too. Neural networks have produced state-of-the-art results in machine translation, sentiment analysis, and topic classification.[15]

The popularity of deep learning models is a direct result of their unmatched power to produce predictive models for difficult tasks such as text and image processing. In other words, they stand out for their ability to build off of existing knowledge to predict new knowledge. For this same reason, deep learning is an important object for humanistic study. Neural network applications are not confined to relatively obscure academic competitions; rather, they are already being employed today behind the scenes in a wide variety of applications. Some of these applications directly serve the public good, such as advances in the automated detection and classification of brain tumors from MRI scans.[16] Others play directly into the needs of mass surveillance.[17] The power of deep learning allows for the automation of wide-scale privacy invasions for national and capitalistic motivations, without the limiting cost of having humans manually analyze each element of data. It is likely that many of the technological advances of the near future, such as self-driving cars, will be built on top of deep learning models.[18] In order to understand how these extant and future applications affect society, it is necessary to also understand the deep learning models themselves. The next section proceeds to explain the internal architecture of deep learning models and the relationship of this structure to their observed predictive strengths.

Layered

The focus of the discussion so far has been on the impressive predictive power of deep learning models in the difficult domains of text and image processing. Other than the original connection of neural networks to neurophysiology, which has largely been lost in modern developments, we have not explained why deep learning is particularly well adapted to these applications. It is this task that we now address. As a starting point, a suitable definition of deep learning is required.

Deep learning models apply a sequence of successive transformations to an input object of study and ultimately produce a modified output value. In the predictive modeling context, the final outputs are the predicted tags, and the transformations are adaptively learned by a training algorithm applied to a large collection of pretagged objects. Each transformation should, at least in theory, assist in moving from "raw" input formats, such as pixel intensities or character streams, toward meaningful features that capture semantic meaning within an image or textual document. Typically, the first few transformations consider interactions only between small groups of nearby pixels or characters. Successive transformations

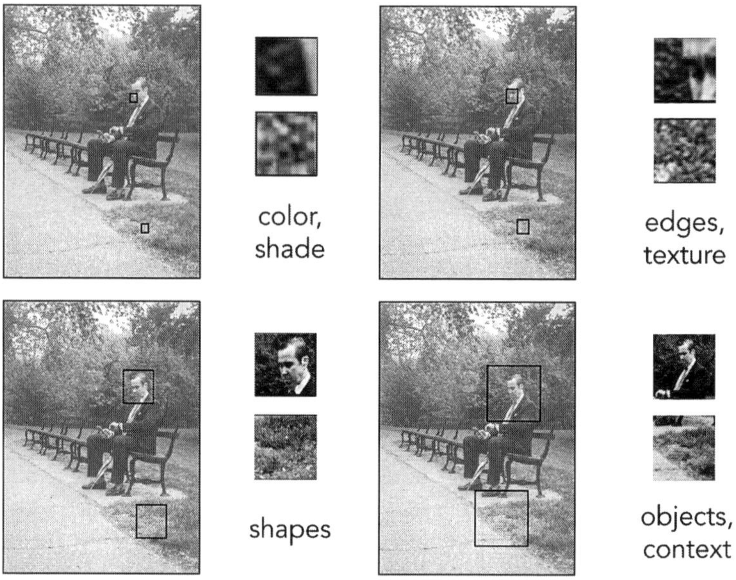

FIGURE 15.1. Conceptual depiction of features detected by subsequent layers in a neural network when applied to a photograph image. Photo by Greg Parish, "NYC Central Park," 2015. Licensed under CC-BY 4.0.

are applied to larger "windows" of the object, with the final layers applied to the entire image.[19] An example of a particular, highly idealized deep learning model is useful to further explain the concept.

Consider the example image in Figure 15.1 and the selected boxes of interest. The first few layers of a neural network may look only at nearby swatches of the image and convert the raw pixels into numbers that at first describe their overall color and shading. A slightly larger view provides information about the texture of the grass and edges that make up the nose of the man. Subsequent layers reveal small objects (noses), larger objects (faces), and finally objects within their context. A final layer, not shown within the boxes, could be applied to the entire image to aggregate information about the individual objects. This layer would capture features about the scene as a whole. Figure 15.2 shows a similar linguistic example. Subsequent layers of the neural network look at larger windows of the text by grouping characters into words, words into phrases, phrases into sentences, and sentences into entire documents.[20] The layered nature of deep learning models, likely the original motivation behind the term

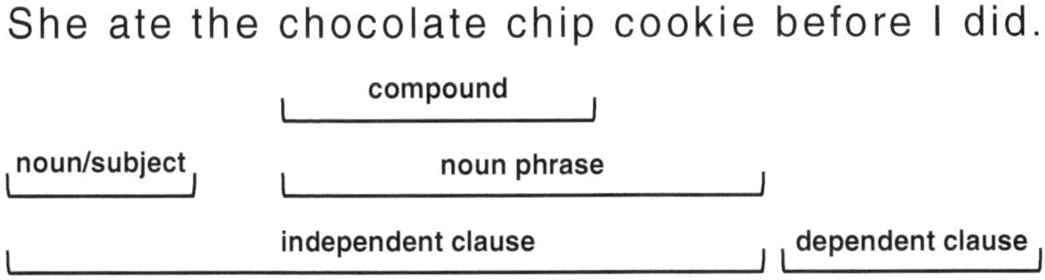

FIGURE 15.2. Depiction of hierarchical features detected applying a neural network algorithm to a sentence of textual data.

"deep," is the fundamental feature differentiating them from other approaches and directly addresses the representational issues presented as the primary challenges to working with text and image data.

It is not an easy task to build deep learning models from scratch. Dozens of complex transformations operating seamlessly together must be created and iteratively modified in an attempt to address the most challenging problems in predictive modeling. Very large datasets are required in order to estimate the hundreds of millions of parameters that describe state-of-the-art neural networks. Public datasets for training image models, such as the ILSVRC and VGGFace2 dataset, typically provide millions of tagged images to produce accurate face-detection models.[21] These datasets are typically constructed by making use of digitized corpora such as MediaWiki and Google Image Search. Once a large dataset is assembled, special hardware in the form of expensive and powerful graphics processing units (GPUs) is required to process such large datasets through the complex architectures of modern neural networks.[22] Even with good training data and the required hardware, the actual construction of neural networks is still a significant challenge. Adjusting the millions of training parameters is known to be an incredibly fraught task; subtle changes to the structure of the network can drastically alter the output of the model.[23] It would appear that the power of neural networks may be restricted to well-funded companies or research groups and available only for a small set of high-impact tasks for which the payoff in time and money is worthwhile. In practice, this is far from the case due to the special layered structure of deep learning models.

When trained on sufficiently large image datasets, the initial transformations described by large neural networks tend to be generalizable to new problems unrelated to the original prediction task. Recall that the first layers in a neural network only work locally over small regions of an image. These initial layers detect general features such as shading, color, and texture. Even layers in the middle of the network correspond to rough shapes and the formation of larger objects. It is only the last few layers that are directly related to the specific predictive modeling tasks of interest. As a result, predictive neural networks can be adapted through the process of transfer learning to predict new outputs by reusing the trained values in the interior layers and only learning the form of the final one to three transformations. This drastically reduces the amount of data, hardware, and expertise required to construct a new model. For example, recently a research group built a highly predictive image-processing neural network using a set of only 443 frontal chest X-ray images through transfer learning applied to the AlexNet model.[24] The researchers copied all but the final layer of the network and trained the relatively small set of final weights with their own data. The ability to perform transfer learning, which drastically increases the number of feasible applications of deep learning, is another direct feature of the layered nature of the models.

The underlying idea of transfer learning—that interior layers in neural networks code generic features that can be adapted to new problems—can also be used to motivate the related concept of "embeddings." An embedding applies a selection of lower-level transformations from a neural network to an object of interest, the output of which can be viewed as a sequence of numeric values. In transfer learning a predictive model is built on top of these embedded values, but there is also intrinsic value in the embedding itself. Embeddings have, for example, recently received attention in applications as diverse as cognitive psychology and the digital humanities.[25] The numbers described by the embedding capture, according to our description of how neural networks function, important semantic features present within the input image or textual document. Each number in the embedding does not directly correspond to a meaningful quantity. Rather, the spatial relationships of the objects within the embedding capture various semantic meanings. Inputs with similar features, in particular, will have similar sequences of numbers. Connecting objects that have similar embeddings to one another has been shown to provide accurate image and document similarity metrics that require no manual tagging or retraining.[26] As an example, Figure 15.3 illustrates a two-dimensional word embedding for a small collection of words. The full embedding these are taken from was trained on the English-language text from Wikipedia containing three hundred thousand words arranged in 300-dimensional space.[27] Food items and verbs/professions are visibly separated in the embedding space. Pairs of closely related terms, such as "journalist-writer," "believe-understand," and "read-write," are embedding next to one

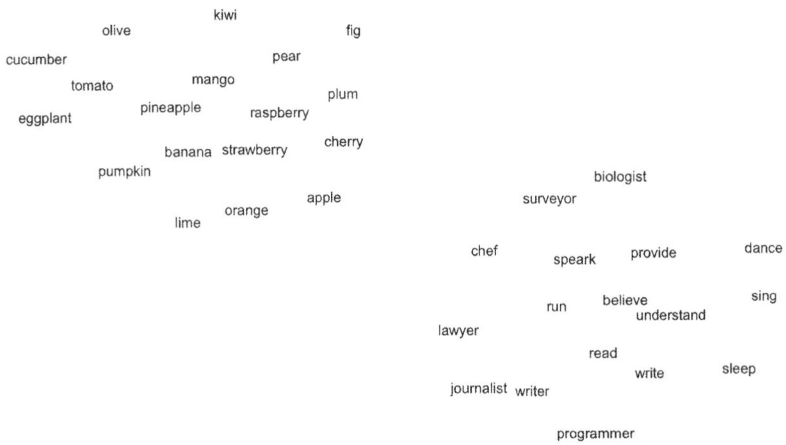

FIGURE 15.3. Two-dimensional word embedding of various fruits, vegetables, occupations, and verbs.

another. Also, the profession "chef" is situated closer to the food items than any other profession. As with transfer learning, the feasibility of embeddings is directly tied to the layered nature of deep learning models.

The layered structure of deep learning models is a direct consequence of the challenges posed by the processing of image and textual data. Without the sequential application of transformations, deep learning would offer no immediate benefit to predictive modeling for these difficult classes of important machine learning problems. The layers also immediately make way for the significant application of transfer learning and embeddings, without which deep learning models would be inaccessible to all but a small number of applications. Unfortunately, the layered nature also comes at the cost of interpretability. It is notoriously difficult, if not outright impossible, to comprehend how neural networks achieve their amazing predictive results. As we witness a proliferation of neural network applications in society, our inability to understand exactly what they are doing poses a number of concerns.

Impenetrable

Modern neural networks for text and image processing typically consist of dozens of layered transformations and hundreds of millions of learned parameters. Our description here of how neural networks transform images, by successively detecting larger and larger regions of interest and stitching them together, is a highly idealized version of how networks actually function. The general concepts have been validated through the efficacy of transfer learning and visualizations of embedding spaces, but the specific meaning of any given internal representation is generally impossible to discern. Because of the complex dependencies present within the layers of a neural network, classic approaches to interrogating a particular model, such as applying small perturbations to a single parameter and watching the result, are rarely very enlightening. The general lack of interpretability in deep learning is a well-known problem; several recent workshops were specifically dedicated to papers on the interpretability of neural network models.[28] A collection of approaches have been proposed in an attempt to build an understanding of how neural networks function.

One approach for understanding the inner workings of neural networks is to focus on the objects in a predictive modeling task that are incorrectly tagged. One simple approach is to investigate those categories that have particularly high error rates. Does the model have trouble with a specific category, or does it struggle to differentiate between a certain set of objects? Analysis of the results can be insightful in understanding the internal mechanisms of the neural network. For example, the ILSVRC revealed that animals with distinctive furs (e.g., foxes, porcupines, and tigers) are particularly easy to classify. On the other hand, long, slender objects (e.g., letter openers, flagpoles, and water bottles) are typically the hardest to detect. Abstract concepts such as "restaurant" and "grocery store" are also among the most difficult categories for algorithms to distinguish.

Taken together, this evidence shows that neural networks are best at understanding localized features and struggle the most on categories that require putting together contextual knowledge across the entire image. Looking at specific objects that are misclassified by a model, the *negative examples,* is another method of understanding the behavior of neural networks. For example, an investigation of the negative examples from the GoogLeNet model—the 2014 winner of ILSVRC—showed particular difficulty with "images that contain multiple objects, images of extreme close-ups and uncharacteristic views, images with filters, images that significantly benefit from the ability to read text [a salt shaker], images that contain very small and thin objects [fishing reel], images with abstract representations."[29] These highlight challenges in the existing model and suggest significant gaps between the way the model understands images and humanlike processing of visual data. Ongoing research in computer vision is often motivated by understanding where, and ideally why, current models fail on certain tasks.

Alternatively, another approach to understanding neural networks is to focus on objects where the model performs well. The motivation behind the use of neural networks is their incredible predictive power. It seems reasonable that if we want to understand how neural networks function, some attention should be paid to the many objects that are correctly tagged. A clever approach to studying these *positive examples* is to occlude part of the object and observe the extent to which these occlusions affect the predicted categories. For an image, this involves replacing a region of the image with a monochromatic box, effectively hiding a region of the image from the neural network.[30] In text analysis, a similar approach removes one or more words or phrases.[31] Visualizing the regions that most directly impact the predicted values, and quantifying how much of the text or image can be removed without significantly impacting the results, provides an additional understanding of how the neural network represents knowledge. Similarly, the embeddings of correctly classified categories can be investigated for each layer of a neural network. Identifying which layers separate specific categories provides a window into the specific role of each layer in the overall prediction task.

Despite the existence of techniques for understanding neural network architectures, there remains a fundamental inability to understand how the network performs the task of transforming inputs into reliable predictions. Negative examples elucidate those abstract features that are generally missed by the network. Positive examples, along with occlusion, hint at those regions and features that are captured by the model. How these features are captured, however, remains a mystery. The fundamental trouble is the depth of the model. Each layer is codependent on all of the others, and understanding the network therefore requires understanding the entire network all at once, which is impossible given the size and depth of modern neural networks. And the problem is only getting worse.

Over time, neural networks have grown deeper and more complex. The winning ILSVRC model "ResNet" from 2015 had a total of 152 layers (for comparison, AlexNet has only 8 layers).[32] By 2016, the ResNet model had expanded to a total of 1,000 layers.[33] Popular models for text analysis now commonly employ recurrent neural networks, which contain complex architectures for storing "memories" as the network cycles through characters and words within a document. As further evidence of our inability to understand neural network models, recent research has revealed strange and unintuitive results from seemingly powerful predictive models. Carefully constructed perturbations can be applied to an image that are imperceptible to the human eye but that cause arbitrarily large changes in the

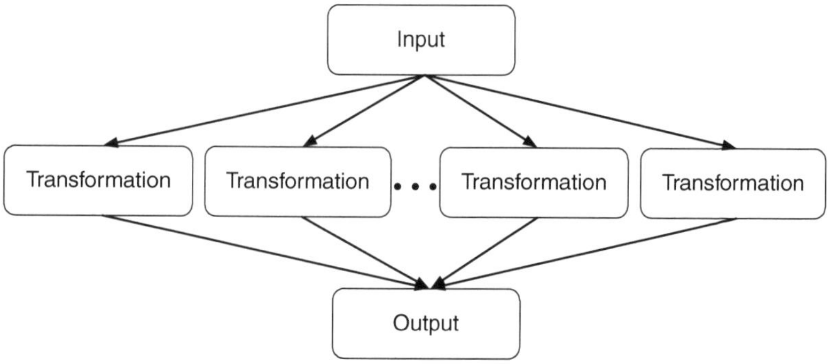

FIGURE 15.4. Schematic visualization of a "shallow learning" predictive model.

predicted tags associated with the image.[34] Conversely, images can be found that appear to be pure noise but are confidently categorized with an extremely high probability on one particular tag. These examples point to a significant gap in the way that neural networks process data compared with the human processing of images and text.

As neural networks become integrated into systems that directly affect people, it becomes increasingly important to understand how deep learning models function. Most of the work on interpretability has so far focused on understanding neural networks in order to modify their architecture and improve the predictive power of future models. However, it is arguably even more important to understand the models from a social perspective. How can we be convinced that an algorithm for tracking passengers at airport security is not motivated by racial profiling? What checks exist to detect when models employed by the medical industry are being optimized for insurance money rather than patient health? Or, what confidence do we have that autonomous vehicles trained in sunny California will accurately deal with snowy New England winters? All of these questions can be addressed on a macroscopic scale through external validation and regulatory transparency, but it becomes difficult for an individual to trust or challenge the results of a specific model that eludes any direct ability to understand its internal mechanisms.

While many machine learning algorithms have been characterized as being uninterpretable black boxes, our characterization of neural networks as impenetrably difficult to understand draws on features unique to deep learning methods. Figure 15.4 displays a schematic representation of a "shallow"—a model that is not deep—predictive model. A collection

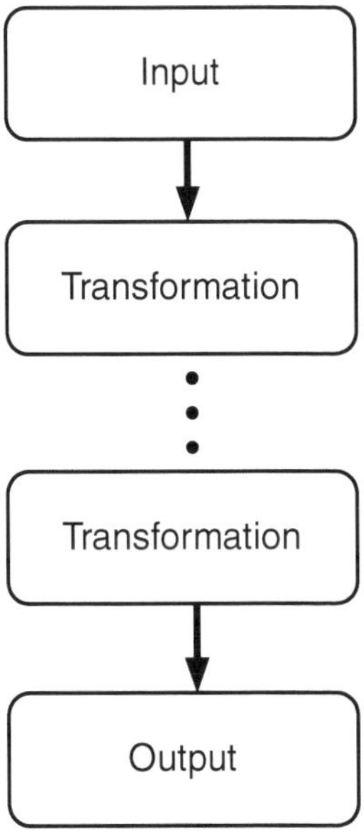

FIGURE 15.5. Schematic visualization of a "deep learning" predictive model.

of transformations is applied to the raw input data and then combined again to produce the output classifications. For comparison, Figure 15.5 provides a diagram of a deep learning model in which transformations are sequentially applied to the input data in order to yield the output categories. Shallow models may become quite complex if there are a large number of transformations. For example, models such as boosted trees also often involve millions of parameters, and it can be difficult to understand how these parameters come together to produce a final set of predicted tags.[35] However, shallow models can be decomposed into individual elements that each act independently on the input variables and produce distinct contributions to the output classification values. On a local level, at least, there is a possibility for understanding how regression and tree-based models construct predictions from their inputs. In contrast, the layered structure of deep learning models makes even this level of understanding impossible. The lack of a local understanding makes it difficult to assess the structure of a neural network and determine whether a specific application is (algorithmically) reasonable or advisable. The layered structure, then, is a fundamental cause of the impenetrable nature of deep learning models.

Unavoidable Trichotomy

We have shown that deep learning models exhibit their depth along three alternative meanings of the term "deep." They exhibit a deep knowledge in understanding image and textual data by producing accurate labels for a range of predictive modeling tasks. This predictive power is achieved through structures that consist of a deep succession of transformations that gradually push the input objects toward the predicted output tags. Finally, these chains of interrelated transformations hide the parameters of the model with an impenetrable depth that obscures exactly how they arrive at their results. Crucially, we have seen that these three elements are related by far more than the polysemous nature of the English word "deep." The layered nature of deep learning models is a necessary feature for their ability to make predictions for hard tasks such as text and image processing, and these layers in turn are fundamentally difficult to interpret. From the unavoidable interdependence between these elements of deep learning, we conclude here with implications for continued study of deep learning as an object of humanistic inquiry.

First, it is important to start describing the concept of a *deep problem* in addition to deep learning. The way in which text and image data are stored, as streams of characters and pixel intensities, necessitates the use of layered models that modify the original data and represent objects within a new space. In other words, the nature of working with text and image data requires deep learning models in order to achieve high levels of accuracy. Analysis of these objects is an intrinsically deep problem, irrespective of the specific models used to study them.

The classification of tasks, rather than the algorithms for performing them, as "deep" is important. It signals that many of the challenges underlying modern machine learning are actually problems of how knowledge is transmitted and represented. In turn, this directly draws connections from machine learning into well-trodden areas of humanistic inquiry such as epistemology, semiotics, and communication theory. A word-embedding model maps directly onto Ferdinand de Saussure's assertion that words draw meaning through their "simultaneous coexistence" with all other words.[36] Autoencoders, a particular class of neural networks, provide a mathematical formulation directly related to Stuart Hall's encoding/decoding model of social communication.[37] Erwin Panofsky's tripartite series of levels to understanding works of art, which starts with the literal subject matter and proceeds up through iconography and iconology, mirrors the layered hierarchy of levels in modern convolutional neural networks and hints at the application of transfer learning.[38] The first level of interpretation is, in theory, universal; cultural considerations become more explicit higher up the chain of understanding. In short, by focusing on the tasks and not their explicit solutions, we find numerous points of contact between predictive modeling tasks and ongoing questions in a wide range of other fields. Providing points of connection across fields allows for more productive critiques and fruitful interdisciplinary interactions.

As a second implication, embeddings—the output of a particular sequence of transformations within a deep learning model—should be considered as an object of study in its own right. We have argued that the intermediate representations offered by the internal layers of a neural network do encode generalizable semantic information that can be utilized in new tasks through transfer learning. The internal representations, unlike the raw inputs, more directly encode useful semantic information. They have the potential to allow for the utilization of shallow models, even for many complex tasks.[39] If we are able to find good general-purpose embeddings that work with shallow models, this would help alleviate some concerns about the lack of interpretability in deep learning models. While the process of converting raw inputs into the embedding space may remain opaque, with time and analysis, a direct characterization of the embedding space could be achieved. Several results suggest that a general-purpose embedding that can be used across all tasks, or a close approximation to one, can be attainable. In image processing, it has been shown that significant sequences of layers in neural networks can be *inverted* to re-create "photographically accurate information" about the image, establishing that relatively little information is being lost in (at least the lower-level) transformations.[40] For text analysis, where transferable embeddings initially proved more difficult to detect, recent work has produced several candidates that appear to have generalized very well to a variety of tasks.[41] The culture in deep learning research of making research, code, and datasets openly available is a great start for making it possible to offer meaningful studies of embedding spaces. We now need more scholars actively engaged in treating these embeddings as an important object of study.

Finally, it is also important to train scholars from a wide range of fields in the technology of deep learning, specifically neural networks. Layered models that successively reparametrize raw inputs are, as we have seen, necessary for sufficiently predictive models. Deep learning techniques will likely remain popular for a considerable amount of time and are poised to become even more integrated into important real-world systems. We need domain experts from fields such as medicine, biology, public policy, law, economics, and across the humanities to understand this technology. To do so opens up avenues for both important innovations and meaningful critiques of current practices. As we have shown, deep learning models are difficult enough to comprehend even for those in the field of machine learning who have been working with them for decades. Due to this complexity, meaningful collaborations between domain experts and researchers in deep learning require a working understanding of the power and challenges of neural networks across disciplinary boundaries.

Deep learning approaches are here to stay. They offer amazing predictive accuracy and a plethora of exciting technological advances, but they also make way for a wide range of troubling applications. As deep learning becomes increasingly ubiquitous in real-world systems, the unavoidable trichotomy between knowledge, layers, and a lack of interpretability has important implications for anyone concerned with the use and proliferation of algorithmic logic in society.[42] Direct humanistic inquiry into the algorithms behind deep learning is needed as we grapple with their cultural and social implications.

Notes

1. Xiaolin Wu and Xi Zhang, "Responses to Critiques on Machine Learning of Criminality Perceptions," *arXiv preprint arXiv:1611.04135* (2016): 1–14, https://arxiv.org/pdf/1611.04135; Yilun Wang and Michal Kosinski, "Deep Neural Networks Are More Accurate Than Humans at Detecting Sexual Orientation from Facial Images," *Journal of Personality and Social Psychology* 114, no. 2 (2018): 246.

2. Trevor Hastie, Robert Tibshirani, and Jerome Friedman, *The Elements of Statistical Learning*, 2nd ed. (New York: Springer, 2009).

3. This is not entirely true for textual data. The characters could be grouped together into words in a process known as "tokenization," and words do have some intrinsic meaning. Many text-processing tasks, such as spam detection and authorship attribute, can be accurately modeled with general-purpose algorithms using only word counts. However, more advanced tasks such as document summarization and automatic language translation require taking word order and high-level grammatical features into account. There is no such analogue for image data, and the problem remains for even relatively simple tasks.

4. While interesting in their own right, the contentious evolutionary details behind these two strengths, and the specific pathways for language acquisition such as Chomsky's language acquisition device (LAD), are not important for the

discussion here. For more details on both, see Simon Thorpe, Denis Fize, and Catherine Marlot, "Speed of Processing in the Human Visual System," *Nature* 381, no. 6582 (1996): 520; and Noam Chomsky, *Aspects of the Theory of Syntax* (Cambridge, Mass.: MIT Press, 1965).

5. Warren S. McCulloch and Walter Pitts, "A Logical Calculus of the Ideas Immanent in Nervous Activity," *Bulletin of Mathematical Biophysics* 5, no. 4 (1943): 115–33.

6. In fact, neural networks are arguably the *only* practical example of a deep-learning algorithm. Often the terms are used interchangeably. In this article, "deep learning" is used to describe the general modeling approach, and the term "neural networks" is used only to refer to specific applications of deep learning.

7. Yoshua Bengio, Dong-Hyun Lee, Jorg Bornschein, Thomas Mesnard, and Zhouhan Lin, "Towards Biologically Plausible Deep Learning," *arXiv preprint arXiv:1502.04156* (2015), 1, https://arxiv.org/pdf/1502.04156.

8. In an effort to reclaim the physiological legitimacy of neural networks, some have called for a renewed partnership with neuroscience, with minimal recent success. See Adam H. Marblestone, Greg Wayne, and Konrad P. Kording, "Toward an Integration of Deep Learning and Neuroscience," *Frontiers in Computational Neuroscience* 10 (2016): 94.

9. Marvin Minsky and Seymour A. Papert, *Perceptrons: An Introduction to Computational Geometry* (Cambridge, Mass.: MIT Press, 1969).

10. Yann LeCun, Bernhard Boser, John S. Denker, Donnie Henderson, Richard E. Howard, Wayne Hubbard, and Lawrence D. Jackel, "Backpropagation Applied to Handwritten Zip Code Recognition," *Neural Computation* 1, no. 4 (1989): 541–51.

11. Olga Russakovsky, Jia Deng, Hao Su, Jonathan Krause, Sanjeev Satheesh, Sean Ma, and Zhiheng Huang, "ImageNet: Large Scale Visual Recognition Challenge," *International Journal of Computer Vision* 115, no. 3 (2015): 211–52.

12. Alex Krizhevsky, Ilya Sutskever, and Geoffrey E. Hinton, "ImageNet Classification with Deep Convolutional Neural Networks," *Advances in Neural Information Processing Systems* 25, no. 2 (2012), 1097–1105. For each image, the model predicts the five most likely categories the image corresponds to and is "correct" if the true category is one of these five. Leeway is provided because some categories are incredibly difficult even for expert human labelers, such as two closely related dog breeds or edge cases over the distinctions between a generic "cup" and a "coffee cup."

13. Jie Hu, Li Shen, and Gang Sun, "Squeeze-and-Excitation Networks," *arXiv preprint arXiv:1709.01507 7* (2017), 1–11, https://arxiv.org/pdf/1709.01507.

14. Yann LeCun, Yoshua Bengio, and Geoffrey Hinton, "Deep Learning," *Nature* 521, no. 7553 (2015): 440.

15. Jeremy Howard and Sebastian Ruder, "Universal Language Model Fine-Tuning for Text Classification," *Proceedings of the 56th Annual Meeting of the Association for Computational Linguistics (Long Papers)* (ACL, 2018), 328–39, https://aclweb.org/anthology/P18{~?~REGENCODE:hyphen}1031.

16. Mohammad Havaei, Axel Davy, David Warde-Farley, Antoine Biard, Aaron Courville, Yoshua Bengio, Chris Pal, Pierre-Marc Jodoin, and Hugo Larochelle, "Brain Tumor Segmentation with Deep Neural Networks," *Medical Image Analysis* 35 (2017): 18–31.

17. Gil Levi and Tal Hassner, "Age and Gender Classification Using Convolutional Neural Networks," *Proceedings of the IEEE Conference on Computer Vision and Pattern Recognition Workshops* (IEEE, 2015), 34–42.

18. Sebastian Ramos, Stefan Gehrig, Peter Pinggera, Uwe Franke, and Carsten Rother, "Detecting Unexpected Obstacles for Self-Driving Cars: Fusing Deep Learning and Geometric Modelling," *Proceedings of the IEEE Intelligent Vehicles Symposium* (IEEE, 2017), 1025–32.

19. Ian Goodfellow and Yoshua Bengio, *Deep Learning* (Cambridge, Mass.: MIT Press, 2016).

20. The models described here are, more precisely, examples of convolutional neural networks (CNNs), which are frequently used in both text and image analysis.

21. Qiong Cao, Li Shen, Weidi Xie, Omkar M. Parkhi, and Andrew Zisserman, "VGGFace2: A Dataset for Recognising Faces across Pose and Age," *Proceedings of the IEEE Conference on Automatic Face and Gesture* (IEEE, 2018), 67–74.

22. Haoxiang Li, Zhe Lin, Xiaohui Shen, Jonathan Brandt, and Gang Hua, "A Convolutional Neural Network Cascade for Face Detection," *Proceedings of the IEEE Conference on Computer Vision and Pattern Recognition* (IEEE, 2015), 5325–34.

23. Yoav Goldberg, "A Primer on Neural Network Models for Natural Language Processing," *Journal of Artificial Intelligence Research* 57 (2016): 345–420.

24. Yaniv Bar, Idit Diamant, Lior Wolf, Sivan Lieberman, Eli Konen, and Hayit Greenspan, "Chest Pathology Detection Using Deep Learning with Non-medical Training," *Proceedings of the IEEE 12th International Symposium on Biomedical Imaging* (IEEE, 2015), 294–97.

25. Siddharth Patwardhan and Ted Pedersen, "Using WordNet-Based Context Vectors to Estimate the Semantic Relatedness of Concepts," *Proceedings of the Workshop on Making Sense of Sense: Bringing Psycholinguistics and Computational Linguistics Together* (2006): 1–8, https://www.aclweb.org/anthology/W06-2501/.

26. Jey Han Lau and Timothy Baldwin, "An Empirical Evaluation of doc2vec with Practical Insights into Document Embedding Generation," *arXiv preprint arXiv:1607.05368* (2016): 1–11.

27. Alexis Conneau, Guillaume Lample, Marc'Aurelio Ranzato, Ludovic Denoyer, and Hervé Jégou, "Word Translation without Parallel Data," *arXiv preprint arXiv:1710.04087* (2017): 1–12, https://arxiv.org/pdf/1710.04087.

28. For example, the NIPS 2017 workshop "Interpreting, Explaining and Visualizing Deep Learning . . . Now What?" and the EMNLP 2018 workshop "Analyzing and Interpreting Neural Networks for NLP."

29. Russakovsky et al., "ImageNet," 243.

30. Matthew D. Zeiler and Rob Fergus, "Visualizing and Understanding Convolutional Networks," in *Computer Vision—ECCV 2014,* ed. D. Fleet, T. Pajdla, B. Schiele, and T. Tuytelaars (Zurich: Springer, 2014), 827.

31. Marco Tulio Ribeiro, Sameer Singh, and Carlos Guestrin, "Why Should I Trust You? Explaining the Predictions of Any Classifier," *Proceedings of the 22nd ACM SIGKDD International Conference on Knowledge Discovery and Data Mining* (ACM SIGKDD, 2016), 1135–44.

32. Kaiming He, Xiangyu Zhang, Shaoqing Ren, and Jian Sun, "Deep Residual Learning for Image Recognition," *Proceedings of the IEEE Conference on Computer Vision and Pattern Recognition* (IEEE, 2016), 770–78.

33. Kaiming He, Xiangyu Zhang, Shaoqing Ren, and Jian Sun, "Identity Mappings in Deep Residual Networks," in *Computer Vision—ECCV 2016,* ed. B. Leibe, J. Matas, N. Sebe, and M. Welling (Zurich: Springer, 2016), 630–645.

34. Seyed-Mohsen Moosavi-Dezfooli, Alhussein Fawzi, and Pascal Frossard, "Deepfool: A Simple and Accurate Method to Fool Deep Neural Networks," *Proceedings of the IEEE Conference on Computer Vision and Pattern Recognition* (IEEE, 2016), 2574–82.

35. Rich Caruana, Yin Lou, Johannes Gehrke, Paul Koch, Marc Sturm, and Noemie Elhadad, "Intelligible Models for Healthcare: Predicting Pneumonia Risk and Hospital 30-Day Readmission," *Proceedings of the 21st ACM SIGKDD International Conference on Knowledge Discovery and Data Mining* (ACM SIGKDD, 2015), 1721.

36. Ferdinand de Saussure, *Course in General Linguistics,* trans. Roy Harris (La Salle, Ill.: Open Court, 1998), 159.

37. Stuart Hall, "Encoding/Decoding," in *Culture, Media, Language,* ed. Stuart Hall, Dorothy Hobson, Andrew Love, and Paul Willis (London: Hutchinson, 1980), 128–38.

38. Erwin Panofsky, *Studies in Iconology: Humanistic Themes in the Art of the Renaissance,* trans. Gerda S. Panofsky (New York: Routledge, 1972).

39. That is, models that are shallow in respect to the embedding layer. They are still deep relative to the raw text or image input data.

40. Aravindh Mahendran and Andrea Vedaldi, "Understanding Deep Image Representations by Inverting Them," *Proceedings of the IEEE Conference on Computer Vision and Pattern Recognition* (IEEE, 2015), 5188–96.

41. Howard and Ruder, "Universal Language Model Fine-Tuning for Text Classification."

42. Safiya Umoja Noble, *Algorithms of Oppression: How Search Engines Reinforce Racism* (New York: New York University Press, 2018).

CHAPTER SIXTEEN

From Stereoscopic Depth to Deep Learning

Brooke Belisle

What is depth? Obvious, and yet elusive, depth is the stuff beyond the surface—the difference between the flatness of an image and the volume of an object. It is the thickness of things and the expanse between them, the dimensionality through which things hold themselves together and apart. Like length and height, it seems like an objective measure to be taken, read off from the shape of the world as the very vector of Descartes's *res extensa* and *partes extra partes*. But depth is also a subjective product of individual perception: it manifests through the coordination of two eyes seeing together from different points of view. As 3D media of all kinds show, depth can also be an illusion, something we seem to see when faced with only a flat screen or a pair of photographs.

Due to this complexity, depth is one of the most difficult challenges when we try to teach computers to see. How can algorithms articulate the perceptual contours of our dimensional world? How can seeing take place entirely in terms of numerical expressions about pixel arrays? "Computer vision" is a metaphor, as well as the name and aim of a rapidly advancing field of computer science. This metaphor mapping human to machine permeates both the vocabulary and the structure of the field: *object recognition* happens through *deep learning* in *neural networks* with linked *perceptrons*. This elision of human and machine seems so persuasive that algorithms already step in to see for us.

News articles in early 2019 exposed how major companies have been using deep learning and computer vision algorithms to screen job candidates.[1] One platform, HireVue, promises faster and better employment decisions by replacing initial, face-to-face interviews with artificial intelligence (AI) video analysis: applicants upload video responses to interview

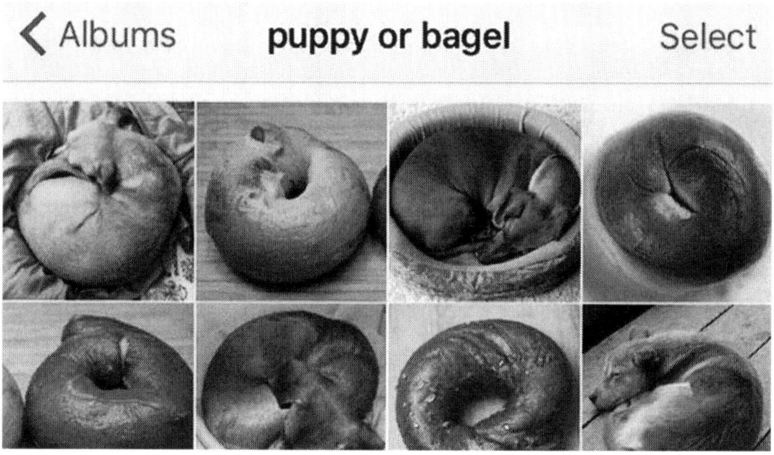

FIGURE 16.1. "Puppy or Bagel?" Posted on Twitter, March 7, 2016, by @teenybiscuit.

questions, and a neural network assesses their voice, posture, and facial expressions in the recording. HireVue's website offers extended assurances that this process not only is unbiased but also helps eliminate human bias.[2] At the same time, critiques of computer vision increasingly take issue with these kinds of claims, demonstrating how bias can be built into these systems.[3]

Popular memes about object recognition, like "puppy or bagel?" (Figure 16.1), deflect more serious misrecognitions, such as the 2015 scandal of Google Photos labeling black people gorillas.[4] In that instance, image recognition software reflected biases structuring the material used to train it: software engineers had developed and tested face-recognition software on sets of photographs that largely excluded people of color. Google addressed the problem by simply removing the classification "gorilla." Recent research continues to expose how computer vision remains biased: black faces are not only less likely to be seen by computer vision systems but also more likely to be mislabeled—misgendered as male, or rated as angry even though they are smiling.[5]

Policing for category errors does not go far enough to solve the multiple forms of blindness and bias that AI can automate. In the case of computer vision, there is a profound misrecognition at stake in the most fundamental ways that computers model and enact "seeing." Computer vision operates not only as if machine processes can replicate and replace embodied, human processes but also as if mathematical representations could stand in for the visible world. To assume that a computer could see is to assume that the way the world appears as visible—the way it opens to vision and affords visibility—is as available to machinic forms of capture as it is to embodied forms of perception. The stakes of this conflation might seem purely philosophical—posing ontological, epistemological, and phenomenological questions about what the world is and how it can be known and experienced. The stakes are quite concrete in each case, however, as computer vision increasingly subtends actions, decisions, and interventions in everyday life. These may range from labeling a face in a photograph to recommending job applicants or determining the target area for a drone strike.[6]

In order to consider what is at stake in the emerging forms of visibility associated with computer vision, I want to turn back to an earlier construction of visibility—one that computer vision directly incorporates just as it seems to leave it behind. As computer vision develops algorithmic techniques for relating human and machine ways of seeing, and for relating the lived world with its visual representation, this reactivates questions that were negotiated by the emerging technology of photography over the second half of the nineteenth century. Photography, and in particular stereoscopic photography, cultivated and relied on a potential slippage between embodied and technical ways of seeing, between things and representations. As the most popular early form of photography, stereoscopic representation helped support persuasive analogies relating binocular vision and camera lenses, objects and images, embodied space and the represented space.

In what is still probably the most influential account of the stereoscope, Jonathan Crary includes it among other optical toys that swerved, temporarily, away from an otherwise monocular epistemology structuring vision and representation at least since the camera obscura.[7] Crary and others have persuasively shown how changing techniques for representing space and time, including stereoscopic and serial photography, participated in the ways that broader patterns of perception and lived experience were structurally deranged by logics of industrial capital.[8] Today, logics of information capital inscribe themselves through algorithmic techniques that increasingly mediate not only how we see and represent the world but also how we are positioned as visible within it.

On the one hand, stereoscopic photography helped pave the way for many of the problematic aspects of computer vision today. The stereoscope also, however, emphasized embodied dimensions of vision that exceed a computational model. The way that the stereoscope was coupled with early photography opened a range of spatial and perceptual logics for this new medium, shaping how photographs could be understood to mediate the visible world. Some of these spatial and perceptual logics subtend the project of computer vision, while others are undermined by emerging structures of algorithmic imaging.

Photographic Depth

In photography's first decades, its images were often described as inferior to drawings and paintings. Martha Sandweiss has explained, for example, how panorama painters used photographs as studies, rather than understanding them as rivals for the market in verisimilitude.[9] Whereas the photograph was celebrated for its capacity to inscribe every minute detail without regard for its relative significance, the impartiality of mechanical inscription was also understood as a flaw; rather than communicating a coherent view, a photograph could seem to render merely a cacophony of detail.[10] A painting might seem to convey a more accurate view of what it pictured to the extent that its subjective and aesthetic rendering was felt to emulate ways that perception already organized visual experience—framing a place as a landscape, a view as a particular perspective. Ways of interpreting accuracy, objectivity, and verisimilitude shifted over the second half of the nineteenth century in relationship to the rise of photography. During this time the most popular photographs were stereographs described and marketed as "views."

The stereoscope (Figure 16.2) and photography were inventions announced within months of one another, and photography was immediately used to make stereoscopic "views." An international boom in stereophotography was set off in 1851, when the stereoscope was a star of the Great Exhibition and the invention of collodion enabled mass production of paper prints. Stereographs circulated through colonial routes on a global scale, as the first form of photographic mass visual culture. By 1854, the London Stereoscopic Company used the tagline "No home without a stereoscope." In a well-known passage of his essay "The Stereoscope and the Stereograph" (1859), Oliver Wendell Holmes exhorts: "Give us a few negatives of a thing worth seeing, taken from different points of view, and that is all we want of it. Pull it down or burn it up, if you please."[11] I will come back to the implicit violence of this comment later, but for the moment I want to emphasize that Holmes says a *few* negatives. Rather than saying a photograph could stand in for the thing itself, he suggests the relationship *between* different photographs could recapitulate the *visibility* of the thing itself.

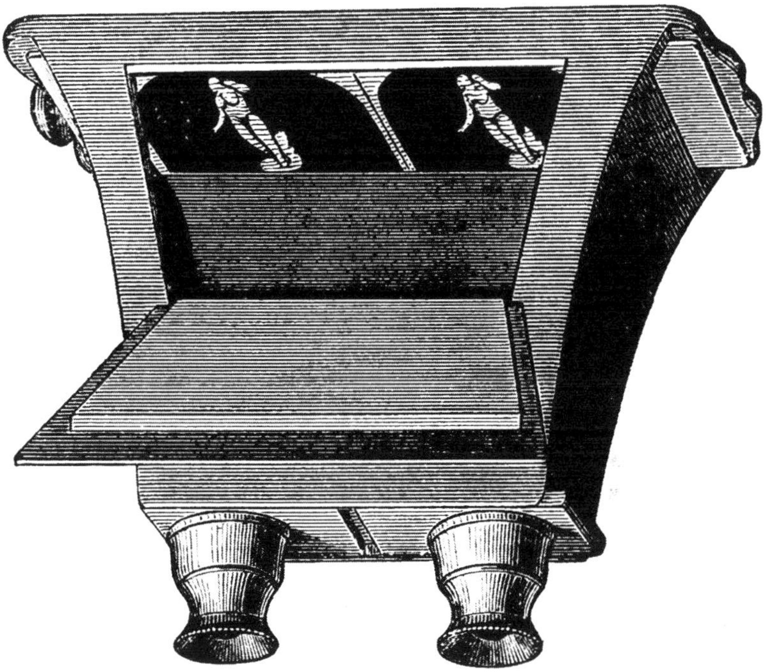

FIGURE 16.2. Brewster-style stereoscope ca. 1850s.

The difference between images is what enables stereoscopic depth, and it also anchors the analogy between eyes and cameras that was used to explain this depth to nineteenth-century spectators. For example, a widely read explanation of the stereoscope, published the year of the Great Exhibition in *Illustrated London News,* claims that "the two plates in the two cameras stand truly for the two eyes, and receive each just such picture, no more, no less, as each eye receives."[12] Robert J. Silverman has explained how "a network of natural theological presumptions" and "sturdy Victorian scientific principles" supported this idea that "because it duplicated the optical circumstances of human binocular vision, the stereoscopic camera functioned like a pair of surrogate eyes and could create truthful pictures of the world. . . . The twin lenses of the stereoscopic camera were often praised as infallible scribes that could etch reality on their photographic tablets."[13] A stereoview was said to be as good as an actual view because cameras had photographically recorded a scene exactly as it would have presented itself to two eyes. This seemed to allow the scene to present itself to the viewer's two eyes, via the stereograph, as it would "in person": as a visual experience that *demanded* perceptual coordination. The very spacing of images in a stereo pair seemed to reiterate the way the world presents itself to embodied perception—as unfolding in space, visible from multiple angles at once.

As one looked through a stereoscope, the perception of depth performed a *visceral* analogy, relating not only eyes with cameras, and things with images, but suggesting that the dimensionality we perceive in the world could be reiterated by the dimensions of photographic representation. The perception of depth that a stereograph could prompt both drew upon and helped authorize an analogy between human vision and photographic imaging that would soon seem self-evident beyond the particular circumstance of a stereoview.

Over the second half of the nineteenth century, the idea that relationships between photographs could reiterate the world's own dimensionality inflected the broader development of photography. If scholarship on art and media has minimized the stereoscope's role in this development, it may be because photographic techniques of parsing space and time interwove in ways that appeared, looking back from the twentieth century, as precinematic. Looking back now from a context of digital imaging, the same trajectory discloses a related history from stereoscopic to digital depth. Eadweard Muybridge, to take the best-known example, made stereographic series before his early motion studies—which he made with stereo cameras.

A number of panels in Muybridge's later motion studies, published in *Animal Locomotion,* capture only one moment from multiple points of view (Figure 16.3). For these he used an alternate arrangement of cameras at angles to his subject, triggered all at once. If the more common motion studies suggest how slices of time could add up to duration, anticipating cinema, these other series suggest how slices of space could add up as volume, anticipating the exploded perspectives of digital modeling.[14]

Less known today than Muybridge, and preceding his experiments, François Willème pursued his own technique for translating between three-dimensional perspectives and photographic series.[15] In 1859, the same year Holmes published his ecstatic essay, Willème invented what he called "photosculpture." A subject would pose on a small circular platform inside a panoramic enclosure, where cameras arranged every fifteen degrees would be triggered simultaneously, to capture images of the subject from twenty-four perspectives. These images would then be projected one by one on a screen, where the subject's silhouette would be traced with

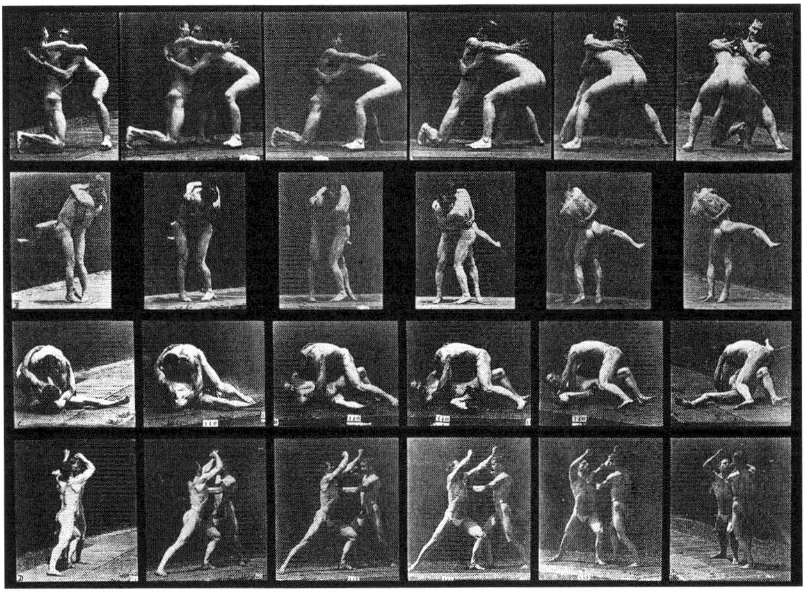

FIGURE 16.3. Plate 520, "Men Wrestling," from Eadweard Muybridge, *Animal Locomotion: An Electro-Photographic Investigation of Consecutive Phases of Animal Movements* (1887).

a pantograph to be transferred as the changing contours of twenty-four sculptural segments (Figure 16.4). These segments were gathered and smoothed into a three-dimensional portrait. The first person to purchase rights to this patent, and develop his own modified technique, was Antoine Claudet, one of the pioneers of stereoscopic photography.

The serial work of Willème and Muybridge relied on and extended an assumption the stereoscope helped cultivate: that spatial relationships between photographs could reiterate the world's own dimensionality. Rather than emphasizing the way an object is inscribed in a single photograph—which would later ground assumptions of indexicality—this assumption invests the relationship between photographs with a form of referentiality. This referentiality is not pictorial but dimensional, positing that the way the images materially and perceptually coordinate rearticulates the way that the material world they depict is materially arrayed and perceptually available. Serial photography in the late nineteenth century was part of a transition between stereoscopic and cinematic ways of relating photographs, at a moment when the terms of verisimilitude were reorganizing

FIGURE 16.4. Series of photographs made in François Willème's photosculpture studio, ca. 1863–67.

such that photographic images would soon seem like the *best* way to record and restage the world's objective visibility.

Today, computer vision incorporates assumptions that early photography helped naturalize, using sets of photographs as proxies for the visible world that computers are taught to see. As the visual archive of photography is uploaded and analyzed to train computer vision, critiques tend to circle back to questions of indexicality—how well a photographic or digital image stands for or stands in for what it pictures. Efforts to redress bias tend to focus on more inclusive datasets for training algorithms, to yield more accurate labeling. But focusing on depth allows us to raise a different question, about how specific techniques of *relating* images suggest different assumptions about how the world is visible and representable. To digitize depth, computer vision almost reenacts techniques from the history of photographically parsing space. But, as computer vision processes sets of photographs, it reworks photographic structures that perceptually triangulate depth with algorithmic structures that calculate it.

Digital Depth

For a computer, an image is a set of numbers describing an array of pixels. In an essay titled "Invisible Images," the artist Trevor Paglen explains how this supports a nonhuman construction of vision:

> The fact that digital images are fundamentally machine-readable regardless of a human subject . . . allows for the automation of vision

> on an enormous scale. . . . In aggregate, AI systems have appropriated human visual culture and transformed it into a massive, flexible training set . . . if we want to understand the invisible world of machine-machine visual culture, we need to unlearn how to see like humans. We need to learn how to see a parallel universe composed of activations, keypoints, eigenfaces, feature transforms, classifiers, training sets, and the like.[16]

These terms become the syntax structuring a ten-minute video, *Behold These Glorious Times!*, that Paglen debuted in a fall 2017 exhibition titled *A Study of Invisible Images*. At the start of a ten-minute loop, a small square blinks into view at the center of a black screen, rapidly moving through different images faster than we can interpret them. Within seconds, another square appears immediately left of the first, and then another to the right, each flashing through a succession of images. Over a few moments we realize that the images in each "tile" are related: one shows birds, another guitars, another typewriters (Figure 16.5). But the tiles are accumulating around the screen so quickly that we cannot keep up, until a nine-by-eleven-inch grid organizes them into what might be pixels of an overarching image. All the images in Paglen's video are taken from datasets used to train computer vision. In this first series, each tile is a montage of an image category, reflecting the labels used to structure training sets. Computational neural nets may compare millions of prelabeled images to derive mathematical expressions of the information patterns most likely to correspond to each label.

Moving faster than we can follow, Paglen's video almost seems to show a computer's point of view as its vision is being trained—as it is fed sets

FIGURE 16.5. Still from Trevor Paglen, *Behold These Glorious Times!* (2017). Ten-minute, single-channel digital video projection. Music composed with Holly Herndon. Courtesy of Metro Pictures and the artist.

of images and attempts to relate them. The way we, as spectators, struggle to see patterns that *just* outrun recognition also suggests, of course, that the video is training us, bending our human vision toward this parallel universe. The video's score syncopates with the image in staccato pulses that blend digital-sounding beeps with choral vocalizations. It was composed in collaboration with Holly Herndon, who trains neural networks to make computer music.[17]

The aesthetics of Paglen's video invoke familiar, avant-garde traditions of montage and structuralist cinema, as if attempting to galvanize new sensibilities with strange juxtapositions, retrain apperception through machinic rhythms, or lay bare the structural devices of deep learning algorithms. But the visual and temporal grammars of cinema can only mistranslate the algorithmic operations of neural networks. The relational structure of neural networks is mathematical; images are not temporally sequenced, but spatially compared at the level of pixels. And these processes are not, themselves, visual; as Paglen himself insists, the "images" of computer vision are not visible in the same sense as the images of this video projection. Paglen is not making machine vision visible. As part of his larger "study in invisible images," this work uses the spatial and temporal relationships of the moving image to explore the relational imaging logics of machine-vision operations.

When an image is fed into a neural network, algorithms analyze its numerical expression for mathematical patterns. A first layer of the network might identify lines by finding adjacent pixels with related properties. A next level might then compare all the lines found in the first layer and assess if any of these lines connect to form corners. Then a next layer might compare all the corners identified to assess whether any connect as bounded shapes, and so on. As an image moves through a neural network, a series of numbers moves through mathematical forms of analysis that identify patterns in those numbers, which are expressed in a new set of numbers, which is then passed to the next level, which will attempt to identify patterns among the patterns, and so on.

The depth in deep learning refers to the relationship between these layers. We may imagine this in terms of spatial depth, like geologic strata—and some diagrams of neural networks encourage this. But the depth of deep learning is much more abstract: across layers, a compounding of relational complexity is expressed as mathematical dimensionality. Binary and linear forms of classification are compounded into hyperplanes of multidimensional classification. This kind of mathematical dimensionality is impossible to visualize, but it is possible to render the numerical expressions at any level of the neural network in terms of an image. If we watch how an image moves through a neural network, looking at visual renderings of numerical information, we see what looks like increasing abstraction or lossy compression of the initial image. The image becomes less recognizable to us, because at each stage we are seeing increasingly complex information patterns rendered as an image. This is what *resolution* looks like for the computer, however, as its algorithms match patterns with patterns, to close in on image recognition.

When computer vision identifies an object, this means it finds a strong correlation between the mathematical patterns found in a given image and the patterns it has already associated with a label. For example, what the computer has learned to label "goldfish" is based on whatever images it has been shown labeled "goldfish" have in common, and how they differ from images with other labels. Given that goldfish are often photographed in round fishbowls, round fishbowls are incorporated into the definition of "goldfish." In his 2013 essay and again in his 2018 retrospective at the Smithsonian, Paglen presented an image taken from the ImageNet dataset, associated with the label "goldfish": a blue halo surrounds a central blur of orange. This image expresses a mathematically derived prediction about how each pixel in an image labeled goldfish is most likely to appear, relative to an image with any other label in the ImageNet dataset.[18] This is not a picture of a goldfish or even an average of many goldfish pictures: it is an expression of relative probabilities that a computer vision system trained on ImageNet would use to identify goldfish-ness.

The convolutions between layers in deep learning networks actually *flatten* how depth appears for a human view, and how we see it in photographs. This flattening begins with the fact that numbers about pixels specify how an image is rendered on a flat coordinate plane. For a computer, the size of an object is about how many pixels it encompasses—so, in the computer's interpretation of a photograph, something actually small that looms large in the foreground might be read as objectively bigger than something very large standing farther from the camera and, therefore, appears small in the background of the photograph. To see dimensionality, a computer has to be taught to extrapolate it from patterns of pixels. This is often done using strategies drawn directly from the era of stereoscopic photography.

One of the most influential training sets for computer vision, COIL-100, developed at Columbia University in 1996, reiterates techniques used by Willème and Muybridge.[19] Each of one hundred objects was placed on a motorized platform, and photographed every five degrees of rotation, to produce seventy-two different views (Figure 16.6). A cross between spatial and temporal depth that manifested in late nineteenth-century photography recurs in datasets like these. For computer vision algorithms, similar information about shape and volume can be extracted from images taken from multiple perspectives in either time or space. The distinction between stereoscopic and cinematic kinds of depth seems less absolute, contingent on relationships between apparatus and spectator that are unimportant in algorithmic analysis.

The ambiguity of spatial and temporal depth in computer vision becomes clear in a later section of *Behold These Glorious Times!* in which Paglen animates datasets like COIL-10. After the initial series of image tiles fills the screen, that colorful grid disappears and a series of single images of fast food—a sandwich, then a salad, then a bagel—spin like

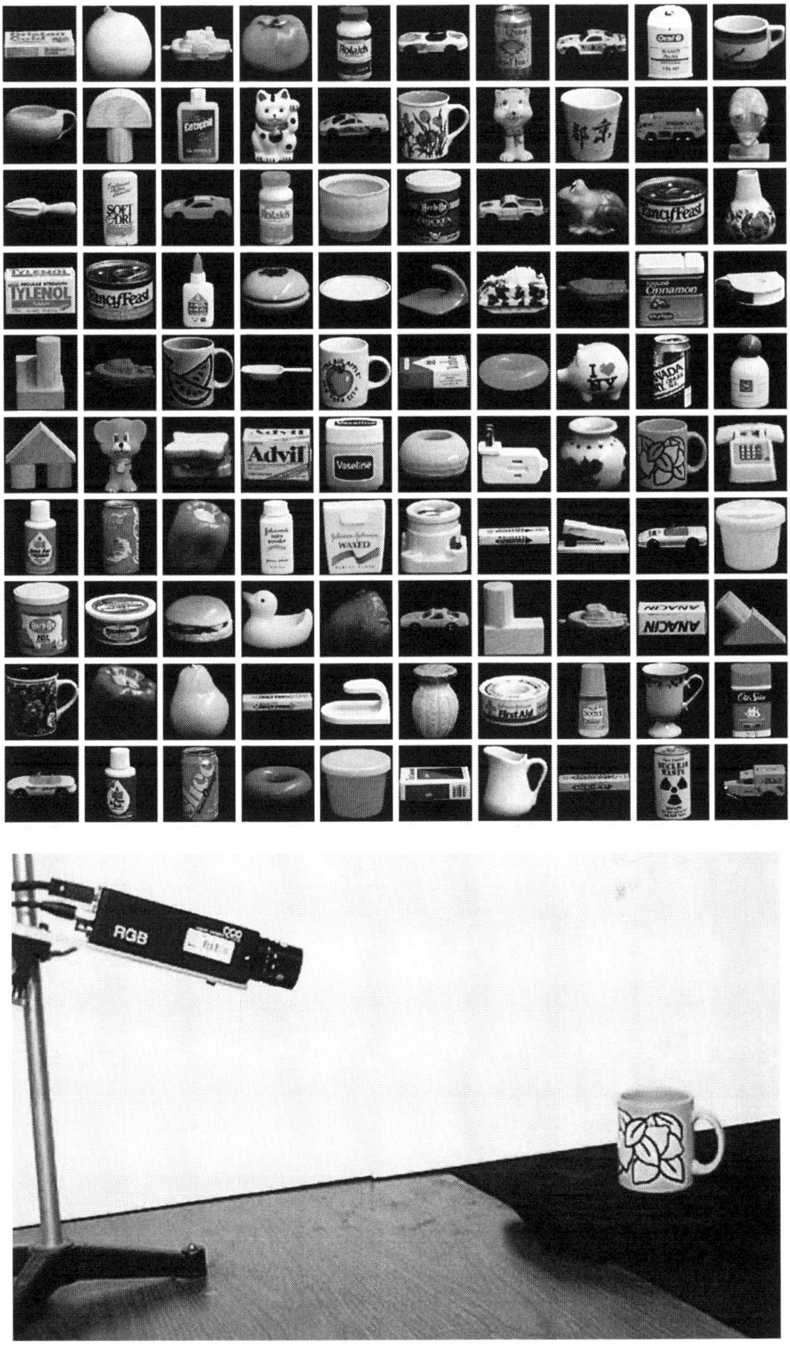

FIGURE 16.6. Objects in the COIL-100 dataset, and documentation of image capture process (1996). By Sameer Nene, Shree Nayar, and Hiroshi Murase. http://www.cs.columbia.edu/CAVE/software/softlib/coil-100.php.

Frisbees in the center of a black screen, with jagged pixel edges marking them as flat cutouts. Then the music slows as the full screen displays what look like real-time, color clips of a black-gloved hand setting one toy object after another on a rotating platform: a goose, a duck, an owl, and so on. The full-screen image then refracts into a grid of smaller tiles that each depict the same rotating object in black and white; as this grid continues to refract into smaller tiles, the images appear to shift from positive to negative, becoming more pixelated and unrecognizable. For a few minutes, the video moves through several figures at different levels of abstraction, and if we can recognize the duck or goose now, it is only because we saw them more clearly moments ago. After the grid parses into tiles so small and abstract that they again begin to look like pixels of a larger, unrecognizable image, the video returns to a full screen with a series of single, rotating figures. A deer is only barely recognizable, turning slowly in black space; its white pixels aggregate in changing opacities, appearing ghostly, like the idea of a deer. As the image becomes increasingly abstract, again, we can only imagine which animal appears (Figure 16.7).

This section of the video follows a series of images as they are parsed through layers of a neural net. Like photosculpture, this process extracts and combines contours to produce a dimensional model of the object. But, rather than manually adding silhouettes into a sculpture, algorithms extract mathematical expressions of how pixels relate across images of the object from different perspectives. This extrapolates dimensionality as the mathematical structure capable of coordinating surface points in a particular way. The interrelationship of multiple views becomes part of the definition of the object, incorporating the variability of vantage points as if perspective was a feature of the *object in itself* rather than a condition of how it is seen. Defining dimensionality this way does not teach computers to see depth as much as do away with it.

The way computer vision models depth may inherit, and rearticulate, an ethos of extraction that also conditioned how nineteenth-century stereographs were often used and understood. Although Oliver Wendell Holmes's cavalier invitation to "tear it down or burn it up, if you please" is to some extent rhetorical flourish, his explanation of the stereograph is filtered through equally violent metaphors: "We have got the fruit of creation now, and need not trouble ourselves with the core. Every conceivable object of Nature and Art will soon scale off its surface for us. Men will hunt all curious, beautiful, grand objects, as they hunt the cattle in South America, for their skins, and leave the carcasses as of little worth."[20] This language overtly privileges surface over substance,

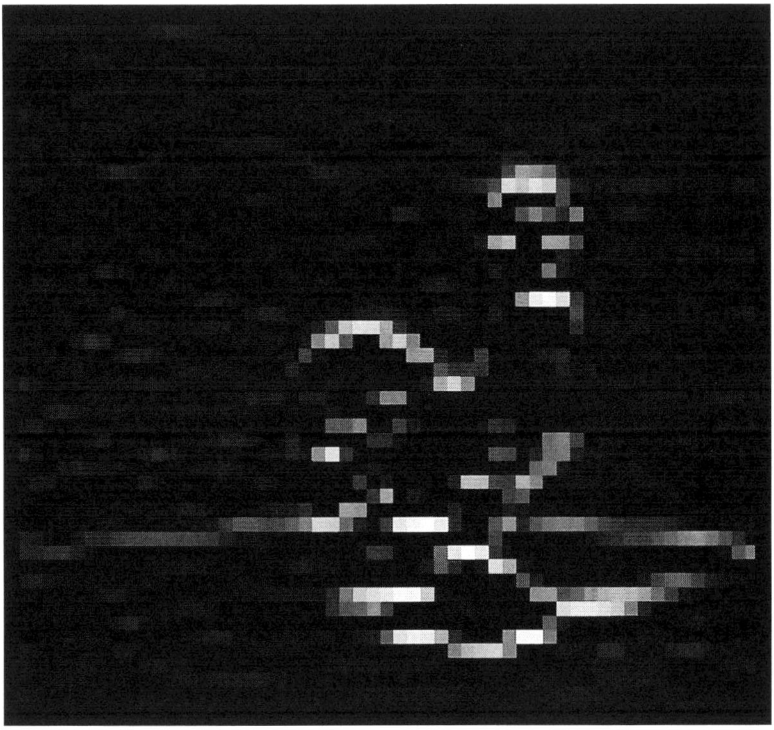

FIGURE 16.7. Still from Trevor Paglen, *Behold These Glorious Times!* (2017), ten-minute, single-channel digital video projection. Music composed with Holly Herndon. Courtesy of Metro Pictures and the artist.

suggesting that the value of "things worth seeing" lies less in the things than in the seeing. This not only devalues the world in favor of its representation but also forgets that representation encodes particular ways of seeing. A stereoview might offer the opportunity to reembody one viewing position: a vantage point inflected by the values of the one who took the picture. But, to be more than a collection of things worth seeing, to be a visible *world,* the space of visibility would have to sustain a plurality of perspectives and would have to remain open to changing ideas of what could be worth seeing and count as seeing, and what perspective or whose point of view would be most important, generalizable, or actionable.

Modeling the world in terms of image relations disregards the way visibility is materially instantiated—always inscribed within specific and contingent relationships between seer and seen. Scholarship on nineteenth-century stereo photography has critiqued how those relationships were

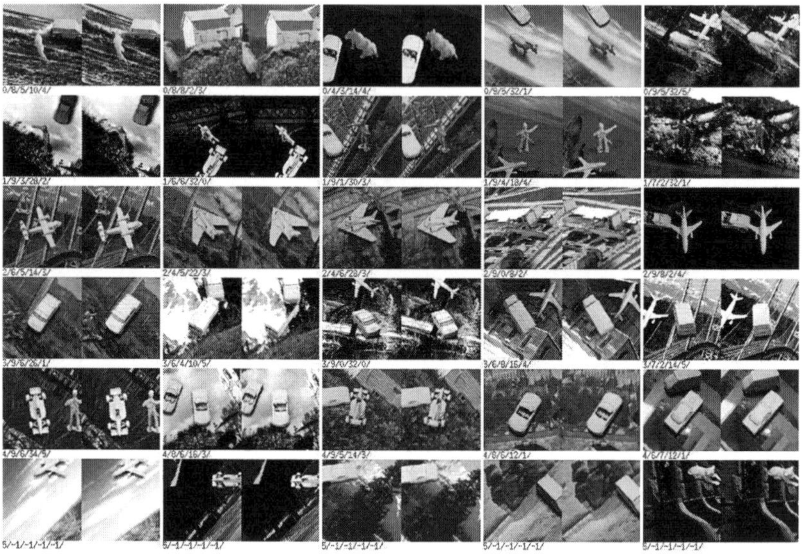

FIGURE 16.8. Documentation of the NORB dataset, showing the figures used for training and testing, and some of the stereoscopic training images produced (2003–present). By Fu Jie Huang, Yann LeCun, and Leon Bottou. https://cs.nyu.edu/~yann/research/norb/.

often conceived through colonial logics: in many stereoviews, "other" people and places appear on display, almost within the viewer's reach, as almost interchangeable objects available to be collected, consumed, and compared from a point of view that is itself presumed to be unseen, unmapped, and universal.[21] When stereoscopic images are produced for machines, they are not "views" in the same sense of older stereographs: they are algorithmically analyzed rather than coordinated through an embodied look. This translation from the terms of human vision to those of computer vision seems to align the machine with the unmarked point of view, as the guarantee of an objective and generalizable visibility.

Although computer vision may work to obviate perspective—along with its implications—its constructions of dimensionality encode specific ways of seeing marked by particular values. For example, consider the stereoscopic images of the NORB dataset (Figure 16.8). Used to train object recognition algorithms, this grayscale image set depicts different combinations of plastic toys from different aerial perspectives.[22] The toys consist of five examples for each of five categories: animal, human, plane, truck, and car. The toys were placed on a rotating, circular platform and photographed from specific angles with a stereo camera. Different background scenes were then digitally added to make object recognition more challenging. After training computer vision algorithms on this dataset, researchers fed the algorithms test images with related toys or actual examples of the five object categories, to assess how well objects would be identified. The NORB training images visually invoke military photographs from the two world wars, both with their aerial perspectives and through the vintage look of the toy soldiers and vehicles. Many of the test images, in contrast, could almost be stills from postwar Hollywood—the bizarre encounters and outlandish scales invoke B-list, 3D horror films.

The NORB images stage a miniature world in which humans corral tiny dinosaurs, every person has a gun, and trucks and planes jumble in traffic jams. Despite the unreality—even absurdity—of these images, the kind of object recognition they train and test has real-world implications for remote sensing and aerial surveillance. The choice of objects and their arrangements communicates assumptions about what computer vision needs to see; the stereoscopic and aerial presentation trains the ways of seeing that computer vision can be used to enact. The goal of this training is to reliably identify objects despite changes of perspective and context; in essence, this is yet another example of factoring out the material specificity of the point of view, incorporating contingent conditions of visibility into algorithmic definitions of the object. Within these definitions, the kinds of contingencies that inhere in point of view are difficult to register.

The kind of computer vision that sets like NORB can be used to train—algorithms that can identity humans and animals, trucks and planes—can be used to selectively see some things and not others. Vision systems for self-driving cars are being trained, for example, to identify and avoid pedestrians. Google Earth uses computer vision to automatically scrub both people and cars out of its model, to picture the most "pretty Earth."[23] In military applications, computer vision can be used, from a distance, to map and speculate about dynamics that might appear differently on the ground and from embedded points of view. One concern is that object recognition makes mistakes: the "google gorillas" debacle continues, with escalating stakes, as black faces are still more likely to be missed or mislabeled.[24] Another, related concern is about the structure of vision and visibility that computer vision models and enacts. Authorizing algorithmic constructs as yielding an objective and actionable view can work to route around, replace, and overwrite other dimensions of embodied vision and relational visibility. It can disavow the fact that every perspective is situated, by imagining mathematical probability could constitute perspective.

Seeing Double

As strategies drawn from nineteenth-century photography are incorporated into techniques of computer vision, embodied processes of depth perception are displaced by algorithmic processes. But this process began before digitization. Photography has long participated in translating a dimensional world into a flat representation, and in abstracting embodied space into the mathematics of a grid. Stereographs were used in the Great Surveys of the American West, as tools for planning railroad lines and extracting resources; time-and-motion studies were used to regulate gestures of industrial labor; anthropometric photographs were used to define identity in terms of facial features. The serial images of Muybridge and Willème display signs of this tendency in the numbers printed and painted within the photographed spaces. These numbers encode actual spatial relations in terms that can be read off from the surface of the photographs, regulating how these representations will then be ordered and interpreted as modeling spatial arrangements. The structure of digital imaging inherits and escalates this logic, encoding every image—both in how it is recorded and how it is displayed—according to the mathematical grid that structures its machine readability.

It seems impossible to imagine an algorithmic avant-garde that could derange the dominant logic of digital imaging today. It also seems overly simplistic to believe that ever-tighter imbrications of human and machine are either fully alienating or a means of creative evolution. I want to suggest that we might, more modestly, reconsider potentials that may reappear each time technological transformations restructure relationships of vision and representation. Walter Benjamin once used stereoscopic seeing as a metaphor for a historical way of thinking that juxtaposed disjunctive elements to open new perspectives. In media studies this approach has been called "media archaeology" or the "perspective of deep time." In bringing together nineteenth-century photography and twenty-first-century computer vision, I am suggesting an alternative reading of each, without claiming that the old simply evolved into the new or that the new simply repeats the old. Instead, I hope to reactivate a less dominant way of thinking about stereoscopic vision against the way it is currently being incorporated into computer vision.

Stereoscopic imaging was conceived in relationship to binocular, human vision and played a critical role in shaping how relationships of vision and representation would be conceived as photography transformed visual culture. Contemporary forms of stereoscopic imaging—now directed more frequently to computer vision than to human perceivers—condition digital transformations of visual culture. Practices of photogrammetry and 3D mapping, which increasingly subtend everyday technologies from Google Maps to smartphone cameras, rely on sets of multi-perspectival images that are automatically captured and processed through computer vision algorithms. Automated and computational forms of stereoscopic imaging are increasingly "black boxed" in technologies ranging from military mapping to consumer photography.

As we consider how this will matter, and what forms of response or critique remain open, it is important to pause to remember that the technologies themselves do not entirely determine the point of view they may seem to enact. Stereographs are not necessarily instantiations of the colonialist perspectives they were used to support; each person who takes up a stereograph, and embodies its dimensions as a view, restages it through an original act of seeing. Though stereoscopic photography may have seemed to prove that dimensionality can be transferred from world to image, it also exposed how dimensionality always triangulates seer and seen. The apparent volume of a stereoview always inscribes the voluminosity of an embodied perceiver, whose two eyes span the gap structuring the stereoview, as its very condition of visibility. Using a stereoscope stages a visceral discovery that depth is not an objective measure to be read off from things, but a condition of visibility, a condition that is provisional, contingent, and irreducibly relational.

To make the world fully explicit as a set of image relations, concretely articulated in numerical terms, would be to eradicate the possibility of any situated view. Every perspective involves blind spots, because things are not visible from all sides at once, and some things occlude others. To be a visible world requires something more than a set of objects defined by their surfaces; it requires depth and spacing, a mutual emplacement of everything relative to everything else that holds every aspect of the world apart and yet gathers it together as a world. The depth between seer and seen could not be removed from the view because it describes how visibility is always inscribed within the contours of a world that includes both seer and seen; their mutual orientation is an aspect of *how* a world unfolds as visible. This kind of interdependent dimensionality is difficult to think about and even harder to represent. It comes into view in specific encounters, with particular bodies, through forms of relationality that elude and exceed calculation.

Notes

1. Mark Blunden, "Graduates Are Taking £9k Courses to Help Beat AI Interviews for City Jobs," *London Evening Standard,* October 2, 2018, https://www.standard.co.uk/tech/ai-interviews-city-jobs-graduates-a3951296.html.

2. Hire Vue company website, accessed March 20, 2019, https://www.hirevue.com/.

3. See, for example, a recent report on discrimination and AI by Simone West, Meredith Whittaker, and Kate Crawford, "Discriminating Systems: Gender, Race, and Power in AI," AI Now Institute, April 2019, https://ainowinstitute.org/discriminatingsystems.html.

4. As of January 2018, the scandal was ongoing, as Google seems to have addressed the error by removing potentially offensive categories rather than changing the recognition algorithms. Jessica Guynn, "Google Photos Labeled Black People 'Gorillas,'" *USA TODAY,* July 1, 2015, https://www.usatoday.com/story/tech/2015/07/01/google-apologizes-after-photos-identify-black-people-as-gorillas/29567465/.

5. See "Computer Programs Recognise White Men Better Than Black Women: Biased Training Is Probably to Blame," *Economist,* February 15, 2018; Lauren Rhue, "Racial Influence on Automated Perceptions of Emotions," November 9, 2018, SSRN, https://ssrn.com/abstract=3281765; Joy Buolawini and Timnit Gehru, "Gender Shades: Intersectional Accuracy Disparities in Commercial Gender Classification," *Proceedings of Machine Learning Research* 81 (2018): 1–15; Benjamin Wilson, Judy Hoffman, and Jamie Morgenstern, "Predictive Inequity in Object Detection," *arXiv preprint, arXiv: 1902.11097* (February 2019), https://arxiv.org/abs/1902.11097. Researcher Lauren Rhue goes so far as to suggest the following: "Until facial recognition assesses black and white faces similarly, black people may need to exaggerate their positive facial expressions—essentially smile more—to reduce ambiguity and potentially negative interpretations by the technology"; Lauren Rhue, "Emotion-Reading Tech Fails the Racial Bias Test," *The Conversation,* January 3, 2019, http://theconversation.com/emotion-reading-tech-fails-the-racial-bias-test-108404.

6. For example, the Department of Defense outsourced work to Google to train computer vision algorithms to recognize "38 classes of objects that represent the kinds of things the department needs to detect, especially in the fight against the Islamic State of Iraq and Syria"; Cheryl Pellerin, "Project Maven to Deploy Computer Algorithms to War Zone by Year's End," July 21, 2017, U.S. Department of Defense, https://www.defense.gov/Newsroom/News/Article/Article/1254719/project-maven-to-deploy-computer-algorithms-to-war-zone-by-years-end/.

7. Jonathan Crary, *Techniques of the Observer: On Vision and Modernity in the Nineteenth Century* (Cambridge, Mass.: MIT Press, 1992).

8. Jonathan Crary, *Suspensions of Perception: Attention, Spectacle, and Modern Culture* (Cambridge, Mass.: MIT Press, 2001); Philip Brookman, "Helios: Eadweard Muybridge in a Time of Change," in *Helios: Eadweard Muybridge in a Time of Change* (Gottingen: Steidl and Corcoran Gallery of Art, 2010), 23–110.

9. Martha A. Sandweiss, *Print the Legend: Photography and the American West* (New Haven, Conn.: Yale University Press, 2004).

10. An exemplary discussion of photography's inferiority to painting, due to its slavish recapitulation of detail, can be found in Lady Elizabeth Eastlake, "Photography," *London Quarterly Review,* no. 101 (April 1857): 442–68.

11. Oliver Wendell Holmes, "The Stereoscope and Stereograph," *The Atlantic,* June 1859, https://www.theatlantic.com/magazine/archive/1859/06/the-stereo scope-and-the-stereograph/303361/.

12. Note that sometimes two cameras were used to produce two images that would then be paired for a stereoview, while other times a stereo camera with two lenses could be used to capture a pair of images in one exposure. "The Stereoscope, Pseudoscope and Solid Daguerreotypes," *Illustrated London News,* January 24, 1852, 77–78. The *Illustrated London News* was among the first illustrated newspapers. It doubled its circulation during the Great Exhibition, publishing images of the event using a new collodion process that printed photographs directly on wood blocks for more photorealistic engravings.

13. Robert J. Silverman, "The Giant Eyes of Science: The Stereoscope and Photographic Depiction in the Nineteenth Century," in *Instruments and the Imagination,* ed. Thomas L. Hankins and Robert J. Silverman (Princeton, N.J.: Princeton University Press, 1999), 163–64.

14. Eivind Rossaak, *Between Stillness and Motion: Film, Photography, Algorithms* (Amsterdam: Amsterdam University Press, 2011); Brooke Belisle, "The Dimensional Image: Overlaps in Stereoscopic, Cinematic, and Digital Depth," *Film Criticism* 37/38, no. 3/1 (2013): 117–37.

15. See Michele Bogart, "Photosculpture," *Art History* 4, no. 1 (1981): 54–65, https://doi.org/10.1111/j.1467-8365.1981.tb00696.x; Robert A. Sobieszek, "Sculpture as the Sum of Its Profiles: François Willème and Photosculpture in France, 1859–1868," *Art Bulletin* 62, no. 4 (1980): 617–30, https://doi.org /10.2307/3050057. Alex Galloway made a similar connection between photosculpture and algorithmic imaging in "Polygraphic Photography and the Origins of 3-D Animation," in *Animating Film Theory,* ed. Karen Redrobe Beckman (Durham, N.C.: Duke University Press, 2014), 54–67. Ian Dawson reconstructed Willème's apparatus with art students and digital imaging technologies in 2012; http://www.iandawsonstudio.com/photosculpture.html.

16. Trevor Paglen, "Invisible Images (Your Pictures Are Looking at You)," *The New Inquiry,* December 8, 2016, https://thenewinquiry.com/invisible-images-your -pictures-are-looking-at-you/.

17. Holly Herndon is an important artist in her own right, innovating the use of AI in music. See Emily McDermott, "Holly Herndon on Her AI Baby, Reanimating Tupac, and Extracting Voices," *Art in America*, January 7, 2020, accessed April 30, 2020, https://www.artnews.com/art-in-america/interviews/holly-herndon-emily-mcdermott-spawn-ai-1202674301/.

18. Paglen, "Invisible Images." ImageNet is an online database of images with hierarchical labels; http://image-net.org, updated 2016.

19. COIL stands for Columbia Object Image Library, and 100 refers to the number of objects in the set. COIL-20 names a related set of images, made at Columbia in a similar way, picturing 20 objects in gray scale. See S. A. Nene, S. K. Nayar, and H. Murase, "Columbia Object Image Library (COIL-100)" (Technical Report CUCS-006-966, February 1996, Department of Computer Science, Columbia University).

20. Holmes, "The Stereoscope and Stereograph."

21. On the colonial perspectives in nineteenth-century stereographs, see Brooke Belisle, "Total Archive: Picturing History from the Stereographic Library to the Digital Database," *Mediascape*, Winter 2013, http://www.tft.ucla.edu/mediascape/Winter2013_PicturingHistory.html; Pauline Stakelon, "Travel through the Stereoscope," *Media History* 16, no. 4 (November 1, 2010): 407–22; Ellen Strain, "Exotic Bodies, Distant Landscapes: Touristic Viewing and Popularized Anthropology in the Nineteenth Century," *Wide Angle* 18, no. 2 (1996): 70–100.

22. NORB was developed at NYU and stands for NYU Object Recognition Benchmark. See "NORB Object Recognition Dataset, Fu Jie Huang, Yann LeCun, New York University," https://cs.nyu.edu/~ylclab/data/norb-v1.0/.

23. Developers who work on Google Earth routinely use the phrase "pretty earth" to refer to the visual composite that uses only the greenest foliage and bluest skies. This version debuted in 2016 and was described as "Pretty Earth" by bloggers who took up Google's own, internal language. See, for example, "Google Earth Gets a Makeover," Google Earth Blog, June 28, 2016, https://www.gearthblog.com/blog/archives/2016/06/google-earth-gets-a-makeover.html.

24. In spring 2019, popular presses published a flurry of stories on race and AI, largely in response to academic research such as the above-cited report from NYU's AI Now Institute by West, Whittaker, and Crawford, "Discriminating Systems," and similar reports by Professors Joy Buolamwini at MIT (Larry Hardesty, "Study Finds Gender and Skin-Type Bias in Commercial Artificial-Intelligence System," *MIT News Office*, February 11, 2018, http://news.mit.edu/2018/study-finds-gender-skin-type-bias-artificial-intelligence-systems-0212), and Amy Morgenstern at Georgia Tech (Sigal Samuel, "A New Study Finds a Potential Risk with Self-Driving Cars: Failure to Detect Dark-Skinned Pedestrians," *Vox*, March 6, 2019, https://www.vox.com/future-perfect/2019/3/5/18251924/self-driving-car-racial-bias-study-autonomous-vehicle-dark-skin).

CHAPTER SEVENTEEN

The Deep Realness of Deepfake Pornography

A Conversation

Shaka McGlotten, Susanna Paasonen, and John Paul Stadler

In what follows, social anthropologist Shaka McGlotten, media studies scholar Susanna Paasonen, and film and media scholar John Paul Stadler engage in a conversation about pornographic deepfakes, which rose to prominence in 2018 and pose a variety of challenging political, ethical, and social questions.

Q: *To what extent do deepfakes have depth? Or, what's necessarily "deep" about deepfake porn?*

JOHN PAUL STADLER: "Deepfakes" are named after the reddit user who spurred an entire (now defunct) subreddit of hyperrealistic digitally altered porn centered primarily on female celebrities (and, in that regard, their emergence capitalized on the 2014 hack and leak of various female celebrities' intimate photos). Deepfakes' use of technology to alter images, video, and audio belongs to a long lineage of media falsification, perhaps best known by Photoshop in the preceding decades. Even though deepfakes took their name from this reddit username, I am interested in how the "deep" here marks a difference from the mediated fakes that preceded them. Notably, what neural networks and machine learning software like fakeapp have facilitated is widespread access and ease in creating such hyperrealistic falsifications. While the "deep" of deepfakes would at first seem to signal increasing layers of falsification, the expansive availability of this media forgery, or its democratizing effect, would be more accurately described through its spreadability. Secondarily, if we take depth to imply profundity, the deep of deepfakes can be conceived of as the sheer awe in being able to suture one's likeness to a stranger's body convincingly, although just what the threshold of believability is deserves examination. I do not think, for instance, that deepfake porn needs to be fully believable to still enjoy widespread popularity, because what deepfakes do is turn porn spectatorship into something more like a video game that we control and manipulate. They alter the reception practices and socialization patterns of pornography into something else than what we've seen before.

SUSANNA PAASONEN: The deepness of deepfakes has to do with their verisimilitude based on photorealism: they simply look real to the degree that, when well made, their fakeness can be virtually impossible to identify. Here, deepfakes build on a longer trajectory of "faking it" that cuts through the history of pornography from the mostly knowingly clumsy and stylized "Tijuana Bibles" published in the United States from the 1920s to perhaps the 1960s, featuring not only popular cartoon characters but also movie stars in throes of obscene acts to more realistic graphic renditions of mainstream celebrities gone wild. This visual tradition has been one of still images that have, with the introduction of 3D graphics, grown increasingly photorealistic while regularly remaining fantastic in the scenarios depicted—as in "Hellywood 3D," a site featuring images of female pop stars and actors engaging in largely nonconsensual sexual acts with frisky monsters, demons, goblins, and zombies. So, the deepness of deepfakes playing out as photorealism reminds me of mid-1990s discussions on how the truth-value of photography (and here, that of videography) based on indexicality becomes obscured and disturbed with the introduction of digital manipulation and modeling. Lev Manovich argued around that time that the codes of photorealism become fetishized rather than threatened in the process, given that they operate as the aspirational representational goals of digital imaging. Manovich proposed that this enables a recontextualization of photography (and videography) as graphics, as etymologically belonging to painting or drawing, rather than as transparent, somehow immediate traces of moments captured in space and time.

SHAKA MCGLOTTEN: I'm chiming in late here, and I think you've both done a great job historicizing questions of depth in relation to deepfakes. To this historicization, I would add fan art, which is where I first encountered images reworking characters and celebrities from popular media franchises. The ur-example is

Kirk/Spock. Fan and slash fiction have a curious relationship to the sorts of celebrity that seem to be the focus of deepfake pornography insofar as there was, I think, an emphasis on the characters rather than the actors portraying them. Of course, this is a generalization, given the tentacular vastness of fan fiction networks. One can certainly find many examples of fan fiction that play with different levels of mediation. The stars of the still still-running *Supernatural*—Jensen Ackles and Jared Padalecki—might be featured as fictional versions of themselves playing the Winch brothers they portray on the program.

Screen media images introduce a problematic that I'm not sure troubles fan fiction in the same way, though I'd be happy to be corrected here, namely, questions of consent, especially as they are connected with gender. Framed through the lens of affect, the deep in deepfakes might also be conceived as the depth of feeling impacts—violation, betrayal, shame, anger, among others. I think this is especially the case for women, for whom the penalties for possessing or expressing sexual autonomy remain. In contrast, Tom Felton, who played Draco Malfoy in the *Harry Potter* films, joked amiably about erotic fan art, even noting that his brother had used one of the more popular images as the home screen on his phone.

Q: *What issues do deepfakes raise for pornographic media, or how do deepfakes plug into conversations we've already been having about pornography in the twenty-first century?*

JPS: There are a couple ways to think about deepfake porn. The first is as an extension of virtual reality pornography. So much of the innovation around VR porn, which has been an ongoing obsession of adult media, has revolved around the Oculus Rift. The porn produced under this platform seeks to place the viewer within the body of the porn performer and "send" them within the diegesis of the porn world. Much like the film *Being John Malkovich* (Spike Jonze, 1999), the "virtual" here becomes the inhabiting of another person's reality, but one for which we have a first-person perspective, donning a new skin and seeing from a new set of eyes. Deepfakes allow for the production of another virtuality, one that blurs two realities into an amalgamation, or augmented reality. Notably, though, this virtuality maintains a third-person perspective—not sending viewers *into* the porn, but keeping them on the outside—a perspective from which viewers can marvel at something wholly unreal. In this way, it is very much a continuation of remix culture. To the extent that the "deep" in deepfake can be understood spatially, the name is misleading, because its innovation is all about surface modifications (albeit with 3D modeling), and viewers remain in the traditional position of porn spectatorship—that is, outside of it (but with the possibility of sending facial avatars into it).

The second, and more common, way to think of deepfakes is in terms of consent and the alarming potential for this technology to produce a new kind of revenge porn. In this understanding, deepfake porn constitutes a grave threat for the proliferation of nonconsensual porn that can be deployed to harass, embarrass, and harm anyone who has a digital presence, with the most likely target continuing to be women. Oftentimes, what is "deep" about deepfakes concerns their point of origin—that is, one typically will not find the user who manipulated the video, nor will such victims be able to easily halt their proliferation. This is a problem of the internet more broadly but is especially unique for deepfake porn because the laws we have—here, I am speaking in the U.S. context—largely fail to protect against such a unique phenomenon, which could be argued to be a kind of parody and, in regard to the question of harm, is troubled by the actual "unrealness" of the media produced, or its mixed ontology. The two legal avenues for recourse are misappropriation of image and antidefamation laws, but much of this remains murky territory made no less complicated by Section 230 ("The Good Samaritan Act"), which has historically been lauded for keeping the internet "open" by not holding platforms liable for users' content, so long as a good faith effort is made on behalf of the platform to remove objectionable content.

SP: As John points out, deepfakes are both about the pornographic adaptations of novel technological frontiers aiming for increased immersion and verisimilitude while at the same time remaining highly predictable in their imageries and functions. Most deepfake porn currently in circulation focuses on the bodies of female celebrities, actors such as Scarlett Johansson being perennially popular. And as the technology allows for modeling any person's likeness, there are no obvious limits to who can be imag(in)ed doing what with whom and how. As Shaka suggests above, the gendered dynamics here are striking, and clearly a product of homosocial straight male geek cultures: the novelty of the technology comes applied in reproducing disappointingly predictable gendered and sexual hierarchies. Despite the lack of limits of what digitally modeled bodies can do, and how they may look, people end up approximating the visual codes and standard scenes of mainstream commercial U.S. heteroporn. This could be interpreted simply as lack of imagination but is, of course, more accurately understood as an aim to technologically master deepfaking to the point of fully reaching the aspired-to aesthetic, that of straight porn clips. Deepfakes allow for extensions of revenge porn just as they do for masturbatory visual fantasizing about unattainable bodies, acts, and scenarios.

The interesting thing for me here is how the risk of shame and shaming becomes attached to the people whose likeness is being modeled and what this tells about the affective dynamics of sexuality in popular discourse where shame sticks to women as sexual subjects and objects of desire alike. And, indeed, what all this says about sex and shame, especially in the context of U.S. culture.

SM: It's clear we're all lined up in thinking about some of the politics of gender and sexuality as they interface with histories of pornographic media and homosocial misogyny. Deepfakes, like all so-called new media, to paraphrase Wendy Hui Kyong Chun, update pornographic media while remaining much the same. When I put on my anthropologist hat, what I'd want to know is more about the production, distribution, and consumption of deepfakes. What forms of technical expertise are necessary, through which channels do they travel, and, crucially, what forms of pleasure are attendant to the genre?

I'm thinking here of an update with a difference (and there's always a difference, right?), namely, the now ordinary availability of deepfake software that produces highly realistic versions of one's younger or older self. FaceApp is perhaps the best known as of this writing. So, again thinking anthropologically, what happens when this particular capacity is used to produce pornographic images not just of the famous, but of oneself or one's friends? Using apps like these allows one to activate and transgress taboos. I'm thinking here of a specific example: child pornography. Recently, perusing the feed of my NSFW Twitter, I came across a Snap that featured the user's underage face on his adult body. There was a prominently featured disclaimer: "SNAPCHAT APP!!! My 16 yo face on me jerking."

JPS: Both Susanna and Shaka raise compelling points about the affective dimension(s) of deepfakes and the ways in which their production and dissemination in largely homosocial misogynist forums will continue to alter the aims to which they are put. While perhaps naively utopian, one fascinating article I came across on this topic concerned a paraplegic man who was considering having a deepfake porn made of himself to reexperience the sex he was no longer able to have. While by no means the common usage of deepfake technology, this particular example speaks to Susanna's point that shame attaches differently to male bodies than female bodies within this representational regime. Partially, too, this gendered gap is structured on the notable minimization—if not more often outright absence—of faces for the male performers in the mainstream heteroporn that is being remixed, although there is nothing stopping users from overlaying male celebrities onto gay porn. To Shaka's point, deepfakes will certainly pose ethical questions for the new category of "deepfake child pornography," as well as a whole new dilemma for media forensics in distinguishing between the two, and I could easily imagine an episode of *Black Mirror* where pedophiles are "treated," in a kind of substitutive logic, with deepfake porn.

Q: *Pornography's relationship to authenticity is a fraught one. How do deepfakes change the way we think authenticity in pornography?*

JPS: One question that continues to interest porn studies centers on discerning whether the pleasure on display was acted (and so, false, commercial) or experienced (and so, genuine, amateur). I want to state up front that I think this binary is overly simplistic, but nonetheless useful for broadly framing what deepfakes make visible. Orgasm is supposedly uncontrollable, and in that lack of control it indexes authentic pleasure. Yet we all know that pornography is performative, too, and so the degree to which an orgasm is authentic then becomes an open question, most notably for women, for whom orgasm can easily be faked, as female orgasm lacks the overt visual signification of the male money shot. It is no surprise, then, that the face becomes the primary marker of pleasure for female performers, or, as Linda Williams notes, an adoption of the man's money shot comes to stand in for her own pleasure.

Deepfakes are largely the replacement of a porn performer's face with someone else's. As one of the more common indicators of pleasure, the face swap here becomes the ultimate fabrication of pleasure. In a way, deepfakes lay bare the pornographic conceit by producing a kind of Kuleshov effect of their own: Gal Gadot's facial expression, culled from an interview or promotional video and meant to express benign engagement, gets mapped and reconstituted as an expression of sexual longing. In other words, deepfake pornography illustrates the semiotic structure of pornography and destabilizes it by reminding the viewer of the performative and editorializing component of all pornography. In that regard, it might also be thought of as having a kind of Brechtian alienation effect. This, though, relies on the idea that, regardless of how good the falsification is, viewers always discern the fabrication on some affective or subtextual level (the uncanny valley effect). My hypothesis is that the nagging falseness of these videos—though believable, as many are—is an inherent feature of their pleasure. Here, then, the deep may not suggest the difficulty in discerning falseness as much as an intensification of the suspicion we have always brought to depictions of pleasure.

SP: Yes, the conventions of cinematic and video porn have revolved around authenticity as the realness of bodies, the acts depicted, and the intensities of sensation experienced (as verified through those standard money shots). Such authenticity, and realness, is perhaps nowhere more noticeable than in the contemporary abundance of amateur porn on online platforms, or in cam sites promising immediate and possibly interactive access to performers. But just having people fuck on camera does not good porn make. The imperative of visibility that Williams addresses means that bodies are arranged for maximal visibility with the aid of lighting and camerawork, making displays of authenticity to a degree fantastic, or at least staged.

At the same time, the aesthetics and codes of porn revolve equally around excess and hyperbole: there is an abundance of bodies, bodily excretions, potential acts and intensities to be discovered and displayed. Porn is, centrally, "more than" sex as stylized displays of what bodies can do and feel, which, depicted through audiovisual means, are focused on showing how all this looks and sounds. There is therefore something of a default gap in corporeal mediation when it comes to touch, feel, scent, or taste. Here, authenticity has to do with those instances when the depiction of bodies moving on a screen somehow moves the bodies of those watching—when something resonates and leaves an impression, no matter how momentary. These instances can involve a gesture, a movement, a connection, a recollection, or something else. In the fakeness of deepfakes, or the uncanny valley that John addresses, visual verisimilitude meets artifice manifested in facial registers and nuances, possibly giving rise to additional registers of resonance, or at least to those of pleasure. These pleasures can range from technical mastery (especially for those making the deepfakes) to imaginary visual control over the bodies depicted: yet other kinds of intensities can certainly emerge as well.

I am not proposing here a binary between authenticity and fakeness (excess, hyperbole, or artifice) as a conceptual framework for making sense of pornographic aesthetics and conventions. On the contrary, it is my argument that these come intermeshed, or even as embedded in one another, the question then being how they play out in any particular image, video clip, or text, and what kinds of intensities of sensations and experience they afford.

In an extrapornographic framework, it is precisely this uncanny valley, coupled with faces shifting from one to another—from Jack Nicholson to Jim Carrey; from Rick Astley to David Bowie; or from Arnold Schwarzenegger to Sylvester Stallone; and back again—that seem to have allowed for the most visible public discussion on the potential uses of deepfakes through the YouTube channel of Ctrl Shift Face. The deepfake eyes may be vacant or vacuous, but the fact of a face not quite staying on, and bleeding from one iconic (male) mainstream celebrity to another, packs a powerful affective address.

To date, public debates have revolved around its applications in porn and politics (in a somewhat narrow meaning of representational and party politics), often in ways that isolate these fields of cultural production, commentary, and impact from one another. I think our brief exchange here points to a more fundamental entanglement of things that pushes critical inquiry to go horizontal ways in order to figure out the current and, of course even more pressingly, the potential future resonances and implications of deepfake technology to how we believe our own eyes, how we enjoy fakeness, realness, and shifts between them. Here, porn and politics really can't be pulled apart.

SM: So I want to respond to this in two ways.

I'll start with the Twitter post I described above. The poster publishes a lot of material on his Twitter, where he directs users to his Only Fans site, where his full videos are posted. There one finds dozens of films; many of them are thematically linked by

Daddy/Son role-play. The videos themselves are largely shot on smartphones and so aesthetically convey what I think of as a kind of pornographic ordinary. The filter is ordinary too; anyone can do it. Such videos already constitute a genre. Desire attaches to all of the things John and Susanna mention above—an expression, gesture, "impressions," and the uncanny valley itself—and they attach to genre. The FaceApp filter isn't convincing, but it's doing it for some people and creating an array of affordances, from finding media like it to consume and all the fantasies they induce, to creating it oneself for oneself. Perhaps I'm thinking more about experimentation than authenticity, experimentations with media forms and genres, and with the pleasures immanent to them.

This is my second point, and it moves from the pornographic to the political (yes, I haven't forgotten that porn is always political!). Porn has always been at the forefront of technological innovation. It is a forefront and a testing ground. While I'd known about deepfake porn in 2017, my first encounter with the software was a video of President Barack Obama in which he appeared to be delivering a speech he'd never in fact delivered, his face, mouth, and voice altered via algorithm. It was eerie, but not convincing. We are living in a *Black Mirror* episode (I like John's episode pitch a lot) and fake news and dis/misinformation campaigns increasingly shape our media ecologies. It's clear that the uncanny valley will be overcome, probably pretty soon. So this is where we are. Deepfakes have already been weaponized if we think of the ways that in pornographic media the technology violates the consent of those featured. And they are being weaponized on the political front. We should fully expect to see some deepfakes prominently featured on Fox in 2020. And Google, YouTube, Facebook, WhatsApp, and Instagram. While digital forensics experts are developing tools to detect deepfakes, they acknowledge that theirs will be an ongoing effort as deepfakes become ever more convincing. We can thus think of the realness, or even the deep realness, of deepfake pornography as a frontline in an AI arms race. That's some deep shit.

JPS: Indeed, it is. In June 2019, the United States House Intelligence Committee held their first open hearings on deepfakes and AI, and already there is legislation—the DEEPFAKES Accountability Act (acronym "Defending Each and Every Person from False Appearances by Keeping Exploitation Subject to Accountability Act")—that has been proposed to stem the potential damage of synthetic media purporting to be real. The question will be to what extent the terms of this debate get adequately articulated and nuanced and how this bill would remediate (in both senses of the word) said harm. Current language in the bill would require digital watermarks to authenticate the inauthenticity of deepfakes (which, in the bill, are not exclusively pornographic), but watermarks are easily cropped out, and the very "spreadability" of such media makes locating an original poster—and person behind that post—nearly impossible to prosecute. In this regard, the DEEPFAKES Accountability Act, if passed, might function more like a game of "whack-a-mole."

As Shaka mentions above, pornography often operates at the forefront of technological development, but in debates surrounding deepfakes, its origin, the pornographic version, is typically treated as little more than obvious ill in need of being stamped out. I don't dispute that in many cases deepfake porn can and does produce harm, but I want to caution scholars to seek to understand more capaciously what other reception practices, affects, and registers it might engage. Deepfake porn hits a cultural nerve, no doubt, one that reveals the deep-seated suspicion we have for how the internet makes sex—real, fake, and somewhere in between—public. This is a conversation that Susanna, Shaka, and I have only begun to have. Going forward, we should be thinking more broadly and systemically about why pornography drives technology as it does and how it can serve as a kind of prophetic vision for the mediascapes of tomorrow.

ACKNOWLEDGMENTS

First, we want to acknowledge the fantastic research assistance of Helen Stuhr-Rommereim. She prepared the manuscript with meticulous care and kept us on track throughout the process. Thanks also to all of our authors, who have been sources of inspiration. We are also very grateful to everyone at the University of Minnesota Press for smoothly and enthusiastically pushing the project forward. We are grateful to Ideas on Fire for indexing the collection. And our anonymous readers offered constructive perspective that strengthened the coherence of the volume.

From Karen

I would first like to thank Jeff Scheible. Jeff's January 2016 lecture in the Penn Cinema and Media Studies colloquium, "Debts to Depth," provided the catalyst for this volume. Working with him has been intellectually energizing and an utter pleasure. Thank you, Jeff, for your generosity, rigorous thinking, inspiration, and humor. In the summer of that same year, Iggy Cortez submitted a proposal to the Society for Cinema and Media Studies for a panel titled "Mediating Infinitude," which included Iggy, Karl Schoonover, Eugenie Brinkema, and me. The conversation was dazzling, and the thoughts and questions generated there, in addition to my ongoing conversations with Iggy about our field, have informed this volume in numerous and particular ways. In the midst of working on this volume, I began collaborating with Dagmawi Woubshet on an African Humanities Project at the University of Pennsylvania with the support of a Penn SAS grant. Working with Dag, as well as with our partners—Professor Elizabeth Waldis Giorgis at Addis Ababa University, and Louis Massiah and

Marcellus Armstrong at Scribe Video Center—has provided me with profound sources of hope and joy in a political landscape that tries so hard to be demoralizing. Thanks to them all for their sustaining and inspiring selves. For research support, I am grateful to Michael Leja and the Department of History of Art at the University of Pennsylvania, as well as to Xiaoyu Yang, Michael Prendergast, and Nathan Emery for research assistance. Thank you to David Young Kim for our exchanges about mining and images, and to Julia Alekseyeva, Timothy Corrigan, Peter Decherney, Kathy DeMarco, Meta Mazaj, and Rahul Mukherjee for the ongoing conversation about what cinema and media studies might be. For the remarkable staff support in Penn's Program of Cinema and Media Studies, the Department of the History of Art, and the Wolf Humanities Center that is the source of time for research, thank you to Dru Baker, Nicola Gentili, Darlene Jackson, Sarah Milinski, Libby Saylor, and Sara Varney. I'm grateful to my first-grade neighbor, Kieran Nayak-Bole, who, during COVID-19–inspired porch hangouts, generously offered suggestions on titles, subtitles, book covers, and my overall research trajectory! And for making life so crazy-beautiful and fun, thanks to those who have my heart: Paul M. Cobb, Bea Ballou, and Siduri, Lua, and Bruno Beckman. While working on this book, I lost two of the friends who taught me the most not only about how to watch movies and think with others but about friendship itself. Douglas Crimp and Jonathan Kahana have both, in quite different ways, fundamentally shaped the kind of scholar and person that I am, and I miss them deeply. I dedicate this book to their memories and to the wide and wonderful circles of friendship they fostered.

From Jeff

Living in London while collaborating on this volume with a colleague based in Philadelphia has helped me keep a foot in my hometown in ways that ended up being more important than I could have foreseen. Thank you, Karen, for your insights, initiative, and radiant spirit. Working together has been a blast. Thanks to Rahul Mukherjee and Timothy Corrigan for paving the way for this collection's possibility through their invitation to speak at the University of Pennsylvania. I started researching depth while I was a Banting Fellow at Concordia University. Thanks to everyone in the Film Studies program at Concordia, especially Martin Lefebvre, for sponsoring me. Zach Melzer and Valdis Silnis helped with useful preliminary research while there. I am grateful to have many wonderful colleagues in the Film Studies Department at King's College who have supported this project in ways big and small. Nicole Starosielski's engagement in all things deep is something I always treasure. I began thinking about depth and film theory through numerous conversations and exchanges with my dissertation supervisor, Edward Branigan, who passed away while we were working on this collection. The way this volume approaches depth—as a word that has many different shades of related meanings—is inspired by Edward's expansive way of seeing, and it saddens me to know that he will not be able to read the book. I dedicate *Deep Mediations* to his memory and to his lasting influence.

CONTRIBUTORS

LAUREL AHNERT is visiting lecturer in the Department of Media and Screen Studies at Northeastern University.

TAYLOR ARNOLD is assistant professor of statistics in the Department of Math and Computer Science at the University of Richmond. He is coauthor of *Humanities Data in R: Exploring Networks, Geospatial Data, Images, and Text* and *A Computational Approach to Statistical Learning*.

ERIKA BALSOM is senior lecturer in film studies at King's College London. She is author of *An Oceanic Feeling: Cinema and the Sea*; *After Uniqueness: A History of Film and Video Art in Circulation*; and *Exhibiting Cinema in Contemporary Art*, as well as coeditor of *Artists' Moving Image in Britain since 1989* and *Documentary across Disciplines*.

BROOKE BELISLE is assistant professor in the Department of Art at Stony Brook University.

JINHEE CHOI is a reader in film studies at King's College London. She is author of *The South Korean Film Renaissance: Local Hitmakers, Global Provocateurs*. She edited *Reorienting Ozu: A Master and His Influence* and coedited, with Mattias Frey, *Cine-Ethics: Ethical Dimensions of Film Theory, Practice, and Spectatorship*; with Mitsuyo Wada-Marciano, *Horror to the Extreme: Changing Boundaries in Asian Cinema*; and with Noël Carroll, *Philosophy of Film and Motion Pictures: An Anthology*.

JENNIFER FAY is professor of English and professor and chair of cinema and media arts at Vanderbilt University. She is author of *Theaters of Occupation: Hollywood and the Reeducation of Postwar Germany* (Minnesota, 2008) and *Inhospitable World: Cinema in the Time of the Anthropocene*.

LISA HAN is assistant professor of film and media studies in the Department of English at Arizona State University.

JEAN MA is associate professor in the Department of Art and Art History at Stanford University, where she teaches in the Film and Media Studies Program. Her publications include *Still Moving: Between Cinema and Photography*; *Melancholy Drift: Marking Time in Chinese Cinema*; and *Sounding the Modern Woman: The Songstress in Chinese Cinema*. She is coeditor of the book series Music, Sound, and Media at the University of California Press.

SHAKA McGLOTTEN is a maker and author of *Virtual Intimacies: Media, Affect, and Queer Sociality* and *Dragging: Or, in the Drag of a Queer Life*. They are professor of anthropology and media studies at Purchase College–SUNY.

SUSANNA PAASONEN is professor of media studies at the University of Turku, Finland, and author of *NSFW: Sex, Humor, and Risk in Social Media* (with Kylie Jarrett and Ben Light); *Many Splendored Things: Thinking Sex and Play*; and *Carnal Resonance: Affect and Online Pornography*.

JUSSI PARIKKA is professor at the University of Southampton's Winchester School of Art and a visiting scholar at FAMU at the Academy of Performing Arts, Prague. His books include *Digital Contagions: A Media Archaeology of Computer Viruses*; *Insect Media: An Archaeology of Animals and Technology* (Minnesota, 2010); *A Geology of Media* (Minnesota, 2015); *What Is Media Archaeology?*; and, most recently, the short coauthored book *Remain* (Minnesota and Meson Press, 2019). Among many other volumes, he is coeditor of *Writing and Unwriting (Media) Art History: Erkki Kurenniemi in 2048*. With Darren Wershler and Lori Emerson, he is coauthor of *The Lab Book* (Minnesota, 2021).

ALESSANDRA RAENGO is associate professor of moving image studies at Georgia State University. She is author of *On the Sleeve of the Visual: Race as Face Value* and *Critical Race Theory and "Bamboozled."*

POOJA RANGAN is associate professor of English and film and media studies at Amherst College. She is author of *Immediations: The Humanitarian Impulse in Documentary.*

KAREN REDROBE is the Elliot and Roslyn Jaffe Professor of Cinema and Modern Media in the Department of the History of Art at the University of Pennsylvania. She is author of *Vanishing Women: Magic, Film, and Feminism* and *Crash: Cinema and the Politics of Speed and Stasis*; editor of *Animating Film Theory*; and coeditor of *Still Moving: Between Cinema and Photography* and *On Writing with Photography* (Minnesota, 2013).

KATHERINE ROCHESTER is associate director of curatorial research at VIA Art Fund in Boston. She is editor, with Lou Cantor, of *Intersubjectivity Volume II: Scripting the Human.*

JEFF SCHEIBLE is lecturer in film studies at King's College London and author of *Digital Shift: The Cultural Logic of Punctuation* (Minnesota, 2015).

JORDAN SCHONIG is visiting assistant professor of film studies in the Department of English at Michigan State University.

KARL SCHOONOVER is professor of film and television studies at the University of Warwick (UK). With Rosalind Galt, he wrote *Queer Cinema in the World* and edited *Global Art Cinema: New Theories and Histories.* He is author of *Brutal Vision: The Neorealist Body in Postwar Italian Cinema* (Minnesota, 2012).

JOHN PAUL STADLER is lecturer in film studies at North Carolina State University. He is author of the chapbook *Prehistoric.*

NICOLE STAROSIELSKI is associate professor in the Department of Media, Culture, and Communication at New York University. She is author of *The Undersea Network* and coeditor of *Signal Traffic: Critical*

Studies of Media Infrastructure and *Sustainable Media: Critical Approaches to Media and Environment.*

LAUREN TILTON is assistant professor of digital humanities in the Department of Rhetoric and Communication at the University of Richmond. She is coauthor of *Humanities Data in R: Exploring Networks, Geospatial Data, Images, and Text.*

INDEX

Page references in italics refer to illustrations.